Inequality, Development, and Growth

Edited by

Günseli Berik,
Yana van der Meulen Rodgers,
and Stephanie Seguino

Routledge
Taylor & Francis Group
LONDON AND NEW YORK

First published 2011 by Routledge
2 Park Square, Milton Park, Abingdon, Oxon, OX14 4RN

Simultaneously published in the USA and Canada
by Routledge
270 Madison Avenue, New York, NY 10016

Routledge is an imprint of the Taylor & Francis Group, an informa business

This book is a reproduction of *Feminist Economics*, vol.15, issue 3. The Publisher requests to those authors who may be citing this book to state, also, the bibliographical details of the special issue on which the book was based.

Typeset in Baskerville by Taylor & Francis Books
Printed and bound in Great Britain by CPI Rowe, Chippenham, Wiltshire

British Library Cataloguing in Publication Data
A catalogue record for this book is available from the British Library

ISBN13: 978-0-415-59944-3 (hbk)
ISBN13: 978-0-415-60994-4 (pbk)

Disclaimer
The publisher would like to make readers aware that the chapters in this book may be referred to as articles as they had been in the special issue. The publisher accepts responsibility for any inconsistencies that may have arisen in the course of preparing this volume for print.

Contents

Notes on Contributors ix

1. Feminist Economics of Inequality, Development, and Growth
Günseli Berik, Yana van der Meulen Rodgers, and Stephanie Seguino 1

2. Gender Equality and Economic Growth in the World Bank *World Development Report 2006*
Diane Elson 35

3. Gender Disparity in Education and the International Competition for Foreign Direct Investment
Matthias Busse and Peter Nunnenkamp 61

4. The Impact of Gender Inequality in Education and Employment on Economic Growth: New Evidence for a Panel of Countries
Stephan Klasen and Francesca Lamanna 91

5. Do Gender Disparities in Employment Increase Profitability? Evidence from the United States
Ajit Zacharias and Melissa Mahoney 133

6. Women's Employment and Family Income Inequality during China's Economic Transition
Sai Ding, Xiao-yuan Dong, and Shi Li 163

7. Do Economic Reforms Influence Home-Based Work? Evidence from India
Uma Rani and Jeemol Unni 191

8. Gender Disparities and Economic Growth in Kenya: A Social Accounting Matrix Approach
Bernadette Mukhwana Wanjala and Maureen Were 227

9. Globalization, Gender, and Poverty in the Senegal River Valley
Jeanne E. Koopman 253

10. Modeling Gender Effects of Pakistan's Trade Liberalization
Rizwana Siddiqui 287

11. Gender, Monetary Policy, and Employment: The Case of Nine OECD Countries
Yelena Takhtamanova and Eva Sierminska 323

Index 355

This book was previously published as a special issue of *Feminist Economics*, the official journal of the International Association for Feminist Economics (IAFFE). All contributions have been subjected to the journal's rigorous peer review process and comply with the journal's editorial policies, as overseen by the editor, Diana Strassmann, and the journal's editorial team, including the associate editors, the editorial board, numerous volunteer reviewers, and the journal's in-house editorial staff and style editors. The special issue and book have been made possible by the very generous financial support of Rice University, the Friedrich Ebert Stiftung, the United Nations Department of Economic and Social Affairs and Division for the Advancement of Women.

Notes on Contributors

Günseli Berik is Professor of Economics at the University of Utah, where she teaches feminist economics, development economics, and political economy of gender, class, and race/ethnicity in the US. Her research examines the relationship between development, labor market inequalities, and well-being. Her latest research focuses on strategies for improving labor standards, gendered labor market outcomes of different kinds of industrial policy, and the Genuine Progress Indicator (GPI). She has conducted research for the United Nations and the World Bank and is Co-editor of *Feminist Economics.*

Matthias Busse is Professor of Economics at the Ruhr-University of Bochum, Germany. Previously, he was Head of the World Economy Program at the Hamburg Institute of International Economics (HWWI). Before joining the Hamburg Institute, he worked as an economist at the German Federal Chancellery, Bonn, and as a management consultant. He received his PhD and habilitation degree in economics from the University of Hamburg, Germany. His research interests focus on international trade, foreign direct investment, and development economics.

Sai Ding is Associate Professor at the Institute of Ethnology and Anthropology at the Chinese Academy of Social Sciences. She has been a visiting scholar at Gothenburg University, Sweden, for the project "Income Distribution during China's Economic Transition" since 2005 and is an adjunct faculty member of the Hubert H. Humphrey Institute of Public Affairs at the University of Minnesota. Her research focuses on income distribution, Chinese ethnic minority issues, and gender/women's issues.

Xiao-yuan Dong is Professor of Economics at the University of Winnipeg in Canada, an adjunct professor at the China Center for Economic Research (CCER) at Beijing University, and co-director of the Chinese Women Economists Research and Training Program. She has published extensively on China's economic transition and development and on gender/women's issues. She was a Guest Editor for a special issue of *Feminist Economics* on

Gender, China, and the World Trade Organization and currently serves on the board of the International Association of Feminist Economics.

Diane Elson is Professor of Sociology and member of the Human Rights Centre at the University of Essex. She is a former Vice President of the International Association of Feminist Economists and former Associate Editor of *Feminist Economics*. She has published widely on gender and development, with a particular focus on macroeconomics. She is currently researching methods of auditing economic policy from a human rights perspective.

Stephan Klasen is Professor of Economics at the University of Göttingen, Germany. He is also coordinator of the recently founded Courant Research Centre "Poverty, Equity, and Growth in Developing and Transition Countries." He holds a PhD from Harvard University and has since held positions at the World Bank, King's College (Cambridge, UK), and the University of Munich. An important research focus is determinants, measurement, and consequences of gender inequality in developing countries. He is Co-managing Editor of the *Review of Income and Wealth*, the leading international journal on the measurement and interpretation of poverty and inequality issues.

Jeanne E. Koopman is Research Fellow at Boston University's African Studies Center. She was a Fulbright lecturer in Senegal in 2002–2003 where she taught environmental economics and began the research project on which her study is based. Her previous research has focused on African rural economies with particular attention to gender issues and the way international economic relations affect male and female farmers.

Francesca Lamanna is Economist in the Human Development Network in the Latin American and Caribbean Region at the World Bank Group. Previously she worked as Researcher at the Universities of München and Göttingen, Germany, and she consulted for various units at the World Bank. Francesca holds an MA in economics from University College, London, and she is finishing her PhD in development economics at the University of Göttingen. Her research interests include gender, growth, informality, and labor market reforms.

Melissa Mahoney is a doctoral student in economics at the New School for Social Research in New York City. Her research interests include economics of education, gender disparities, distribution of income, and public finance.

Peter Nunnenkamp is currently senior fellow at the Kiel Institute for the World Economy, where he headed the "Global Division of Labor" research area until 2009. Between 1987 and 2005, he headed the "International Capital Flows" research division. He earned his PhD in economics from the University of Giessen, Germany. His current fields of specialization include consequences of globalization in industrialized and developing countries, determinants and effects of foreign direct investment, and aid allocation and aid effectiveness.

Uma Rani is Senior Development Economist at the International Institute of Labour Studies. She holds a PhD in Economics from the University of Hyderabad, India. She has held Visiting Fellow positions at the Institute of Developing Economies, Japan, and the Institut de Recherche pour le Développement, Paris, to undertake research on precarious and non-standard forms of work. She co-authored the books *Social Income and Insecurity: a Study in Gujarat* (Routledge 2010) and *Flexibility of Labour in Globalizing India: The Challenge of Skills and Technology* (Tulika Books 2008). Her research interests include development economics, the informal sector, social policies, and gender.

Yana van der Meulen Rodgers is Associate Professor of Women's and Gender Studies at Rutgers University. She teaches courses and conducts research on quantitative methods in feminist research; gender and economic development; women and global labor movements; and economics of the family. Many of her studies have focused on East and South Asian economies, and she has travelled to and lived in Asia to conduct her research. She maintains a regular consulting relationship with the World Bank and the United Nations, and she serves as Associate Editor for *Feminist Economics.*

Stephanie Seguino is Professor of Economics at the University of Vermont. Her research explores the macroeconomic relationship between inequality, growth, and development. Recent work explores parallels in the macro-economic role of race and gender inequality; explores differential gender and racial unemployment effects of contractionary monetary policy; and considers the macroeconomic effect of gender inequality under conditions of balance-of-payments constrained growth. She serves as Associate Editor for *Feminist Economics*, consults with the United Nations, and teaches in the African Programme on Rethinking Development Economics, a training program in development economics for policy-makers, researchers, and civil society from Africa and other developing countries.

Li Shi is Professor in the School of Economics and Business and Director of the Center for Income Distribution and Poverty Studies at Beijing Normal University. His publications include several edited volumes: *China's Retreat from Equality* (M.E. Sharpe 2001, with R. Zhao and C. Riskin), *Unemployment, Inequality and Poverty in Urban China* (Routledge 2006, with H. Sato), and *Income Inequality and Public Policy in China* (Cambridge University Press 2008, with B. Gustafsson and T. Sicular), as well as articles in a range of English- and Chinese-language scholarly journals.

Rizwana Siddiqui is Senior Research Economist at the Pakistan Institute of Development Economics. She holds an MSc from Quaid-i-Azam

University and an MA from the Institute of Social Studies, The Netherlands. She specializes in econometrics, quantitative models, development finance, and structural adjustment. Her research focuses on gender, globalization, and poverty issues. She developed a SAM-based computable general equilibrium model for Pakistan to assess the impact of trade liberalization policies on poverty and welfare. It has been used to analyze issues such as remittance inflow, foreign capital inflow, gender division of labor, intrahousehold allocation of resources, and financial liberalization.

Eva Sierminska is Research Economist at CEPS/INSTEAD, Luxembourg, and Research Affiliate at DIW Berlin. In the past, she was Director of the Wealth Project (LWS) at the Luxembourg Income Study and Researcher at Georgetown University. Her current research focuses on cross-country and demographic differences in labor market attachment, income and wealth distribution, the link between consumption, income, and wealth, inequality measurement, and methodological issues in cross-country wealth analysis. She received her PhD in economics from Johns Hopkins University.

Yelena Takhtamanova is Economist at the Federal Reserve Bank of San Francisco. Prior to joining the Federal Reserve Bank of San Francisco, she was Assistant Professor at California State University, Sacramento. Her current research focuses the effect of exchange rate changes on inflation, inflation-output tradeoff (the Phillips curve), and the link between changes in household wealth and consumption. She received her PhD in economics from Johns Hopkins University.

Jeemol Unni is RBI Chair Professor at the Institute of Rural Management, Anand (IRMA), India. She holds a PhD and MPhil in Economics and undertook postdoctoral research at the Economic Growth Center, Yale University. She is on the Editorial Board of the *Indian Journal of Labour Economics*. Her research interests are in labor economics, the informal sector, education economics, social policy, and gender. Her recent publications are *Social Income and Insecurity: A Study in Gujarat* (co-author, Routledge 2010), *Flexibility of Labour in Globalizing India: The Challenge of Skills and Technology* (co-author, Tulika Books 2008).

Bernadette Wanjala is PhD Fellow in economics at the Development Research Institute, Tilburg University, The Netherlands. She has wide research experience and publications in macroeconomics (with focus on fiscal policy), macro modeling, development economics, and gender-aware macroeconomics. She previously worked as an Assistant Policy Analyst in the Macroeconomics Division, Kenya Institute for Public Policy Research and Analysis.

Maureen Were works at the Research Department of the Central Bank of Kenya. She previously worked for the Kenya Institute for Public Policy Research and Analysis and has undertaken a number of research projects on the Kenyan macroeconomy and other pertinent socioeconomic issues relating to employment, gender, trade, finance, and development.

Ajit Zacharias is Senior Scholar at Levy Economics Institute of Bard College. His main area of research is distribution of income and wealth. Zacharias received an MA from the University of Bombay and a PhD from the New School for Social Research.

FEMINIST ECONOMICS OF INEQUALITY, DEVELOPMENT, AND GROWTH

Günseli Berik, Yana van der Meulen Rodgers, and Stephanie Seguino[1]

ABSTRACT

This study examines connections between intergroup inequality and macroeconomic outcomes, considering various channels through which gender, growth, and development interact. It upholds the salience not only of equality in opportunities but also equality in outcomes. The contribution argues that inequalities based on gender, race, ethnicity, and class undermine the ability to provision and expand capabilities, and it examines the macroeconomic policies that are likely to promote broadly shared development. It explores how the macroeconomy acts as a structure of constraint in achieving gender equality and in turn how gender relations in areas like education and wage gaps can have macro-level impacts. Further, it underscores that the interaction of the macroeconomy and gender relations depends on the structure of the economy, the nature of job segregation, the particular measure of gender inequality, and a country's international relations. Finally, it outlines policies for promoting gender equality as both an intrinsic goal and a step toward improving well-being.

INTRODUCTION

Increased global economic integration, the adoption of market-oriented reforms, and a circumscribed role for the state in managing economies over the last few decades has caused income and wealth inequality to expand both within and between countries (Branko Milanovic 2005; International Labour Organization [ILO] 2008).[2] This trend is consistent with research findings in feminist economics, which has demonstrated that such policy reforms have worked against development and have generated intergroup inequality in gender, race/ethnicity, and class terms (Diane Elson and Nilüfer Çağatay 2000; Günseli Berik and Yana van der Meulen

Rodgers 2008). Nation-states have attempted to avert rising inequality through a variety of policies (including labor market, social, and fiscal policies). However, much more research is needed to understand the appropriate balance of government regulation and market liberalization to set the stage for growth that reduces intergroup inequality (hereafter, inequality).

In this contribution, we reflect on linkages between inequality, development, and growth from a feminist economics perspective. We examine both the effect of macroeconomic policies and economic growth on inequalities in material resources and well-being and the effects of inequality on economic growth in an effort to identify policies that promote broadly shared development.

We argue that macroeconomic theory and policy should be constructed within the broader framework of human well-being, rather than being solely concerned with how economies function and the achievement of macroeconomic fundamentals such as price stability and robust growth rates. Human well-being requires at a minimum adequate provisioning (through interconnected paid labor and unpaid care activities and entitlements from the state or community); capabilities (the ability to do or be, based on provisioning); and agency (the ability to participate in decision making so as to shape the world we live in). This definition of well-being is consistent with that envisioned by the capabilities approach (Amartya Sen 1999; Martha Nussbaum 2003). This evaluative framework draws on the argument that social conditions and policies should be assessed according to the extent to which people have the capabilities to lead the kind of lives they want to lead and to be the person they want to be, such as the ability to be healthy and to seek education. Accordingly, development – what we refer to as broadly shared development – is synonymous with expansion of capabilities. In this framework, income inequality constrains the achievement of human well-being because it translates into unequal political and social power. This power differential inhibits not only equality of opportunities in access to education and health, but also agency and voice, which are constrained by the social and political institutions that emerge to justify material imbalances.

These linkages make clear why we argue not only for equality of opportunities but also equality of outcomes. By outcomes we refer not only to capabilities but also to income, wealth, and other assets. The quest for equality of outcomes in the case of incomes and other measures of resource control does not refer to the goal of attaining equality across all individuals. Rather, we envision equality of outcomes as a condition of similar group distributions, such that no one group is systematically disadvantaged even though within-group inequality may exist. In the case of capabilities, we interpret the goal of equality of outcomes to be one of expanding capabilities of all without, however, the pursuit of equality through downward harmonization. For example, in countries where women live longer than men or have higher completion rates in education, we do not seek a process that reduces women's well-being in order to achieve equality of outcomes.

While feminist economists emphasize the gender-equitable achievement of an adequate level of provisioning and the expansion of capabilities, many feminist economists are also concerned with other types of inequality that may intersect with gender inequality (Lourdes Benería and Gita Sen 1982; Marilyn Power 2004). This broader concern with inequality is based on the premise that women and men are not homogeneous groups and that any systemic form of stratification based on invidious group characteristics inhibits the ability of the subordinate group to provision, with multiple forms of inequality compounding these disadvantages.[3]

We view economic growth as a means for expanding capabilities, especially in very low-income economies. Growth can add to the entitlements that one's labor and asset ownership, governments, and community-based arrangements make available for provisioning. In low-income countries, high-growth is more conducive to institutionalize and implement equitable policies that require a larger allocation of funds. In high-income countries, however, policies that focus on redistribution rather than economic growth will provide more scope for achieving expansion of capabilities (Hülya Dağdeviren, Rolph van der Hoeven, and John Weeks 2004).[4] In either case, however, achieving an equitable expansion of capabilities depends crucially on how countries achieve growth and how they utilize the proceeds of growth.[5] Growth is not sufficient to ensure expansion of capabilities because policies enhancing equality are likely to generate distributional conflict and resistance from groups who benefit from the status quo distribution. For example, dominant groups could point to added costs as a basis for resisting policies designed to strengthen social protection and to create jobs that would enable adequate provisioning.

In this contribution we build upon research in feminist economics that has sought to integrate gender into macroeconomic theory and develop gender-equitable macroeconomic policy recommendations. Since the early 1980s this body of research has examined the links between gender equality and macroeconomic aggregates such as trade, investment, and economic growth, and it has established that macroeconomic policies have gendered effects. In this contribution we provide further insight into the connections between inequality related to gender, class, and ethnicity on the one hand, and macroeconomic outcomes on the other. Our goal is to examine more closely than previous studies the multifaceted linkages between inequality, development, and growth, and to integrate insights from this volume's studies to show the relevance of gendered analysis of macroeconomics.

We begin with a consideration of contrasting notions of equality that shape differing policy agendas, and we argue for the salience of equality of outcomes in the pursuit of broad-based development. Our examination of the impacts of macroeconomic policies on inequalities in light of contributions in this volume adds new evidence to earlier conclusions on the inimical effects of market reforms on human well-being. We also present a clear case that gender inequality in alternative measures can hinder as well as promote economic growth. In view of this analysis we aim to identify macroeconomic policies that can promote gender equality in its various dimensions and to delineate the appropriate roles for the state and market in helping to achieve broadly shared development.

FEMINIST AND MAINSTREAM PERSPECTIVES ON INEQUALITY AND MACROECONOMICS

Distinct differences in the approaches of feminist and mainstream economists have emerged in the burgeoning research on the interrelationship of inequality and growth. Contrasting views are apparent at the outset as evidenced in the framing of the inequality problem. We consider first the perspective of mainstream economics that underlies the influential policy documents of the World Bank, including the 2006 *World Development Report* (hereafter *WDR* 2006) evaluated by Diane Elson (2009) in this volume. This perspective, which is also embodied in standard economics textbooks and thinking, does not fully reflect the growing sophistication of mainstream economics, but it does have a heavy influence in policy and the market reforms spearheaded by the World Bank and the International Monetary Fund (IMF) in developing economies.

The mainstream perspective emphasizes equality of opportunity, in the sense of formal, legal equality but is reluctant to promote equality of outcomes based on the argument that it would undermine efficiency. As Elson's (2009) textual analysis of *WDR* 2006 indicates, the mainstream perspective argues that promoting equality of opportunity can achieve economic efficiency (or "prosperity," as it is put throughout *WDR* 2006). Inequality of opportunity, in turn, is linked to poorly functioning markets that must be fixed by fostering greater competition. This approach has led to policy prescriptions that privilege market competition through liberalization and privatization. The notion of competition underlying the *WDR* 2006 and similar documents envisions an idealized society of small producers as the economic agents who will spur economic growth, a far cry from actual economies in which unequal bargaining power between corporations and wage workers abounds. Moreover, the mainstream concept of competition does not recognize the social embeddedness of markets and that their operation reproduces the power inequalities and social norms that are inscribed within these institutions.

Further underlying the mainstream perspective is a vision of modernization that sees inequality as a holdover of past unequal opportunities (see, for example, James R. Kluegel and Eliot R. Smith [2007]). As Elson (2009) describes, the *WDR* 2006 reflects a particularly narrow variant of this notion: inequality is a characteristic of traditional (preindustrial) societies where concentration of power creates self-reinforcing ''inequality traps,'' a term frequently used in the *WDR* 2006. And the locus of gender inequality, according to the *WDR* 2006, is rural South Asia and inequalities between men and women in the ownership of assets. Thus, the *WDR* 2006 does not view gender inequality as a feature of industrial societies or high-growth East Asian economies.[6] Moreover, despite widely accepted microeconomic analysis in which women's unpaid labor constrains their labor market participation and contributes to occupational segregation and gender wage inequality, the *WDR* 2006 gives scant attention to both labor market inequality and women's burden of unpaid labor.[7] Consistent with the mainstream perspective, however, *WDR* 2006 views removing legal barriers to women's participation in labor markets and access to land rights as sufficient for achieving gender equity.[8]

In contrast to the mainstream perspective, most feminist economists seek equality of outcomes, broadly understood to encompass occupations, activities, and resources, including income and assets. We see equality of opportunity and equality of outcomes as closely related, such that systemic inequality in outcomes contributes to unequal power and, as a result, unequal opportunities.[9] Likewise, promoting equal opportunity will not be sufficient to ensure equality of outcomes, given the disadvantages that may arise from past history and present social arrangements. Market processes, far from alleviating the inequality problem, can exacerbate it. Gender norms are embedded in labor markets, and fostering competition can perpetuate gender inequality. For example, when women enter the labor market, they are often paid less than men on the assumption that they are dependent on men. Assigning men the role of breadwinner also provides a rationale for hiring men into jobs with upward mobility. Women, in turn, are slotted into low-wage, insecure jobs considered to be fitting for their assumed role as secondary wage earner. Further, in the absence of policy to address women's unpaid housework and caring responsibilities or paid work arrangements that accommodate caring labor, competition in labor markets is stacked against women who have difficulty maintaining labor force attachment levels equal to those of men. These barriers, in turn, lead to persistent gender disparities in occupational outcomes and wages.

Feminist economists' analyses of the interrelationship between inequality, development, and growth underscore that the macroeconomy provides the structural conditions under which equality is sought. In addition, gendered assumptions are embedded in models that guide macroeconomic policies. In this framework, individuals seek to provision for themselves and their families in the context of the macroeconomy. No matter how hard individuals work, how many sacrifices they make, and how much schooling they seek for themselves and their children, their families' ability to provision will depend on the structure and functioning of the aggregate economy. Macroeconomic events can present hurdles for individuals and families in a number of contexts, including a recession; a structural change and thus a mismatch between the individual's skills and those in demand in labor markets; international agreements that have opened a country to trade competition and financial volatility, leading to instability in prices, interest rates, asset prices, and exchange rates, with consequent effects on employment; and liberalization of foreign direct investment (FDI) that gives employers the potential to bargain down wages. These examples indicate that the macroeconomy acts as a structure of constraint in the achievement of broadly shared well-being and may contribute to inequality.

Further, the macroeconomy is itself a gendered structure, as evidenced by differences in women's and men's employment distribution and reservation wages, the latter due to variations in responsibility for unpaid caring labor. In addition, erroneous or unrealistic gendered assumptions are embedded in models that guide macroeconomic policies (for example, assumptions that men are breadwinners and that labor is an unreproduced commodity), and as a result, those policies can worsen gender equality.

This understanding provides the framework for a large body of feminist economics research that critiques market-oriented policies for generating inequality and setbacks in achieving development. These policies, adopted *en masse* by developing and industrialized economies since the early 1980s, have accelerated their integration into the international economy and reduced government regulation over the domestic economy. Macroeconomic stabilization policies have sought to reduce inflation, budget deficits, and balance-of-payments deficits through restrictive monetary and fiscal policies and currency devaluation. Longer-term reforms in the area of trade liberalization, capital account liberalization, deregulation of government controls, and the privatization of public services and state-owned enterprises have become key components of structural adjustment programs. These stabilization policies and reforms have subsequently become normalized as "sound" macroeconomic policies.

A series of financial crises in East Asia, South America, and Russia, and most recently the global financial crisis that started in 2008, have brought widespread critique in policy and scholarly circles of the neoliberal policy agenda, with calls for a new international financial architecture and a move away from unfettered deregulation and liberalization (Barry Eichengreen 1999; Narcis Serra and Joseph Stiglitz 2008). Yet well before this clamor for change, feminist economists had critiqued the mainstream policy agenda for its uneven distributional consequences across gender, ethnicity, and class (Lourdes Benería and Shelley Feldman 1992; Pamela Sparr 1994; Nilüfer Çağatay, Diane Elson, and Caren Grown 1995). Feminist economists have argued that the deflationary bias and the commodification bias of these macroeconomic policies result in entitlement failures for low-income groups and more generally domestic groups that are not internationally mobile (Elson and Çağatay 2000). Budget cuts in basic public services along with privatization of these services and social protection increase livelihood insecurity and shift the burden of social reproduction onto these groups. Women in low-income groups, in particular, have to not only search for paid work in economies that generate, at best, weak employment growth but also put in more time and effort to provision with non-market substitutes to make ends meet. Further, the costs of increased vulnerability to global financial crises brought on by financial liberalization are borne by the same domestically locked-in groups who are least able to bear them. Thus, low inflation targets, budget surpluses, and efficiency are achieved by shifting costs and risks away from financial interests and wealthy domestic groups. Feminist economists have not only questioned the soundness of these macroeconomic policies but also made theoretical contributions to macroeconomic theories that recognize the implications of inequality (Berik and Rodgers 2008). We discuss our interpretations of this literature and this volume's contributions in the following two sections.

IMPACT OF MACROECONOMIC POLICIES ON INEQUALITY

Developing countries have adopted remarkably similar macroeconomic policies since the 1980s, in large part due to the influence of the World Bank and IMF. Those policies have included a reduced role for the state in directing investment, fiscal austerity, inflation-targeting, coupled with trade, investment, and financial liberalization. This set of policies has had mixed effects on women's employment. In some countries, women have experienced increased access to employment in export-oriented labor-intensive manufacturing (Guy Standing 1999). These gains in employment have been accompanied by precarious working conditions, however, due to labor deregulation and deflationary macroeconomic policies. In other developing countries, trade liberalization has resulted in the demise of domestic industries and loss of formal employment. Strapped by IMF and World Bank conditionality, which is even more stringent than the World Trade Organization (WTO) regulatory structure, governments continue to have fewer policy options to implement active industrial policies to generate employment (Shahrukh Rafi Khan 2007). These policy constraints have led to the rapid expansion of a range of informal jobs that lack basic legal and social protections and are not subject to formal economic regulations. In manufacturing, jobs are often dead-end with no opportunity to move up the job ladder to higher-wage, skilled jobs or to supervisory positions. Firms have increasingly turned to flexible and informal work arrangements that are temporary, seasonal, or casual, with women slotted for those jobs (Radhika Balakrishnan 2001).

The increasing informalization of the global workforce has brought a growing tendency of final-goods producers to subcontract toward smaller-scale, home-based operations (Marilyn Carr, Martha Alter Chen, and Jane Tate 2000). Home-based workers are predominantly women who work for lower pay (often on a piece-rate basis), receive few if any fringe benefits, pay their own utility costs, work long hours, and remain uncovered by most national labor laws. Many women resort to this type of work if they have lost formal-sector jobs or if they need to combine paid work with childcare obligations (Lourdes Benería 2007).

Given the fairly widespread nature of home-based work as an inherent structure in many developing economies, an interesting question is how macroeconomic policy reforms have affected the home-based work decisions of women and men. Uma Rani and Jeemol Unni (2009), in this volume, use both household survey data and macroeconomic data to tackle this question in the case of India's trade and industrial policy liberalization of the 1990s. Like many developing countries after World War II, India had utilized an import substitution industrialization strategy as a basis for development planning. However, in the early 1990s, a series of external, political, and macroeconomic shocks precipitated a financial crisis to which the Indian government responded by requesting stand-by assistance from the IMF. In exchange for IMF aid, the government agreed to a fairly standard policy prescription of stabilization and structural adjustment policies, including a major reduction in tariff rates across the board. Additional waves of trade and industrial policy reforms followed.

In exploring how India's trade and investment liberalization affected home-based workers, Rani and Unni (2009) find more of an impact on men. The authors argue that home-based work was already a prominent feature of the female labor market in India before the reforms, and that cultural norms and socioeconomic status more so than macroeconomic policy reforms determined women's home-based work. However, a relatively small proportion of men had engaged in home-based work before the liberalization. Men's labor proved more responsive to the increased employment opportunities in home-based work that followed the reforms. The increase in men's home-based work was especially pronounced in import-competing industries producing machinery. Since this activity was generally considered heavy work, it was socially more acceptable for men to engage in this work. When reforms led to outsourcing, firms preferred male workers even when the activity was home-based. Caste also played a role, with men in lower-status castes being more likely to participate in low-paid home-based jobs, since men in higher-status castes had more employment options outside the home. Hence liberalization policies in India brought men closer to women in the incidence of home-based work, resulting in downward harmonization of pay and work conditions, which is not a viable approach to achieving gender equality. Rani and Unni's (2009) study is unique for its use of micro and macro data to examine the effect of macroeconomic policies on the relative composition of visible work in the market economy and of invisible home-based work.

More broadly, the informal economy is a vitally important structure that permeates the various links between gender and the macroeconomy. To the extent that women are overrepresented in informal work, macroeconomic reforms to boost aggregate demand can lead to employment gains that disproportionately favor men. In this volume, Bernadette Mukhwana Wanjala and Maureen Were (2009) conduct a multiplier analysis using a Social Accounting Matrix (SAM) for Kenya to examine how domestic investment strategies targeting sectors with high linkages affect employment and pay. They show that women workers in Kenya benefit relatively less from new domestic investment in manufacturing since they predominantly work in sectors where the stimulus package creates low-paid, unskilled jobs. The authors conclude that financing for development by promoting domestic investment must support women's skills acquisition, primarily through higher education and training opportunities, so that they have improved access to formal and skilled jobs.

Just as gender-neutral policy reforms to stimulate domestic investment can have gendered effects due to women's concentration in the informal economy, public sector downsizing may be gender-neutral in intent but have differential effects in practice. Public sector employment retrenchment, an integral part of broader economic reform strategies, is motivated by the need to trim government budget deficits, correct staffing and skill imbalances in public enterprises, improve efficiency of public sector operations, and refocus the priorities of national governments. Downsizing often involves lay-offs for employees, particularly women, who have lower levels of tenure, less education, and lower status positions. As Jieyu Liu (2007) argues, during China's public sector retrenchment in the late 1990s, women experienced disproportionate job losses primarily due to the nature of gendered job segregation (that is, women's concentration in less-skilled jobs), which also constrained women's post-lay off job prospects.

Sai Ding, Xiao-yuan Dong, and Shi Li (2009), in this volume, examine how changes in the employment and earnings of married women in China affected overall income inequality from 1988 to 2002, a period of profound economic reforms and substantial public sector retrenchment. They argue that when women generate monetary incomes in the paid labor market, their earnings contribute to the household's purchasing power and potentially to a lessening in overall income inequality if their spouses are in low-paid jobs. The authors use a decomposition procedure involving the coefficient of variation of total household income and find that the disproportionate job losses of women during the retrenchment contributed to rising overall inequality in urban China, which worked against the otherwise equalizing effect that their earnings would have had on inequality. These results provide valuable new evidence that a market-oriented reform strategy may be ostensibly gender-neutral but in practice may contribute to greater gender disparity in employment rates. This distorts the otherwise equalizing effect of women's labor force participation and worsens overall income inequality.

Building social provisioning criteria into macroeconomic models constitutes an important step toward examining the gender implications of macroeconomic policies. Such efforts have precedents in the theoretical models of William Darity (1995) and Korkut Ertürk and Nilüfer Çağatay (1995), along with a small but growing number of studies that add women's unpaid work and gendered power relations to Computable General Equilibrium (CGE) models. CGE analysis, which has a fairly long history as a planning tool in scholarly and policy discourse, can be used to demonstrate that macroeconomic policies and shocks affect men and women differently through multiple sectoral linkages in the economy. In this volume, Rizwana Siddiqui (2009) constructs a gendered CGE model for Pakistan and conducts a series of simulations involving the liberalization of trade policy. The model incorporates several innovations, including social reproduction activities, labor disaggregated by gender, and male- and female-headed households. Siddiqui's results indicate that trade reforms led to a higher gender gap in domestic workloads, literacy rates, and infant mortality rates among poor households. Because overall welfare was reduced, Siddiqui concludes that poverty reduction and income redistribution policies need to accompany trade liberalization.

Jeanne E. Koopman (2009) provides the only analysis in this volume of the impact of macroeconomic policies on an agrarian economy. In an historical account of the modernization of agriculture in the Senegal River Valley since the 1970s, she explains how the implementation of market-oriented reforms from 1985 onward undercut a fledgling labor- and capital-intensive farming system that was supposed to promote food security. The construction of dams and irrigation schemes to support modern agriculture contributed to Senegal's unsustainable debt burden, which was followed by the country's structural adjustment program. These policies increased the cost of farming by cutting credit and subsidies to smallholders. Consistent with the outcomes of agricultural trade liberalization in other countries in Sub-Saharan Africa and in Latin America in the 1990s (Mamerto Perez, Sergio Schlesinger, and Timothy A. Wise 2008), family farmers in Senegal were further squeezed by falling prices for their output when trade liberalization exposed them to import competition, and the government eliminated its program to purchase the output of farmers.

A decline in caste inequality accompanied the shift from traditional to modern irrigated farming in the Senegal River Valley, as the government distributed equal-sized plots to all heads of household. Men's migration, to make up for the elimination of government support for farming, also contributed to the decline in caste-based income inequality, as migrants were disproportionately from artisan and ex-slave castes. However, the government's model of irrigated plot distribution left gender inequality in access to land unchanged, as only a small proportion of women could obtain land rights as household heads. Unlike other parts of Africa, married women in Senegal did not have customary land-use rights nor did they have substantial gender-specific food provisioning responsibilities. As the labor-intensive farming was phased in and men's migration increased, women were called upon to work on male-controlled household plots. Based on time-use survey data from 1958 and 1991–2, Koopman documents the shift in agricultural work burden from men to women and children. Surprisingly, this shift in burden was accompanied by a decline in the absolute amount of time devoted to farming, which according to Koopman is symptomatic of policy failure. As of 2008, rice farming and migration are no longer viable, and these smallholders, who make up half the population in Senegal, are faced with rising food insecurity. Koopman's village case study shows that the farm income generated by women on small garden plots is vital for household livelihoods. Yet, both their insecure land rights and competition from subsidized European food imports constrain women's attempts to grow vegetables for the market and household subsistence.

Also in this volume, Ajit Zacharias and Melissa Mahoney (2009) explore the gender implications of the shift in power relations in the US from 1982 to 1997 that led to an increase in profitability. This phenomenon was contemporaneous with structural change in the economy as evidenced by the growing share of labor-intensive jobs, primarily in services. The authors investigate the impact of the feminization of employment on the profit rate during the "leaden age," as it is denoted in the post-Keynesian literature, due to the combination of economic growth with downward pressure on wages.[10] Surprisingly, the driving factor in rising profitability was not the incorporation of women into the economy at lower wages than men's. Rather, declines in unionization and the liberalization of FDI and trade contributed to declining employment and wages in primarily male-dominated, blue collar manufacturing jobs. One result was that men's wages fell, accounting for three-quarters of the increase in the gender wage ratio during this period. Hence, as Rani and Unni (2009) also demonstrate, macro-level policies had a gender inequitable effect in a way that disadvantaged men more than women. And, as other contributions to this volume underscore, gender job segregation shaped the gendered effects of macroeconomic policy. While feminist economics research in recent years has produced a good deal of evidence that women's livelihoods have been made more precarious by the shift to policies that promote market and trade liberalization and a reduced role for the state, clearly there are countries in which men have been disproportionately negatively affected.

Yelena Takhtamanova and Eva Sierminska (2009), in this volume, offer another study on a developed economy, with an investigation of the gendered employment impact of contractionary monetary policy on member countries of the Organisation for Economic Cooperation and Development (OECD). In contrast to recent empirical evidence from developing countries indicating that the costs of reducing inflation are disproportionately borne by women (Elissa Braunstein and James Heintz 2008), Takhtamanova and Sierminska do not find any statistically significant employment effects by gender for nine OECD countries for the period 1980–2004. The results, based on both single equation estimation and vector autoregression (VAR) techniques, indicate that there is no statistically significant difference in male and female employment elasticities in response to a change in short-term interest rates. The authors' VAR results, however, do show statistically significant negative employment effects of monetary policy shocks on men and women for most countries in the sample. The absence of a gendered effect could be attributable to women's concentration in sectors that are less susceptible to disruption during cyclical fluctuations. In the US, one of the countries in their analysis, a body of evidence indicates that men and women in subordinate ethnic groups bear the burden of joblessness in response to contractionary monetary policy, suggesting that sometimes ethnic inequality can substitute for gender inequality (John D. Abell 1991; Willem Thorbecke 2001; Seth B. Carpenter and William M. Rodgers, III 2004). Unfortunately, sparse or nonexistent racially disaggregated employment data in other OECD countries hampers the possibilities for determining whether the costs of monetary shocks are similarly distributed to subaltern groups in those countries.

Consistent with emerging standards in the field of feminist economics, this volume's studies utilize a diverse set of methodologies to analyze inequality. While large-scale surveys are a key source of evidence, several studies rely on methodologies that go beyond econometric analysis to provide valuable descriptions of changes in inequality. On one end is Koopman's (2009) historical study that draws upon large-scale survey data on time use by gender and age and a recent village sample survey on women's income contribution to the household. At another point along the spectrum, Ding, Dong, and Li (2009), as well as Zacharias and Mahoney (2009), rely on decomposition techniques to identify the sources of changes in inequality. We also see a variety of regression techniques applied to country-specific data, such as logit regressions of work decisions (Rani and Unni [2009]), and vector autoregressions and ordinary least squares regressions of monetary policy effects on employment (Takhtamanova and Sierminska [2009]). Likewise, the unit of analysis ranges from a region within a country or a village that yields rich insights on process (Koopman [2009]), to all households or a set of macroeconomic aggregates within a country (Siddiqui [2009]), to a large set of countries (exemplified by

Stephan Klasen and Francesca Lamanna's [2009] and Matthias Busse and Peter Nunnenkamp's [2009] contributions discussed in the next section).

The volume also includes gendered applications of multi-sector planning models similar to those used by governments and international agencies to simulate the outcomes of macroeconomic reforms through multiple channels in the economy (Wanjala and Were [2009]; Siddiqui [2009]). While other types of gendered macro models follow an economy-wide approach and link aspects of the monetary economy with those of the household economy, they do not allow for connections with detailed sectors (Marzia Fontana and Yana van der Meulen Rodgers 2005). An engendered CGE approach fills this gap with the simultaneous analysis of all individual sectors of the monetary economy, the relations among them, and the linkages and feedback effects between the monetary economy and the household economy. Yet SAM- and CGE-based techniques are still evolving, and readers need to be careful to assess the underlying assumptions and parameter choices that help to determine the simulation results.[11] That said, analyses by Wanjala and Were (2009) and Siddiqui (2009) shed light on important gender-related reallocation mechanisms through which macroeconomic reforms might operate, mechanisms that conventional analyses fail to capture.

IMPLICATIONS OF INEQUALITY FOR GROWTH

The formulation of efficacious policies to promote societal development and raise living standards requires a clear understanding of how gender relations can affect progress toward those goals. Moreover, we want to know how gender and the macroeconomy interact so as to devise policies that enable gender equality to be compatible with economic growth. An emerging body of research, with considerable policy relevance, explores the implications of the gender distribution of capabilities, income, and other resources for economic growth (Janet Saltzman Chafetz 1989; Stephan Klasen 2002; Stephanie Seguino 2008b).

In this research, scholars have theoretically traced out the channels through which gender affects macroeconomic outcomes, with a number of cross-country studies that have empirically tested the theories. The evidence thus far suggests that macroeconomic effects of gender inequality can be contradictory: gender inequality may stimulate some macroeconomic aggregates while having negative effects in other areas (Janet Stotsky 2006; Berik and Rodgers 2008; and Elissa Braunstein 2008). These contradictory findings, which reflect differences in theoretical frameworks, have given rise to an important debate on whether the net effect of gender inequality is a stimulus or a drag on growth.[12]

One group of scholars emphasizes the long-run determinants of productivity growth. This research generally assumes full employment and well-functioning labor markets, thus placing less emphasis on short-run outcomes.[13] The second group, encompassing heterodox approaches (including Keynesianism) highlights the potential for demand-side disturbances in the short run that can lead to excess capacity and bargaining power differentials, the latter resulting in wages diverging from productivity. The emerging debate also shows that the relationship between growth and gender depends on which measure of gender inequality, and thus which transmission mechanism, is under consideration. Some measures of gender inequality (such as gender wage gaps) are fast acting variables, influencing aggregate demand, employment, and output in the short run. The effects of others are slower to manifest. For example, the macroeconomic effect of differential investments in girls and boys today may not be visible until sometime in the future. Gender effects also differ according to the structure of the economies under consideration (post-industrial, industrial, or agricultural). The gender division of labor varies with economic structure and will therefore influence the transmission mechanisms by which gender affects growth.

The compelling body of work offering evidence that gender inequality slows the long-run rate of economic growth uses gender gaps in education, life expectancy, and employment as explanatory variables (M. Anne Hill and Elizabeth King 1995; David Dollar and Roberta Gatti 1999; Klasen 2002; Stephen Knowles, Paula Lorgelly, and P. Dorian Owen 2002; Berta Esteve-Volart 2004). Influenced by neoclassical theories, these studies do not consider the implications of short-run macroeconomic fluctuations. For the most part, by relying on cross-country regressions, this research implicitly assumes that the role of gender inequality is similar across countries; that is, that we can make universal claims about the effect of gender inequality on economic growth. This research strategy also does not evaluate the effect of differences in economic structure among countries.[14]

Gender relations affect macroeconomic outcomes through several channels in this body of work. Educational gender gaps, for example, are linked to higher rates of fertility and lower saving rates. Rising fertility can reduce investment in children's education and health. Moreover, educational inequality can contribute to women's unequal household bargaining power, affecting the distribution of household resources, given women's greater tendency to allocate spending to children's needs (Lawrence Haddad, John Hoddinott, and Harold Alderman 1997; Rae Lesser Blumberg 2004). By lowering the resources invested in children, inequality is theorized to lower the quality of the future labor supply and long-run productivity growth.

In addition to micro-level effects, scholars such as Anne Boschini (2003) have noted that systematic differences in investments in girls' and boys' education can be inefficient due to selection distortion. Overinvesting in less talented men while underinvesting in able women, reduces the average skill level in the economy with negative effects for aggregate productivity. Educational investments may be distorted due to gender norms and stereotypes that slot men and women into gendered occupations. Unequal educational outcomes and the resulting occupational segregation do not need to be based on discrimination to have a negative effect. Boschini (2003) finds that internalized norms may influence gender-specific educational choices, which may result in a suboptimal allocation of ability. She presents evidence based on a cross-country sample from 1970 to 1988 that the presence of gender stereotypes lowers the rate of skill acquisition in the economy, the rate of technological change, and the rate of economic growth.

Using an updated data set on educational attainment, Klasen and Lamanna (2009), in this volume, confirm the substantial negative effect of educational gaps on growth previously reported in the literature (Hill and King 1995; Klasen 2002; Knowles, Lorgelly, and Owen 2002). They trace both direct and indirect effects (the latter including the mediating variables of investment, population, and labor force growth) and explore the effects of employment inequality on growth, using labor force participation rates as a proxy due to data limitations.[15] Their analysis, which covers ninety-three countries over the period 1960 to 2000, finds that countries with wider gender differences in labor force participation rates grow more slowly, with simulations suggesting that growth in the Middle East and Northern Africa (MENA) and South Asia regions is reduced due to this effect.[16]

A second body of research in the gender and macroeconomics literature emphasizes the demand-side effects of inequality in wages and employment in both the short and long run (Ertürk and Çağatay 1995; Robert Blecker and Stephanie Seguino 2002; Stephanie Seguino and Mark Setterfield 2009).[17] This research is further differentiated from the supply-side literature by its attention to structural features of economies that influence how gender interacts with macroeconomic aggregates. In this kind of research, a country's economic structure combined with the gender division of labor is an important factor in determining the nature of the interaction between gender inequality and growth. Feminist economics research on semi-industrialized economies finds evidence that gender wage inequality can stimulate two important macroeconomic aggregates: investment and exports (Stephanie Seguino 2000a, 2000b). Developing countries are heavily reliant on exports to finance imported intermediate and capital goods in order to relieve a balance of payments constraint to growth (A.P. Thirlwall 1979; Mark Setterfield 2006). Since the 1970s, women's labor has become a primary source of foreign exchange earnings that has helped relieve this constraint in many semi-industrialized economies (Stephanie Seguino 2008a). Women's low wages, due to women's job segregation in export industries that are subject to intense price competition and downward pressure on wages (especially in garments, textiles, and electronics), have been key in the "feminization of foreign currency earnings" (Vidyamali Samarasinghe 1998). While the concentration of women in export manufacturing has received the most attention, even in some agricultural economies, women's seasonal or daily wage labor on farms has proven critical to keeping costs low and export demand high.

In agricultural economies, however, the effect of gender on growth prospects is linked to the gender division of labor within the agricultural sector, and gender inequality in land ownership and loan access (C. Mark Blackden and Chitra Bhanu 1999; Cheryl Doss and Michael L. Morris 2000). In this structure the salient measures of gender inequality will differ as well, with the relatively greater importance of primary educational gaps, gender differences in loan access, and land rights. Therefore, gender equality in access to land and technology, rather than gender inequality in wages, may hold the key to increasing productivity in food production. Consistent with such an argument, Koopman (2009) argues that tiny plots and tenuous land rights for women in the Senegal River Valley constrain food output and marketable surpluses.

Also in this volume, Busse and Nunnenkamp (2009) explore the effect of gender educational gaps on FDI. As much of the development literature has shown, robust investment is an important driver in stimulating growth, and countries are in competition to attract FDI to make up for the shortfall in domestic investment. Based on cross-country regressions using an unprecedented large dataset (seventy-seven developing host countries and twenty-eight source countries), Busse and Nunnenkamp find that foreign firms responded positively to gender equality in education over the 1980–2005 period. This positive and statistically significant effect is confined to middle-income, developing host countries and developed source countries for FDI. The effect of educational inequality on FDI in low-income, developing countries and on the FDI emanating from developing host countries is statistically insignificant. The authors interpret the disparity in results for low- and middle-income countries in terms of differences in the nature of FDI, which is related to diversity in economic structure. In low-income countries, FDI is resource seeking (concentrated in extractive industries), and the availability of skilled labor does not figure strongly into investment. Likewise, the authors interpret the non-responsiveness of developing source country FDI to educational inequality in terms of the nature of FDI from these countries: efficiency-seeking (that is, low labor-cost searching) FDI relies less on skilled labor in developing host countries.

Busse and Nunnenkamp's (2009) main finding is robust and points to the complementarity between the equality and growth goals for countries that strive to reduce gender education gaps. Greater equality in education will not only boost FDI by expanding the pool of skilled labor but also enhance growth, since FDI-related spillovers are contingent on the presence of qualified labor. They also indicate that if developing countries do not take educational equality seriously they could end up stuck in a low-wage, low-labor-productivity, footloose FDI trap. Moving up the industrial ladder, however, takes more than educational equality. Boosting the skilled labor supply would have to complement a set of selective credit, subsidy, and import protection policies that target specific industries.

Busse and Nunnenkamp (2009) cautiously point out that their findings do not rule out the possibility that gender wage inequality might be an added attraction for FDI that flows to middle-income developing countries. More education for women contributes to higher labor productivity, and this could explain the positive effect on FDI, but the key nexus here might be the impact of the combination of gender wage inequality and educational equality on foreign firms' profitability. The two combine to lower unit labor costs below what would have been the case if women had greater bargaining power to negotiate for wage levels that fully reflected their productivity. The lower unit labor costs, in turn, stimulate profits and product demand. Busse and Nunnenkamp note that wage data constraints do not allow them to differentiate among the productivity and wage effects that are proxied by the gender educational inequality variable. Likewise, they are also unable to sort the effects of gender inequality on different types of FDI in a cross-country regression analysis. Analogously, while Klasen and Lamanna (2009) find that gender equality in labor force participation stimulates growth, their research does not address whether higher growth is due to the stimulus to profits and thus investment resulting from women's low wages, which are examined by Ertürk and Çağatay (1995) and Korkut Ertürk and William Darity, Jr. (2000).[18]

A comprehensive analysis of the growth effects of educational equality requires an assessment of whether women are able to capture the full extent of their increased productivity in the form of higher wages. Women's ability to do so will depend on structural features of the economy, labor market institutions such as labor unions, and rules on capital flows, including FDI. If women are concentrated in industries in which the mobility of FDI limits their bargaining position in wage setting, women could benefit from one form of greater equality – education – without any assurance that gender wage equality will ensue. This constraint suggests that efforts to promote gender equality must also pay attention to the ability of women to translate increased skills into commensurate remuneration.

Global evidence on trends in gender wage gaps is mixed. Some evidence that gaps are closing has been found, in part due to narrowing educational gaps. For several developing countries, including several in Asia, however, the discriminatory portion of gender wage gaps has increased (Günseli Berik, Yana van der Meulen Rodgers, and Joseph Zveglich 2004; Doris Weichselbaumer and Roger Winter-Ebmer 2005; Nidhiya Menon and Yana van der Meulen Rodgers 2009). In addition, Remco Oostendorp (2009) finds evidence that FDI net inflows contribute to wider gender wage gaps in high-skill occupations in poorer economies.

Despite the contributions of cross-country regression analyses, as shown by the Klasen and Lamanna (2009) and Busse and Nunnenkamp (2009) studies in this volume, this methodology is unable to identify country-specific factors that may influence outcomes. There is growing recognition that cross-country regressions must be coupled with local case studies to determine the context that underlies the association between dependent variables and structural forces (Francisco Rodríguez and Dani Rodrik 2001; Joseph E. Stiglitz 2005).[19] Exceptional cases are also sources of insight in helping countries determine policies that they could either adapt or avoid (John A. Donaldson 2008). Indeed, Busse and Nunnenkamp identify country case studies as a useful methodology to sort out questions about the unobservable transmission mechanisms between gender educational equality and FDI. This move toward methodological complementarity is consistent with feminist economists' interest in understanding process and agency as well as outcomes.[20]

Apart from methodological caveats, the supply-side analyses on inequality in education, labor force participation, and employment have made a convincing case that not only women but society as a whole could benefit from greater gender equality. If gender-equitable change will promote both efficiency and fairness, then why is there resistance to change? As suggested by the demand-side perspectives, the efforts that enable women to raise their wages may lead to economic contraction due to negative effects on profitability, investment, and export sales. This short-run disturbance in demand could cause not only a fall in men's employment and output but also make it difficult to achieve long-run growth. Thus even if gender equality could produce positive supply-side effects on labor force quality in the long run, in the short run, gender equality might induce shocks that drive economies off their long-run growth paths. This argument is contrary to the view of some growth theorists that such shocks result only in transitory departures from trend normal output growth, where output growth is assumed to be fully determined by supply side factors (Amitava Dutt and Jaime Ros 2007). In this way, the macroeconomy acts as a constraint on gender equality. However, as we will discuss in the next section, policy changes can serve to make gender wage equality compatible with short-run growth.

Feminist economists have also attributed the perpetuation of gender inequality to rent-seeking behavior on the part of men who have an incentive to maintain structures underpinning their privileged economic position (Amartya K. Sen 1990; Bina Agarwal 1997; Dipankar Purkayastha 1999; and Braunstein 2008). Through collective action men may create and perpetuate social norms and rules that benefit them but are socially costly.

Thus, male workers might resist gendered job integration that could increase women's bargaining power vis-à-vis employers and reduce the persistent gender wage gaps. This potential for within-class distributional strife would have to be addressed in order to advance the goal of gender equality.

POLICIES TOWARD EQUITABLE DEVELOPMENT

Given the new evidence on the interlinkages between equality and growth, we next draw attention to the challenge of determining the policies required to ensure equality with growth. This argument implies that post-1980 policies that sought market liberalization with a reduced role for the state in managing the development process must be redesigned with the goal of promoting the compatibility of equality and growth. New feminist economics research in this volume provides additional insights into policies to consider for promoting gender equality as both an intrinsic goal and a step in the process to facilitate broadly shared development.

Achieving equitable development requires full employment, jobs at decent wages, the ability of people to combine paid with unpaid work, and the equitable distribution between men and women of paid work opportunities and unpaid work responsibilities.[21] In some countries, this goal implies a need to increase labor's share of income by turning profit-led economies, in which corporations possess substantial power because of the threat effect that comes from firm mobility, into wage-led economies (Stephanie Seguino 2007). Industrial policy that increases the incentives to shift to higher productivity and higher wage production processes is one tool (Stephanie Seguino and Caren Grown 2006). Skill- and capital-intensive goods and services tend to be more income elastic and less price elastic, both of which make higher wages less contractionary. Developmental banking, credit subsidies, and investment performance requirements to move the economy up the industrial ladder are important components of such a strategy (Robert Wade 2003; Helen Shapiro 2007). In addition, regulation of FDI can slow the mobility of firms, which could then benefit from efficiency wage effects of higher female wages. These approaches can promote growth and thereby reduce the resistance to implementing equitable policies among dominant groups of workers (in particular, men or privileged ethnic groups).

Industrial policy that raises labor productivity would also help resolve the potential distributional strife between employers and workers and make possible improvements in working conditions (Seguino 2008b; Günseli Berik and Yana van der Meulen Rodgers, forthcoming). In addition, affirmative action and training programs that could reduce gender job segregation would help to boost productivity and skills acquisition. Women's movement into higher-skilled jobs could thus potentially alleviate the pressures of higher relative female wages on short-run disturbances to growth. In turn, higher and gender-equitable pay, improved health and safety in the workplace, and union rights are the means to improve livelihoods and counter the widening class and gender income inequalities engendered by the expansion of global production systems.

However, the pursuit of industrial policies to move economies to a higher productivity path requires policy space at the country level, especially in developing countries. This policy space is currently narrowed by both the WTO rules and the IMF and World Bank conditionality. This bottleneck to achieving a more equitable society calls for reforms of the global rules for trade and capital mobility. Moving away from the current global regime of unregulated capital flows would release the deflationary bias of fiscal and monetary policies by reducing the ability of footloose financial interests and rentier groups to threaten to flee (Elson and Çağatay 2000). Changing the WTO's mission from maximizing the global volume of trade to reducing global poverty would be a major step (Dani Rodrik 2007). This shift would enable countries to pursue growth strategies tailored to the needs and conditions of the domestic economy to reduce poverty. Likewise, if the IMF and the World Bank could replace their standard conditionality with the promotion of basic political freedoms, the chances of promoting equitable development would be greatly enhanced. While Rodrik's (2007) suggestion for reform is based on the strong association between economy-wide (household) equality and participatory democracy, the same argument could be made for reducing intergroup inequality as well.

Koopman's (2009) contribution on Senegal also illustrates the urgent need to reform global trade rules. While Koopman argues that strengthening women's land rights and access to technology is a key part of the solution to the current food crisis in the Senegal River Valley, she also recognizes that providing land rights for women is not an adequate strategy.[22] Koopman's study offers an indictment of both foreign-directed, large-scale agricultural modernization projects and agricultural trade liberalization in generating vulnerability, undermining sustainable rural livelihoods, and unleashing migration. It is urgent to reform trade rules so as to allow policy space for developing countries to regulate imports that compete with local food crops that are key to subsistence (Perez, Schlesinger, and Wise 2008). Also crucial are efforts to bring back state support for small farmers by reprioritizing local food security.

Promoting broadly shared development also requires a reorientation of central bank policies away from inflation targeting. Inflationary pressures are diverse in their causes, but inflation targeting primarily aims at controlling inflation by reducing aggregate demand and can contribute to employment declines and downward pressure on wages. As Takhtamanova and Sierminska (2009) show, tight monetary policies have imposed costs on workers in the form of job losses in their OECD sample: job shortages produce competition for the scarce supply of remaining jobs. This competition is often gendered and racialized with dominant groups asserting their right to a job when jobs are scarce. These costs underscore the importance of searching for alternative approaches to assuring price stability without losing sight of the primary macroeconomic goal of ensuring that individuals are able to provision for themselves and their families. There is a growing critique of inflation targeting, with concerns about its effectiveness in promoting price stability relative to approaches that may be less costly in terms of employment (Gerald Epstein and Erinç Yeldan 2008). Further, several scholars have provided evidence that annual inflation rates of up to 15 percent are not harmful to growth (Michael Bruno and William Easterly 1996; Robert Pollin and Andong Zhu 2006).[23] These critiques suggest the importance of developing a more refined context-specific approach to controlling inflation that also provides space for government to pursue the goal of employment creation.

In developing countries, many of the problems of inflation result from supply side bottlenecks – high food production costs, poor transportation networks, and high labor costs due to pervasive poor health. Public investment, not tight money policy, can best tackle these problems. Directing public spending to extension services, subsidized agricultural inputs, and credit for resource-constrained women farmers can address high food costs in places such as Sub-Saharan Africa. Evidence from this region shows that by equalizing women's access to necessary inputs and credit, agricultural productivity could rise by 10 to 20 percent (Katrine Saito, Hailu Mekonnen, and Daphne Spurling 1994; Christopher Udry 1996). Further, women's low yields in Ghana, for example, have been linked to insecure land tenure rights (Markus Goldstein and Christopher Udry 2008). These findings suggest that efforts to reduce inflation linked to high food prices require gender equalizing public investment in farming and changes to the legal code that give women secure land rights, as also argued by Koopman in this volume. Inflation targeting may not be the appropriate tool to achieve these goals, and indeed, by lowering output and employment, it could reduce public sector revenues that could be used to alleviate inflationary pressures.[24]

An alternative approach, adopted by Sweden, combines inflation targeting with labor market policies and has achieved very low unemployment rates. The approach includes a centralized and coordinated wage bargaining system that promotes full employment while fostering moderation of wage demands during economic expansions and the implementation of countercyclical active labor market policies to enhance employment opportunities during downturns (Dominique Anxo and Harald Niklasson 2008). Other developed economies might adopt similar approaches, with the understanding that such policies reduce not only gender but also ethnic competition over jobs.

Busse and Nunnenkamp (2009) and Klasen and Lamanna (2009), in this volume, make apparent the societal benefits to closing gender gaps in education. The volume's case studies of China, Pakistan, and Kenya also show the need for policy measures that build women's educational qualifications and strengthen the social safety net to support women in the adjustment process. Education goals include not only gender equality at all levels of education but also better access for women to vocational education. This may be especially useful for women who are home-based workers or who lose their jobs as a result of increased trade competition. Strengthening the social safety net supports provisioning and thus fosters equitable development together with growth. But, as Elson (2009) points out in this volume, systems of social protection and labor market regulation need to be redesigned to recognize the positive contribution of unpaid work to the monetized economy.

Indeed, we argue that recognition of women's disproportionate responsibility for unpaid domestic labor is a prerequisite for tackling persistent gender inequalities in the labor market. Results on closing employment gaps in Klasen and Lamanna (2009) suggest the need for parental leave policies and other public measures to solve the childcare problem for working parents and to enforce anti-discrimination legislation. While policies that enhance women's employment and earnings capacities are an enormous step in the right direction, they do not speak to women's domestic responsibilities and other structural impediments. Public provision of daycare services for young children and after-school care will help to relieve the time and budgetary constraints that women workers, in particular, experience. Stronger enforcement of equal pay and equal opportunity legislation will reduce discriminatory pay and employment practices that contribute to the gendered impacts of macro policy reforms. These policies can help women translate greater education and labor market participation into fair wages and jobs that utilize women's skills and establish good working conditions.

Several contributions in this volume conclude that gender equality of education and labor force participation (as a proxy for employment) are a stimulus to FDI and growth. These measures of gender gaps are not, however, adequate to capture well-being, and indeed, we cannot be sure they do not inadvertently capture exploitation. Educational improvements do not always translate into higher wages. Being in the labor force does not always equate with a decent job with stable earnings and benefits. This ambiguity is a reflection of data inadequacies that all researchers exploring the relationship between gender equality and growth face. The data needs for accurately estimating overall income, hence gauging women's access to resources, are enormous (Seguino 2008b).[25] In this sense, although the evidence in this volume suggests that educational and employment equality are good for growth, there remains a possibility that this does not ensure equality in other dimensions of material well-being, including wages and security of income stream. We thus have a long way to go in fleshing out a macroeconomics policy agenda that is both good for growth and good for gender equality. Such a framework, we argue, would also require, more generally, a strategy that results in broadly shared development by class and ethnicity as well.

ISSUES FOR FUTURE RESEARCH

In this study, we have presented the feminist conceptual framework linking inequality and growth, examined new evidence on how macroeconomic policies affect inequality, explored the implications of gender inequality for economic growth, and presented an agenda for gender-equitable policy alternatives. We have argued that a gender-aware lens on macroeconomic policies shows that gender inequality may be used to stimulate growth, that macroeconomic policies have gender-differentiated effects, and that these policies may exacerbate gender inequality. Our study has also highlighted the reciprocal relationship between inequality and growth. That is, while macroeconomic policies may exacerbate gender inequality and other forms of inequality, inequality also has macroeconomic effects. We close with suggestions for new research in three areas related to macroeconomic aggregates and gendered well-being.

First, more empirical work is needed to show how privatization, liberalization, and economic crises affect the ability of men and women to provision for their families. For example, measures of children's nutritional status such as stunting and wasting can indicate illness or nutritional deprivation due to catastrophic events and major economic shocks. With the wide availability of developing country health survey data, it would be quite feasible to examine how children's nutritional status varies during a period of structural adjustment and macroeconomic reform. This work would also build on a large body of micro-based analyses demonstrating that educating girls also has a functional importance in terms of benefits for the next generation, as the socioeconomic status and actions of more educated mothers during pregnancy and child rearing can have a large impact on children's nutritional status, health, and well-being (David Pelletier 1998, Paul Glewwe 1999; Michael Boyle, Yvonne Racine, Katholiki Georgiades, Dana Snelling, Sungjin Hong, Walter Omariba, Patricia Hurley, and Purnima Rao-Melacini 2006). A woman's education can also give her autonomy and bargaining power within the household and affect her children's nutritional status. However, little is known about how the increased burdens associated with macroeconomic adjustment policies affect the power of mothers within the household to make choices about their children's food and healthcare that increase their children's chances for optimal physical and social development.

Second, we argue for a renewed focus on how macroeconomic policies can affect gender equality in autonomy, access to resources, and sexual rights. Understanding the associations between individual-level decision making and the macroeconomic environment can lead to important insights into the spread of HIV/AIDS and the effectiveness of policy interventions. As Cecilia Conrad and Cheryl R. Doss (2008) discuss, an array of macroeconomic variables can affect individual decisions related to the spread of HIV/AIDS, including income-generating opportunities for individuals and communities, the availability of imported medical goods, and structural-adjustment-type programs. And, the gender discrimination and social structures that inhibit gender equality and women's rights are instrumental in the feminization of HIV/AIDS in the developing world, particularly in Africa. For example, India's macroeconomic policy reforms, which contributed to an increase in home-based work as discussed in this volume by Rani and Unni (2009), also made women more susceptible to HIV/AIDS infection (Ushma D. Upadhyay 2000). Because the reforms cut agricultural subsidies, women shifted to jobs in the urban, informal sector, including sex work, which increased their risk of becoming infected with HIV. Decision-making power for women is closely related to their access to schooling and remunerative employment, their relations with their partners, and their reproductive rights. Understanding women's empowerment can shed new light on the particularly rapid spread of HIV/AIDS among women, since their ability to practice safe sex and seek treatment depends on their bargaining power.

Third, in the absence of widely available alternative measures, feminist empirical analyses of growth have used GDP per capita, which has been the subject of longstanding feminist critique (Lourdes Benería 1981; Marilyn Waring 1988). As a tally of the monetary transactions, GDP not only leaves out the contributions of unpaid care activities and services of the environment to human well-being, it also disregards the nature of the growth generated, the composition of goods produced, and the depletion of resources in the course of growth. Thus feminist economists have engaged with mainstream economists on their turf, using this flawed measure, which generally overestimates well-being due to its lack of a debit side to account for the costs generated by the output expansion. While feminist economists have critically assessed the nature of growth, their critique has largely focused on low-level equilibrium traps generated by labor-intensive, low-technology growth strategies, for example, in export manufacturing. The next step in feminist economics analyses of inequality, growth, and development is to problematize the nature of growth more broadly by using the principle of sustainability as the yardstick and goal in the pursuit of equality.[26]

Finally, our argument for the development of policies that promote adequate livelihoods and equality implies a useful collaboration between feminist economists, heterodox macroeconomists, whose primary focus has been on class inequality, and economists concerned with racial and ethnic inequality. Indeed, many of the policies that we have highlighted – such as industrial policies and social protection policies – are beneficial not only to women but also more broadly to all those at the bottom of the distribution whose well-being has been compromised by an excessive reliance on liberalized markets to promote growth since the early 1980s.

ACKNOWLEDGMENTS

This volume benefitted greatly from the support and dedicated participation of many people. We are indebted to Diana Strassmann, the editor of *Feminist Economics*, for her extraordinary efforts in overseeing this project on inequality, development, and growth and we appreciate her comments on this essay. We would also like to express our gratitude to the journal's editorial staff, particularly Gemini Wahhaj, Mónica Parle, and Raj Mankad, for their invaluable contributions to the entire volume and to the preparation of the May 2008 United Nations workshop where the volume contributors presented their work. The UN workshop and follow-up events in Torino, Italy and in Doha, Qatar were made possible by the generous support of the Friedrich Ebert Foundation, the UN Division for the Advancement of Women, and the UN Department of Economic and Social Affairs. We thank Jürgen Stetten, Carolyn Hannan, Manuel Montes, Werner Puschra, and Sara Burke for creating the intellectual climate that fostered discussion among authors and discussants. Finally, we are indebted to a large number of colleagues and scholars who served as reviewers of papers and workshop discussants.

NOTES

[1] Authors are listed in alphabetical order. Each author contributed equally to this project.

[2] Some scholars have reservations about the statistical significance of the results and argue that it is too early to confirm this trend (Sudhir Anand and Paul Segal 2008).

The World Bank (2006), which distinguishes among three types of inequality, concurs that inter-country inequality has risen since 1980 but reports that global inequality (assessed for the 1993–2000 period only) has not changed much, and international inequality (taking country population size, and therefore the rise in average incomes in China and India, into account) has declined.

3 Thus, we share the methodological premises of the emerging social provisioning perspective in feminist economics (Power 2004). This perspective broadens the longstanding concern of feminist economists with gender inequality to include attention to multiple forms of inequality. It also emphasizes attention to unpaid domestic and caring work as integral parts of the economic system and insists on judging the success of economic policies by their ability to promote human well-being. As such, the focus of economic analysis changes from individual pursuit of financial gains and competition toward social provisioning through cooperation.

4 Using simulation exercises, Dağdeviren, van der Hoeven, and Weeks (2004) show that redistribution of current income rather than distribution-neutral economic growth is the most effective means for poverty reduction in all but the very low-income economies. Redistribution with growth is the second best alternative.

5 Our interest in the nature of growth includes both the composition of output and the technologies of production. We believe that in both low- and high-income countries environmental sustainability should be integral to the goal of expanding availabilities. We are concerned about the pursuit of growth at any cost through dismantling, or not putting in place, environmental regulations since this strategy undermines livelihoods and capabilities.

6 Elson (2009) points out that the *WDR* 2006 downplays gender wage inequality as a problem, as it views the expansion of women's employment opportunities in export manufacturing as a solution to gender inequality.

7 While human capital theory integrates unpaid work into its analysis of labor market inequalities, it regards women's care responsibilities as a matter of choice. See Michael Levin (1984) for an argument that dismisses the feminist concern with unequal labor market outcomes on this basis and rules out any policy measures beyond creating the legal equal opportunity for employment.

8 Elson (2009) contends that while *WDR* 2006 argues in favor of gender equity, its analysis of the persistence of inequality of opportunity and therefore its solution to gender inequality is flawed. Specifically, she argues that it fails to acknowledge women's unpaid work as a constraint on equality of opportunity and does not recognize that gender inequality often underpins economic growth. Moreover, she demonstrates that the *WDR* 2006 is not an entirely coherent document. Even as it continues to advocate liberalization and privatization, it acknowledges that in many countries powerful groups have controlled the course and reaped the benefits of liberalization and privatization – the so-called "elite capture" gaining attention in the literature – which has become a source of inequality.

9 Anne Phillips (2004) argues that equality of outcome should be considered as a reasonable test for whether equality of opportunity is available.

10 This period of stagnation stands in contrast to the "golden age of capitalism" that extended from 1945 to 1973, an era of rapid growth, low unemployment, and rising real wages in the industrial economies of Europe and North America.

11 For example, the restrictive assumption of fixed prices in Wanjala and Were (2009) prevents them from incorporating relative price effects into the multiplier analysis of the stimulus package. And the closure rules in Siddiqui's (2009) CGE model prevent a complete representation of the various channels by which trade liberalization affects the economy.

12 Scholarship in this area has focused almost exclusively on economic growth as the macroeconomic variable of interest. The research has not yet systematically explored the developmental impact of gender wage inequality on capabilities (for example, on societal health outcomes and education).

13 The long run and the short run do not refer to specific lengths of time, but rather are distinguished by the flexibility decision makers have. In the short run, some inputs are fixed while at least one can be varied. The long run is a period of time in which the quantities of all inputs can be varied. With regard to gender variables, the productivity of the labor supply is a variable that can lead to change in the long run, via more education or increased investments in children, but is fixed in the short run.

14 A number of empirical analyses do include dummy variables to capture regional differences in relationships between gender and macro outcomes. However, the authors emphasize cultural differences between regions more than economic structure as a motivation for the inclusion of regional dummies (Dollar and Gatti 1999; Klasen 2002).

15 However, labor force participation is a poor proxy for employment. For example, we know that in a number of countries, in the Caribbean in particular, labor force participation may not correlate well with employment since women have higher unemployment rates than men.

16 These results are consistent with Esteve-Volart's (2004) study investigating the impact of the share of women among managers and workers across Indian states. She found that the average productivity of workers and talent of managers was smaller in cases of employment discrimination (manifested as occupational segregation), with negative implications for innovation, technology adoption, and growth.

17 In addition, see Elissa Braunstein (2000); Stephanie Seguino (2000a, 2000b); Matthias Busse and Christian Spielmann (2006); and Shaianne Osterreich (2007).

18 The stimulus to profits results from the discriminatory portion of the gender wage gap, that is, the portion unaccounted for by productivity differentials between men and women.

19 One proposed solution is to apply a growth diagnostics method that helps the researcher to identify binding constraints to growth at the country level such that when a constraint is relaxed, there is a payoff in terms of higher growth (Ricardo Hausmann and Dani Rodrik 2005).

20 Feminist economists' interest in examining how an outcome came about renders case studies invaluable. To convey insights about process, a single researcher may use complementary methodologies or draw upon case study evidence produced by others in interpreting cross-country regression results.

21 The concepts of "decent wages" and "decent work" are part of the ILO's decent work agenda, which calls for productive work that ensures fair pay, workplace security, support for families, opportunities for personal growth, freedom to associate and organize, and no discrimination along with employment generation, promotion of social protection, and social dialogue.

22 Koopman's argument is consistent with the literature that is critical of the disproportionate attention given to women's legal rights to land in the context of liberalization. For example, Shahra Razavi (2007) points out the contradictions in the stance of some advocates for women's land rights. She indicates that they do not pay as much attention to gender inequalities in access to complementary inputs and technology, and they tend to overlook the fact that the promotion of land titling and land markets has reduced women's access to land in the course of liberalization in Africa. Razavi also takes issue with the argument that rectifying gender inequality in land rights is a win-win scenario for promoting efficiency, gender equality, and poverty reduction. She argues that not only is the empirical basis of the efficiency argument weak, but also

the efficiency of small farms is often achieved on the basis of distress and intensification of women's labor, either as unpaid family workers or own account workers.

[23] Moreover, Ben Bernanke, Thomas Laubach, Frederic Mishkin, and Adam Posen (1999) find that inflation targeting is less successful in reducing the "sacrifice ratio" compared to other methods of controlling inflation. In the macroeconomics literature, sacrifice ratio refers to the output cost of reducing inflation.

[24] Inflation targeting in Africa is pursued along with import liberalization, which together aim to solve the supply-side bottlenecks by making lower-priced food imports available. The policy mostly benefits urban consumers at the expense of local small farmers who, as Koopman (2009) argues, cannot compete with imported food produced by capital-intensive and often heavily subsidized agricultural systems. Agricultural trade liberalization also contributes to trade deficits and exacerbates the debt burden.

[25] Labor force participation may not correlate well with employment if women have substantially higher unemployment rates than men. Further, employment data do not tell us about the quality of the job, wages, benefits, and gender differences in the volatility of earnings associated with the positions that women and men hold. The level of income is also dependent on hours of reproductive labor, leisure, and recuperation and on cash transfers from the state.

[26] While Human Development Index (HDI) and Gender-related Development Index (GDI), which were developed by the Human Development project, emphasize the expansion of human capabilities as the goal of development, they incorporate GDP per capita (as proxy for the means for expanded capabilities) and thus do not address the question of nature of growth. Genuine Progress Indicator (GPI) is a more promising alternative that addresses several shortcomings of GDP per capita including feminist critiques (John Talberth, Clifford Cobb, and Noah Slattery 2007). While GPI estimates have been calculated recently for several industrial economies and several states within the US, it has not yet achieved the status of an internationally comparable measure.

REFERENCES

Abell, John D. 1991. "Distributional Effects of Monetary and Fiscal Policy: Impacts on Unemployment Rates Disaggregated by Race and Gender." *American Journal of Economics and Sociology* 50(3): 269–84.

Agarwal, Bina. 1997. "'Bargaining' and Gender Relations" *Feminist Economics* 3(1): 1–51.

Anand, Sudhir and Paul Segal. 2008. "What Do We Know About Global Income Inequality?" *Journal of Economic Literature* 46(1): 57–94.

Anxo, Dominique and Harald Niklasson. 2008. "The Swedish Model: Revival After the Turbulent 1990s?" Discussion Paper 189, International Institute for Labour Studies.

Balakrishnan, Radhika, ed. 2001. *The Hidden Assembly Line: Gender Dynamics of Subcontracted Work in a Global Economy.* Bloomfield, CN: Kumarian Press.

Benería, Lourdes. 1981. "Conceptualizing the Labor Force: The Underestimation of Women's Economic Activities." *Journal of Development Studies* 17(3): 10–28.

———. 2007. "Gender and the Social Construction of Markets," in Irene van Staveren, Diane Elson, Caren Grown, and Nilüfer Çağatay, eds. *Feminist Economics of Trade*, pp. 13–32. London and New York: Routledge.

Benería, Lourdes and Shelley Feldman, eds. 1992. *Unequal Burden: Economic Crises, Persistent Poverty, and Women's Work.* Boulder, CO: Westview.

Benería, Lourdes and Gita Sen. 1982. "Class and Gender Inequalities and Women's Role in Economic Development – Theoretical and Practical Implications." *Feminist Studies* 8(1):157–76.

Berik, Günseli and Yana van der Meulen Rodgers. 2008. "Engendering Development Strategies and Macroeconomic Policies: What's Sound and Sensible?" in Günseli Berik, Yana van der Meulen Rodgers, and Ann Zammit, eds. *Social Justice and Gender Equality: Rethinking Development Strategies and Macroeconomic Policies*, pp. 1–43. London: Routledge.

———. Forthcoming. "Options for Enforcing Labour Standards: Lessons from Bangladesh and Cambodia." *Journal of International Development.*

Berik, Günseli, Yana van der Meulen Rodgers, and Joseph Zveglich. 2004. "International Trade and Gender Wage Discrimination: Evidence from East Asia." *Review of Development Economics* 8(2): 237–54.

Bernanke, Ben, Thomas Laubach, Frederic Mishkin, and Adam Posen. 1999. *Inflation Targeting: Lessons from the International Experience.* Princeton, NJ: Princeton University Press.

Blackden, C. Mark and Chitra Bhanu. 1999. "Gender, Growth, and Poverty Reduction." 1998 Status Report on Poverty in Sub-Saharan Africa, World Bank Technical Paper 428, Special Program of Assistance for Africa, World Bank.

Blecker, Robert and Stephanie Seguino. 2002. "Macroeconomic Effects of Reducing Gender Wage Inequality in an Export-Oriented, Semi-Industrialized Economy." *Review of Development Economics* 6(1): 103–19.

Blumberg, Rae Lesser. 2004. "Extending Lenski's Schema to Hold up Both Halves of the Sky: A Theory-Guided Way of Conceptualizing Agrarian Societies That Illuminates a Puzzle about Gender Stratification." *Sociological Theory* 22(2): 278–91.

Boschini, Anne. 2003. "The Impact of Gender Stereotypes on Economic Growth." Research Papers in Economics 2003: 4, Department of Economics, Stockholm University.

Boyle, Michael, Yvonne Racine, Katholiki Georgiades, Dana Snelling, Sungjin Hong, Walter Omariba, Patricia Hurley, and Purnima Rao-Melacini. 2006. "The Influence of Economic Development Level, Household Wealth and Maternal Education on Child Health in the Developing World." *Social Science and Medicine* 63(8): 2242–54.

Braunstein, Elissa. 2000. "Engendering Foreign Direct Investment: Family Structure, Labor Markets, and International Capital Mobility." *World Development* 28(7): 1157–72.

———. 2008. "The Feminist Political Economy of the Rent-Seeking Society: An Investigation of Gender Inequality and Economic Growth." *Journal of Economic Issues* 42(4): 959–79.

Braunstein, Elissa and James Heintz. 2008. "Gender Bias and Central Bank Policy: Employment and Inflation Reduction." *International Review of Applied Economics* 22(2): 173–86.

Bruno, Michael and William Easterly. 1996. "Inflation and Growth: In Search of a Stable Relationship." *Federal Reserve Bank of St. Louis Review* 78(3): 139–46.

Busse, Matthias and Peter Nunnenkamp. 2009. "Gender Disparity in Education and the International Competition for Foreign Direct Investment." *Feminist Economics* 15(3): 61–90.

Busse, Matthias and Christian Spielmann. 2006. "Gender Inequality and Trade." *Review of International Economics* 14(3): 362–79.

Çağatay, Nilüfer, Diane Elson, and Caren Grown. 1995. "Introduction." *World Development* 23(11): 1827–36.

Carpenter, Seth B. and William M. Rodgers, III. 2004. "The Disparate Labor Market Impacts of Monetary Policy." *Journal of Policy Analysis and Management* 23(4): 813–30.

Carr, Marilyn, Martha Alter Chen, and Jane Tate. 2000. "Globalization and Home-Based Workers." *Feminist Economics* 6(3): 123–42.

Chafetz, Janet Saltzman. 1989. "Gender Equality: Toward a Theory of Change," in Ruth Wallace, ed. *Feminism and Sociological Theory*, pp. 135–60. Newbury Park, CA: Sage Publications.

Conrad, Cecelia and Cheryl R. Doss. 2008. "The AIDS Epidemic: Challenges for Feminist Economics." *Feminist Economics* 14(4): 1–18.

Dağdeviren, Hülya, Rolph van der Hoeven, and John Weeks. 2004. "Redistribution Does Matter: Growth and Redistribution for Poverty Reduction," in Anthony Shorrocks and Rolph van der Hoeven, eds. *Growth, Inequality, and Poverty*, pp. 125–53. New York: Oxford University Press.

Darity, William. 1995. "The Formal Structure of a Gender-Segregated Low-Income Economy." *World Development* 23(11): 1963–8.

Ding, Sai, Xiao-yuan Dong, and Shi Li. 2009. "Women's Employment and Family Income Inequality during China's Economic Transition." *Feminist Economics* 15(3): 163–90.

Dollar, David and Roberta Gatti. 1999. "Gender Inequality, Income, and Growth: Are Good Times Good for Women?" Policy Research Report on Gender and Development, Working Paper Series 1, World Bank.

Donaldson, John A. 2008. "Growth is Good for Whom, When, How? Economic Growth and Poverty Reduction in Exceptional Cases." *World Development* 36(11): 2127–43.

Doss, Cheryl and Michael L. Morris. 2000. "How Does Gender Affect the Adoption of Agricultural Innovations? The Case of Improved Maize Technology in Ghana." *Agricultural Economics* 25(1): 27–39.

Dutt, Amitava and Jaime Ros. 2007. "Aggregate Demand Shocks and Economic Growth." *Structural Change and Economic Dynamics* 18(1): 75–99.

Eichengreen, Barry. 1999. *Toward a New International Financial Architecture: A Practical Post-Asia Agenda*. Washington, DC: Institute for International Economics.

Elson, Diane. 2009. "Gender Equality and Economic Growth in a World Bank *World Development Report*." *Feminist Economics* 15(3): 35–59.

Elson, Diane and Nilüfer Çağatay. 2000. "The Social Content of Macroeconomic Policies." *World Development* 28(7): 1347–64.

Epstein, Gerald and Erinç Yeldan. 2008. "Inflation Targeting, Employment Creation and Economic Development: Assessing the Impacts and Policy Alternatives." *International Review of Applied Economics* 22(2): 131–45.

Ertürk, Korkut and Nilüfer Çağatay. 1995. "Macroeconomic Consequences of Cyclical and Secular Changes in Feminization: An Experiment at Gendered Macromodeling." *World Development* 23(11): 1969–77.

Ertürk, Korkut and William Darity, Jr. 2000. "Secular Changes in the Gender Composition of Employment and Growth Dynamics in the North and the South." *World Development* 28(7): 1231–8.

Esteve-Volart, Berta. 2004. "Gender Discrimination and Growth: Theory and Evidence from India." The Suntory and Toyota International Centres for Economics and Related Disciplines (STICERD) Development Economics Papers 42, London School of Economics.

Fontana, Marzia and Yana van der Meulen Rodgers. 2005. "Gender Dimensions in the Analysis of Macro-Poverty Linkages." *Development Policy Review* 23(3): 333–49.

Glewwe, Paul. 1999. "Why Does Mother's Schooling Raise Child Health in Developing Countries? Evidence from Morocco." *Journal of Human Resources* 34(1): 124–59.

Goldstein, Markus and Christopher Udry. 2008. "The Profits of Power: Land Rights and Agricultural Investment in Ghana." *Journal of Political Economy* 116(6): 981–1022.

Haddad, Lawrence, John Hoddinott, and Harold Alderman. 1997. *Intrahousehold Resource Allocation in Developing Countries: Models, Methods, and Policy*. Baltimore, MD: Johns Hopkins University Press.

Hausmann, Ricardo and Dani Rodrik. 2005. "Self-Discovery in a Development Strategy for El Salvador." *Economía* 6(1): 43–101.

Hill, M. Anne and Elizabeth King. 1995. "Women's Education and Economic Wellbeing." *Feminist Economics* 1(2): 21–46.

International Labour Organization (ILO). 2008. *World of Work 2008*. Geneva: International Labour Organization.

Khan, Shahrukh Rafi. 2007. "WTO, IMF and the Closing of Development Policy Space for Low-Income Countries: A Call for Neo-Developmentalism." *Third World Quarterly* 28(6): 1073–90.

Klasen, Stephan. 2002. "Low Schooling for Girls, Slower Growth for All? Cross-Country Evidence on the Effect of Gender Inequality in Education on Economic Development." *World Bank Economic Review* 16(3): 345–73.

Klasen, Stephan and Francesca Lamanna. 2009. "The Impact of Gender Inequality in Education and Employment on Economic Growth: New Evidence for a Panel of Countries." *Feminist Economics* 15(3): 91–132.

Kluegel, James R. and Eliot R. Smith. 2007. *Beliefs About Inequality: Americans' Views of What Is and What Ought to Be*. Piscataway, NJ: Transaction Publishers.

Knowles, Stephen, Paula Lorgelly, and P. Dorian Owen. 2002. "Are Educational Gender Gaps a Brake on Economic Development? Some Cross-Country Empirical Evidence." *Oxford Economic Papers* 54(1): 118–49.

Koopman, Jeanne E. 2009. "Globalization, Gender, and Poverty in the Senegal River Valley." *Feminist Economics* 15(3): 253–85.

Levin, Michael. 1984. "The Earnings Gap and Family Choices," in Phyllis Schafly, ed. *Equal Pay for Unequal Work*, pp. 125–39. Washington, DC: Eagle Forum Education and Legal Defense Fund.

Liu, Jieyu. 2007. "Gender Dynamics and Redundancy in Urban China." *Feminist Economics* 13(3/4): 125–58.

Menon, Nidhiya and Yana van der Meulen Rodgers. 2009. "International Trade and the Gender Wage Gap: New Evidence from India's Manufacturing Sector." *World Development* 37(5): 965–81.

Milanovic, Branko. 2005. *Worlds Apart: Measuring International and Global Inequality*. Princeton, NJ: Princeton University Press.

Nussbaum, Martha. 2003. "Capabilities as Fundamental Entitlements: Sen and Social Justice." *Feminist Economics* 9(2/3): 33–59.

Oostendorp, Remco. 2009. "Globalization and the Gender Wage Gap." *World Bank Economic Review* 23(1): 141–61.

Osterreich, Shaianne. 2007. "Gender, Trade, and Development: Labor Market Discrimination and North-South Terms of Trade," in Irene Van Staveren, Caren Grown, Diane Elson, and Nilüfer Çağatay, eds. *The Feminist Economics of Trade*, pp. 55–77. London and New York: Routledge.

Pelletier, David. 1998. "Malnutrition, Morbidity and Child Mortality in Developing Countries," in United Nations, ed. *Too Young to Die: Genes or Gender?*, pp. 109–32. New York: Department of Economic and Social Affairs, Population Division, United Nations.

Perez, Mamerto, Sergio Schlesinger, and Timothy A. Wise. 2008. *The Promise and the Perils of Agricultural Trade Liberalization: Lessons from Latin America*. Washington, DC and Medford, MA: Washington Office on Latin America (WOLA) and The Global Development and Environment Institute (GDAE), Tufts University.

Phillips, Anne. 2004. "Defending Equality of Outcome." *Journal of Political Philosophy* 12(1): 1–19.

Pollin, Robert and Andong Zhu. 2006. "Inflation and Economic Growth: A Cross-Country Nonlinear Analysis." *Journal of Post-Keynesian Economics* 28(4): 593–614.

Power, Marilyn. 2004. "Social Provisioning as a Starting Point for Feminist Economics." *Feminist Economics* 10(3): 3–19.

Purkayastha, Dipankar. 1999. "Patriarchal Monopoly and Economic Development." *Feminist Economics* 5(2): 61–78.

Rani, Uma and Jeemol Unni. 2009. "Do Economic Reforms Influence Home-Based Work? Evidence from India." *Feminist Economics* 15(3): 191–225.

Razavi, Shahra. 2007. "Liberalisation and the Debates on Women's Access to Land." *Third World Quarterly* 28(8): 1479–500.

Rodríguez, Francisco and Dani Rodrik. 2001. "Trade Policy and Economic Growth: A Skeptic's Guide to the Cross-National Literature," in Ben Bernanke and Kenneth S. Rogoff, eds. *NBER Macroeconomics Annual 2000*, pp. 261–338. Cambridge, MA: MIT Press.

Rodrik, Dani. 2007. *One Economics, Many Recipes: Globalization, Institutions, and Economic Growth*. Princeton, NJ: Princeton University Press.

Saito, Katrine, Hailu Mekonnen, and Daphne Spurling. 1994. "Raising the Productivity of Women Farmers in Sub-Saharan Africa." Discussion Paper 230, World Bank.

Samarasinghe, Vidyamali. 1998. "The Feminization of Foreign Currency Earnings: Women's Labor in Sri Lanka." *Journal of Developing Areas* 32(3): 303–26.

Seguino, Stephanie. 2000a. "Accounting for Gender in Asian Economic Growth." *Feminist Economics* 6(3): 22–58.

———. 2000b. "Gender Inequality and Economic Growth: A Cross-Country Analysis." *World Development* 28(7): 1211–30.

———. 2007. "Is More Mobility Good? Firm Mobility and the Low Wage-Low Productivity Trap." *Structural Change and Economic Dynamics* 18(1): 27–51.

———. 2008a. "Gender, Distribution, and Balance of Payments Constrained Growth in Developing Countries." Working Paper 133, Political Economy Research Institute.

———. 2008b. "The Road To Gender Equality: Global Trends and the Way Forward," in Günseli Berik, Yana van der Meulen Rodgers, and Ann Zammit, eds. *Social Justice and Gender Equality: Rethinking Development Strategies and Macroeconomic Policies*, pp. 44–71. London: Routledge.

Seguino, Stephanie and Caren Grown. 2006. "Gender Equity and Globalization: Macroeconomic Policy for Developing Countries." *Journal of International Development* 18(8): 1081–104.

Seguino, Stephanie and Mark Setterfield. 2009. "Gender Equality and the Sustainability of Steady State Growth Paths," in Mark Setterfield, ed. *Handbook of Alternative Theories of Economic Growth*. Cheltenham, UK; Northampton, MA, USA: Edward Elgar Publishers, Ltd.

Sen, Amartya K. 1990. "Gender and Cooperative Conflicts," in Irene Tinker, ed. *Persistent Inequalities*, pp. 123–49. Oxford: Oxford University Press.

Sen, Amartya. 1999. "The Ends and Means of Development," in *Development As Freedom*, pp. 35–53. New York: Alfred Knopf.

Serra, Narcis and Joseph Stiglitz. 2008. *The Washington Consensus Reconsidered: Towards a New Global Governance*. London and New York: Oxford University Press.

Setterfield, Mark. 2006. "Thirlwall's Law and Palley's Pitfalls: A Reconsideration," in Philip Arestis, John McCombie, and R. Vickerman, eds. *Growth and Economic Development: Essays in Honour of A.P. Thirlwall*, pp. 47–59. Cheltenham: Edward Elgar.

Shapiro, Helen. 2007. "Industrial Policy and Growth." Working Paper 53, United Nations Department of Economic and Social Affairs.

Siddiqui, Rizwana. 2009. "Modeling Gender Effects of Pakistan's Trade Liberalization." *Feminist Economics* 15(3): 287–321.

Sparr, Pamela. 1994. *Mortgaging Women's Lives: Feminist Critiques of Structural Adjustment*. London: Zed Press.

Standing, Guy. 1999. "Global Feminization through Flexible Labor: A Theme Revisited." *World Development* 27(3): 583–602.

Stiglitz, Joseph E. 2005. "The Overselling of Globalization," in Michael M. Weinstein, ed. *Globalization: What's New?*, pp. 228–61. New York: Columbia University Press.

Stotsky, Janet. 2006. "Gender and its Relevance to Macroeconomic Policy: A Survey." Working Paper 06/233, International Monetary Fund.

Talberth, John, Clifford Cobb, and Noah Slattery. 2007. *The Genuine Progress Indicator 2006: A Tool for Sustainable Development.* Oakland, CA: Redefining Progress.

Takhtamanova, Yelena and Eva Sierminska. 2009. "Gender, Monetary Policy, and Employment: The Case of Nine OECD Countries." *Feminist Economics* 15(3): 323–53.

Thirlwall, A.P. 1979. "The Balance of Payments Constraint as an Explanation of International Growth Rate Differences." *Banca Nazionale del Lavoro Quarterly Review* 128(March): 45–53.

Thorbecke, Willem. 2001. "Estimating the Effects of Disinflationary Monetary Policy on Minorities." *Journal of Policy Modeling* 23(1): 51–66.

Udry, Christopher. 1996. "Gender, Agricultural Production, and the Theory of the Household." *Journal of Political Economy* 104(5): 1010–46.

Upadhyay, Ushma D. 2000. "India's New Economic Policy of 1991 and Its Impact on Women's Poverty and AIDS." *Feminist Economics* 6(3): 105–22.

Wade, Robert. 2003. "What Strategies Are Viable for Developing Countries Today? The World Trade Organization and the Shrinking of 'Development Space.'" *Review of International Political Economy* 10(4): 621–44.

Wanjala, Bernadette Mukhwana and Maureen Were. 2009. "Gender Disparities and Economic Growth in Kenya: A Social Accounting Multiplier Approach." *Feminist Economics* 15(3): 227–51.

Waring, Marilyn. 1988. *If Women Counted: A New Feminist Economics.* New York: HarperCollins.

Weichselbaumer, Doris and Roger Winter-Ebmer. 2005. "A Meta-Analysis of the International Gender Wage Gap." *Journal of Economic Surveys* 19(3): 479–511.

World Bank. 2006. *World Development Report.* Washington, DC: World Bank.

Zacharias, Ajit and Melissa Mahoney. 2009. "Do Gender Disparities in Employment Increase Profitability? Evidence from the United States." *Feminist Economics* 15(3): 133–61.

Gender Equality and Economic Growth in the World Bank *World Development Report 2006*

Diane Elson

ABSTRACT

This contribution examines how gender equality features in the World Bank's *World Development Report 2006: Equity and Development*, focusing on its conceptual framework, use of empirical evidence, and policy recommendations. It concludes that despite acknowledging that liberalization and privatization have been captured by elites for their own benefit, the report still clings to a neoclassical understanding of how markets and competition work. Moreover, although the report emphasizes gender inequality in opportunities as a trap that hinders economic growth, it shows no understanding of economic growth as a gendered process in which old forms of gender inequality are weakened but new forms of gender inequality emerge.

INTRODUCTION

It is widely agreed that the Washington Consensus – the simplistic view that restrictive monetary and fiscal policy, market liberalization, and privatization promote better and faster development – has been superseded. The Washington Consensus, shared by the International Monetary Fund (IMF), the World Bank, the US Treasury, and the US Agency for International Development (USAID), shaped the stabilization and structural adjustment policies of the 1980s and early 1990s. By the late 1990s, the disappointing results of these policies were evident, and the Washington Consensus was in some disarray. The World Bank, in particular, had made some changes in both its theory and policy, with more focus on empowerment and participation of poor people. There was talk of transition to a new period in development policy and analysis – a "post-Washington Consensus" – in which more attention is paid to social aspects of development.[1]

This paper argues that the *World Development Report 2006: Equity and Development* (hereafter referred to as the *WDR2006*) is emblematic of that shift. The *World Development Report* is the annual flagship publication of the

World Bank, designed to be accessible to a wide audience and an attractive resource for teachers, students, journalists, and civil society activists, as well as development policy analysts in government and international agencies. It has an important influence on discourses of development, on what many people take to be "common sense" about development. Each year it has a special theme, and in 2006, in response to mounting criticism of growing inequality within and between countries, the theme was "equity and development." In the *WDR2006*, it was argued that equity matters in its own right and should be an objective of development policy, not only an instrument to achieve other goals. However, the report makes clear that its focus is not on equality in outcomes, but on equality in opportunities. Thus, its policy focus is on the distribution of assets, access to markets, and political voice – not on the distribution of income. In addition, the report hedges its bets by buttressing its focus on equity with the argument that greater equity could also lead to greater efficiency, and by arguing that some equity-promoting policies might conflict with efficiency (as defined by neoclassical economics) and that such policies should be rejected.[2]

There was some recognition in the *WDR2006* that the policies of liberalization and privatization had flaws. In what I take to be an important innovation in World Bank thinking, the report acknowledges that liberalization and privatization have in many cases been captured by elites and become a source of inequality (World Bank 2006: 182). Nevertheless, the authors of the report clearly feel that equity is a controversial topic, and that they may face criticism for focusing the report on equity, rather than on absolute poverty. This may be related to the fact that the political climate in the US at the time when the report was being prepared was not favorable to an emphasis on equity as a goal of public policy. There are large variations in tone among different sections of the report, and considerable tacking backwards and forwards between different viewpoints on the relevance and desirability of equity.[3] Of course, as Shahra Razavi (2006) points out, the links between changes in the discourse offered by *WDR2006* and the policy conditions attached to World Bank loans (and spelled out in Memoranda of Understanding between the World Bank and governments that borrow from the World Bank) are somewhat tenuous. Nevertheless, discursive shifts in key World Bank documents are noteworthy to the extent that they widen the intellectual space available for debating development with powerful actors in development processes and for challenging and changing "common sense" about development. This study discusses the ways in which gender features in the *WDR2006* and affects the economic analysis it provides. It argues that although the *WDR2006* makes considerable departures from standard neoliberal prescriptions, it does not have an adequate understanding of capitalist development and its gendered characteristics, and as a result fails to provide policy recommendations that address the ways in which gender inequality is not only weakened but also recreated and sustained by capitalist development.

The World Bank did not pay much attention to gender issues in its research or practice before the early 1990s. However, since 1995, gender inequality has been given more attention, culminating in the publication of a policy research report *Engendering Development Through Gender Equality in Rights, Resources, and Voice* (World Bank 2001). A series of operational tools for incorporating gender analysis into the work of the World Bank were also developed (described by Zafiris Tzannatos 2006). For instance, in 1994, an operational policy statement on gender was issued (Operational Policy 4.20) focusing on five sectors – agriculture, education, health, financial services, and labor. But, as Tzannatos (2006: 22) notes, structural adjustment programs were not included. In 2001, a new procedure was introduced: a Country Gender Assessment has to be produced for all borrowing countries. However, there is no *requirement* for country directors or project task team leaders to include attention to gender equality in their operations. Based on her assessment of institutional mechanisms for gender mainstreaming in the World Bank, Carolyn Long concludes: "There have been no incentives for including gender-related activities or sanctions for not doing so" (2006: 45). Attention to gender equality depends on the presence of individual staff prepared to raise gender issues; it is not built into the institutional routines of the World Bank. As Long points out, staff members are still rewarded primarily for getting loans approved (48), and attention to gender is not a requirement for approval of a loan. For example, the production of an acceptable Poverty Reduction Strategy Paper (PRSP) is a condition of approval of program loans,[4] but there is no requirement for the adequate treatment of gender, and very few PRSPs treat gender issues in any depth (Elaine Zuckerman 2002).

Despite the lack of specific gender-related incentives and sanctions, some attention is paid to gender inequality in the *WDR2006*, and recommendations are made for policies to reduce such inequality. Nevertheless, the report has fundamental limitations, stemming from the conceptual framework in which the questions of gender inequality are posed and the scope of the empirical evidence from which it chooses to draw. Gender is implicitly considered within a "modernization" framework, in which gender inequality is viewed as a feature of "traditional" societies and is therefore not inscribed in "modern" commercial, industrial societies. The research on gender equality cited in the report is largely confined to research carried out within the World Bank or by neoclassical economists working within a paradigm shared by the World Bank, although there are a few references to the work of feminist economists in the domain of microeconomics.

Many of the limitations of the *WDR2006* are similar to those of *Engendering Development,* which is extensively critiqued in a collection edited by Drucilla Barker and Edith Kuiper (2006). Nonetheless, there are some interesting differences in the production and positioning of the two reports, and it is thus useful to subject the *WDR2006* to feminist scrutiny. The production of the *WDR2006* involved a large team, most of whom had no specific responsibility to consider gender equality issues, and it is read by a large global audience, many of whom will have no specific interest in or commitment to gender equality. The *WDR2006* reaches a much wider audience than *Engendering Development*. A close reading of the report reveals the way and the extent to which gender issues are understood and incorporated in analysis by the "mainstream" within the World Bank, and also reveals tensions and fissures in that analysis.

THE CONCEPTUAL FRAMEWORK OF THE *WDR2006*

What does the *WDR2006* mean by "equity"? It frequently uses the terms "equity" and "equality" interchangeably. This is in contrast to the distinction that has often been drawn between "equity" and "equality" in the discussion of the Platform for Action, agreed upon at the Fourth United Nations Conference on Women in Beijing in 1995, and in relation to the Convention on the Elimination of All Discrimination Against Women (CEDAW).[5] In these contexts, "equity" is often used to mean de jure or formal equality (usually with reference to the laws of a country and the formal rules of organizations), whereas "equality" is understood as substantive, de facto equality in outcomes. Thus, with reference to the labor market, "equity" is understood to mean the absence of explicitly discriminatory laws and practices, while "equality" is understood to mean the ending of gender wage gaps and occupational segregation. One of the reasons for this distinction is that, as feminist political philosopher Anne Phillips points out:

> We can only be confident that opportunities were equal when the outcome is equal too. Any systematic disparity in outcomes – whether this be a concentration of certain groups at certain points of the social hierarchy or a marked segregation of occupations and roles – alerts us to a likely inequality in initial opportunities. (2004: 13)

The *WDR 2006* is much more comfortable with calling for equity in opportunities than for equality of outcomes. It appeals to the notion of "fairness," which the introduction to the *WDR2006* defines in terms of two basic principles:

> *Equal opportunity*. The outcome of a person's life, in its many dimensions, should reflect mostly his or her efforts and talents, not his or her background. Predetermined circumstances – gender, race,

> place of birth, family origins – and the social groups a person is born into should not help determine whether people succeed economically, socially and politically.
>
> *Avoidance of absolute deprivation.* The road from opportunities to outcomes can be tortuous. Outcomes may be low because of bad luck, or even because of a person's own failings. Societies may decide, for insurance or for compassion, that its members will not be allowed to starve, even if they enjoyed their fair share of the opportunity pie, but things somehow turned out badly for them. (World Bank 2006: 18–9)

In this definition, there is absolutely no allowance for structural factors that might make the link between equality of opportunities and equality of outcomes particularly "tortuous" in profit-driven capitalist economies.[6] There is no allowance for the fact that in such economies, large numbers of people work in hierarchical organizations in which there are only a few places at the top, irrespective of how hard people work or how talented they are; for the fact that the commercial markets on which people depend for their livelihoods are intrinsically uncertain institutions and subject to herd behavior, so that individual precautionary behavior is no guarantee against loss of livelihood; or for the fact that societies will be reproduced only if some people are willing to take on responsibility for unpaid care work, even though this tends to put them at a disadvantage in capitalist labor markets.[7] Individual bad luck and personal failings may play a part in individual outcomes, but a considerable degree of inequality of outcomes is "hard-wired" into the functioning of capitalist economies.

The concern with outcomes in the report's definition of equity/equality is limited to an avoidance of absolute deprivation. Moreover, the avoidance of absolute deprivation is not couched in terms of rights of citizens, even though in 2005 the World Bank took the lead in producing the "Arusha Statement on Social Policy," which emphasized the transformation of subjects and beneficiaries into citizens with universal rights (Global Social Policy Forum 2006: 261).[8] Rather, as the quotation above demonstrates, the *WDR2006* makes its avoidance of absolute deprivation a matter of political prudence or charity.

However, the World Bank is convinced that "people prefer fairness" (2006: 80), based on behavioral economics, game theory, and social psychology. But the critical question of what determines people's perceptions of what is "fair" is not discussed. In unequal societies, rich and powerful groups have the capacity to influence the meanings attached to fairness in ways that perpetuate their power. In fact, there are some international standards relating to fairness set out in human rights treaties and the recommendations produced by the UN bodies that monitor their implementation. The *WDR2006* does briefly mention international human rights law, and its fundamental principles of equality and non-discrimination, in buttressing the argument that it is appropriate for the report to focus on equity (79). But, the report does not appeal to human rights norms to clarify the meaning and application of such principles.[9]

The report does not engage in any explicit discussion of the meaning of gender, but it frequently invokes gender as part of a list of so-called "predetermined circumstances," which also include, at various points, race, caste, religion, place of birth, sexual orientation, and family background. Gender is understood primarily as a characteristic of individuals, not as an unequal social institution that flourishes even in societies that are not "patriarchal" in the classic sense of being dominated by the rule of the fathers.

The report finds it important to isolate "predetermined circumstances" because it considers them "morally irrelevant" (World Bank 2006: 4), meaning that a person cannot be blamed for them. The separation of what a person can and cannot be held responsible for is central to the ethical framework of the *WDR2006*, as it considers a concern for equity to be: "the quest for a situation in which personal effort, preferences, and initiative – rather than family background, caste, race or gender – account for the differences among people's economic achievements" (74). Clearly, there is no performative element to such a concept of gender, no allowance for the variety of ways to choose to live as a woman or man, no allowance for any disruption of the binary of male/female – no ambiguities. This understanding of gender as a pre-determined personal characteristic confuses gender and sex (more precisely, "sex-at-birth"'). Indeed, the report sometimes uses "sex" and "gender" interchangeably.[10]

This inadequate understanding of gender is coupled with an inadequate understanding of social class. There is reference to groups that dominate and those that are dominated (World Bank 2006: 2). But the groups that dominate tend to be described as "elites" and "oligarchs," and there is little mention of modern capitalist corporations and their chief executive officers. The examples of oligarchic dominance provided include cases of "extreme predation," such as Zaire under Mobutu and Haiti under the Duvaliers, and cases of rent seeking through alliances between economic and political elites, such as the Philippines under Marcos and "much of Latin America in past decades" (130). A few historical examples are given for rich countries (for instance, banking in the US in the early 1800s), but "oligarchic dominance" is clearly seen as something "pre-modern" that is not systematically found in developed economies, despite the lobbying and political influence of large corporations.

Little attention is paid to capital-labor relations. The implicit vision of the *WDR2006* is that the self-employed, small farmers and small businesses can be the engines of growth, provided that self-serving elites and oligarchs do not impede them. But, while self-employment, family farming and small businesses provide a lot of employment, rapid growth has always been driven by medium- and large-scale companies employing wage labor.

The *WDR2006* argues that there are complementarities between equity and economic growth (or "prosperity," the term frequently used in the report to mean much the same thing) such that some equity-promoting policies also promote increases in output (often referred to by the report as "economic efficiency"). The overview of the report identifies two broad sets of factors leading to such complementarities. The first concerns "imperfections" in markets for credit, insurance, land, and human capital that prevent resources from flowing where returns are highest, and instead channel them to those who have more wealth. In line with standard welfare economics, the *WDR2006* argues that the best policy is to correct such market failures. But, if this is not feasible, "some forms of redistribution – of access to services, assets, or political influence – can increase economic efficiency" (World Bank 2006: 2).[11]

The second set of factors relates to inequitable non-market institutions. For instance, inequitable political institutions, controlled by elites, direct resources to those with the greatest political influence rather than those with the greatest capacity to use resources efficiently. This is said by the report to lead to less well-off groups having "unexploited talent" (World Bank 2006: 2), and to be more inefficient for society as a whole.

The *WDR2006* argues that inequitable political institutions reinforce market imperfections by rigging markets, so that they are not "level playing fields" in which all can compete on equal terms (World Bank 2006: 129). The "level playing field" metaphor is, of course, widely used by neoclassical economists in the discussion of market competition. The metaphor suggests that it makes sense to evaluate market competition in terms of a game played in an arena constructed and maintained by some external neutral arbiter, who can guarantee that the terrain gives the same opportunities to all and that all players abide by the rules. The *WDR2006* calls upon an "accountable state" to level the field and to promote equitable access, though it is not clear how a country is supposed to transform inequitable political institutions into an accountable state.

This metaphor is consistent with the Walrasian concept of competition, in which all market agents are price-takers and all rights over resources are "given." Of course, mainstream economists recognize many ways in which real markets depart from this ideal, but they continue to use it (as does the *WDR2006*) as a benchmark against which markets should be judged and policy formulated.

Heterodox economists have always had a different understanding of market competition in modern capitalist economies as a dynamic process that is inherently social and political and in which firms are not passive price-takers but instead use a variety of ways to create and keep a competitive advantage.[12] For instance, Karl Polanyi (1967) analyzes markets as social constructions that necessarily embody particular forms of social power. He argues that the creation of modern capitalist market systems required the deliberate use of state power to create markets for land and labor through measures such as the enclosure of common land and punitive laws to control the poor. Market competition was fuelled by the "[f]ear of starvation with the worker, lure of profit with the employer" (Karl Polanyi 1947: 111). The metaphor he uses to depict markets in capitalist economies was that of a "double movement," an ongoing tension between market competition and the demands for social protection that market competition calls forth.

The social and political character of market competition is analyzed by Ha-Joon Chang (2001) in terms of varying norms about the legitimacy of the rights and obligations underpinning specific forms of market competition. These rights and obligations cannot be taken as given, since they vary between different societies and are contested and change over time.[13] His analysis implies that what is perceived as a "level playing field" from one perspective may be judged as decidedly tilted from another.[14] He argues that markets cannot be depoliticized and that efficiency criteria can only be established in the context of an agreed set of rights and obligations.

Feminist heterodox economists have been particularly concerned to show that what may seem to be a "level playing field" from a male perspective is, in practice, tilted against women because of presumptions that they, more than men, have the obligation to provide unpaid care for others.[15] For instance, Diane Elson (1999) analyzes labor markets as "gendered institutions" in which both formal rules and informal practices are instantiations of the gender order prevailing in the society in question. Lourdes Benería (1999) builds upon Polanyi's analysis of the double movement to explore both how women are being transformed by the operation of global markets and how feminism may in turn contribute to the transformation of those markets.

A common thread in the heterodox approach to markets is that there is always a question of who gains and who loses from particular ways of instituting markets. Unfairness in markets is an issue that has to be continually addressed and re-addressed, because competition is not just competition within a given structure of rights and obligations, but also competition to secure a favorable structure of rights and obligations. Moreover, competition also takes the form of technological innovation, and thus is continually disrupting the value of assets and the ease of access to markets. Competition is both an equalizing and an unequalizing process.

Throughout its discussion of the complementarity of equity and prosperity, the *WDR2006* offers little recognition of the possible tensions between the two, such as: the cases in which rapid economic growth has been achieved at the expense of equality; the cases in which growth has entailed increases in absolute deprivation following the dispossession of poor people's lands and the concentration of land holdings in the hands of big commercial farmers; and the cases in which growth has been achieved through a denial of equal opportunities in the labor market. Recognition of such tensions does not mean that there is an inevitable trade-off between equality and economic growth. It does mean recognizing that these are two different objectives, and policies that maximize the possibility of achieving one do not necessarily maximize the possibility of achieving the other.[16]

The report recognizes that it must answer the question of why inequalities of opportunity persist if they are both unfair and also constrain national prosperity.

The answer it provides is "inequality traps" (World Bank 2006: 20). Powerful groups may perceive inequity as beneficial to their immediate interests and act so as to preserve inequity. Political, economic, and sociocultural inequalities in opportunities act in a mutually reinforcing way and "reproduce themselves over time and across generations" (2).

The *WDR 2006* identifies the distribution of wealth as a key factor in creating inequality traps. Those with wealth reinforce their domination through "overt and covert use of power" including "political manipulation or the explicit use of violence" (World Bank 2006: 2). Quite radical sentiments for a World Bank report, one might think, but the critical edge is blunted by locating such inequality traps primarily in "traditional" societies. There are very few examples given for "prosperous" countries – a brief reference to intergenerational social immobility in the US is an exception (6). Many of the detailed examples of inequality traps given in the report are located in rural settings in South Asia.[17] The impression is given that inequality traps are a feature of "traditional" pre-development settings, not "modern" post-development settings. Gender features strongly in the presentation of inequality traps. Indeed, the report states: "Gender inequity is the archetypical 'inequality trap'" (51), and it explains this with reference to "patriarchal societies" in which women are "denied property and inheritance rights" and "have their freedom of movement restricted" and are confined to "inside ... spheres of activity" (20). In such societies, women are economically dependent on men and participate less in decision making inside or outside the home. Women's own role in perpetuating such inequality is discussed, with reference to their enforcing compliance with existing social norms by their daughters and daughters-in-law. In elaborating the gender inequality trap, there is much more focus on women's lack of individual property rights than on their low wages.

The report is hopeful that "changes in labor markets and interventions by the state can break this inequality trap" by enabling women to participate more in paid work (54). The evidence cited is largely from Asia, with much being made of the positive impact of the expansion of the garment industry in Bangladesh (drawing from the work of Naila Kabeer [1997]). There is no consideration of the possibility that new forms of gender inequality traps may emerge, as old ones disintegrate (as argued by Diane Elson and Ruth Pearson [1981]). Women may be trapped at the bottom of the hierarchy in paid employment with low pay, little social protection, and few prospects for promotion. They may be under pressure from advertising, films, and television to turn themselves into sexually attractive commodities to attract a male partner in the marriage market.

Although the *WDR2006* occasionally cites evidence from high-income countries, it does not discuss the existence of "gender inequity traps" in such countries. Little attention is paid to the structural interaction between paid and unpaid work (a key aspect of how any society reproduces itself) as an important determining factor. It is acknowledged that women work longer hours than men, and a chart showing this for a small group of high-, middle-, and low-income countries is included (World Bank 2006: 53). But the importance the report attaches to this is signified by the fact that this chart is hopelessly out of date, as it is taken from the United Nations Development Programme's (UNDP) *Human Development Report 1995* and uses data going back to 1975. Much more data is now available, but the World Bank failed to invest any of its considerable resources in constructing a more comprehensive and up-to-date chart. Thus, the *WDR2006* conceptualizes the gender inequality trap in a way that is quite congruent with a neoliberal agenda that sees the removal of barriers to women's participation in markets as the key policy that will enable both growth and equity to be achieved.

The idea of development "traps" is not new, but previous formulations have not linked such "traps" to inequality within countries, instead pointing to factors such as demographic trends (for example, Harvey Leibenstein [1954]) and geographic endowments (for example, Jeffrey Sachs [2005]). The idea of a trap can be a helpful metaphor, in highlighting the strength of constraints, but unless carefully specified, it can create the impression that the trap can only be sprung through outside assistance, with little attention paid to the collective mobilization of some of those caught in the trap as the critical factor.[18] The *WDR2006* posits better policies within countries as the critical factor in getting free from inequality traps (with enlightened technocrats, advised by the World Bank, as the unspoken agents of change), and perfectly competitive markets as the benchmark against which policies should be judged.

EMPIRICAL EVIDENCE IN THE *WDR2006* ON INEQUALITY, GROWTH, AND INVESTMENT

The report presents a range of empirical evidence in chapters 2, 3, 5, and 6 on inequality, growth, investment, and state institutions. It includes many references to gender. Here I comment on the ways in which gender inequality is treated, highlighting both what is included and what is omitted.

The report makes considerable use of decomposition analysis, a technique that purports to show what share of inequality can be attributed to differences within groups and to differences among groups. Decomposition analysis is applied to inequality in education (measured in terms of years of schooling) and inequality in income or consumption. The decomposition of inequality in education includes gender (or rather, sex) as one of the variables, but not the decomposition of inequality in income or consumption.

With respect to education, the report states: ''Roughly a quarter of global inequality in educational attainment is attributable to differences between men and women but this gap is again declining over time, from 31 percent in the oldest cohort in our sample, to 16 percent in the youngest'' (World Bank 2006: 61).[19] The size of the share of between-sex inequality is typical of inequality decompositions, which generally show the between-group shares to be relatively low, as the report notes (40). The report is to be commended for not drawing the conclusion from these decompositions that gender inequality in years of schooling is too small to merit much attention. According to Ravi Kanbur (2003a), some economists at the World Bank would have been inclined to do so. He suggests that similar research by Deon Filmer (1999) on social disparities in education, which finds that differences in wealth and location account for more inequality than gender, has been used within the World Bank to argue that the gender dimension of educational inequality is not of much consequence. It is inappropriate to draw such conclusions. As Ravi Kanbur (2003b) points out, it is not valid to compare a binary decomposition between just two groups, such as men and women, with a decomposition between multiple groups (such as groups with different levels of wealth or different locations). Increasing the number of categories is likely to increase the between-group component of inequality. Moreover, the size of a between-group share of inequality is not a good guide to its social salience. Inequalities associated with discrimination might be held to merit priority attention, irrespective of the results of decomposition exercises.

In addition to decompositions of educational inequality, the *WDR2006* presents a series of between-group decompositions of inequality in household income (or consumption expenditure).[20] The groups are variously defined in terms of household heads' social group, education, and occupation, and urban (or rural) location. Using data from both rich and poor counties, the report graphs the relationship between overall income/consumption inequalities and the between-group share of inequality. The higher the overall degree of inequality, the higher the share attributed to between-group inequality for all four types of groups. The report argues that these correlations are consistent with mutually reinforcing patterns of between-group inequality and that the between-group differences "account for, and possibly explain, a non-negligible portion of overall inequality" (World Bank 2006: 43). No attention is paid to gender in these decompositions of income (consumption) inequality.[21]

The decomposition approach is also applied at a global level, distinguishing between global inequality, international inequality, and inter-country inequality. Global inequality is defined as relating to the distribution of individual incomes, irrespective of which country a person is living in. As the *WDR2006* explains, "each person has his or her real income." The report defines international inequality as relating to the distribution of country mean incomes, weighted by their population size, so "each person has his or her country's mean income." Inter-country inequality is defined as relating to the unweighted country mean incomes, so "each country has one representative at its mean income" (World Bank 2006: 57). These distinctions prove useful in clarifying debates about whether income inequality in the world as a whole has been increasing or decreasing. According to data presented in the *WDR2006,* inter-country inequality has been increasing, especially since 1980; international inequality has been declining, mainly because of rapid growth in China and India; and global inequality (measured only for the 1993–2000 period due to data constraints) has not changed much.

But it is misleading to argue that the measure of global inequality used in the calculations made for the *WDR2006,* and in the research by Branko Milanovic (2005) that it cites, assigns to each person his or her own income. Instead, *WDR2006* calculations assign individuals their household per capita income, while the calculations made by Milanovic (2005) assign individuals the average income for their decile (as explained in World Bank [2006: 64]). Since there are pervasive intrahousehold inequalities in income, global inequality will be underestimated by these measures.

Nowhere does the *WDR2006* discuss the distribution of individual income and attempt to decompose this by sex.[22] Inequality in individual income is likely to be much greater than inequality in individual consumption, as some people have little or no income of their own and rely on interpersonal transfers for their consumption. Data on wage earnings by sex are more widely available than data on income by sex, but the report makes no attempt to make use of such data. To do so might have called into question the easy assumption, made at the end of chapter 2, that an increase in labor-market opportunities for women is able to break the gender inequality trap. There is no acknowledgement of research showing that the East Asian and Latin American countries with the most equitable distribution of household income have the widest gender wage gaps (Stephanie Seguino 2005).

Much is made of restrictions to women's property rights in the "majority of [developing] countries outside of Europe and Central Asia and Latin America and the Caribbean" (World Bank 2006: 52). But it is noteworthy that much of the evidence cited to show the operation of restrictions on women's land rights is from South Asia, which is indeed a key site of what Deniz Kandiyoti has called "classic patriarchy" (1988: 274).

The influence of the experience of South Asia on the writers of the report is probably what explains the extraordinary claim: "Throughout the developing world, women are much less likely to be enrolled in secondary school or university than men" (World Bank 2006: 52). This is scarcely consistent with the statement a few pages later that "Latin America and the Caribbean, East Asia and Europe and Central Asia seem to have reached gender parity in education" (61). In fact, the United Nations Educational Scientific and Cultural Organization (UNESCO) data on enrollments in secondary school show that there is a sizable group of developing countries, mainly in the Caribbean and Latin America, in which girls' enrollment rate in secondary school is higher than that of boys (Diane Elson and Hande Keklik 2002). The gender inequity trap in such countries operates in different (and perhaps less obvious) ways than in countries that experience classic patriarchy, but there is no systematic discussion of this. The report does supplement the discussion of patriarchy with an endorsement of bargaining models that allow for systematic inequality within households, and even allows that intrahousehold behavior may be inefficient. On the other hand, it is problematic that violence against women in the family is mentioned as "another type of inefficiency" (World Bank 2006: 54), rather than a violation of women's human rights.

The report's presentation of evidence on the relationship between inequality and growth is organized around the Kuznets hypothesis, that in the course of development, inequality in incomes initially increases as average income increases, but at a later stage the relationship is reversed. The report is concerned to argue against the theory that faster growth in developing countries is associated with increasing income inequality. It discusses empirical evidence on the Kuznets hypothesis and casts doubt on the validity of using cross-country data to analyze dynamic processes. It emphasizes the sensitivity of econometric results to specification, sample composition, and time period, and it concludes: "No straightforward relation between income [per capita] and equality can be established" (World Bank 2006: 44). The report advocates country-specific studies, such as the studies of six East Asian and Latin American countries conducted by Francois Bourguignon, Francisco Ferreira, and Nora Lustig (2005). Many feminist economists might agree with these arguments, but they would be surprised by the absence of any discussion of the empirical literature on gender inequality and economic growth produced in the late 1990s and early years of the twenty-first century.

Neither the studies that support the idea that gender inequality hampers growth, nor the studies that have found that gender inequality can promote growth, are mentioned in the report, despite the fact that some prominent contributors are World Bank economists or have worked as World Bank consultants (for example, Anne Hill and Elizabeth King [1995], David Dollar and Roberta Gatti [1999], and Stephen Klasen [1999, 2002]). Cross-country econometric research, framed in the neoclassical paradigm, and showing a negative relationship between gender inequality in education and economic growth, featured prominently in the World Bank policy research report, *Engendering Development through Gender Equality in Rights* (World Bank 2001), but the *WDR2006* ignores such research. Perhaps less surprising is the absence of discussion of research showing a positive relationship between gender inequality in the labor market and economic growth, since this has been produced by feminist economists working within heterodox paradigms. This research includes case studies of particular economies (Günseli Berik 2000; Stephanie Seguino 2000a), as well as cross-country econometric analysis (Stephanie Seguino 2000b). However, it has been published in heterodox journals such as *Feminist Economics* and the *Cambridge Journal of Economics*, while the report tends to cite mainly research in orthodox journals and its own research.

In any case, the *WDR2006* much prefers microeconomic evidence to macroeconomic evidence. Using evidence from microeconomic studies of markets for credit, insurance, land, and human capital, chapter 5 of the *WDR2006* argues that markets frequently fail to enable the rich and the poor to compete on equal terms: the poor pay more for credit than the rich, the poor find it harder to get insurance than the rich, and the poor have less secure land rights than the rich. All of these inequalities lead to underinvestment by the poor in productive assets (and overinvestment by the rich).

Among the microeconomic research that is included, the report does cite two microeconomic empirical studies with a gender focus. One study shows that women's lack of secure land rights in Ghana restricts their ability to invest in the productivity of their land by leaving it fallow, and as a result their land is less productive than men's (Markus Goldstein and Christopher Udry 2002). In contrast, women's secure pension rights in South Africa enabled them to invest in their grandchildren, improving their nutrition and increasing their height-for-age ratio (Esther Duflo 2003). The *WDR2006* treats labor market discrimination only as a source of static inefficiency in investment in human capital, and does not treat it as a violation of human rights. Social groups that are discriminated against in the labor market suffer from underinvestment in their health and education (by their parents and themselves) (World Bank 2006: 94–6). The report draws the conclusion from these micro studies that inequalities result in a reduction in productivity below that which could be obtained if markets did not fail to ensure equal treatment, regardless of income, wealth, social status, or gender.

POLICY RECOMMENDATIONS IN THE *WDR2006*

The policy recommendations are framed in a way that is congruent with neoclassical welfare economics, which can be used to buttress both neoliberal policies and policies that promote more social solidarity.[23] There is some tension in the *WDR2006* as it seeks to steer between right-wing and centrist versions of welfare economics, addressing sensibilities that prioritize private enterprise and sensibilities that support a welfare state. One symptom of this is a shifting view of the merits of taxation. Taxation to fund policies that prevent absolute deprivation is described at an early stage in the report as expropriating "some fruits of the efforts of hard-working men and women"; and it is stated: "This might be seen as violating property rights or the right to appropriate the fruits of one's own labor, again creating unfair processes" (World Bank 2006: 20). However, at other points, the report supports taxation.[24] Indeed there is a whole "box" on taxation later in the report that argues for efforts to increase tax revenue and sets out some principles for doing this in ways that "minimize efficiency costs, while not undermining equity" (176–7).

The policy recommendations in the *WDR2006* focus on human capacities; justice, land, and infrastructure; markets and the macroeconomy; and global markets and institutions. In contrast to chapters 1–6, which present the evidence on the extent of inequality and an analysis of why inequality hampers development, there is little focus on gender inequality in the chapters that deal with the policy recommendations (chapters 7–10).

There are a few mentions of women in the chapters dealing with policy, but there is no systematic analysis of how the policies are expected to have an impact on gender as a structure of social power. Thus, chapter 7, on human capacities, advocates preschool education programs, and mentions that they also help poor mothers participate in the labor market (World Bank 2006: 134). Policies that have been successful in increasing the enrollment of girls in school are also mentioned (138). Mexico's Health, Nutrition and Education Program (known by its Spanish acronym PROGRESA), a conditional cash transfer program, is commended for increasing poor mothers' visits to health clinics, resulting in improvements in the health of newborns and children below the age of three (143). Positive evaluations (for instance by Laura Rawlings [2004]) of PROGRESA's impact on the degree to which women have control of household resources are mentioned (the program transfers cash benefits to women provided they send their children to school and a health clinic for immunizations and checkups). It is acknowledged that the program puts more demands on women's time, but no mention is made of criticism by feminists that this type of program serves to reinforce the view that children's health and education are the responsibility of mothers not fathers and fails to challenge the unequal gender division of labor.

Conditional cash transfer programs of this type are much more effective in reducing income poverty than weakening unequal systems of gender and class power.

Similarly, there is a box on reductions in maternal mortality in Malaysia and Sri Lanka (144), but no discussion of what has prevented similar improvements in other countries. The discussion of financing affordable healthcare does not include any gender analysis, such as the problems of ensuring that women get access in their own right to insurance-based health systems and not just as dependents of a "male breadwinner."

The same absence marks the discussion of social protection. The report argues for social protection and provides evidence of the ways in which it can improve equality of opportunity but does not mention gender issues in social protection. To liberate women from the gender inequality trap, it is vital that women's access to social protection is an unconditional right, unconnected to their relationships to men. There is no systematic analysis of this right, just a brief mention that women's participation in public works programs "can be enhanced through non-discriminatory wages, the provision of on-site child care, and adequate private latrines" (World Bank 2006: 152). It is also noted that contributory pension programs have low coverage, and that elderly women who have not worked outside the home are particularly vulnerable to poverty in old age (153). But there is no discussion of how to ensure that social protection covers women and men on an equal basis.

There are similar scattered mentions of women in chapter 8. The issue of discrimination against women in many systems of customary law (World Bank 2006: 159) and the problem of violence against women (162) are mentioned. Considerable attention is paid to gender and land rights, and joint titling is recommended (165). There is some recognition of the problems that poor people have in exercising their land rights and of the fact that "land sales markets have ambiguous effects on equity" (167), as poor people may be forced by adverse circumstances into "distress sales" of their land. There is no mention of the gender dimensions of these issues. There is no recognition, for instance, of the ways in which social norms may pressure women not to exercise their land rights (as discussed by Bina Agarwal [1997]). Nor is there a discussion of the ways in which women face specific disadvantages in land markets (as discussed by Shahra Razavi [2007]).

The *WDR2006* rightly notes that investments in basic water and energy infrastructure can increase gender equity (World Bank 2006: 169), but it does not discuss how to ensure that such investment is designed in a way that meets the needs of poor women. The report is far more cautious about privatization than many earlier World Bank documents, concluding that the evidence is mixed on its benefits for poor people (171). It notes the disadvantages for poor people of ending possibilities for cross-subsidization via measures such as charging all users the same price for a connection to the piped water system, irrespective of the difference of cost in supplying remote rural locations and nearby urban locations. It also notes the disadvantages to poor people of setting tariffs at cost recovery levels, but offers no analysis of the differential impact on poor women and poor men. The report recommends that voice and accountability be strengthened in systems of infrastructure provision but offers no guidance on how to make sure that women are equally represented with men.

The *WDR2006* makes some allowance for an international dimension to inequality traps, though it is careful never to use the phrase "inequality trap" in describing the position of poor countries in the global economy. Instead, chapter 3 refers to "global inequalities in power" (World Bank 2006: 66), illustrated by differences in the voting power of rich and poor countries in the World Bank, and in the size of the delegations that rich and poor countries maintain in Geneva, seat of the World Trade Organization.

As noted earlier, the *WDR2006* argues that markets are not "level playing fields" because of "oligarchic dominance." Liberalization is the usual neoclassical prescription to undermine "oligarchic dominance," but in a considerable innovation in World Bank thinking, the report acknowledges that liberalization can be captured by elites, especially when it is accompanied by privatization (World Bank 2006: 182). This is said to have happened in the financial markets in Chile in the 1970s, Mexico in the 1980s, and the Russian Federation in the 1990s: in all of those cases, state-owned assets were privatized to small elite groups, and no effective steps were taken to design market regulation in ways that promoted competition, including ease of access for new entrants. To counteract elite capture, the *WDR2006* recommends greater public scrutiny of any liberalization and privatization measures, and emphasizes the need for appropriate regulation of markets rather than a simple push for deregulation. "Potential actors to help oversee the process include associations of small firms, consumer groups, NGOs, media and labor unions" (184). There is no discussion of an alternative strategy in which such groups could, through their oversight, improve the efficiency and equity of the public sector in ways that would remove the need for so much liberalization and privatization.

The *WDR2006* recognizes that the design of market regulation and macroeconomic policy is as important for interhousehold equity as the provision of public services and infrastructure, something that feminist economists have long argued (see for instance Diane Elson and Nilüfer Çağatay [2000]). However, the report does not extend this recognition to gender. There is no gender analysis of market regulation, and there are very few references to women: one reference in the discussion of the regulation of financial markets (World Bank 2006: 184), two references in the discussion of labor market regulation (187, 190), and none in the discussion of regulation of product markets. Markets are not recognized as "gendered institutions," shaped by gender norms and stereotypes, as a result of which any structure of market regulation is likely to have different implications for women and for men (an aspect of markets revealed by feminist analysis; see Elson [1999] and Barbara Harriss-White [1998], for example).

There is absolutely no mention of gender in the treatment of macroeconomic policy. It is recognized that economic crises and their resolutions tend to have inequitable distributional effects among rich and poor people (World Bank 2006: 200–1), but the question of whether the effects are even more adverse for poor women than for poor men is not raised. Only the effect of macroeconomic policy on market income and access to public services is considered. No mention is made of the impact on hours spent in paid and unpaid work, an issue raised in feminist economics (see, for example, Maria Sagrario Floro [1995]). There is no recognition that gender-blind macroeconomic policy tends to produce gender asymmetric effects. The report calls for stronger regulation of financial systems, the introduction of comprehensive insurance mechanisms, and an anti-cyclical rather than pro-cyclical macroeconomic policy, with all of which feminist economists might agree. But such measures need to be supplemented by gender-aware fiscal and monetary policies. The ups and downs of the macroeconomy must be monitored, with attention to the different impacts on women and men and on paid and unpaid work. Most importantly, decent work (that enables men and women alike to combine paid employment with unpaid care responsibilities), for women equally with men, needs to become an objective of macroeconomic policy. Any fiscal stimulus prepared to counteract a severe economic downturn should pay regard to creating jobs for women as well as men.

The final chapter of the report (chapter 10), which is devoted to achieving greater global equity, also fails to include any gender analysis. It recommends greater international labor mobility; more access for producers in poor countries to markets in rich countries; more equal participation of rich and poor countries in setting the global rules for trade, international property rights, and international capital flows; and improvements in development assistance. The World Bank's vision is of a world in which barriers to market access and lack of voice in setting the rules by which markets operate are the key reasons for global inequality. If only global markets can be brought closer to the World Bank's ideal of competitive markets, the world will be a fairer and more efficient place. There is no recognition that the spread of market competition may itself be part of the problem rather than the solution, creating market societies in which every part of life is commodified and submitted to a calculus of money costs (Beneria 1999).

Ironically, the two brief mentions of women in chapter 10 do point toward the drawbacks of increasing market access and competition. The first mention refers to the possible costs of migration from poor to rich countries, noting concerns in poor countries that the "migration of women creates major deficits in child rearing, family support and care for the elderly" (World Bank 2006: 209), imposing costs on those left behind. We may question the assumption that these activities have to be carried out by women, but may wish to applaud the recognition that migration entails non-market costs. We may note that migration often tears people unwillingly from their homes and communities, resulting in loneliness and misery. People would often prefer to stay in their own communities and enjoy the love and affection of family and friends, if only they could make a decent living there. The second mention of women refers to the need for measures to combat the "trafficking of girls and women" (210). Implicit in this is a view that limits should be placed on what can be bought and sold, but this view is not brought into the open and explored further. If free markets are good for other commodities and other forms of labor, why not for the sex trade? And if free markets are not good for sexual services, why are they good for other kinds of labor service?

What is missing from the policy recommendations is any understanding of the centrality of policies to enable people to combine paid work, in decent conditions, with unpaid work, such as taking care of their families and friends, with equal sharing of both between men and women. The *WDR2006* does recognize the importance of reducing those forms of unpaid work that are drudgery, such as collecting water and fuel, through investment in infrastructure. But it does not recognize the need to design systems of social protection and labor market regulation to acknowledge the positive contribution of unpaid work and to promote the equal sharing of unpaid work between women and men.

Also missing is the recognition that to secure equality (including gender equality) together with growth, economies must be wage-led, in the sense that production is oriented toward supplying a broad-based domestic market based on rising labor productivity and rising wages, rather than toward supplying an export market based on keeping wage increases below rises in productivity and channeling the proceeds to increase the share of profits in the national income (Stephanie Seguino and Caren Grown 2007). This requires an active industrial strategy that provides incentives for the development of new types of production based on technological innovation to create more and better jobs for both women and men. It also requires an active policy of managing cross-border flows of trade and investment, rather than simply liberalizing international markets. But that requires a much bigger departure from the Washington Consensus than the *WDR2006* is prepared to make. These and other policies that are required are spelled out in more detail in a very different international report, issued in 2005 by the United Nations Research Institute for Social Development, entitled *Gender Equality: Striving for Justice in an Unequal World.*[25]

CONCLUSION

The *WDR2006* argues for greater gender equality in opportunities as an objective in its own right, as well as for its instrumental value in promoting faster growth, and that is to be welcomed. But it is not concerned to address inequalities in outcomes. Moreover, its analysis of what sustains gender inequality is seriously flawed. It emphasizes gender inequality as an important "inequality trap" that hinders development, but it situates this trap in rural, pre-industrial settings, and overgeneralizes on the basis of evidence that is largely from South Asia. It shows no understanding that the process of economic growth and development is a gendered process in which old forms of gender inequality may be weakened but new forms are created and sustained even in the richest countries in the world. The report makes an important innovation in World Bank thinking in recognizing that liberalization and privatization can be, and have been, captured by elites. It calls for public policy by accountable states to regulate markets in ways that promote equal access (creating a "level playing field"), but private enterprise and competition are still seen as the solution rather than part of the problem. The way in which competition itself continually tilts the playing field this way and that is not recognized. The report's discussion of how markets and the macroeconomy need to be reshaped pays no attention to gender issues. The report is marked by an optimism that better land rights and access to labor markets can liberate women from the gender inequality trap, without any thorough acknowledgment of the way that the unequal division of responsibility for unpaid domestic work constrains women from competing equally with men. Cooperative as well as competitive solutions are required if gender inequality, even in opportunities, is to be fully established.

ACKNOWLEDGMENTS

I would like to thank the three reviewers and the editors for their helpful comments. Also, thanks to the Institute of Political Economy at Carleton University for providing facilities to enable me to revise this paper while a Visiting Professor in Fall 2008.

NOTES

[1] For a useful discussion of this, see Global Social Policy Forum (2006).

[2] The same is true of the World Bank Policy Research Report *Engendering Development through Gender Equality in Rights, Resources, and Voice* (World Bank 2001).

3 The variety of views of World Bank Executive Directors is accommodated with a typical "get-out clause": "This report will not prescribe what is equitable for any society. That is the prerogative of its members to be undertaken through decision-making processes they regard as fair" (World Bank 2006: 20).

4 Program loans support a sector or countrywide program of new policies.

5 The CEDAW Committee, which monitors implementation of the convention, has argued the convention calls not for "equity" but for "equality" (see, for example, United Nations [2005: 47] and United Nations [2007: 4]).

6 The *WDR2006* allows for some structural, system-wide economic, social, and political factors in preventing equal opportunities, but once equal opportunities have been established by removing these impediments, only individual factors, like luck and personal qualities, are perceived as hindering fair outcomes.

7 Phillips (2004) notes that this oversight is also prevalent in much contemporary academic writing on inequality, which focuses more on individual variation in talents and preferences than on structural factors.

8 It is pertinent to note that the Universal Declaration of Human Rights refers to the right to "an adequate standard of living," and states have an immediate obligation to ensure that "minimum core standards" are met in realizing this right (Henry Steiner and Philip Alston 1996: 256–328).

9 In merely gesturing toward human rights, the *WDR2006* appears to share the view, widespread among mainstream economists, that human rights norms and standards do not provide guidance on how to deal with policy in the presence of resource constraints (for an expression of this view, see Tzannatos [2006: 31]). However, while human rights norms and standards are not able to determine all the details of economic policy, they do provide guidance on what policies violate human rights obligations and on how to improve policies to secure greater compliance with human rights (Diane Elson 2006; Radhika Balakrishnan 2007).

10 For instance, on the opening page of the report, a contrast is drawn between the opportunities of a poor black girl and a rich white boy in South Africa, and we read that they "could hardly be held responsible for their family circumstances: their race, their parents' income and education, their urban or rural location, or indeed, their *sex*" (italics added). And in the next paragraph, the point is made that the opportunities of this girl and boy are very different "by virtue of their *gender*, socialization, their geographic location, and their access to schools" (World Bank 2006: 1, italics added).

11 This is reminiscent of "Redistribution with Growth," the strategy espoused by the World Bank in the early 1970s (Hollis Chenery, John Duloy, and Richard Jolly 1974).

12 See, for example, Sam Bowles, Herb Gintis, and Bo Gustafsson (1993) and Richard Arena and Christian Longhi (1998).

13 The examples Chang discusses include child labor, polluting production processes, and workers' rights. Measures to ban imports produced with child labor, or by polluting production processes, or with low-paid non-union labor may be seen as legitimate from a developed country point of view; but as means of protection of developed country businesses from a developing country point of view.

14 Thus, attempts to incorporate labor and environmental standards in international trade agreements may be judged by firms and governments in developing countries as tilting the playing field against them.

15 See, for example, Randy Albelda and Chris Tilly (1994) and Jane Humphries and Jill Rubery (1995).

16 This point is argued in more detail by John Roemer (2006) in his critique of the *WDR2006*.

[17] For example, the concept is explained at length in a two-page box entitled "Inequality traps stifle economic development in a north Indian village" (World Bank 2006: 26–7). There is no comparable box entitled "Inequality traps stifle development in a low-income, ethnic minority district in a North American/Western European city."

[18] The Sachs version of the trap is an example of this danger: foreign aid is the key factor that springs the trap (Sachs 2005: chapter 3).

[19] This claim is based on Caridad Araujo, Francisco Ferreira, and Norbert Schady, (2004).

[20] The report correctly notes that income and consumption capture different dimensions of economic welfare, with income better seen as a measure of opportunity and consumption better seen as a measure of achievement (World Bank 2006: 38). But, since some countries have data on household income and some on household expenditure, this difference is not systematically maintained, and data referring to income is merged with data referring to expenditure.

[21] This is not to suggest that decomposition by sex of household head should have been included. Rather, it would have been useful to draw attention to the point that such decompositions are based on household survey data sets, and measure only interhousehold inequality, while assuming intrahousehold inequality is zero. This would have been consistent with the report's recognition that there is inequality within households in its discussion of the inequality trap for women (World Bank 2006: 53).

[22] Of course, data to do this are not readily available, but that needs noting and criticizing.

[23] For more discussion of the ambiguities of welfare economics, see Chang (2001).

[24] Though there is no human rights treaty that explicitly justifies taxation, the clarification of rights and obligations produced by the various UN bodies responsible for monitoring the implementation of treaties, and the reports of the Special Rapporteurs appointed by the UN Commission on Human Rights, make it plain that taxation is not in itself a form of expropriation or violation of property rights, and indeed is a necessary instrument for the realization of human rights (Elson 2006).

[25] Several feminist economists contributed to this report, which is reviewed in *Feminist Economics* by Caren Grown (2007).

REFERENCES

Agarwal, Bina. 1997. "'Bargaining' and Gender Relations: Within and Beyond the Household." *Feminist Economics* 3(1): 1–51.

Albelda, Randy and Chris Tilly. 1994. "Towards a Broader Vision: Race, Gender and Labour Market Segmentation in a Social Structure of Accumulation Framework," in David Kotz, Terrence McDonough, and Michael Reich, eds. *Social Structures of Accumulation: The Political Economy of Growth and Crisis,* pp. 212–30. Cambridge: Cambridge University Press.

Araujo, Caridad, Francisco Ferreira, and Norbert Schady. 2004. "Is the World Becoming More Unequal? Changes in the World Distribution of Schooling." Informally published document, World Bank, Washington, DC.

Arena, Richard and Christian Longhi, eds. 1998. *Markets and Organization.* Berlin: Springer-Verlag.

Balakrishnan, Radhika. 2007. "Exploring Collaborations: Heterodox Economics and an Economic Social Rights Framework." *Feminist Economics* 13(1): 93–101.

Barker, Drucilla and Edith Kuiper, eds. 2006. *Feminist Economics and the World Bank: History, Theory and Policy.* New York: Routledge.

Benería, Lourdes. 1999. "Globalization, Gender and Davos Man." *Feminist Economics* 5(3): 61–84.

Berik, Günseli. 2000. "Mature Export-Led Growth and Gender Wage Inequality in Taiwan." *Feminist Economics* 6(3): 1–26.

Bourguignon, Francois, Francisco Ferreira, and Nora Lustig. 2005. *The Microeconomics of Income Distribution Dynamics in East Asia and Latin America.* New York: World Bank and Oxford University Press.

Bowles, Sam, Herb Gintis, and Bo Gustafsson, eds. 1993. *Markets and Democracy.* Cambridge: Cambridge University Press.

Chang, Ha-Joon. 2001. "Breaking the Mould: An Institutionalist Political Economy Alternative to the Neoliberal Theory of the Market and the State." Social Policy in a Development Context Programme Paper 6, United Nations Research Institute for Social Development (UNRISD).

Chenery, Hollis, John Duloy, and Richard Jolly, eds. 1974. *Redistribution with Growth: Policies to Improve Income Distribution in Developing Countries in the Context of Economic Growth.* Oxford: Oxford University Press.

Dollar, David and Roberta Gatti. 1999. "Gender Inequality, Income and Growth: Are Good Times Good for Women?" Policy Research Report on Gender and Development Working Paper Series 1, World Bank, Washington, DC.

Duflo, Esther. 2003. "Grandmothers and Granddaughters: Old Age Pensions and Intrahousehold Allocation in South Africa." *World Bank Economic Review* 17(1): 1–25.

Elson, Diane. 1999. "Labour Markets as Gendered Institutions: Equality, Efficiency and Empowerment Issues." *World Development* 27(3): 611–27.

———. 2006. *Budgeting for Women's Rights: Monitoring Government Budgets for Compliance with CEDAW.* New York: United Nations Development Fund for Women (UNIFEM).

Elson, Diane and Ruth Pearson. 1981. "Nimble Fingers Make Cheap Workers: An Analysis of Women's Employment in Third World Export Manufacturing." *Feminist Review* (7): 87–107.

Elson, Diane and Nilüfer Çağatay. 2000. "The Social Content of Macroeconomic Policies." *World Development* 28(7): 1347–78.

Elson, Diane and Hande Keklik. 2002. *Progress of the World's Women 2002.* New York: United Nations Development Fund for Women (UNIFEM).

Filmer, Deon. 1999. "The Structure of Social Disparities in Education: Gender and Wealth." Washington, DC: World Bank.

Floro, Maria Sagrario. 1995. "Economic Restructuring, Gender and the Allocation of Time." *World Development* 23(11): 1913–30.

Global Social Policy Forum. 2006. "The World Bank and Social Development Policy-Turning the Tide." *Global Social Policy* 6(3): 259–87.

Goldstein, Markus and Christopher Udry. 2002. "Gender, Land Rights and Agriculture in Ghana." Informally published document, Yale University, New Haven, CT.

Grown, Caren. 2007. "Book Review: Gender Equality: Striving for Justice in an Unequal World." *Feminist Economics* 13(2): 397–401.

Harriss-White, Barbara. 1998. "Female and Male Grain Marketing Systems: Analytical and Policy Issues for West Africa and India," in Cecile Jackson and Ruth Pearson, eds. *Feminist Visions of Development,* pp. 189–213. London: Routledge.

Hill, Anne and Elizabeth King. 1995. "Women's Education and Economic Well-Being." *Feminist Economics* 1(2): 21–46.

Humphries, Jane and Jill Rubery, eds. 1995. *The Economics of Equal Opportunities.* Manchester: Equal Opportunities Commission.

Kabeer, Naila. 1997. "Women, Wages and Intra-Household Power Relations in Urban Bangladesh." *Development and Change* 28(2): 261–302.

Kanbur, Ravi. 2003a. "Education, Empowerment and Gender Inequalities," in B. Pleskovic and Nick Stern, eds. *The New Reform Agenda,* pp. 217–33. Oxford: Oxford University Press.

———. 2003b. "The Policy Significance of Inequality Decompositions." Paper presented at the Cornell University, London School of Economics, and United Nations University – World Institute for Development Economics Research (UNU-WIDER) Conference on Spatial Inequality and Development.

Kandiyoti, Deniz. 1988. "Bargaining with Patriarchy." *Gender and Society* 2(3): 227–90.

Klasen, Stephen. 1999. "Does Gender Inequality Reduce Growth and Development? Evidence from Cross-Country Regressions." Policy Research Report on Gender and Development Working Paper Series 7, World Bank, Washington, DC.

———. 2002. "Low Schooling for Girls, Slower Growth for All? Cross-Country Evidence on the Effect of Gender Inequality in Education on Economic Development." *World Bank Economic Review* 16(3): 345–73.

Leibenstein, Harvey. 1954. *A Theory of Economic-Demographic Development.* Princeton, NJ: Princeton University Press.

Long, Carolyn. 2006. "An Assessment of Efforts to Promote Gender Equality at the World Bank,"in Drucilla Barker and Edith Kuiper, eds. *Feminist Economics and the World Bank: History, Theory and Policy,* pp. 40–56. New York: Routledge.

Milanovic, Branko. 2005. *Worlds Apart: International and Global Inequality.* Princeton, NJ: Princeton University Press.

Phillips, Anne. 2004. "Defending Equality of Outcome." *Journal of Political Philosophy* 12(1): 1–19.

Polanyi, Karl. 1947. "Our Obsolete Market Mentality." *Commentary* 3: 109–117.

———. 1967. *The Great Transformation.* Boston: Beacon Press.

Rawlings, Laura. 2004. "A New Approach to Social Assistance: Latin America's Experience with Conditional Cash Transfer Programs." Social Protection Discussion Paper Series, World Bank, Washington, DC.

Razavi, Shahra. 2006. "'New Frontiers of Social Policy?' and the Silences of the 'Arusha Statement.'" *Global Social Policy* 6(3): 278–81.

———. 2007. "Liberalization and the Debates on Women's Access to Land." *Third World Quarterly* 28(8): 1479–500.

Roemer, John. 2006. "The 2006 World Development Report: Equity and Development." *Journal of Economic Inequality* 4: 233–44.

Sachs, Jeffrey. 2005. *Investing in Development: A Practical Plan to Achieve the Millennium Development Goals.* London: Earthscan.

Seguino, Stephanie. 2000a. "The Effects of Structural Change and Economic Liberalization on Gender Wage Differentials in South Korea and Taiwan." *Cambridge Journal of Economics* 24(4): 437–59.

———. 2000b. "Gender Inequality and Economic Growth: A Cross-Country Analysis." *World Development* 28(7): 1211–30.

———. 2005. "All Types of Inequality are Not Created Equal: Divergent Impacts of Inequality on Economic Growth.". Working Paper 433, Levy Economics Institute, Bard College, Annandale-on-Hudson, NY.

Seguino, Stephanie and Caren Grown. 2007. "Gender Equity and Globalization: Macroeconomic Policy for Developing Countries," in Irene van Staveren, Diane Elson, Caren Grown, and Nilüfer Çağatay, eds. *The Feminist Economics of Trade,* pp. 292–315. London: Routledge.

Steiner, Henry and Philip Alston. 1996. *International Human Rights in Context.* Oxford: Clarendon Press.

Tzannatos, Zafiris. 2006. "The World Bank, Development, Adjustment and Gender Equality," in Drucilla Barker and Edith Kuiper, eds. *Feminist Economics and the World Bank: History, Theory and Policy*, pp. 13–39. New York: Routledge.

United Nations. 2005. *Report of the Committee on the Elimination of Discrimination against Women. Concluding Comments of the Committee on Paraguay*. Supplement 38(A/60/38). New York: United Nations.

———. 2007. *Report of the Committee on the Elimination of Discrimination. Concluding Comments of the Committee on Nicaragua.* CEDAW/C/NIC/CO/6. New York: United Nations.

United Nations Development Programme (UNDP). 1995. *Human Development Report 1995*. New York: UNDP.

United Nations Research Institute for Social Development (UNRISD). 2005. *Gender Equality: Striving for Justice in an Unequal World.* Geneva: UNRISD.

World Bank. 2001. *Engendering Development Through Gender Equality in Rights, Resources, and Voice.* Policy Research Report, World Bank, Washington, DC.

———. 2006. *World Development Report 2006: Equity and Development.* Washington, DC: World Bank.

Zuckerman, Elaine. 2002. *A Primer on Poverty Reduction Strategy Papers and Gender.* Washington, DC: Gender Action.

Gender Disparity in Education and the International Competition for Foreign Direct Investment

Matthias Busse and Peter Nunnenkamp

ABSTRACT

With few exceptions, the empirical literature on foreign direct investment (FDI) continues to be gender blind. This paper contributes to filling this gap by assessing the importance of gender inequality in education as a determinant of FDI. The authors estimate a standard gravity model on bilateral FDI flows that is augmented by educational variables, including different measures of gender inequality in education. The analysis covers an unprecedented number of both host and source countries of FDI, thereby reducing the risk of distorted results because of a sample selection bias. The results support the view that foreign investors are more likely to favor locations where education-related gender disparities are small. However, the discouraging effects of gender disparity on FDI are restricted to middle-income (rather than low-income) developing host countries and to investors from developed (rather than developing) countries.

INTRODUCTION

The question of whether gender inequality hinders or helps the integration of countries into the international division of labor has received only scant attention in the empirical literature. Some evidence exists on the links between gender inequality and trade. Matthias Busse and Christian Spielmann (2006) find that wage inequality is positively associated with comparative advantage in labor-intensive exports, whereas inequality in terms of labor-market participation and education is negatively related with such exports. According to Stephanie Seguino (1997), wage inequality may have contributed to the export success of countries such as South Korea.[1] However, the role of gender inequality has been largely ignored in studies about the countries' attractiveness for foreign direct investment (FDI).

This is fairly surprising in light of the fierce international competition for FDI. Policy-makers are falling over themselves to entice foreign investors, for example, by offering tax breaks and outright subsidies, in the hope that FDI inflows would induce higher growth and employment. Yet, it is still open to debate what actually drives FDI inflows.[2] In particular, the sizeable literature on FDI determinants has generally been gender blind (Elissa Braunstein 2006).

This paper attempts to fill this gap by assessing the role of gender disparity with respect to host countries' attractiveness for FDI. The focus will be on *education-related* gender disparity and its effects on FDI flows to developing countries, for which the linkage is of particular concern.[3] Opposing hypotheses in this regard call for empirical analyses. On the one hand, gender disparity in education may stimulate FDI by offering cost advantages if it leads to lower average wages at a given level of labor productivity. On the other hand, FDI may be discouraged if foreign investors increasingly rely on the local availability of skilled labor, which gender disparity in education is likely to constrain.

We estimate a gravity model on bilateral FDI flows, covering as many (developing) host countries of FDI as possible to avoid a sample selection bias. The standard gravity model is augmented by educational variables, including different measures of gender inequality in education. We chose this rather indirect approach of assessing the FDI effects of gender disparity as disparity measures directly capturing wage costs, labor productivity, and the qualification of the workforce by gender are unavailable or subject to serious data constraints.

Our results clearly reject the view that foreign investors favor locations where education-related gender disparities may offer cost advantages. Rather, we find that gender disparity discourages FDI inflows. However, the strength of this relation depends on the level of education, being most pronounced with respect to secondary and tertiary education. Additional robustness tests reveal that the discouraging effect of gender disparity becomes statistically insignificant when considering only low-income host countries and developing source countries.

PREVIOUS STUDIES AND GENDER DISPARITY MEASURES

Even though the literature on FDI determinants does not address gender issues, a strand of this literature on social factors and FDI relates to the analysis in this paper. Several studies raise the question of whether FDI tends to go where social standards are low and worker rights are repressed to save costs, or rather where social and political conditions are similar to those prevailing in the home country.[4] Howard J. Shatz (2003) focuses on education as a determinant of FDI but does not consider gender gaps in education. Shatz finds that better educated workers attract more FDI. The counter-hypothesis is rejected, according to which FDI is undertaken "in countries with low levels of education to escape the high compensation costs with which higher levels of education and skill are associated" (Shatz 2003: 188). The question addressed in the following analysis – that is, whether gender inequality attracts or rather discourages FDI inflows – resembles this strand of the literature on FDI determinants in that there are two opposing hypotheses.

On the one hand, gender disparity in education could be associated with higher FDI inflows. In the process of economic globalization, multinational companies appear to face mounting cost pressure. They increasingly refer to vertical types of FDI (also labeled efficiency-seeking FDI), which provides a means to allocate specific steps of the production process to where the relevant comparative advantages can be utilized. Consequently, this type of FDI tends to be sensitive to international cost differentials. In particular, vertical FDI is often associated with the relocation of labor-intensive parts of the value chain to lower-wage locations. This may strengthen the incentives of multinational companies to exploit less-skilled, low-wage female labor. The movement of FDI in so-called footloose industries, such as textiles and clothing, to countries with segmented labor markets may provide cases in point.[5]

On the other hand, multinational companies may be more interested in drawing on sufficiently qualified labor rather than just cheap labor. David Kucera (2002) refers to survey results in which the managers of multinational companies rated the quality of labor in the host country to be more important than the cost of labor. Indeed, empirical evidence suggests that the labor demand of multinational companies is biased toward relatively skilled workers in developing host countries (Overseas Development Institute 2002). Furthermore, multinational companies are increasingly under pressure, notably from nongovernmental organizations (NGOs), to show good corporate behavior (Matthias Busse 2004). As a consequence, they may shy away from host countries with pervasive social injustice in general and gender inequality in particular.[6]

It follows that the impact of gender inequality in education on FDI is theoretically ambiguous. Unit labor costs tend to decline to the extent that gender inequality in education involves lower average wages at a given level of labor productivity, with less educated women entering the labor force.[7] Locations where education-related gender inequality is more pronounced might then have a competitive edge in attracting cost-oriented FDI of the vertical type. However, gender inequality may also be associated with higher unit labor costs, and thus less vertical FDI, if it is mainly associated with lower average labor productivity. In other words, gender inequality in education has opposing effects on unit labor costs. Moreover, the impact of gender inequality in education on FDI inflows would still be indeterminate even if unit labor costs declined on balance. In contrast to vertical FDI, the horizontal type of FDI (also labeled market-seeking FDI) may be unaffected by changes in unit labor costs. This type of FDI essentially duplicates the parent company's production at home in the host countries. Market access motivations dominate over cost considerations, and factor intensities of production in the host countries largely resemble those at home. Hence, the importance of unit labor costs for overall FDI inflows is likely to depend on the composition of FDI, which – though difficult to measure exactly – tends to vary considerably across host countries (see also Kucera [2002]).

Ideally, we would like to cover several aspects of gender disparity and their effects on FDI inflows, including gender wage gaps, differences in labor-force participation rates between males and females, and education-related differences. The focus on education-related disparity measures implies some limitations. Inferences about the FDI effects of gender disparity in general remain indirect and incomplete. First, education-related measures tend to capture the *net* effects of two transmission mechanisms running through wages and labor productivity, without being able to disentangle them. Second, any positive FDI effects of less disparity in education may be associated with gender wage disparity to the extent that an improved qualification of female workers does not lead to a corresponding pay rise. Consequently, concerns about gender equity and fairness would not necessarily be overcome if only less gender disparity in education resulted in more FDI.

However, wage disparity measures and differences in labor-force participation rates are not particularly useful as possible determinants of FDI in the present context of a large panel of host countries and a time span of about twenty-five years because of the following reasons:

- Data on wage differences are only available for selected years and a limited number of countries.[8] The insufficient country coverage especially may cause seriously biased results when analyzing FDI determinants (Shatz 2003; Matthias Busse, Jens Königer, and Peter Nunnenkamp 2008). Moreover, when available, wage data typically refer to the manufacturing sector only (Kucera 2002; Busse and Spielmann 2006).[9] This limitation is problematic, as FDI in developing countries increasingly consists of FDI in the services sector (United Nations Conference on Trade and Development [UNCTAD] 2004; Braunstein 2006). And finally, the problem of reverse causation running from FDI to wages and wage disparity would be all but impossible to resolve.
- Similar arguments apply to labor-force participation rates. Again, problems of reverse causality loom large (Braunstein 2006). The statistically insignificant results Kucera (2002) achieves when adding the proportion of female workers in the industry to his list of FDI determinants may well reflect that causality between FDI and female employment shares goes both ways (see also Elissa Braunstein

[2002]). Moreover, gender-specific labor-market participation rates do not necessarily reflect discrimination but rather may be based on voluntary decisions of female workers (Busse and Spielmann 2006).

Consequently, education-related gender disparity appears to be the first choice when analyzing FDI determinants. While theory indicates that the level of education in a host country should influence FDI inflows (Shatz 2003), the possibility of reverse causation – meaning that higher FDI results in better education – seems to be rather remote in comparison with wages and employment. The empirical studies of Shatz (2003) as well as Jonathan Eaton and Akiko Tamura (1996), considering education among the determinants of FDI, find that better educated workers in host countries attract higher FDI inflows. However, both studies cover only selected FDI source countries (United States FDI in the case of Shatz, US and Japanese FDI in the case of Eaton and Tamura). Furthermore, Braunstein's (2006) verdict that most FDI studies are gender blind applies to both Shatz (2003) and Eaton and Tamura (1996).

To the best of our knowledge, Kucera (2002) is the only exception in that he considers gender-specific educational variables as determinants of FDI. He does not find evidence suggesting that education-related gender disparity resulted in higher FDI inflows. Yet, his results are far from robust. The positive effect of (relative) female educational attainment on FDI is statistically significant only when high-income host countries are included in the sample, and the coefficient of this variable even changes its sign once the regressions are run with regional dummies.

Moreover, Kucera's study has some shortcomings that we attempt to overcome in the following analysis. First of all, it is purely cross-sectional, while we use a panel analysis to examine changes over time in the relation between gender gaps in education and FDI. Second, we employ a gravity model on bilateral FDI flows, and we explicitly account for the fact that various host countries have not attracted any FDI flows from particular source countries. Third, we draw on a large, new dataset to cover essentially all (developing) host countries as well as a large number of source countries and thereby avoid, or at least substantially reduce, a sample selection bias.

In the regressions reported below, we measure gender gaps in education by comparing females and males with respect to average years of schooling. While we also consider three different levels of education when estimating the Tobit model later in this paper, we confine the subsequent presentation of stylized facts to gender gaps in education at all levels of schooling combined, in order to save space. We compare the situation prevailing in 1980 with that in the most recent years (average of 2000 and 2005). The mean and the range of gender differences at specific levels of schooling are presented in the Appendix.

In Figure 1, ratios far below one reflect larger gender gaps in education working against women. On the other hand, women are overrepresented in some countries with ratios above one (notably in several Latin American countries). Not surprisingly, high-income countries, on average, have a relatively narrow gender gap in education, whereas the gap is widest in low-income countries. This applies to both 1980 and the most recent years. In contrast to what one might expect, however, there is also considerable variation over time.[10] Middle-income countries, on average, caught up with high-income countries in terms of narrowing the gender gap; in recent years, middle-income countries resembled the high-income group in that the gender gap in education was less than 10 percent. At the same time, low-income countries, while still lagging behind, made remarkable progress in expanding the schooling of females relative to males.

Moreover, the group averages reported in Figure 1 conceal considerably different developments in particular countries. This may be exemplified by three middle-income countries in Latin America. Colombia and Honduras started with a ratio of close to one in 1980 but through subsequent developments diverged: females spent 24 percent more time in education than males in Colombia in recent years, whereas the ratio of females to males deteriorated to 0.67 in Honduras. Bolivia, starting with a pronounced gender gap (0.68), made substantial progress in closing this gap (to 0.88 in 2000/2005). Similar discrepancies apply to low-income countries in sub-Saharan Africa. Mozambique reported a large gender gap (0.23) at the beginning of the period of observation but a relatively narrow one recently

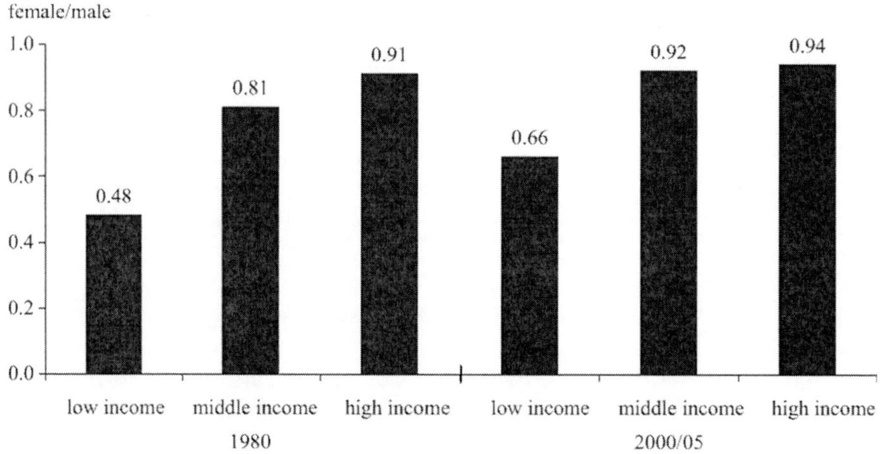

Figure 1 Gender disparity in schooling,[a] 1980 and 2000/2005
Note: [a]Average years of schooling at all levels combined: females divided by males; 2000/2005 represents the average for 2000 and 2005.
Sources: Robert J. Barro and Jong-Wha Lee (2001) and UNESCO (2007).

(0.69). Ghana and Sudan both started at a ratio of females to males in education of about 0.4. While this ratio increased to 0.62 in Sudan, it declined slightly in Ghana.

APPROACH AND DATA

We follow a standard approach in the large empirical FDI literature[11] and estimate a gravity-type model on the determinants of FDI. Gravity models are widely used to analyze the movement of goods, services, and factors of production between different locations within or across countries. The common intuition is to portray spatial transactions analogous to Newton's Law of Gravity. Consequently, mass and distance are core elements of this class of models. In cross-country contexts as the present one, the focus is on economic size (in terms of income and/or population) and geographical distance between each pair of countries. Economic interaction is supposed to be an increasing function of the economic size of partner countries and a decreasing function of the distance between them; larger countries with higher income are thus expected to be involved in more transactions with nearer-by and larger countries. Various extensions of this basic model structure have been suggested in the literature. The extended version we use is specified below.

As noted by Alan V. Deardorff (1998), this class of models first appeared in the empirical economics literature on bilateral trade flows. Deardorff also shows that simple gravity models can be derived from standard trade theories. More recently, gravity models have also been applied to analyze financial flows. The explanatory power of gravity models on financial flows is comparable with that of models on trade flows (Philippe Martin and Hélène Rey 2004). According to Richard Portes and Hélène Rey, this is hardly surprising as the gravity approach "emerges naturally" from theories of asset trade (2005: 275). Recent examples employing gravity models to analyze bilateral FDI include Shatz (2003) and John H. Mutti and Harry Grubert (2004).

Hence, in contrast to Avik Chakrabarti's earlier verdict of "measurement without theory" (2001: 90), there appears to be widespread agreement by now on the appropriate analytical framework to guide empirical work on the determinants of FDI. Indeed, variables such as market size and openness to trade that the extreme bounds analysis of Chakrabarti (2001) found to be fairly robust determinants of FDI represent important cornerstones of the gravity model. The particular advantage of the extended gravity model in explaining the determinants of bilateral FDI flows is the fact that differences between source and host country characteristics can be used as explanatory variables. A standard FDI analysis using aggregated FDI flows for each country would not be suitable for that task.

While the core variable set of gravity models helps prevent fragile results due to ad-hoc choices on control variables, the estimation results may still be sensitive to sample selection. Shatz's (2003) analysis of US FDI clearly reveals that sample selection matters for empirical results.[12] Consequently, we cover as many countries as possible in our baseline regressions and, at the same time, perform robustness tests for specific sub-samples.[13]

Furthermore, when applying gravity models to FDI flows, one must take into account the concentration of FDI in a few host countries. During the period under consideration (1978–2004), about 80 percent of FDI flows to all (150) middle- and low-income countries were concentrated in just twenty countries (World Bank 2006). Bilateral FDI flows are often equal to zero; this applies to roughly three-quarters of all observations in our sample. The censored nature of this variable implies that the results from OLS estimations would very likely be biased. Therefore, we use a non-linear method of estimation such as Tobit.

The Tobit model represents our preferred option among alternative approaches suggested in the literature to avoid biased results when the dependent variable is censored.[14] This model estimates FDI flows between a particular pair of countries in one step. The underlying assumption is that the explanatory variables have the same impact on (1) the probability of receiving any bilateral FDI at all (selection decision) and (2) the amount of FDI allocated thereafter (allocation decision). This assumption appears to be reasonable in the context of bilateral FDI flows; it would be difficult to find an exclusion variable that affects selection but does not affect allocation, as two-step models such as the Heckman model would require.

In our empirical approach, we principally follow David L. Carr, James R. Markusen, and Keith E. Maskus (2001), who estimate the so-called knowledge-capital model that integrates the previously separate concepts of horizontal (market-seeking) and vertical (efficiency-seeking) FDI into a single model by considering the determinants of both types of FDI within a single estimation equation.[15]

Our basic specification reads as follows:

$$\text{In}(FDI_{ijt}) = \alpha_0 + \alpha_1 \ln(FDI_{ijt-1}) + \gamma' X_{jt} + \phi' Y_{ijt} + \alpha_2\, GenderInequality_{jt} + \lambda_t + \varepsilon_{ijt} \tag{1}$$

where FDI_{ijt} stands for foreign direct investment of country i in country j at period t, FDI_{ijt-1} corresponds to FDI inflows in the previous period t-1, X_{jt} represents a set of host country control variables, Y_{ijt} denotes the difference between source and host country characteristics, λ_t is a set of year dummies, and $GenderInequality_{jt}$ corresponds to gender inequality in education between males and females in the host country. The error term of the random effects estimation can be written as:

$$\varepsilon_{ijt} = v_{ijt} + u_{ijt} \tag{2}$$

where u_{ijt} is the random unobserved bilateral effect and v_{ijt} represents the remaining error.[16]

For the dependent variable, we use two measures of FDI: first, FDI flows from the source to the (developing) host country in percent of host country GDP (the variable is labeled *FDI1*), and second, the share of FDI attracted by a specific (developing) host country in total FDI flows from the source country under consideration to all developing host countries (*FDI2*) included in our sample. The second measure captures the attractiveness of a particular country relative to other host countries. We calculate three-year averages to smooth the considerable fluctuation of annual bilateral FDI flows. At the same time, this approach ensures that we have enough variation in the data.[17]

The limited host country coverage of previous analyses of bilateral FDI flows is overcome by fully exploiting the (largely unpublished) data available upon request from UNCTAD's Data Extract Service. Yet, some data limitations remain. Most importantly, it is not possible to differentiate between different types of bilateral FDI flows. For instance, vertical FDI should be affected more strongly by gender inequality in education than horizontal FDI; it is mainly the former type of FDI that is supposed to depend on international cost differences as well as the availability of sufficiently qualified labor in the relevant literature. Likewise, the impact of gender inequality in education may be stronger in the case of greenfield FDI, compared with mergers and acquisitions (M&As), which amount to a change in ownership of *existing* production facilities and may be driven by asset-seeking motives in the first place.[18] Tax-induced distortions in international FDI patterns are minimized by excluding FDI flows to offshore financial centers (see also below); but the problem remains that FDI channeled through offshore centers to the ultimate host country cannot be accounted for appropriately.

We include the lagged dependent variable on the right-hand side of the regression equation for two reasons. First, this solves the potential problem of autocorrelation in the pooled time-series regressions.[19] Second, this procedure is theoretically plausible as foreign investment in the previous period is highly relevant for FDI in the current period. Above all, countries that already have considerable FDI inflows are much more likely to attract multinational corporations. This has been shown, for example, by Victor M. Gastanaga, Jeffrey B. Nugent, and Bistra Pashamova (1998); the lagged FDI variable is always highly statistically significant in their regressions. By including lagged FDI flows, the econometric specification becomes a dynamic panel.

We employ a fairly standard set of controls, including total host country population and real GDP growth for market-seeking FDI (labeled *population* and *growth*, respectively),[20] host country inflation (*inflation*), host country openness to trade (*openness*), the difference in GDP per capita between the source and the host country for vertical FDI (*DiffGDPpc*), and a dummy for the existence of a bilateral or regional trading agreement – that is, a free trade agreement or customs union (*RTA*). We expect a positive association of *population, growth, DiffGDPpc,* and *RTA* with FDI; the opposite applies to *inflation,* as this variable can be interpreted as a proxy for macroeconomic distortions. Exact definitions and data sources for all variables as well as descriptive statistics can be found in the Appendix.

As for time invariant variables, we also closely follow the empirical literature on gravity models and incorporate dummies for a *common border,* a *common language,* and *colonial ties* as well as the distance between the source and the host country (*distance*). The first three control variables are expected to be positively associated with FDI flows, whereas the sign of *distance* is unclear. On the one hand, management and transport costs are likely to increase if two countries are located far away from each other; on the other hand, remote markets might be better served through local production, that is, FDI in the host country. Hence, the net impact on FDI is uncertain.

To reduce the skewness in the data, we take the natural logarithm of *population, FDI1, FDI2, DiffGDPpc, distance,* and *inflation.* But this would mean that we would lose observations with negative values or zeros. To overcome this problem, we use the following logarithmic transformation that reduces the skewness in the data and, at the same time, retains negative and zero observations:

$$y = \ln\left(x + \sqrt{(x^2 + 1)}\right) \tag{3}$$

Using this transformation leaves the sign of x unchanged, while the values of x pass from a linear scale at small absolute values to a logarithmic scale at large values.

In addition to these standard control variables, we include the institutional development of host countries, proxied by political constraints on the executive branch (*political constraints*). Poor institutions may discourage FDI by giving rise to uncertainty (for example, with respect to the protection of property rights [Jeong-Yeon Lee and Edwin Mansfield 1996; Witold J. Henisz 2000]) and additional costs (for example, in the case of corruption [Shang-Jin Wei 2000]). We use the index for political constraints that was developed by Henisz (2000). In contrast to alternative institutional indicators, this variable is available for a large number of countries and years. *Political constraints* focuses on the political discretion of the executive branch. Less discretion is supposed to render credible commitments to (foreign) investors more likely. The indicator ranges from zero (total political discretion) to one (no political discretion). Thus, we expect a positive link between *political constraints* and FDI flows. Finally, we include two variables that control for investment liberalization: (1) *CapOpen* for unilateral capital account liberalization of the host country (Menzie D. Chinn and Hiro Ito 2005) and (2) *BIT* for a bilateral investment treaty ratified between the source and the host country (Busse, Königer, and Nunnenkamp 2008). Both measures are expected to stimulate higher FDI flows.

Lastly, we measure the variable of principal interest, gender inequality in education, as the difference between the male and female score for average years of schooling in the population aged 25 and above (*education inequality*).[21] In additional estimations, we use more detailed information of gender inequality in primary, secondary, and tertiary education. This allows us to examine at which level of education gender inequality matters most for the host countries' attractiveness to FDI. Needless to say, we also control for years of schooling of both sexes combined with respect to either all levels of schooling (*education*) or specific levels of schooling (*primary education, secondary education,* and *tertiary education*).

Our analysis covers the period 1978–2004, that is, optimally nine observations of three-year averages for all indicators. UNCTAD's Data Extract Service provides FDI data since 1970, but very few countries report FDI flows for the 1970s at a bilateral level. To avoid any biases arising from an extremely small sample of reporting countries, we start with 1978. We exclude financial offshore centers, such as Panama, the Bahamas, or the Cayman Islands.[22] Extending the sample to include a large number of poor developing host countries is crucial to avoid a sample selection bias and to assess the chances of these countries becoming more attractive to FDI. Our sample consists of seventy-seven developing host countries, based on the World Bank's classification of low- and middle-income countries.[23] By covering twenty-eight FDI source countries, including various non-OECD source countries, we at least partly capture the recent surge of FDI flows from developing countries to other developing countries. The Appendix includes lists of the source and host countries.

MAIN RESULTS

Following the model specification and the introduction of the variables, we now turn to the empirical results. Table 1 reports the results of the Tobit model for both FDI variables and total years of schooling. The estimations include all control variables introduced before. Apart from *inflation,* all control variables have the expected sign, and the significance of the coefficients is not much affected when considering FDI as a share of GDP (*FDI1*) or FDI shares (*FDI2*) as the dependent variable.

As anticipated, FDI in the past is a strong predictor for current FDI as the coefficient of the lagged dependent variable is positive and highly statistically significant. The strongly positive coefficients of the host countries' populations, GDP growth rates, and the differences in per

Table 1 FDI and education, total years of schooling

Dependent variable	*(1)* *ln (FDI1)*	*(2)* *ln (FDI2)*
ln (FDI_{t-1})	0.299*** (0.012)	0.619*** (0.020)
Education	0.108*** (0.021)	0.035*** (0.005)
Education inequality	-0.128*** (0.043)	-0.050*** (0.009)
ln (population)	0.291*** (0.033)	0.101*** (0.008)
ln (DiffGDPpc)	0.044*** (0.009)	0.007*** (0.002)
Growth	0.027** (0.012)	0.005** (0.002)
ln (inflation)	0.004 (0.026)	0.003 (0.005)
Openness	0.004*** (0.001)	0.001*** (0.000)
Common border	0.674** (0.290)	0.295*** (0.061)
Common language	0.476*** (0.110)	0.080*** (0.023)
ln (distance)	-0.539*** (0.063)	-0.143*** (0.014)
Colonial ties	0.448** (0.210)	0.037 (0.044)
RTA	0.518** (0.200)	0.050 (0.041)
Political constraints	0.710*** (0.190)	0.022 (0.038)
CapOpen	0.081*** (0.029)	0.020*** (0.006)
BIT	0.390*** (0.096)	0.028** (0.012)
Observations	8,299	8,299
Country pairs	1,531	1,531

Notes: Marginal effects, computed at the mean, are displayed; standard errors are reported in parentheses; due to space constraints, the coefficients for constant term and the year dummies are not shown; *** significant at 1 percent level, ** significant at 5 percent level, and * significant at 10 percent level. The p-values of the Wald χ^2 test for the null hypothesis that all explanatory variables equal zero are always statistically significant at the 1 percent level (not reported).

capita income between the host and source countries (*DiffGDPpc*) reveal that FDI flows to the sample countries are driven by both market-seeking and efficiency-seeking motives (horizontal and vertical FDI). The importance of vertical FDI is also indicated by the significantly positive coefficient of *openness*; greater openness to trade reflected in this variable improves the host countries' attractiveness to FDI involving the relocation of particular segments of the value chain and the offshoring of intermediate production.[24] Likewise, less regulated capital transactions are associated with higher bilateral FDI flows, as the coefficient of *CapOpen* is positive and significant at the 1 percent level.

Apart from colonial ties in one specification, all the time-invariant variables traditionally included in gravity models turn out to be statistically significant at the 5 percent level. Bilateral FDI flows between a source and a host country having a common border or speaking the same language are higher than bilateral flows between countries without such common characteristics. The same applies for colonial ties (except column [2]). By contrast, a larger distance between the host and the source country tends to reduce bilateral FDI flows. Distance-related management and transport costs outweigh the source country's incentive to undertake FDI in remote countries and serve these markets through local production.

Results turn out to be weaker for some other control variables. In contrast to our expectations, *inflation* is positive but never significant.[25] *RTA* has the expected positive coefficient but fails to reach the conventional 10 percent significance level in one specification. We obtain a similar outcome for *political constraints* – that is, a positive linkage with FDI in both specifications but only one (highly) significant coefficient. Finally, the ratification of bilateral investment treaties (*BIT*) leads to higher FDI inflows, which is in line with previous findings by Busse, Königer, and Nunnenkamp (2008).

Turning to the education-related determinants of FDI, our results corroborate Shatz (2003) as well as Eaton and Tamura (1996) in that average years of schooling of both sexes taken together (*education*) are associated with higher FDI flows at the 1 percent level. In the present context of gender inequality, it is still more important that *education inequality* is negatively related to bilateral FDI flows. The coefficient of our variable of principal interest, which captures the difference between male and female years of total (primary, secondary, and tertiary) schooling, turns out to be significant at the 1 percent level for the full sample of (developing) host countries. Hence, our panel analysis produces stronger results than the cross-section analysis of Kucera (2002). While Kucera finds no evidence suggesting that gender disparity in education leads to higher FDI inflows, our results support the stronger conclusion that gender disparity in education clearly reduces FDI inflows.

The quantitative effect of less gender disparity in education on FDI inflows is modest but by no means negligible. Taking the estimated coefficient on *education inequality* with *FDI1* as the dependent variable (−0.128) at face value, a decrease in the difference between male and female years of total schooling by 0.25 years (that is, the standard deviation of *education inequality*) would lead – on average – to an increase in the FDI/GDP ratio by some 2.5 percent.[26] The long-run effect would be still more pronounced. The long-run effect can be calculated by dividing the coefficient of *education inequality* by one minus the coefficient of the lagged dependent variable. Based on the estimate reported in column (1) of Table 1, the long-run FDI effect of a decrease in *education inequality* by one standard deviation would amount to 3.6 percent of FDI inflows as a share of GDP.

Overall, the findings for the effect of gender inequality on FDI underscore the findings for the effect of the education of both sexes combined on FDI: In the first place, the attractiveness of host countries to FDI stems from offering foreign investors the opportunity to draw on sufficiently qualified labor, be it male or female workers. This does not rule out that foreign investors aim to reduce wage costs for similarly qualified labor.[27] But the estimation results suggest that the wage-reducing motive of FDI is dominated by the motive to complement FDI-related production techniques with sufficiently qualified labor in the host country. Gender inequality in education tends to constrain this option as it limits the pool of locally available labor that meets the standards required by foreign investors.

In the next step of our analysis, we differentiate the educational variables (average years of schooling of both sexes combined as well as gender disparity related to years of schooling) by considering three levels of schooling separately. In all other respects, the specification of the Tobit model remains as before.[28]

The results shown in Table 2 suggest that *education* at all levels is positively associated with FDI inflows. In contrast to Shatz (2003), we do not find that primary education had stronger effects on FDI than higher levels of education. The pattern found here for various sources of FDI appears to be plausible given that primary education tends to be a weaker indicator of the availability of skilled labor than higher levels of education. US FDI (analyzed by Shatz) may deviate from this pattern because the motives underlying US FDI differ from those underlying FDI from other sources.[29] Off-shoring labor-intensive parts of the production process to lower income host countries appears to figure relatively prominently in US FDI, which may thus depend less on skilled local labor.

Moreover, we do not find any evidence that gender inequality results in higher FDI inflows either at the lower level of primary education or at the higher level of secondary and tertiary education. Rather, as before for total schooling, all coefficients on *education inequality* are statistically significant and have the same negative sign. Apart from inequality in tertiary education, the coefficients reach the 1 percent significance level. However, the results also show that the size of the coefficients at the secondary and tertiary level of education is considerably higher in comparison to the primary level. In other words, changes in secondary or tertiary education disparities have a much stronger impact on FDI inflows than changes at the primary level.

SENSITIVITY ANALYSES

We perform two types of sensitivity analyses in this section. First, we replicate our estimations with average years of schooling at all levels combined for various sub-samples of host and source countries, and second, we perform Tobit fixed-effects estimations to control for country-pair fixed effects.

In the estimations reported in Table 3, we return to average years of schooling at all levels combined as a measure of gender inequality in education. To save space, we show only the results for the variable of principal interest in the present context.[30] To facilitate comparison, the main results from Table 1 are listed again in the first row of Table 3.

The size of the discouraging effect of gender inequality in education on FDI inflows may depend on the stage of development of the host country.

Table 2 FDI and primary, secondary, and tertiary education

	(1)	*(2)*	*(3)*	*(4)*	*(5)*	*(6)*
Education level	*Primary education*		*Secondary education*		*Tertiary education*	
Dependent variable	*ln (FDI1)*	*ln (FDI2)*	*ln (FDI1)*	*ln (FDI2)*	*ln (FDI1)*	*ln (FDI2)*
ln (FDI_{t-1})	0.300*** (0.012)	0.620*** (0.020)	0.302*** (0.012)	0.631*** (0.021)	0.304*** (0.012)	0.639*** (0.021)
Education	0.163*** (0.030)	0.055*** (0.007)	0.213*** (0.062)	0.058*** (0.013)	0.786*** (0.200)	0.230*** (0.042)
Education inequality	-0.181*** (0.070)	-0.070*** (0.015)	-0.413*** (0.110)	-0.135*** (0.023)	-0.749* (0.440)	-0.372*** (0.090)
ln (population)	0.284*** (0.033)	0.098*** (0.008)	0.313*** (0.033)	0.105*** (0.008)	0.282*** (0.030)	0.093*** (0.007)
ln (DiffGDPpc)	0.045*** (0.009)	0.007*** (0.002)	0.037*** (0.009)	0.004** (0.002)	0.035*** (0.009)	0.004** (0.002)
Growth	0.028** (0.012)	0.006** (0.002)	0.023** (0.012)	0.004* (0.002)	0.026** (0.012)	0.005** (0.002)
ln (inflation)	0.001 (0.026)	0.001 (0.005)	0.015 (0.026)	0.006 (0.005)	0.026 (0.026)	0.009* (0.005)
Openness	0.004*** (0.001)	0.001*** (0.000)	0.005*** (0.001)	0.001*** (0.000)	0.006*** (0.001)	0.001*** (0.000)
Common border	0.699** (0.290)	0.303*** (0.061)	0.655** (0.290)	0.282*** (0.061)	0.674** (0.290)	0.278*** (0.061)
Common language	0.476*** (0.110)	0.0808*** (0.023)	0.469*** (0.110)	0.076*** (0.023)	0.466*** (0.110)	0.0704*** (0.023)
Ln (distance)	-0.535*** (0.063)	-0.141*** (0.014)	-0.533*** (0.063)	-0.137*** (0.014)	-0.517*** (0.063)	-0.133*** (0.014)
Colonial ties	0.453** (0.210)	0.0385 (0.044)	0.427** (0.210)	0.027 (0.044)	0.435** (0.210)	0.029 (0.043)
RTA	0.469** (0.210)	0.033 (0.041)	0.659*** (0.200)	0.093** (0.041)	0.620*** (0.200)	0.079* (0.041)
Political constraints	0.755*** (0.190)	0.034 (0.038)	0.767*** (0.190)	0.050 (0.039)	0.896*** (0.190)	0.0871** (0.037)
CapOpen	0.088*** (0.029)	0.022*** (0.006)	0.085*** (0.029)	0.022*** (0.006)	0.100*** (0.029)	0.025*** (0.006)
BIT	0.388*** (0.096)	0.026* (0.016)	0.435*** (0.096)	0.042** (0.019)	0.419*** (0.095)	0.035* (0.019)
Observations	8,299	8,299	8,299	8,299	8,299	8,299
Country pairs	1,531	1,531	1,531	1,531	1,531	1,531

Notes: See Table 1; *** significant at 1 percent level, ** significant at 5 percent level, and * significant at 10 percent level.

Table 3 Robustness checks and extensions, education inequality

Dependent variable	*(1)* *ln (FDI1)*	*(2)* *Ln (FDI2)*
Full sample (as reported in Table 1)	-0.128*** (0.043)	-0.050*** (0.009)
Middle-income countries	-0.246*** (0.059)	-0.066*** (0.013)
Low-income countries	0.075 (0.085)	0.007 (0.011)
Period 1990–2004	-0.204*** (0.060)	-0.107*** (0.017)
Developed source countries	-0.182*** (0.061)	-0.062*** (0.010)
Developing source countries	0.021 (0.039)	-0.003 (0.019)

Notes: To save space, we only report the results for the education inequality variable; *** significant at 1 percent level, ** significant at 5 percent level, and * significant at 10 percent level. See Table 1 for further notes.

For this reason, we test whether a differentiation of the fairly heterogeneous group of developing host countries offers additional insights. Indeed, the discouraging effects of gender inequality on FDI are confined to middle-income countries, which (according to the World Bank's classification) comprise countries with a per capita income of between US$876 and US$10,725 in 2005 (World Bank 2006). By contrast, gender inequality remains completely statistically insignificant as a determinant of FDI in low-income countries, that is, countries with a per capita income of US$875 or less. Some types of FDI undertaken in low-income countries are rather unlikely to be motivated by the availability of qualified labor. For example, this probably applies to resource-seeking FDI in the primary sector, which accounts for the bulk of total FDI flows to various low-income countries. In any case, qualified labor tends to be in extremely short supply in these host countries, and less gender inequality in education is unlikely to improve this situation substantially. Consequently, foreign investors in low-income host countries may care less about gender inequality than in more advanced host countries. It is important to note, however, that even in low-income countries gender inequality does not induce more FDI.

Next, we check whether the impact of gender inequality on FDI has changed over time. One would expect that the discouraging effect had become more pronounced in recent years. The demand of foreign investors for qualified local labor may have risen with the increasing complexity of production techniques transferred to the host countries. In fact, there is support for this proposition as the size of the coefficients is larger (in both regressions) when the estimations are based on the 1990–2004 period, instead of between 1978 and 2004.

Next, we replicate the estimations for two groups of source countries. As mentioned previously, developing countries have increasingly become sources of FDI. Arguably, the motives underlying FDI from developing countries differ from the motives underlying FDI from more advanced source countries: On the one hand, wage-related cost savings could be a less important driving force of FDI undertaken by less developed source countries in other developing countries, since wages tend to be similar in the source and the host country. *Ceteris paribus,* this could have strengthened the discouraging effect of gender inequality on FDI from developing countries. On the other hand, some relatively advanced developing source countries appear to have used FDI as a means to relocate less sophisticated industrial activities to where cost savings could be realized.[31] This type of FDI probably draws less on qualified labor in the lower-income host countries.[32]

It turns out that gender inequality in education enters insignificantly when the estimation is restricted to developing source countries. The results for the full sample of source countries are mainly driven by the discouraging effect of gender inequality on FDI from developed source countries. For the latter, the significance level closely resembles the general pattern reported in Table 1 and the size of the coefficients is somewhat larger.

Finally, the results presented so far are based on a random-effects model, and it may be argued that they are mainly driven by variations across countries rather than over time. To account for this potential weakness of our results, we replicate the analysis from Table 1 using a Tobit fixed-effects model as a robustness check. The results show that the country fixed effects capture a considerable part of the variation in the dependent variables, as a number of independent variables are no longer statistically significant (Table 4). Above all, this applies to *education* and differences in GDP per

Table 4 FDI and total years of schooling, fixed-effects estimation

Dependent variable	*(1)* *ln (FDI1)*	*(2)* *ln (FDI2)*
ln (FDI_{t-1})	0.023* (0.013)	0.199*** (0.012)
Education	0.030 (0.130)	0.000 (0.023)
Education inequality	-0.051* (0.032)	-0.021** (0.011)
ln (population)	0.213* (0.174)	0.241* (0.130)
ln (DiffGDPpc)	-0.028 (0.023)	0.004 (0.004)
Growth	0.018 (0.013)	0.004* (0.002)
ln (inflation)	-0.038 (0.034)	-0.001 (0.006)
Openness	0.008*** (0.003)	-0.001 (0.001)
RTA	0.436 (0.290)	0.096* (0.053)
Political constraints	0.352 (0.280)	0.006 (0.051)
CapOpen	0.114*** (0.044)	0.008 (0.008)
BIT	0.178* (0.101)	0.006* (0.003)
Observations	8,299	8,299
Country pairs	1,531	1,531

Notes: See Table 1; *** significant at 1 percent level, ** significant at 5 percent level, and * significant at 10 percent level.

capita. On the other hand, market size (population), economic growth, openness to trade, joining a regional trade agreement, and liberalizing the capital account through unilateral measures or bilateral investment treaties still matter for FDI flows, though significance levels tend to be weaker in comparison to the random-effects model and the coefficients often remain insignificant in one of our two specifications. Importantly, gender inequality in education is always negatively associated with FDI inflows; the coefficient is significant at the 10 percent level or better. Jointly with the previous evidence from additional regressions in this section, this outcome demonstrates that the link between *education inequality* and FDI inflows is quite robust.

CONCLUSIONS

With few exceptions, the empirical literature on FDI continues to be gender blind. This paper contributes to filling this gap by assessing the importance of gender inequality in education as a determinant of FDI. We estimate a standard gravity model on bilateral FDI flows, which is augmented by educational variables, including measures of gender inequality in education. Since we lack sufficient data on disparity measures such as wages, labor productivity, and worker qualification by gender, this approach takes an indirect route by testing the opposing propositions that gender disparity in education may either stimulate FDI by reducing unit labor costs or discourage FDI by constraining the local availability of sufficiently qualified labor.

We find no evidence whatsoever that multinational companies favor locations where education-related gender disparity exists. Gender disparity in education clearly discourages FDI flows from developed countries to relatively advanced (middle-income) developing countries. However, the effect is statistically insignificant in low-income host countries. The latter finding can be attributed to the prominence of specific types of FDI that rely considerably less on qualified local labor; resource-seeking FDI in the primary sector of low-income countries is a case in point. Likewise, the motivation underlying FDI from developing countries – including resource-seeking and cost-oriented FDI in fairly poor developing countries – provides an explanation for why this group of foreign investors appears to care less about gender inequality in the host countries.

The finding that gender disparity does not attract FDI for any of the subgroups of host and source countries under consideration has important implications for the fierce international competition for FDI inflows. It would clearly be counter-productive if policy-makers entered into a race to the bottom not only by lowering corporate tax rates or corporate contributions to social security systems but also by being lenient about the still widespread gender gaps in education. It is obviously difficult to prove that policy-makers consciously maintained gender gaps in education to contain wage increases for unskilled labor. It cannot be ruled out, however, that policy-makers are tempted not to fight gender gaps in education effectively – in the erroneous belief that having a pool of cheap unskilled labor will attract FDI. Particularly in relatively advanced (middle-income) developing countries, policy-makers would rather be well advised to tackle the persistent gender disparity to improve their countries' attractiveness to FDI, if not for more general reasons of fairness and equity. But even in low-income developing countries, it would not pay to maintain gender gaps in education, if we recall that the effect on FDI was statistically insignificant for these host countries.

This is not to ignore that cost-related dimensions of gender inequality, notably wage discrimination, may offer short-term benefits to investors, help attract FDI that is mainly motivated by the availability of cheap labor, and provide a (temporary) boost to economic growth associated with footloose FDI that is unlikely to stay. In the longer run, however, we argue that policy-makers should be aware of the adverse effects of gender disparity on both FDI inflows and economic growth if persistent inequality in education adds to the supply of cheap female workers. Our estimation results suggest that the negative effects of gender disparity on FDI are quantitatively modest in the short run but clearly become more important over time. This implies that persistent gender disparity in education would run the risk of developing host countries ending up in a trap of low wages, low labor productivity, and footloose FDI.

Multinational companies in the manufacturing and services sectors tend to rely on relatively skilled labor in the host countries. Unskilled labor-intensive FDI – for example, in footloose industries such as clothing and footwear – may have received considerable public attention. But empirical evidence indicates that foreign investors in developing countries typically apply more advanced production techniques than local firms operating in the same industry, and FDI is frequently concentrated in skill-intensive industries (Overseas Development Institute 2002). It also appears that multinational companies are pursuing increasingly complex integration strategies (UNCTAD 1998), in which educated and well-trained labor plays an important role. With labor demand of foreign investors being focused on higher skills, better-educated and high-skilled women would enhance the attractiveness to FDI by adding to the pool of skilled labor available in a host country.

Our findings suggest that less gender disparity in education would promote FDI-related economic growth in the long run. According to the relevant literature, the growth effects of FDI in developing host countries critically depend on the degree to which transfers of technology and know-how are disseminated throughout the host economy.[33] Local absorptive capacity plays an important role with regard to FDI-related spillovers: FDI can only be expected to provide a stimulus to economy-wide productivity gains if local producers and workers are sufficiently qualified to imitate superior technology and acquire advanced skills. According to Eduardo Borensztein, José De Gregorio, and Jong-Wha Lee (1998), local human capital constraints hinder stronger growth effects of FDI. Increasing female education and skills levels can help overcome this constraint and, thereby, help transform larger FDI inflow into higher economic growth.

By analyzing the FDI effects of gender inequality in education, we specify an important transmission mechanism that has received little attention in the literature on gender inequality and economic growth. However, the present paper offers just one more piece of the complex puzzle on gender inequality and economic growth. Further research is clearly required in several respects. First, we do not address dimensions of gender disparity other than education-related disparity. In particular, immediately cost-related dimensions, such as wage discrimination, may have different implications for specific types of FDI. Wage disparity may attract cost-oriented FDI, notably the off-shoring of labor-intensive parts of production. This would resemble the finding of Busse and Spielmann (2006) that wage disparity is positively associated with comparative advantage in labor-intensive export production. Furthermore, the particular dimension of gender inequality matters not only for FDI but also more broadly for the economic development of the host countries (Jean Drèze and Amartya Sen 1989; Lant Pritchett and Lawrence H. Summers 1996; Stephanie Seguino 2000; Stephan Klasen 2002).

Second, disaggregating the different types of FDI may also complement the picture of FDI-related transmissions of gender disparity to growth. Specific types of FDI are likely to respond differently to gender disparity. For example, FDI of the horizontal (or local market-seeking) type may be less affected than FDI of the vertical (or efficiency-seeking) type by gender inequality in terms of both education and labor costs. At the same time, the growth effects may depend on the specific type of FDI. The literature on the growth effects of (aggregate) FDI suggests that attracting more FDI per se is no guarantee to achieve higher growth (for example, Maria Carkovic and Ross Levine 2005). Data constraints render it difficult to assess the transmission mechanisms between gender disparity and growth for specific types of FDI in the context of broad (host and source) country samples. A more promising option could be to conduct case studies for specific host countries attracting different types of FDI. Another option would be to focus on one particular source country, notably the US, which offers detailed data on the operations of foreign affiliates that may allow for a distinction between different types of FDI.

Finally, future research may attempt to provide an integrated account of several transmission mechanisms between gender disparity and growth. An important step in this direction would be to simultaneously account for FDI and trade-related effects. These two transmission mechanisms may well work in opposite directions. This might be the case, for instance, if wage inequality strengthened comparative advantage in labor-intensive exports of developing countries (as found in the trade paper of Busse and Spielmann 2006) but no longer attracted FDI. The tendency of multinational companies to contract out unskilled, labor-intensive work to local firms, and to purchase inputs from them, could explain why wage inequality promoted trade, while leaving FDI unaffected or even reducing it.

On the other hand, both transmission mechanisms may reinforce each other. This possibility arises from the above finding that less gender disparity in education induces more FDI, in combination with the earlier finding of Busse and Spielmann (2006) that less gender disparity in education is positively associated with comparative advantage in labor-intensive exports. From a gender perspective, the equity and fairness implications of such a scenario would still remain unresolved. It would have to be assessed whether and to what extent wage discrimination is underlying the positive export and FDI effects of less gender disparity in education. In other words, overcoming gender disparity in education and reaping any ensuing trade and FDI benefits may come at the cost of violating other dimensions of gender equity, such as wage equity.

NOTES

1 By contrast, Günseli Berik, Yana van der Meulen Rodgers, and Joseph E. Zveglich (2004) consider openness to trade to be a determinant of gender wage gaps, finding that trade openness is inversely related to women's relative wages in South Korean and Taiwanese industries.

2 Avik Chakrabarti (2001) subjects the findings of various studies on FDI determinants to extreme bounds analysis and concludes that few determinants are robust to minor changes in sample selection and the specification of the test equation.

3 Restricting the sample to developing host countries is in line with Bruce A. Blonigen and Miao Grace Wang (2005), who argue strongly against pooling rich and poor countries in empirical FDI studies. Later in this paper, we will further differentiate between low- and medium-income countries within the fairly heterogeneous group of developing countries.

4 Overall, the available evidence seems to be in conflict with the hypothesis that exploiting low social standards and repressed worker rights represents an important motivation of FDI. The survey of Drusilla K. Brown (2000) concludes that poor labor practices did not attract FDI; recent studies include Phillipp Harms and Heinrich W. Ursprung (2002), David Kucera (2002), and Matthias Busse (2003, 2004).

5 Footloose industries are not tied to any location but tend to move from country to country following government incentives and/or low wages.

6 The point made by Shatz (2003) and Matthias Busse, Jens Königer, and Peter Nunnenkamp (2008) about sample selection (see below) suggests a further twist to this debate. While multinational companies may shy away from countries that do not pass a basic threshold in terms of social standards and gender equality, companies may exploit cost advantages once this threshold is passed.

7 As noted by Kucera (2002), labor costs tend to decline when some groups of workers are paid less than others for similarly productive work due to discrimination.

8 Moreover, Remco H. Oostendorp (2004) stresses the heterogeneous format of available wage data.

9 Oostendorp (2004) provides a major exception.

10 Note that Shatz (2003) argues against panel analyses on education-related determinants of FDI, as he suspects variation over time to be marginal.

11 See Assaf Razin and Efraim Sadka (2007) for an overview of the relevant literature.

12 As Shatz notes: "national statistical agencies publish bilateral data about the investment activities of their multinationals only for host countries that have sizeable inflows of FDI. This means that nearly all research on foreign direct investment focuses on the winners, countries that have achieved at least some success in attracting FDI. This is a major problem since policy advice is most often sought by the countries that are excluded from analysis" (2003: 118).

13 By replicating the regressions for specific sub-groups of countries, we assess the sensitivity of results with respect to sample selection, while the extreme bounds analysis of Chakrabarti (2001) is particularly suited to assess the sensitivity of results with respect to variable selection.

14 See Eric Neumayer (2002) for a more detailed discussion of alternative approaches.

15 We divert from the model by Carr, Markusen, and Maskus (2001) in that we use additional control variables. We do not include the interactive terms used by them.

16 A Hausman test showed that there is no clear preference for the random- or fixed-effects model. Depending on the dependent variable or host country sample, we prefer either a random- or a fixed-effects model.

17 Note that bilateral FDI flows take negative values if the source country divests in a particular host country (for example, through selling its equity share to local firms and transferring the proceeds back home). We keep negative values with respect to *FDI1*. However, the results for *FDI1* hardly change if we exclude negative values. By contrast, negative bilateral flows are set equal to zero when calculating the share variable *FDI2*. This helps us include as many observations as possible, while avoiding the somewhat odd notion of negative FDI shares.

18 In contrast to M&As, greenfield FDI creates new or additional assets.

19 While a standard Durbin-Watson test showed that we do not necessarily have (first-order serial) correlation in the regressions, we cannot reject the hypothesis of no correlation either. In fact, the evidence is inconclusive.

20 The growth rate of GDP may suffer from endogeneity, as FDI inflows could have an impact on it. In the present context, however, we are not particularly interested in an unbiased estimate of the coefficient on GDP growth. Crucially, any bias in this respect is unlikely to affect the coefficient on our educational indicators – that is, the main interest of the present empirical analysis.

21 The data have principally been taken from Robert J. Barro and Jong-Wha Lee (2001). We extended their dataset with more recent figures from United Nations Education, Scientific, and Cultural Organization (UNESCO 2007) to ensure that we can run a panel analysis up to the year 2004. We also performed estimations with average years of schooling for the age group of 15 and above. Unreported results proved very similar to those reported below. The results for the age group of 25 and above may be more reliable, however. This is because average years of schooling for this age group would hardly be affected, even if FDI flows had an impact on the educational attainment of younger cohorts. We owe the point that endogeneity problems may be mitigated in this way to the guest editors of this volume.

22 FDI flows to financial offshore centers can hardly be explained in the context of a gravity model that does not capture tax-related motivations of FDI; including financial offshore centers may thus lead to biased estimation results. We exclude all countries that are on the list of offshore financial centers as reported by Eurostat (2005). For a discussion on tax-induced distortions in international capital flows, see Organisation for Economic Co-operation and Development (OECD 2000).

23 Since we use the 2005 World Bank definition for the distinction between developing und developed countries, economies like Taiwan and the Republic of Korea fall into the latter category. While this has not been the case for the entire 1978–2004 period, our results do not change much if both countries are treated as developing countries.

24 Obviously, greater openness to trade encourages trade in finished goods, too. In contrast to trade in intermediates, however, the effect of more trade in final goods on FDI flows tends to be ambiguous. This is because the removal of trade barriers for finished goods reduces the incentive to undertake FDI of the "tariff jumping" kind to penetrate protected host-country markets.

25 The results for the remaining variables do not change much if *inflation* and other insignificant variables are excluded from the analysis. Yet, we include them as they could have an impact on FDI from a theoretical point of view.

26 Note that the mean of 1.06 for *FDI1*, reported in the Appendix, has to be changed using the reversed transformation equation (3), which results in 1.27. The 2.5 percent increase in the dependent variable then results from the product of -0.128 and -0.25 divided by 1.27.

27 Obviously, it would be desirable to control for the wages of skilled and unskilled labor in our estimations. However, the data situation does not allow us to do so.

28 The results for the control variables are essentially unchanged. Therefore, they are not discussed here in any detail.

29 Another reason for different results is that Shatz (2003) performs a pure cross-country analysis, whereas our findings are based on a panel analysis.

30 Complete results are available from the authors upon request.

31 See Gaute Ellingsen, Winfried Likumahuwa, and Peter Nunnenkamp (2006) for a recent analysis of the case of Singapore in this context.

32 Probably, the same applies to resource-seeking FDI undertaken by developing source countries such as China in low-income regions, notably in Africa.

33 See, for example, the extensive survey of the relevant literature by Robert E. Lipsey (2002).

REFERENCES

Barro, Robert J. and Jong-Wha Lee. 2001. "International Data on Education Attainment: Updates and Implications." *Oxford Economic Papers* 53(3): 541–63.

Berik, Günseli, Yana van der Meulen Rodgers, and Joseph E. Zveglich. 2004. "International Trade and Gender Wage Discrimination: Evidence from East Asia." *Review of Development Economics* 8(2): 237–54.

Blonigen, Bruce A. and Miao Grace Wang. 2005. "Inappropriate Pooling of Wealthy and Poor Countries in Empirical FDI Studies," in Theodore H. Moran, Edward M. Graham, and Magnus Blomström, eds. *Does Foreign Direct Investment Promote Development?* pp. 221–44. Washington, DC: Institute for International Economics.

Borensztein, Eduardo, José De Gregorio, and Jong-Wha Lee. 1998. "How Does Foreign Direct Investment Affect Economic Growth?" *Journal of International Economics* 45(1): 115–35.

Braunstein, Elissa. 2002. "Gender, FDI and Women's Autonomy: A Research Note on Empirical Analysis." University of Massachusetts Amherst. http://www.peri.umass.edu/fileadmin/pdf/gls_conf/glw_braunstein.pdf (accessed April 2007).

———. 2006. "Foreign Direct Investment, Development and Gender Equity: A Review of Research and Policy." Occasional Paper 12, United Nations Research Institute for Social Development, Geneva.

Brown, Drusilla K. 2000. "International Trade and Core Labour Standards: A Survey of the Recent Literature." Occasional Paper 43, Organisation for Economic Co-operation and Development.

Busse, Matthias. 2003. "Do Transnational Corporations Care About Labour Standards?" *Journal of Developing Areas* 36(2): 49–68.

———. 2004. "Transnational Corporations and Repression of Political Rights and Civil Liberties: An Empirical Analysis." *Kyklos* 57(1): 45–66.

Busse, Matthias and Christian Spielmann. 2006. "Gender Inequality and Trade." *Review of International Economics* 14(3): 362–79.

Busse, Matthias, Jens Königer, and Peter Nunnenkamp. 2008. "FDI Promotion through Bilateral Investment Treaties: More Than a Bit?" Kiel Working Paper 1403, Kiel Institute for the World Economy.

Carkovic, Maria and Ross Levine. 2005. "Does Foreign Direct Investment Accelerate Economic Growth?" in Theodore H. Moran, Edward M. Graham, and Magnus Blomström, eds. *Does Foreign Direct Investment Promote Development?* pp. 195–220. Washington, DC: Institute for International Economics.

Carr, David L., James R. Markusen, and Keith E. Maskus. 2001. "Estimating the Knowledge-Capital Model of the Multinational Enterprise." *American Economic Review* 91(3): 693–708.

Chakrabarti, Avik. 2001. "The Determinants of Foreign Direct Investment: Sensitivity Analyses of Cross-country Regressions." *Kyklos* 54(1): 89–113.

Chinn, Menzie D. and Hiro Ito. 2005. "What Matters for Financial Development? Capital Controls, Institutions, and Interactions." Working Paper 11370, National Bureau of Economic Research, Cambridge, MA.

Deardorff, Alan V. 1998. "Determinants of Bilateral Trade: Does Gravity Work in a Neo-classical World," in Jeffrey A. Frankel, ed. *Regionalization in the World Economy*, pp. 7–22. Chicago: University of Chicago Press.

Dollar, David and Art Kraay. 2007. Institutions, Trade and Growth Database. http://eron.worldbank.org/WBSITE/EXTERNAL/EXTDEC/O,,ContentMDK:20311740_pagePK:64165401~piPK:64165026~thesitePK:469372,00.html (accessed April 2007).

Drèze, Jean and Amartya Sen. 1989. *Hunger and Public Action.* Oxford: Oxford University Press.

Eaton, Jonathan and Akiko Tamura. 1996. "Japanese and U.S. Exports and Investment as Conduits of Growth," in Takatoshi Ito and Anne O. Krueger, eds. *Financial Deregulation and Integration in East Asia*, pp. 51–75. Chicago: University of Chicago Press.

Ellingsen, Gaute, Winfried Likumahuwa, and Peter Nunnenkamp. 2006. "Outward FDI by Singapore: A Different Animal?" *Transnational Corporations* 15(2): 1–40.

Eurostat. 2005. *European Union Foreign Direct Investment Yearbook 2005.* Luxembourg: European Communities.

Gastanaga, Victor M., Jeffrey B. Nugent, and Bistra Pashamova. 1998. "Host Country Reforms and FDI Inflows: How Much Difference Do They Make?" *World Development* 26(7): 1299–314.

Harms, Phillipp and Heinrich W. Ursprung. 2002. "Do Civil and Political Repression Really Boost Foreign Direct Investment?" *Economic Inquiry* 40(4): 651–63.

Henisz, Witold J. 2000. "The Institutional Environment for Multinational Investment." *Journal of Law, Economics, and Organization* 16(2): 334–64.

———. 2007. *The Political Constraint Index (POLCON) Dataset*. http://www-management.wharton.upenn.edu/henisz/ (accessed January 2007).

Klasen, Stephan. 2002. "Low Schooling for Girls, Slower Growth for All? Cross-Country Evidence on the Effect of Gender Inequality in Education on Economic Development." *World Bank Economic Review* 16(3): 345–73.

Kucera, David. 2002. "Core Labour Standards and Foreign Direct Investment." *International Labour Review* 141(1–2): 31–68.

Lee, Jeong-Yeon and Edwin Mansfield. 1996. "Intellectual Property Protection and U.S. Foreign Direct Investment." *Review of Economics and Statistics* 78(2): 181–6.

Lipsey, Robert E. 2002. "Home and Host Country Effects of FDI." Working Paper 9293, National Bureau of Economic Research, Cambridge, MA.

Martin, Philippe and Hélène Rey. 2004. "Financial Super-Markets: Size Matters for Asset Trade." *Journal of International Economics* 64(2): 335–61.

Mutti, John H. and Harry Grubert. 2004. "Empirical Asymmetries in Foreign Direct Investment and Taxation." *Journal of International Economics* 62(2): 337–58.

Neumayer, Eric. 2002. "Is Good Governance Rewarded? A Cross-National Analysis of Debt Forgiveness." *World Development* 30(6): 913–30.

Organisation for Economic Co-operation and Development (OECD). 2000. "Towards Global Tax Co-operation." Report to the 2000 Ministerial Council Meeting and Recommendations by the Committee on Fiscal Affairs. http://www.oecd.org/dataoecd/9/61/2090192.pdf (accessed April 2008).

Oostendorp, Remco H. 2004. "Globalization and the Gender Wage Gap." Policy Research Working Paper 3256, World Bank, Washington, DC.

Overseas Development Institute. 2002. "Foreign Direct Investment: Who Gains?" Briefing Paper, Overseas Development Institute, London.

Portes, Richard and Hélène Rey. 2005. "The Determinants of Cross-Border Equity Flows." *Journal of International Economics* 65(2): 269–96.

Pritchett, Lant and Lawrence H. Summers. 1996. "Wealthier is Healthier." *Journal of Human Resources* 31(4): 841–68.

Razin, Assaf and Efraim Sadka. 2007. *Foreign Direct Investment: Analysis of Aggregated Flows*. Princeton: Princeton University Press.

Seguino, Stephanie. 1997. "Gender Wage Inequality and Export-Led Growth in South Korea." *Journal of Development Studies* 34(2): 102–37.

———. 2000. "Gender Inequality and Economic Growth: A Cross-Country Analysis." *World Development* 28(7): 1211–30.

Shatz, Howard J. 2003. "Gravity, Education, and Economic Development in a Multinational Affiliate Location." *Journal of International Trade and Economic Development* 12(2): 117–50.

United Nations Conference on Trade and Development (UNCTAD). 1998. *World Investment Report 1998: Trends and Determinants*. New York: United Nations.

———. 2004. *World Investment Report 2004: The Shift Towards Services*. New York: United Nations.

———. 2007a. *Bilateral Investment Treaties* (online database). http://www.unctadxi.org/templates/DocSearch_779.aspx (accessed April 2007).

———. 2007b. *Foreign Direct Investment Statistics* (online database). http://www.unctad.org/Templates/StartPage.asp?intItemID=2921&lang=1 (accessed April 2007).

United Nations Education, Scientific, and Cultural Organization (UNESCO). 2007. *UNESCO Institute for Statistics.* http://www.uis.unesco.org/ev_en.php?ID=2867_201&ID2=DO_TOPIC (accessed April 2007).

Wei, Shang-Jin. 2000. "How Taxing is Corruption on International Investors?" *Review of Economics and Statistics* 82(1): 1–11.

World Bank. 2006. *World Development Indicators 2006: Data on CD-Rom.* Washington, DC: World Bank.

World Trade Organization (WTO). 2007. *Regional Trade Agreements.* http://www.wto.org/english/tratop_e/region_e/region_e.htm (accessed April 2007).

APPENDIX 1

Definition of variables and data sources

Variable	*Definition*	*Source*
FDI1	Bilateral FDI flows from source to (developing) host country in percent of host country GDP (times 10,000)	World Bank and UNCTAD (2007b) and World Bank (2006)
FDI2	Bilateral FDI flows from source to (developing) host country in percent of total FDI to all (developing) countries included in our sample	UNCTAD (2007b)
Population	Total population of host country	World Bank (2006)
DiffGDPpc	Difference between source and host GDP per capita, constant 2,000 US dollars	World Bank (2006)
Growth	Real GDP growth rate of host country in percent	World Bank (2006)
Inflation	Inflation rate of host country in percent (GDP deflator)	World Bank (2006)
Openness	Sum of imports and exports in percent of GDP (host country)	World Bank (2006)
Common border	Common border between source and host country	Dollar and Kraay dataset (2007)
Common language	Common language between source and host country	Dollar and Kraay dataset (2007)
Distance	Distance in km between source and host country	Dollar and Kraay dataset (2007)
Colonial ties	Colonial ties between source and host country	Dollar and Kraay dataset (2007)
RTA	Dummy regional trade agreement, 0-1	World Trade Organization (2007)
Political constraints	Political constraints III, 0-1	Henisz (2007)
CapOpen	Indicator for capital account openness; Chinn-Ito index on financial openness	Chinn and Ito (2005); data kindly provided by Hiro Ito
BIT	Bilateral investment treaty, ratified between source and (developing) host country	UNCTAD (2007a)
Education	Average years of (total) schooling, total population, age 25+	Barro and Lee (2001) and UNESCO (2007)

(*continued*)

(*Continued*)

Variable	*Definition*	*Source*
Education inequality	Average years of (total) schooling, male minus female score, age 25+	Barro and Lee (2001) and UNESCO (2007)
Primary education	Average years of primary schooling, total population, age 25+	Barro and Lee (2001) and UNESCO (2007)
Primary education inequality	Average years of primary schooling, male minus female score, age 25+	Barro and Lee (2001) and UNESCO (2007)
Secondary education	Average years of secondary schooling, total population, age 25+	Barro and Lee (2001) and UNESCO (2007)
Secondary education inequality	Average years of secondary schooling, male minus female score, age 25+	Barro and Lee (2001) and UNESCO (2007)
Tertiary education	Average years of tertiary schooling, total population, age 25+	Barro and Lee (2001) and UNESCO (2007)
Tertiary education inequality	Average years of tertiary schooling, male minus female score, age 25+	Barro and Lee (2001) and UNESCO (2007)

Descriptive statistics

Variable	*Observations*	*Mean*	*Std. Dev.*	*Minimum*	*Maximum*
ln (FDI1)	9,743	1.06	2.51	-10.61	11.53
ln (FDI2)	9,743	0.35	0.49	0.00	5.30
ln (population)	9,743	16.44	0.14	13.21	20.98
ln (DiffGDPpc)	9,743	8.94	1.55	-9.92	11.21
Growth	9,743	3.58	2.59	-9.90	16.38
ln (inflation)	9,743	2.99	1.09	-2.45	9.44
Openness	9,743	68.02	13.12	9.31	230.27
Common border	9,743	0.02	0.13	0.00	1.00
Common language	9,743	0.13	0.33	0.00	1.00
ln (distance)	9,743	8.95	0.63	5.21	9.89
Colonial ties	9,743	0.03	0.18	0.00	1.00
RTA	9,743	0.04	0.11	0.00	1.00
Political constraints	9,743	0.27	0.20	0.00	0.68
CapOpen	9,743	-0.20	0.94	-1.75	2.62
BIT	9,743	0.17	0.20	0.00	1.00
Total education	9,743	4.48	0.61	0.30	10.31
Total schooling inequality	9,743	1.06	0.25	-1.22	3.34
Primary education	9,743	3.15	0.35	0.24	7.88
Primary education inequality	9,743	0.65	0.20	-1.04	2.30
Secondary education	9,743	1.12	0.24	0.04	3.27
Secondary education inequality	9,743	0.32	0.09	-0.48	1.27
Tertiary education	9,743	0.22	0.06	0.01	0.84
Tertiary education inequality	9,743	0.08	0.02	-0.17	0.37

Source country sample

Argentina, Australia, Austria, Belgium-Luxembourg, *Brazil, Chile, Colombia,* Denmark, Finland, France, Germany, Iceland, Japan, Republic of Korea, *Malaysia, Mexico,* Netherlands, New Zealand, Portugal, Spain, Sweden, Switzerland, Taiwan, *Thailand, Turkey,* United Kingdom, United States, *Venezuela*

Note: Developing source countries in italics.

Host country sample

Albania, Algeria, Angola, Argentina, Bangladesh, Bolivia, Botswana, Brazil, Bulgaria, Burkina Faso, Cameroon, Chile, China, Colombia, Republic of Congo, Costa Rica, Côte d'Ivoire, Croatia, Dominican Republic, Ecuador, Egypt, El Salvador, Estonia, Ethiopia, Gambia, Ghana, Guatemala, Guyana, Haiti, Honduras, Hungary, India, Indonesia, Jordan, Kazakhstan, Kenya, Latvia, Lithuania, Malaysia, Mali, Mauritius, Mexico, Mongolia, Mozambique, Namibia, Nicaragua, Niger, Nigeria, Oman, Pakistan, Papua New Guinea, Paraguay, Peru, Philippines, Poland, Romania, Russian Federation, Saudi Arabia, Senegal, Slovenia, Sri Lanka, Sudan, Swaziland, Syrian Arab Republic, Tanzania, Thailand, Togo, Trinidad and Tobago, Tunisia, Turkey, Uganda, Ukraine, Uruguay, Venezuela, Vietnam, Zambia, Zimbabwe

THE IMPACT OF GENDER INEQUALITY IN EDUCATION AND EMPLOYMENT ON ECONOMIC GROWTH: NEW EVIDENCE FOR A PANEL OF COUNTRIES

Stephan Klasen and Francesca Lamanna

ABSTRACT

Using cross-country and panel regressions, we investigate to what extent gender gaps in education and employment (proxied using gender gaps in labor force participation) reduce economic growth. Using the most recent data and investigating an extended time period (1960–2000), we update the results of previous studies on education gaps on growth and extend the analysis to employment gaps using panel data. We find that gender gaps in education and employment considerably reduce economic growth. The combined "costs" of education and employment gaps in the Middle East and North Africa, and South Asia amount respectively to 0.9–1.7 and 0.1–1.6 percentage point differences in growth compared to East Asia. Gender gaps in employment appear to have an increasing effect on economic growth differences between regions, with the Middle East and North Africa, and South Asia suffering from slower growth in female employment.

INTRODUCTION

There are many reasons to be concerned about existing gender inequalities in important well-being-related dimensions such as education, health, employment, or pay. From a well-being and equity perspective, such gender inequalities are problematic as they lower well-being and are a form of injustice in most conceptions of equity or justice.[1] While such a view would argue for reducing gender inequalities in these dimensions of well-being on intrinsic grounds, recently, a literature has developed that has investigated the instrumental effects of gender inequality on other important development outcomes, with a particular focus on economic growth. Without denying the importance of reducing gender inequality on intrinsic grounds, this paper is a contribution to this latter literature.

An important focus of this literature has been to examine the impact of gender inequality in education on economic growth.[2] A number of theoretical contributions have suggested a negative link between gender inequality and economic growth (for example, Oded Galor and David N. Weil [1996] and Nils-Petter Lagerlöf [2003]). This literature shows that, largely due to the impact of female education on fertility and the creation of human capital of the next generation, a lower gender gap will spur economic development. The next section will briefly summarize the main findings from this literature.

In parallel, an empirical literature has also examined these effects. While some earlier studies suggested that gender inequality in education might actually increase economic growth (Robert Barro and Jong-Wha Lee 1994; Robert Barro and Xavier Sala-i-Martin 1995), more recent work has shown that the opposite appears to be the case (M. Anne Hill and Elizabeth M. King 1995; David Dollar and Roberta Gatti 1999; Kristin Forbes 2000; Stephen Knowles, Paula Lorgelly, and Dorian Owen 2002; Stephan Klasen 2002; Steven Yamarik and Sucharita Ghosh 2003; Dina Abu-Ghaida and Stephan Klasen 2004). These studies not only differ from previous analyses in their findings of the impact of gender inequality on economic growth, but they also explain why earlier studies found the opposite effect and why more careful econometric techniques yield the new finding that gender inequality in education reduces economic growth.[3]

These macro studies are also consistent with findings using micro data showing that girls have a higher marginal return to education, which is even higher if the impact of female education on fertility and education of the next generation is included (Hill and King 1995; World Bank 2001; Elizabeth M. King, Stephan Klasen, and Maria Porter 2008).

The effects found are quite large for the regions where gender inequality is sizable, such as South Asia or the Middle East and North Africa (MENA). In fact, Klasen (2002) estimated that 0.9 percentage points of the 1.8 percentage point annual per capita growth difference between the countries in MENA and those in East Asia and the Pacific (EAP) can be attributed to higher initial gender inequality in education there as well as a slower closing of the gap vis-à-vis EAP.[4]

While these results are instructive, they are based on information on education and economic performance until 1990. Since new data on education achievement and economic performance that now stretch to 2000 have recently become available, one purpose of the paper is to update the findings of the impact of gender inequality on economic growth. We will do this by using an updated and extended data set and the same econometric specification that was used in Klasen (2002). For some regions (including the MENA region), an update is particularly germane, as the gender gaps in education have recently been closing more rapidly, so one would expect smaller but still remarkable costs for the existing gender gap in education.

A subject that has not been investigated in great detail is the impact of gender inequality in *employment* and *pay* on economic growth. The relatively small theoretical literature on the subject yields conflicting results (for example, Robert Blecker and Stephanie Seguino [2002], Berta Esteve-Volart [2004], and Tiago de Cavalcanti and José Tavares [2007]). While there is some empirical literature suggesting that high *earnings* gaps, combined with high female labor force participation rates, helped spur export-oriented economic growth in some Asian countries (for example, Stephanie Seguino [2000a, 2000b] and Matthias Busse and Christian Spielmann [2006]), there has not been a thorough empirical investigation of the role of gender gaps in *employment* on economic growth, and the few existing studies have to be treated with caution due to problems of endogeneity, unobserved heterogeneity, and poor data availability and quality.

These issues can best be treated in a panel framework, where one considers the impact of initial employment on subsequent economic growth, and thus can at least partly address issues of endogeneity and unobserved heterogeneneity. Unfortunately, such panel data is only available for labor force participation rates by sex, not for employment by sex; we show below, however, that available data suggest that gender gaps in labor force participation and employment are closely correlated, so one can well proxy for the other. With forty years of data, an analysis of the gender gaps in labor force participation is now possible, and therefore a second aim of the paper is to investigate the impact of gender gaps in labor force participation (as a proxy for gender gaps in employment) on economic growth in such a panel framework.

GENDER INEQUALITY AND ECONOMIC PERFORMANCE: THEORY AND EVIDENCE

There have been a number of theoretical and empirical studies finding that gender inequality in education and employment reduces economic growth.[5] The main arguments from the literature, which are discussed in detail in Stephan Klasen (1999, 2002, 2006), are briefly summarized below.

Regarding gender inequality in education, the theoretical literature suggests as a first argument that such gender inequality reduces the average amount of human capital in a society and thus harms economic performance. It does so by artificially restricting the pool of talent from which to draw for education, thereby excluding highly qualified girls (and taking less qualified boys instead; see, for example, Dollar and Gatti [1999]). Moreover, if there are declining marginal returns to education, restricting the education of girls to lower levels while taking the education of boys to higher levels means that the marginal return to educating girls is higher than that of boys, and thus would boost overall economic performance (World Bank 2001; Knowles, Lorgelly, and Owen 2002).

A second argument relates to the externalities of female education. Promoting female education is known to reduce fertility levels, reduce child mortality levels, and promote the education of the next generation. Each factor in turn has a positive impact on economic growth. Thus, gender gaps in education reduce the benefits to society of high female education (see, for example, Galor and Weil [1996]; Lagerlöf [2003]; World Bank [2001]; and King, Klasen, and Porter [2008]). There is also an important timing issue involved here. Reduced fertility levels will, after some twenty years, lead to a favorable demographic constellation which David E. Bloom and Jeffrey G. Williamson (1998) refer to as a "demographic gift." For a period of several decades, the working-age population will grow much faster than the overall population, thus lowering dependency rates with positive repercussions for per capita economic growth.[6]

A third argument relates to international competitiveness. Many East Asian countries have been able to be competitive in world markets through the use of women-intensive export-oriented manufacturing industries, a strategy that is now finding followers in South Asia and individual countries across the developing world (see, for example, Stephanie Seguino [2000a, 2000b]).[7] For such competitive export industries to emerge and grow, women need to be educated and there must be no barrier to their employment in such sectors. Gender inequality in education and employment would reduce the ability of countries to capitalize on these opportunities (World Bank 2001; Busse and Spielmann 2006).[8]

Regarding gender gaps in employment, there are a number of closely related arguments. First, the literature argues that it distorts the economy, as do gender gaps in education. It artificially reduces the pool of talent from which employers can draw, thereby reducing the average ability of the workforce (see, for example, Esteve-Volart [2004]). Such distortions would not only affect the dependent employed, but similar arguments could be made for the self-employed in agricultural and non-agricultural sectors where unequal access to critical inputs, technologies, and resources would reduce the average productivity of these ventures, thereby reducing economic growth (see Mark Blackden, Sudharshan Canagarajah, Stephen Klasen, and David Lawson [2007]). As self-employment (including in agriculture) is included in our empirical assessment, these arguments might have some empirical relevance in accounting for the results.

A second and also closely related argument suggests that gender inequality in employment can reduce economic growth via demographic effects. A model by Cavalcanti and Tavares (2007) suggests that gender inequality in employment would be associated with higher fertility levels, which in turn reduce economic growth.

Third, the results by Seguino (2000a, 2000b) on the impact of gender gaps in pay on international competitiveness imply that gender gaps in employment access would also reduce economic growth, as it would deprive countries' use of (relatively cheap) women's labor as a competitive advantage in an export-oriented growth strategy.

A fourth argument relates to the importance of women's employment and earnings for their bargaining power within families. There is a sizable literature that demonstrates that women's employment and earnings increase their bargaining power in the home (for example, Amartya Sen [1990]; Lawrence James Haddad, John Hoddinott, and Harold Alderman [1997]; Duncan Thomas [1997]; World Bank [2001]; Stephan Klasen and Claudia Wink [2003]; and King, Klasen, and Porter [2008]). This greater bargaining power not only benefits the women concerned, but can also have a range of growth-enhancing effects. These could include higher savings, as women and men differ in their savings behavior (see, for example, Stephanie Seguino and Maria Sagrario Floro [2003]), more productive investments and use and repayment of credit (see Janet Stotsky [2006]), and higher investments in the health and education of their children, thus promoting the next generation's human capital, and therefore economic growth (see, for example, Thomas [1997] and World Bank [2001]).

A fifth argument relates to governance. There is a growing but still rather speculative and suggestive literature that has collated evidence that women workers, on average, appear to be less prone to corruption and nepotism than men workers (World Bank 2001; Anand Swamy, Omar Azfar, Stephen Knack and Young Lee 2001). If these findings prove to be robust, greater levels of women's employment might be beneficial for economic performance in this sense as well.[9]

There is a related theoretical literature that examines the impact of gender discrimination in pay on economic performance. Here, the theoretical literature is quite divided. On the one hand, studies by Galor and Weil (1996) and Cavalcanti and Tavares (2007) suggest that large gender pay gaps will reduce economic growth. Such gender pay gaps reduce female employment, increase fertility, and lower economic growth through these participation and demographic effects. In contrast, Blecker and Seguino (2002) highlight a different mechanism, leading to contrasting results. They suggest that high gender pay gaps and associated low female wages increase the competitiveness of export-oriented industrializing economies and thus boost the growth performance of these countries. The most important difference in this study, in contrast to the models considered above, is that it focuses more on short-term, demand-induced growth effects, while the other models are long-term growth models where growth is driven by supply constraints. Clearly, both effects can be relevant, depending on the time horizon considered, an issue that is also discussed briefly below.

It is important to point out that it is difficult to theoretically separate the effects between gender gaps in education, employment, and pay. In fact, in most of the models considered above, gender gaps in one dimension tend to lead to gender gaps in other dimensions, with the causality running in both directions.[10] For example, gender gaps in education might automatically lead to gender gaps in employment, particularly in the formal sector, where employers will prefer educated workers and thus will not consider the applications of uneducated women. Conversely, if there are large barriers to female employment or gender gaps in pay, rational parents (and girls) might decide that the education of girls is not as lucrative, which might therefore lead to lower demands for female education and the resulting gender gaps in education.[11] Thus, gender gaps in education and employment are closely related.[12]

Gender gaps in education and employment are not measuring the same thing, however, and thus it is important to investigate them separately. For one, it might be the case that the two issues are largely driven by institutional factors that govern education and employment access and do not therefore greatly depend on each other. For example, one might think of an education policy that strives to achieve universal education and thus reduces gender gaps, while there continue to be considerable barriers to employment for women in the labor market. This might be particularly relevant to the situations in the MENA and most recently South Asia. Moreover, the externalities of female education and female employment are not the same. For example, female education is likely to lead to lower fertility and child mortality of the offspring, while the effect of female employment on these items is likely to be much smaller and more indirect (working mainly through greater women's bargaining power; and there may also be opposite effects, including that the absence of women in the home might in some cases have a negative impact on the quality of childcare). Conversely, the governance externality applies solely to female employment, not to female education.

On the empirical evidence, there is a considerable literature now documenting that gender gaps in education reduce economic growth. Elizabeth M. King and M. Anne Hill (1993) as well as Knowles, Lorgelly, and Owen (2002) use a Solow-growth framework, and find that gender gaps in education have a large and statistically significant negative effect on the level of gross domestic product (GDP). Dollar and Gatti (1999), Forbes (2000), Yamarik and Ghosh (2003), Elizabeth N. Appiah and Walter W. McMahon (2002), and Klasen (2002) investigate the impact of gender gaps on economic growth, and all find that gender gaps in education have a negative impact on subsequent economic growth. They also find that the earlier results by Barro and Lee (1994), that female education might negatively impact economic growth, do not stand up to closer econometric scrutiny.

There are far fewer empirical studies on the impact of gender gaps in employment and pay on economic growth, which is largely due to the data and econometric issues discussed above. Klasen (1999) found that increases in female labor force participation and formal-sector employment were associated with higher growth in a cross-country context. Differences in female participation and employment might have accounted for another 0.3 percentage points in the growth difference between the MENA region and EAP. But these findings have to be treated with caution as they may suffer from reverse causality. In particular, it might be the case that high growth draws women into the labor force (rather than increasing female participation promoting economic growth). There are no easy ways to correct for this econometrically, as there are unlikely to be valid instruments that can be used. Also, there are questions about the international comparability of data on labor force participation and formal-sector employment rates. To the extent that the problems of comparability affect levels but not trends over time, these problems might be avoided in a fixed effects panel setting as the one we are undertaking here.

At the sub-national level, Esteve-Volart (2004) has found statistically significant negative effects of gender gaps in employment and managerial positions on economic growth of India's states using panel data and controlling for endogeneity using instrumental variables.

There are some papers by Seguino (2000a, 2000b) that support the contention that the combination of low gender gaps in education and employment with large gender gaps in pay (and resulting low female wages) were a contributing factor to the growth experience of export-oriented, middle-income countries. A paper by Busse and Spielmann (2006), which finds for a sample of twenty-three developing countries that a combination of low gender gaps in education and employment and large gender gaps in pay helped promote exports, supports this empirical claim. Unfortunately, there are no comprehensive, standardized, and comparable data on gender pay gaps across many countries, so these analyses have been based on relatively small and rather specific samples of countries.[13]

Also empirically, there are some questions about the separation of the effects of gender gaps in education and labor force participation or employment. Regressions that only consider the effect of gender gaps in education might implicitly also measure the impact of gender gaps in employment, particularly if the two are highly correlated. Such high correlation might also make it difficult to separately identify the effects when both are included in a regression (due to the multicollinearity problem).[14] Also, it will be difficult to assess which of the two is the causal driver of the other, given the close and plausible theoretical and empirical linkage.

In sum, there is considerable theoretical support for the notion that gender gaps in education and employment are likely to reduce economic performance (while the literature on the effect of gender gaps in pay is more divided). The empirical results also point to negative effects of gender gaps in education, but there is little reliable cross-country evidence on gender gaps in employment. In the following section, we will discuss the gender gaps in education and employment by developing region before estimating the impact of these gaps on economic performance.

EDUCATION, LABOR FORCE PARTICIPATION, EMPLOYMENT, AND ECONOMIC PERFORMANCE

In this section, we will present data on growth, education, labor force participation, and employment in different world regions, with particular focus on MENA,[15] Sub-Saharan Africa, and South Asia – the areas with particularly high gender gaps in education and/or employment. The data sources and definitions are shown in Table 1.

As shown in Figure 1, the fastest-growing region in the past forty years according to our data set has been the region of EAP. The real per capita annual growth rate between 1960 and 2000 in this region was 4.05 percent. On the contrary, the region that registered least growth is the Sub-Saharan Africa region (0.57 percent). Latin American and Caribbean countries (LAC) did not experience high growth rates either: they grew 1.53 percent annually. The Middle East and the Organisation for Economic Co-operation and Development (OECD) countries' growth rates are in-between at 2.24 percent and 2.66 percent annual growth per capita respectively. To better analyze the pattern of the per capita growth rate, we will decompose it into the decades of the past forty years (1960s, 1970s, 1980s, and 1990s) and consider the different world region's growth rates in the different decades.

Considering the growth rate per decade in Figure 2 allows us to take into account the growth rates of Eastern Europe and Central Asia (ECA) because after 1990 the data available for this region increases considerably. During the nineties those countries were in transition, and their rate of per capita growth was very low (0.26 percent). But also in Sub-Saharan Africa, the annual per capita growth rate decreased in the last four decades, and actually shows negative growth in the nineties (-0.21 percent).

In other world regions, the per capita growth rate was generally higher in the 1960s and 1970s, and then it decreased in the 1980s and 1990s, with the exception of the South Asia region (SA), where the annual growth rate grew quickly in 1980s and was maintained almost at the same level in the 1990s. This result was largely driven by India and Sri Lanka. But their neighbors (EAP countries) still remain the countries that experience largely higher annual per capita growth rate in each decade. The region of MENA, together with Latin America, seems to be successfully recovering from very low growth in the 1980s. One should point out that the data for MENA included in the analysis do not consider many of the oil-exporting Arab states including Saudi Arabia, Kuwait, UAE, Oman, and Libya, for which there is no income data over time.[16] Nevertheless, the growth experience is, to a considerable extent, influenced by the direct and indirect impact of oil prices on oil-producing (and neighboring) countries.[17]

Non-economic indicators of well-being show a similar pattern, although some differences emerge (see Appendix Table 2). The three indicators

Table 1 Variables names, definitions, and data sources[a]

Variable name	*Definitions*	*Data source*
G	Per capita annual compound growth rate in purchasing power, parity-adjusted GDP per capita	Penn World Table 6.1 (Alan Heston, Robert Summers, and Bettina Aten 2002)
GDP60(00)	Real GDP per capita in PPP-terms in 1960 (2000)	Penn World Table 6.1 (Heston, Summers, and Aten 2002)
INV	Average investment rates	Penn World Table 6.1 (Heston, Summers, and Aten 2002)
POPGRO	Growth rate of total population	Penn World Table 6.1 (Heston, Summers, and Aten 2002)
OPEN	Average of exports plus imports as a share of GDP	WDI (World Bank 2002)
LFG	Growth rate of working-age population (15–64)	WDI (World Bank 2002)
FERT60(00)	Level of fertility 1960 (2000)	WDI (World Bank 2002)
M560(00)	Under 5 mortality rate 1960 (2000)	WDI (World Bank 2002)
Life	Life expectancy measured in years	WDI (World Bank 2002)
ED	Number of years of schooling for the male population (15+ and 25+)	Robert Barro and Jong-Wha Lee (2000)
AED	Number of years of schooling for the population	Barro and Lee (2000)
GED	Absolute (annual) growth in male years of schooling	Barro and Lee (2000)
GEDF	Absolute (annual) growth in female years of schooling	
GAED	Absolute growth in total years of schooling	Barro and Lee (2000)
RED	Female–male ratio of schooling	Barro and Lee (2000)
RGED	Female–male ratio of the growth in the years of schooling	Barro and Lee (2000)
MACT	Male economic activity rate (15–64)	ILO Laborsta (ILO 2003)
FACT	Female economic activity rate (15–64)	ILO Laborsta (ILO 2003)
RACT	Female–male ratio of activity rates (15–64)	ILO Laborsta (ILO 2003)
TACT	Total economic activity rate (15–64)	ILO Laborsta (ILO 2003)
FLFT	Female share of the total labor force (15–64)	ILO Laborsta (ILO 2003)

Note: [a]WDI is abbreviation for the report *World Development Indicators*.

shown – under 5 mortality, fertility, and life expectancy – all show larger improvements than the income measures. But the pace of improvements is similar to the growth indicator, with EAP showing the fastest improvements on most indicators, while Sub-Saharan Africa shows the slowest. Here, the MENA region compares very favorably with rapid improvements in life expectancy and under 5 mortality, and large reductions in fertility,

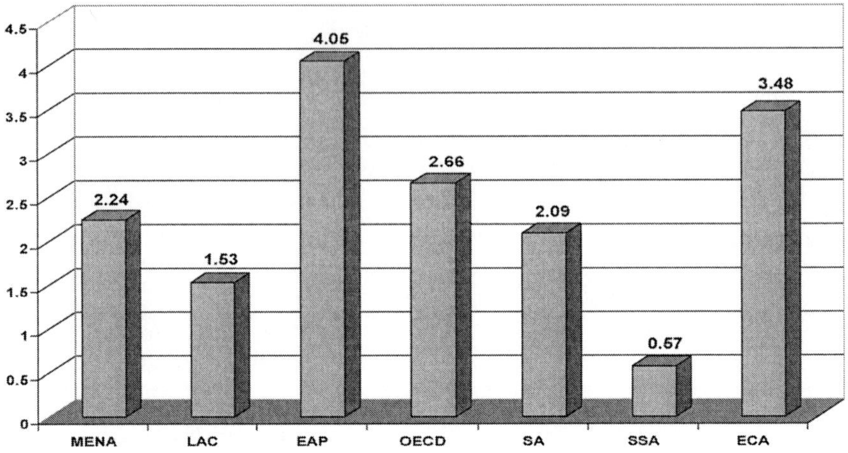

Figure 1 Real regional per capita annual growth rate 1960–2000
Source: Penn World Table 6.1 (Heston, Summers, and Aten 2002).
Notes: The sample of countries included is restricted due to data availability. See the Appendix for a detailed listing. Figures refer to unweighted averages. World regions: MENA (the Middle East and North Africa), LAC (Latin America and the Caribbean), EAP (East Asia and Pacific), OECD (industrialized countries members of the Organisation for Economic Co-operation and Development [OECD]), SA (South Asia), SSA (Sub-Saharan Africa), and ECA (Eastern Europe and Central Asia).

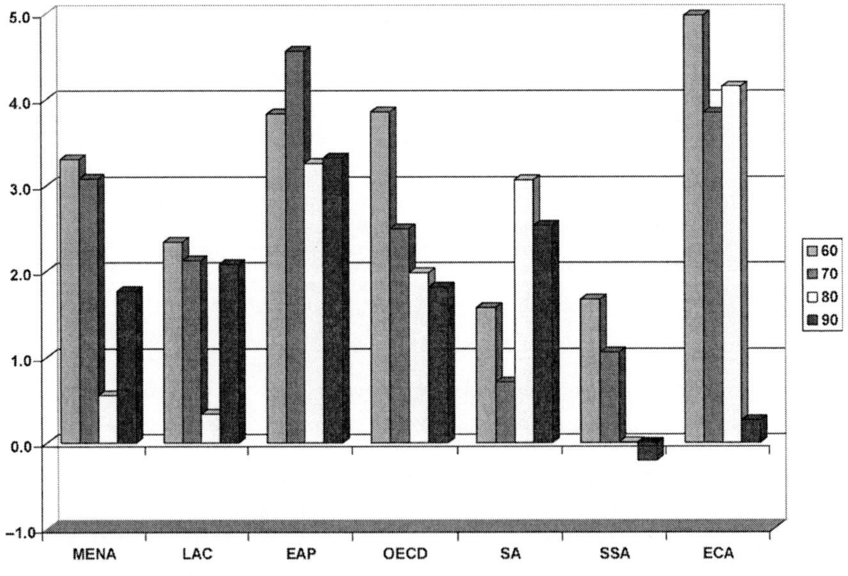

Figure 2 Real regional per capita annual growth rate by decade
Source: Penn World Table 6.1 (Heston, Summers, and Aten 2002).

particularly in the past twenty years, while in South Asia the improvement was generally smaller.

Turning to the indicators of concern here, gender inequality in education, labor force participation, and employment, Appendix Tables 3 and 4 show the development by decade in the regions between 1960 and 2000. These tables show that in all the regions, the education level of the adult population has increased considerably since 1960. Male and female adults have between 1.8 and 4.4 more years of education in 2000 than in 1960, with Sub-Saharan Africa showing the slowest progress and East Asia and the MENA region the fastest. Regarding gender inequality, the data show considerable gender inequality in education in 1960 for most regions. The worst affected were South Asia, Sub-Saharan Africa, and the MENA region, where women had about half or less the education level than men. In all regions, this gap has been reduced, but the gap remains sizable in some. In South Asia, women still only have about 60 percent of the educational achievement of men, and the gap has closed quite slowly in Sub-Saharan Africa. The gaps have been closing faster in EAP and also in the MENA region, where women (15 and older) now have about 73 percent of the education of men.

Appendix Table 4 examines the data on labor force participation rates by gender, the female share of the labor force, and the rates of formal-sector employment. The data show that inequality in labor force participation is also considerable, although the gaps have been narrowing. From these data, a consistent pattern emerges. In particular, EAP as well as Latin America show rapidly declining gender gaps in labor force participation and formal-sector employment. Sub-Saharan Africa shows declines in female labor force participation, but from a previously high level,[18] and the MENA region has the lowest female labor force participation rate and formal sector participation of women throughout the period. The gaps in labor force participation rates in MENA (as in other regions) have also narrowed in recent decades, but by less than most other regions.[19] In South Asia, the gender gap in labor force participation in the past four decades has only marginally reduced.

From our theoretical discussion, we would expect that excluding women from the pool of talent is particularly damaging to formal-sector employment, which may predominantly depend on having the best talent. Thus, using the gender gap in formal-sector employment might be most appropriate. On the other hand, these data are available from the International Labour Organization (ILO) for a much smaller pool of countries, and it appears that measurement error and international comparability is particularly problematic using these data. Therefore, we will use the gender gaps in labor force participation only for the empirical analysis that follows.

Even if formal-sector employment data are not readily available and comparable, one might still want to use the overall employment rate (that is, employed women as a share of the working-age population) rather than labor force participation data, as the presumed theoretical effects are related to employment rather than participation. The difference between the two is, of course, the unemployment rates. While we do not have reliable employment data at the national level, the Key Indicators of the Labour Market (KILM) data of the ILO (2007) suggest that, first, unemployment rates are below 10 percent in all regions except the MENA region (where they are believed to hover around 12–14 percent), and second, the differences in male and female unemployment rates are quite low (usually less than 1 percentage point), so labor force participation data appear to be reasonable proxies for employment levels by sex.[20] Thus, we believe that the data on gender gaps in labor force participation rates will be reasonable proxies for gender gaps in overall employment rates.

In general, however, the quality and comparability of the ILO labor force data is also open to question. The data are estimates based sometimes on very patchy primary data. The comparability problems are likely to be larger in level differences across countries than in trends over time. Despite these problems, we are forced to rely on the available ILO labor force data as the only available cross-country panel data for our analysis. Inherent measurement error in all the labor force estimates leads to the well-known downward bias of coefficients in regression analyses. Thus, any effect that we find is likely to understate the true extent of the effect. Unfortunately, it is very difficult to econometrically control for measurement error. We know little about the structure of the measurement error, nor are there good instruments to address it. We hope that our panel analyses will at least partly reduce this problem to the extent that measurement error and comparability problems are lower across time than they are across space and can therefore be partly controlled for by using country-specific effects.

DATA AND ESTIMATION PROCEDURE

Since the early 1990s, a good deal of empirical growth research using cross-country data was inspired by new growth theories and the availability of better data. In our estimation strategy, we make use of cross-country and panel growth regressions that were pioneered by Robert Barro (1991) and used in a large literature since. Our particular estimation strategy for the cross-section analysis follows Klasen (2002); the panel regressions will be extended to include additional employment variables. As our focus is on long-run economic growth, the most basic specification will use purely cross-country data where the period 1960–2000 will be treated as a single observation for each country. To partly control for possible endogeneity issues and unobserved heterogeneity, we will also consider panel regressions that treat each decade as one observation and use initial values of the covariates. Those panel regressions will also allow us to properly study the impact of gender inequalities in labor force participation on economic growth.

We include a number of regressors that were found to affect economic growth in the literature, including population growth, growth in the working-age population, openness (exports plus imports as a share of GDP), the investment rate, human capital, and regional dummy variables to capture region-specific effects, which are invariably not captured in such cross-country regressions and can include common geographic, institutional, policy, trade, or conflict experiences within regions.[21]

To avoid some of the methodological problems of earlier studies on gender inequality and economic growth, we do not separate male and female education level in our equations. Instead, we generate four different education variables, one for the initial level of education in 1960, one for the gender gap in the level of education in 1960, one for the growth in the level of education in the period 1960–2000, and one for the growth rate of the female-male education level ratio for the period 1960–2000. For the level of education, we could use the average, the male, or the female education level. Each would make different assumptions about the possibilities to affect the gender gap. Using the male education level as a proxy for average education provides an upper-bound estimate for the effect of gender inequality in education on economic growth, as it implicitly assumes that one could improve the gender gap in education by sending more girls to school without having to take out boys (as the male education level is held constant this way).[22] In the alternative specification, when we use average education and the gender gap in average education in our equations, we assume that any increase in female education means an equal-sized reduction in male education and thus constitutes a lower-bound estimate of the effect of gender inequality on economic growth.

It may well be the case that gender inequality in education has a direct impact on economic growth; but gender inequality may also affect economic growth through its effects on investment rates, overall population growth, and growth in the working-age population. Our interest is in capturing both the direct and indirect effects of gender inequality on economic growth. Following Klasen (2002), we will estimate a set of regressions to capture these two effects.

The data used in this paper come from different data sources. Table 1 provides information on data sources and a description of the computation of the main variables of interest. Using the variables defined in Table 1, the equations estimated (using OLS) in the cross-country analysis are the following[23]:

$$g = \alpha + \beta_1 INV + \beta_2 POPGRO + \beta_3 LFG + \beta_4 ED60 + \beta_5 GED + \beta_6 RED60 + \beta_7 RGED + \beta_8 X + \epsilon \quad (1)$$

$$INV = \alpha + \beta_9 POPGRO + \beta_{10} LFG + \beta_{11} ED60 + \beta_{12} GED + \beta_{13} RED60 + \beta_{14} RGED + \beta_{15} X + \epsilon \quad (2)$$

$$POPGRO = \alpha + \beta_{16} OPEN + \beta_{17} ED60 + \beta_{18} GED + \beta_{19} RED60 + \beta_{20} RGED + \beta_{21} X + \epsilon \quad (3)$$

$$LFG = \alpha + \beta_{22} OPEN + \beta_{23} ED60 + \beta_{24} GED + \beta_{25} RED60 + \beta_{26} RGED + \beta_{27} X + \epsilon \quad (4)$$

$$G = \alpha + \beta_{28} OPEN + \beta_{29} ED + \beta_{30} GED + \beta_{31} RED60 + \beta_{32} RGED + \beta_{33} X + \epsilon \quad (5)$$

$$G = \alpha + \beta_{34} INV + \beta_{35} POPGRO + \beta_{36} LFG + \beta_{37} AED60 + \beta_{38} GAED + \beta_{39} RED60 + \beta_{40} RGED + \beta_{41} X + \epsilon \quad (6)$$

$$G = \alpha + \beta_{42} AED + \beta_{43} GAED + \beta_{44} RED60 + \beta_{45} RGED + \beta_{46} X + \epsilon \quad (7)$$

The first equation measures the direct impact of education and the gender bias in education on economic growth, as it controls for investment, population, and working-age population growth. In all regressions, we do control for regional variation.[24] Education and gender bias in education could, however, influence population growth, investment, and growth in the working age population in the future. Therefore, there is a need to consider the indirect impact of education and gender inequalities on economic growth via these variables (Equations 2–4). The total effect of gender inequality in education on growth is determined by the path analysis, in which we simply sum the direct effect and indirect effects of gender inequalities in education on growth (see Klasen [2002]).

The fifth equation is the so-called "reduced form" regression. In this equation, we omit investment, overall population, and working-age population growth variables. We expect the coefficients on education of this regression to measure the total effect of gender bias in education directly. The results should then be comparable to the sum of direct and indirect effects calculated using the path analysis.

Equations 6–7 consider the total number of years of schooling as a measure for the average human capital, generating a lower bound estimate of these effects.

The model is then reestimated using panel data where dependent and explanatory variables refer to the following decades: 1960–9; 1970–9;

1980–9; and 1990–2000. Using panel data would allow us to partly control for endogeneity of the education and labor force participation variables by using initial values of each decade and address unobserved heterogeneity and/or measurement error using country-specific effects.[25] This way, we feel we are able to generate more robust estimates, particularly regarding the labor force participation variables where endogeneity and measurement error are likely to be particularly problematic.

We will use several variables to investigate the impact of gender inequalities in employment on growth across the world. In a first specification, we will add the female share of the labor force to our equation. This specification holds the total labor force fixed and just adjusts the female share of the labor force, assuming that higher female employment could only come about through increased total employment. While this might be the best specification, it does not allow for possible influences of male labor force participation on economic growth, which might bias the results.[26] We use a similar technique to that used in the cross-country growth regression model for the education variables with employment. We generate upper- and lower-bound estimates. We use male activity rates together with the female–male ratio as upper bound estimates (the assumption is that the female–male ratio could be increased without reducing male activity rates, leading to basically more jobs in total) and the total activity rate together with the female–male ratio as lower bound (the assumption is that any additional female job would lead to fewer male jobs). As with the education estimates, we believe that the true effects are closer to the former than the latter specification. Using fixed effects to control for unobserved heterogeneity turns out to be the best panel specification.[27]

Compared with Klasen (2002), the country sample is smaller due firstly to changes in data availability from the Penn World Tables Version 6.1 (Alan Heston, Robert Summers, and Bettina Aten 2002); secondly, to the elimination of apparently inconsistent data for education in two countries; and thirdly, to the lack of data for many transition countries before 1990.[28]

Table 2 shows the descriptive statistic of some variables of interest for the cross-country analysis. This includes a number of variables typically used in cross-country growth models. We have already commented above on trends and regional differences in GDP growth, education, labor force, and non-income indicators of well-being by decade. One point of note is the variable *RGED*, which measures the female–male ratio of growth in education in the period 1960–2000. This variable clearly reflects the different progress made in reducing the gender gap in education in a region. While the ratio is far above 1 in EAP, suggesting that women expanded their education faster than men, the reverse is the case especially in South Asia (0.77) but also in the MENA region (0.87). The figures for SSA show that women expanded their education about as fast as men. Table 2 also includes data on other regressors, including the investment rate, population growth, and

Table 2 Descriptive statistics for cross-section analysis

	TOTAL	*MENA*	*LAC*	*EAP*	*OECD*	*SA*	*SSA*	*ECA*
G	1.78	2.24	1.53	4.05	2.66	2.09	0.57	3.48
INV	15.48	13.18	13.96	20.53	23.92	11.21	10.45	17.31
OPEN	72.98	71.41	79.37	87.82	57.26	38.60	74.76	81.91
M560	166.65	233.75	135.50	139.56	37.45	228.00	273.08	80.78
M500	64.35	45.13	32.00	31.77	6.62	80.65	147.42	16.38
POPGRO	1.89	2.75	1.79	2.01	0.73	2.20	2.50	0.91
FERT60	5.31	7.12	6.12	5.69	2.88	6.30	6.49	3.24
FERT00	3.15	3.32	2.70	2.27	1.67	3.45	5.09	1.47
GDP60	3,377	1,971	3,299	1,813	8,473	930	1,478	2,233
GDP00	8,693	4,462	6,897	12,033	23,153	2,186	2,375	7,910
LFG	2.02	2.95	2.35	2.69	0.86	2.33	2.46	1.00
RED60	0.70	0.39	0.91	0.59	0.93	0.29	0.47	0.73
RGED	1.03	0.87	1.09	1.24	1.02	0.77	0.97	1.05
EDF60	3.41	0.65	3.26	2.74	6.56	0.89	1.19	5.24
GEDF	0.07	0.11	0.07	0.10	0.07	0.06	0.05	0.09

Sources: Authors' computations based on data from WDI (World Bank 2002), Penn World Table 6.1 (Heston, Summers, and Aten 2002), and Robert Barro and Jong-Wha Lee (2000).
Note: In addition to the dependent and explanatory variables of our cross-country model, we do report child mortality (under 5 years of life) in 1960 (M560) and in 2000 (M500), the fertility rate (FERT), and the real GDP per capita in PPP for 1960 and 2000 for each region.

working-age population growth. Here, well-known differences emerge. The region of EAP is notable for its high investment rates, high level of openness, high growth in the working-age population, and moderate population growth. The reverse is basically the case for Sub-Saharan Africa: investment rates are low and population growth rates are high. The MENA region shows very high levels of population growth but also sizable investment rates and levels of openness, while South Asia shows relatively high rates of population growth and a low level of openness and investment.[29]

RESULTS

Table 3 shows the basic set of cross-country regressions using the approach from Klasen (2002) as shown above but with the new data that now stretch from 1960 to 2000. We start by considering the basic regression in column 1. Before turning to the education variables, we briefly comment on the other regressors. Compared with Klasen (2002), we observe a considerably better fit of the regression results, which might partially be due to the slightly smaller (and more homogeneous) sample. Also, all the direct and reduced-form regressions pass the omitted variable test.[30] The substantive results confirm many of the findings from the empirical growth literature. First, we see a strong conditional convergence effect. Second, there is a sizable positive impact of investment on economic growth and a large negative impact of population growth, while we also observe a large positive

Table 3 Gender inequality in education and economic growth

Dependent variable	*Growth (1)*	*INV (2)*	*POPGRO (3)*	*LFG (4)*	*Growth (5)*	*Growth (6)*+	*Growth (7)*+
LOGGDP60	-2.27***	-3.51	-0.18	-0.21	-2.47***	-2.29***	-2.52***
	0.50	3.1	0.34	0.36	0.63	0.52	0.65
POPGRO	-2.80***	0.91				-2.79***	
	0.53	2.25				0.53	
LFG	2.33***	0.04				2.32***	
	0.47	2.10				0.47	
OPEN	-0.001	0.041**	-0.003	-0.002	0.005*	-0.0005	0.006*
	0.003	0.02	0.002	0.002	0.004	0.003	0.004
INV	0.06***					0.06***	
	0.02					0.02	
RED60	0.68	5.84**	-0.4	-0.17	1.75**	0.76	1.72**
	0.85	3.08	0.32	0.33	0.89	0.89	0.91
ED60	0.01	0.92**	-0.02	0.01	0.16**	0	0.13*
	0.07	0.44	0.05	0.06	0.09	0.08	0.10
GED	10.42***	35.42	-1.01	0.85	17.33***	10.59***	18.31***
	4.35	28.95	1.94	2.14	4.46	4.78	4.86
RGED	0.70***	2.07	0.001	0.05	0.95***	0.47**	0.62**
	0.29	2.19	0.25	0.25	0.37	0.25	0.34
SA	-0.07	-3.58	-0.17	-0.46**	-0.90*	-0.02	-0.85*
	0.59	3.07	0.24	0.24	0.64	0.61	0.65
SSA	-0.83*	-6.92***	0.40**	-0.06	-2.49***	-0.81*	-2.47***
	0.57	2.76	0.22	0.22	0.70	0.58	0.71
ECA	-0.1	3.57	-0.91**	-1.32***	-0.46	-0.1	-0.46
	0.63	2.80	0.41	0.54	0.87	0.63	0.88
LAC	-0.87*	-4.87**	0.08	-0.17	-1.79***	-0.87*	-1.81***
	0.56	2.73	0.28	0.27	0.74	0.56	0.74
MENA	-0.17	-3.77	0.72**	0.48	-1.26**	-0.12	-1.24**
	0.53	3.77	0.42	0.41	0.66	0.52	0.65
OECD	0.47	4.81*	-1.07***	-1.64***	-0.12	0.55	0.01
	0.60	3.04	0.37	0.38	0.83	0.60	0.82
CONSTANT	7.35***	13.65	3.26***	3.39***	7.16***	7.65***	7.73***
	1.84	11.80	1.06	1.11	2.10	1.85	2.14
ADJ R2	0.76	0.66	0.64	0.62	0.63	0.76	0.64
OV Test	passed	passed	failed	passed	passed	passed	passed
OBS	93	93	93	93	93	93	93

Notes: Heteroscedasticity-adjusted standard errors reported under the coefficients. *** Refers to 1 percent, ** to 5 percent, and * to 10 percent significance level using a one-tail test. + indicates regression with total education instead of male education only. OV test refers to the Ramsey Reset test for omitted variables.

impact of growth in the working-age population. These findings confirm that the timing of the demographic transition can have a powerful impact on economic growth (Bloom and Williamson 1998). The size of the effect is considerably larger now than it was in Klasen (2002). When population growth is falling due to lower fertility, but working-age population growth is still high due to past high fertility, countries are receiving a "demographic gift" of a low dependency burden (Bloom and Williamson 1998), which allows higher savings, a higher ratio of workers to population, and higher investment demand. Given that fertility in the MENA and South Asia regions is falling rapidly, one would expect the region to enter this phase of the "demographic gift" in the coming decades. To what extent they will be able to capitalize on this opportunity will depend largely on the ability to generate employment for the large numbers of young people entering the working-age population and the labor force in coming decades.

Of the regional dummy variables, only those for Sub-Saharan Africa and Latin America have a (marginally) significant negative coefficient. The size of the coefficients are much smaller than in Klasen (2002), suggesting that the model is better able to explain the growth differences between regions than was possible in Klasen (2002).

Turning to the education variables, the initial male education and the growth of male education have the expected positive signs, although only the education growth variable is significant. The initial female–male ratio of education has the expected positive sign, but it is not significant (compared to Klasen [2002], where it was marginally significant). In contrast, the female–male ratio of growth in adult years of schooling is significant and larger in magnitude than found in Klasen (2002). As these coefficients express the direct effect of gender inequality on economic growth, it appears that the direct effect of *initial* gender inequality on economic growth is relatively small, while gender inequality in the *growth* of education has a sizable direct impact on economic growth.[31]

Columns 2–4 of Table 3 estimate the indirect impact of gender inequality in education on economic growth through the effects they have on investment, population growth, and labor force growth. The investment regression shows that the initial female–male ratio of education has a significant positive effect on economic growth, while the impact of gender inequality in the growth of education is also positive but not significant. In the population growth and working-age population growth regressions, the impact of gender inequality in education is in the right direction, though not significant.[32]

Column 5 of Table 3 shows the reduced form regression, which omits the investment, population growth, and working-age growth variables, and thus gives a direct estimate of the total effect of gender inequality in education on economic growth. The coefficients on both the initial ratio as well as the ratio of educational growth are considerably larger than in column 1, and now both are highly significant. This suggests that gender inequality in education, both initial as well as gaps in educational growth, has a significant negative impact on growth. A comparison between columns 1 and 5 shows that the initial gender gap in education has mainly an indirect impact on economic growth (it appears from column 2 to be via investment), while the female–male ratio of educational growth has mainly a direct impact.

Regressions 6 and 7 of Table 3 use average education and thus estimate a lower bound effect of the impact of gender inequality on economic growth. The effects are generally predictably smaller and somewhat less statistically significant.

In Table 4, we calculate to what extent gender bias in education can explain growth differences between the various regions of the world. We do this for the upper and lower bound estimates. Fortunately, the difference between these two estimates is fairly small.

We also note that the sum of direct and indirect effect (regression 1–4) gives results very similar to the direct estimate from the reduced form (regression 5). As expected, the regions with the largest gender gaps in education – South Asia, Sub-Saharan Africa, and the MENA region – suffer the largest losses in terms of economic growth. But there are big differences here. In contrast to Klasen (2002), where both South Asia and the MENA region were suffering similar losses of about 0.9 percentage points in

Table 4 Gender inequality and growth differences between regions

	Difference SSA-EAP	*Difference SA-EAP*	*Difference MENA-EAP*	*Difference SSA-EAP*	*Difference SA-EAP*	*Difference MENA-EAP*
Total annual growth difference	3.48	1.96	1.74	3.48	1.96	1.74
	Upper bound estimate			*Lower bound estimate*		
Accounted for by:						
Direct effect of gender inequality in education (1)	0.26[a]	0.52	0.38	0.22	0.45	0.33
Initial ratio (RED60)	0.08	0.20	0.14	0.09	0.23	0.15
Ratio of educational growth (RGED)	0.18	0.31	0.24	0.13	0.22	0.17
Indirect effects: via investment	0.08	0.17	0.12	0.07	0.14	0.07
via population growth (3)	0.14	0.33	0.22	0.10	0.26	0.17
via labor force growth (4)	-0.02	-0.06	-0.04	-0.01	-0.04	-0.02
Total indirect effect	0.22	0.34	0.30	0.16	0.36	0.22
Initial ratio (RED60)	0.13	0.32	0.22	0.12	0.29	0.14
Ratio of educational growth (RGED)	0.07	0.12	0.09	0.04	0.07	0.04
Total direct and indirect effect	0.46	0.95	0.69	0.38	0.81	0.55
Total effect using reduced form (5)	0.47	0.97	0.70	0.38	0.81	0.41
Of which: RED60	0.22	0.52	0.36	0.21	0.52	0.24
Of which: RGED	0.25	0.45	0.35	0.17	0.29	0.16

Note: [a]Sums do not add up precisely due to rounding.

annual per capita growth per year, the losses are now slightly larger for South Asia, around 1 percentage point, and very much smaller for the MENA region, about 0.7 percentage points per year. The difference for the diverging performance lies in the faster expansion of female schooling in the MENA region which has contributed to closing the gender gap in education, while progress in South Asia has been much more modest.

When examining the pathways through which gender inequality in MENA, South Asia, and Sub-Saharan Africa lead to lower growth, there is a sizable direct effect that amounts to about 60 percent of the total difference. This direct effect refers mainly to the lowering of the quality of human capital as a result of gender inequalities in education. But this is actually somewhat smaller than what was found in Klasen (2002), where for MENA about 75 percent of the total effect was accounted for by the direct effect. The indirect effect via investment has become somewhat smaller, while the indirect effect via demographic variables it has become more important. Clearly, all pathways investigated contribute to the resulting growth difference, and the magnitudes have shifted toward a greater importance of the demographic pathway, which suggests that higher female education lowers population growth, which in turn helps improve economic growth.

Table 5 shows the result of panel regressions using fixed effects, which was found to be the preferred specification based on the Hausman test. Also here, the empirical findings in these regressions are consistent with the empirical and theoretical literature: we find conditional convergence; a positive effect on growth of the working-age population; and a negative effect of population growth, though the latter two effects are statistically significant in only some specifications.[33] Investment rates statistically significantly promote growth, and openness has a small positive but rarely significant impact.

The specification in regression 8 of Table 5 only examines the impact of gender gaps in education on economic growth. In contrast to the panel results in Klasen (2002) and the cross-section results shown here, the positive effect of a high female–male years of schooling ratio among the adult population (the female–male ratio of education of adults 25 or older) is relatively small and not statistically significant. Further investigations show that this is not driven by a slightly different composition of sample but by the addition of the 1990s. If the 1990s are dropped, a higher female–male ratio of years of schooling has a large and significant effect (not shown here). In fact, it is due to the two regions Latin America and Sub-Saharan Africa in the 1990s. If we exclude these regions for that time period, regression 9 shows that then the positive effect of higher gender equality in education is again sizable and statistically significant.[34] It appears that the moderate to poor growth performance in these two regions, despite falling gender gaps in education, is important enough to reduce the overall effect of educational

Table 5 Gender inequality and economic growth

	(8)	*(9)*	*(10)*	*(11)*	*(12)*	*(13)*	*(14)*	*(15)*	*(16)*
LOGGDP	-5.54***	-7.82***	-10.37***	-6.08***	-10.81***	-6.99***	-6.14***	-8.48***	-11.09***
	1.42	1.33	1.31	1.43	1.32	1.28	1.48	1.41	1.28
POPGRO	-0.57*	-0.44	-0.22	-0.47	-0.23	-0.47*	-0.59*	-0.45	-0.20
	0.42	0.35	0.40	0.40	0.39	0.37	0.42	0.37	0.39
LFG	0.31	0.46*	0.32	0.38	0.34	0.48*	0.45*	0.54**	0.29
	0.27	0.31	0.40	0.31	0.40	0.30	0.31	0.31	0.37
FLFT	–	–	–	7.86**	4.17	–	–	–	–
	–	–	–	3.49	3.36	–	–	–	–
OPEN	0.002	0.005	0.006	0.000	0.006	0.001	0.001	0.003	0.007
	0.004	0.005	0.008	0.005	0.007	0.005	0.004	0.005	0.007
INV	0.09***	0.10***	0.13***	0.10***	0.14***	0.12***	0.10***	0.10***	0.14***
	0.03	0.03	0.02	0.03	0.02	0.03	0.03	0.03	0.02
OED25+	0.00	0.08	–	0.00	–	–	0.00	0.05	–
	0.16	0.17	–	0.16	–	–	0.16	0.16	–
ORED25+	0.43	2.30**	–	1.01	–	–	1.14	3.09**	–
	1.45	1.28	–	1.43	–	–	1.51	1.41	–
YED15+	–	–	0.31**	–	0.31***	–	–	–	0.29***
	–	–	0.13	–	0.12	–	–	–	0.12
YRED15+	–	–	3.33**	–	3.66**	–	–	–	4.42***
	–	–	1.65	–	1.70	–	–	–	1.76
RACT	–	–	–	–	–	5.41***	3.72**	2.97**	1.93*
	–	–	–	–	–	1.48	1.51	1.37	1.49
MACT	–	–	–	–	–	-0.70	3.85	-0.91	-6.60
	–	–	–	–	–	6.69	6.90	7.03	5.73

(*continued*)

Table 5 (Continued)

	(8)	(9)	(10)	(11)	(12)	(13)	(14)	(15)	(16)
1960S	0.12	-0.65	-1.32***	0.59	-0.97*	0.61	0.40	-0.21	-0.49
	0.57	0.59	0.51	0.61	0.59	0.58	0.70	0.76	0.74
1970S	0.04	-0.52	-1.04***	0.37	-0.80**	0.30	0.28	-0.18	-0.47
	0.38	0.41	0.38	0.41	0.44	0.37	0.46	0.51	0.54
1980S	-0.60**	-1.07***	-0.62***	-0.44*	-0.52**	-0.31	-0.46	-0.86***	-0.33
	0.26	0.29	0.25	0.27	0.26	0.26	0.29	0.33	0.30
Constant	20.20***	26.79***	34.93***	18.53***	34.58***	21.45***	16.04**	27.53***	40.98***
	4.87	4.78	4.73	4.89	4.55	7.80	8.03	7.51	6.32
R2	0.32	0.43	0.60	0.34	0.61	0.36	0.34	0.44	0.62
OBS	341	296	143	341	307	441	341	296	143

Notes: Heteroscedasticity-adjusted standard errors reported under the coefficient. *** Refers to 1 percent, ** to 5 percent, and * to 10 percent significance level using a one-tail test. In regressions 9 and 15, the sample excludes Sub-Saharan Africa and Latin America for the 1990s. In regressions 10, 12, and 16, only the OECD, East Asian, and South Asian countries are included.

gender gaps to insignificance. It seems plausible to assume that the poor growth performance, particularly of Sub-Saharan Africa, was not related to the reduced gender gaps in education but to many other factors that have been analyzed in the literature (for example, Paul Collier and Jan Willem Gunning [1999] and World Bank [2006]). Conversely, regression 9 suggests that in all other regions, the impact of gender gaps in education on growth remains as strong in the 1990s as before (in fact, slightly stronger).

In Table 5, regression 10, we replace the education variable with the education of adults 15 or older. This is to also capture the effects of high employment rates of educated women in the young age group 15–24, which might have a particularly large impact on growth. It turns out that in this specification the effect of gender gaps in education on growth are only significant if we limit the analysis to OECD, East Asian, and South Asian countries. But there, the effect is very large and highly significant. This appears plausible, as these are the regions where young, educated women have been particularly active in the labor market.

In Table 5, regressions 11–16, we consider the full sample again and include various labor force participation variables.[35] We consider two different explanatory variables for the labor force participation: the female share of the total labor force (FLFT) and the ratio of female–male economic activity rates (RACT = FACT/MACT). In regression 11, the female share of the labor force (FLFT) has a positive, large significant coefficient on economic growth; that is, countries where the (initial) female share increased from decade to decade were able to achieve higher rates of subsequent economic growth. The effect of gender gaps in education (ORED 25+) in this specification is considerable but not statistically significant. If we exclude Sub-Saharan Africa and Latin America in the 1990s, the effect becomes much larger and highly significant.[36] In regression 12, we use the other education variable (YRED 15+), which shows a large impact of education gaps on growth, and a smaller and no longer significant impact of female shares of the labor force, again reduced to OECD, East Asia, and South Asia.

In regression 13, we use the male labor force participation rate (MACT) and the ratio of the female–male labor force participation rates (RACT) as an alternative way to capture the gender gap in employment. This female–male ratio is highly significant and positive, while the male economic activity rate has a non-significant negative sign. If we add the education gap in regression 14, the coefficient on the gender gap in labor force participation is still positive and significant but smaller, while the coefficient on the male activity rate is now positive but still insignificant. The coefficient on educational gaps is not significant. In the reduced sample (excluding Sub Saharan Africa and Latin America for the 1990s), it also becomes significant in this specification, while the impact of activity rates becomes slightly smaller but remains significant (see regression 15). Lastly, we limit our sample to the OECD countries, East Asia, and South Asia, and use the alternative education variable. We find that then education gaps have a very large impact on growth, while gaps in activity rates have a smaller (and only marginally significant) impact on growth.

Since the coefficient on MACT is small and insignificant, altering MACT when one increases FACT would not have a significant impact on growth. Thus, in contrast to the education regressions in Table 3, it is not necessary to calculate an upper- and lower-bound regression, as the male activity rate seems to be immaterial for growth.[37]

On the whole, these results suggest that gender gaps in labor force participation have a negative impact on economic growth; since these gaps proxy for gaps in employment (see discussion above), gender gaps in employment similarly negatively affect economic growth. For the MENA and South Asia regions, where female employment is still very low, this could have a significant impact on economic growth. The results also give some interesting insights into the relative importance of education and employment gaps in different time periods. In the full sample of countries, educational gender gaps are not so important, while employment gaps have a particularly large impact on economic performance. This is largely due to the experience of the 1990s, when gender gaps in employment appear to be more consequential than those in education. Once Sub-Saharan Africa and Latin America in the 1990s are excluded, however, education and employment gaps have a similar impact on economic growth. If we change to an education variable that includes young people, the results indeed suggest that education gaps are more important than employment gaps, at least in the OECD, East Asia, and South Asia. This suggests that previous studies that only examined gender gaps in education were partly implicitly capturing the effects of gender gaps in employment, and it is indeed useful to consider the two jointly as we have done here. It also suggests, however, that it is not easy to clearly answer the question which one of the two is of more relative importance, as the answer appears to be quite sensitive to the sample, time period, and education variable used. This will become more apparent below.

In further analyses, we also considered some interaction terms. Of particular interest is to interact the effect of openness with gender gaps in labor force participation to see whether the effects of gender gaps in labor force participation rates are different in countries that are more exposed to international trade. The results (not shown here) show a positive (but not significant) interaction term, while the coefficient on RACT is now smaller and still highly significant in all specifications. This provides some supporting evidence that in countries that are strongly exposed to international trade, lower gender gaps in labor force participation are particularly beneficial to economic growth, in line with some of the arguments made above.

Once again, we simulate the impact of gender inequality in education and employment (using gender gaps in labor force participation as our

Table 6 Gender inequality in education and employment and growth impact (EAP-MENA) by decades

	1960s	*1970s*	*1980s*	*1990s*
Growth difference EAP-MENA	0.53	1.48	2.71	1.55
Regression 9				
Education effect (ORED)	0.41	0.65	0.61	0.54
Regression 11				
Education effect (ORED)	0.18	0.29	0.27	0.24
Employment effect (FLFT)	0.75	0.86	0.96	1.06
Total effect	0.93	1.15	1.23	1.30
Regression 13				
Employment effect (RACT)	1.15	1.36	1.62	1.73
Regression 14				
Education effect (ORED)	0.20	0.32	0.30	0.27
Employment effect (RACT)	0.79	0.94	1.11	1.19
Total effect	0.99	1.26	1.41	1.45
Regression 15				
Education effect (ORED)	0.55	0.88	0.82	0.72
Employment effect (RACT)	0.63	0.75	0.89	0.95
Total effect	1.18	1.62	1.71	1.67

Notes: Computations are based on Table 5. Since regressions 10, 12, and 16 did not include data from the MENA region, they are not included in the simulations.

proxy) based on these panel regressions. In Table 6, we show to what extent the difference in economic growth between EAP and MENA can be accounted for by differences in gender inequality in education and employment. Estimates based on regression 9 already show that gender gaps in education can account for a sizable portion of growth differences, but this difference is declining, due to a shrinking difference in gender gaps in education between the two regions. Once gender gaps in employment are included, the share of growth differences explained by these combined gaps increases significantly; in fact, in the 1960s, 1970s, and 1990s, the gaps can account for all of the growth differences, or even more than that in some specifications, suggesting that the MENA region would have grown faster than East Asia in the absence of the gaps. The growth costs, compared with East Asia, of gender gaps in employment, are increasing over time as the gender gaps in employment are shrinking much faster in East Asia than in MENA. In most specifications, the gender gaps in employment explain a larger share of the growth differences with East Asia, suggesting that MENA is particularly held back by its low female labor force participation rates, a subject much discussed in the literature (see, for example, World Bank [2004]).

Table 7 shows to what extent the growth differences between South Asia and East Asia can be explained by gender gaps in education and employment. Here, the impact of larger educational gender gaps in South Asia plays a particularly large role. Depending on the specification, it can

Table 7 Gender inequality in education and employment and growth impact (EAP-SA) by decades

	1960s	*1970s*	*1980s*	*1990s*
Growth difference EAP-SA	2.26	3.86	0.19	0.79
Regression 9				
Education effect (ORED)	0.57	0.50	0.67	0.73
Regression 10				
Education effect (YRED)	0.69	0.88	0.95	0.78
Regression 11				
Education effect (ORED)	0.25	0.22	0.29	0.32
Employment effect (FLFT)	-0.17	0.09	0.34	0.45
Total effect	0.08	0.31	0.63	0.77
Regression 12				
Education effect (YRED)	1.08	1.11	1.19	1.00
Employment effect (FLFT)	-0.09	0.05	0.18	0.24
Total effect	0.98	1.15	1.37	1.24
Regression 13				
Employment effect (RACT)	-0.37	-0.02	0.43	0.60
Regression 14				
Education effect (ORED)	0.28	0.25	0.33	0.36
Employment effect (RACT)	-0.26	-0.01	0.29	0.42
Total effect	0.03	0.24	0.63	0.78
Regression 15				
Education effect (ORED)	0.77	0.67	0.90	0.99
Employment effect (RACT)	-0.20	-0.01	0.24	0.33
Total effect	0.56	0.66	1.14	1.32
Regression 16				
Education effect (YRED)	1.30	1.34	1.44	1.21
Employment effect (RACT)	-0.13	-0.01	0.15	0.22
Total effect	1.17	1.33	1.59	1.43

Notes: Computations are based on Table 5.

account for a growth difference between 0.2 and 1.4 percentage points. In contrast, the impact of employment effects is generally smaller but is increasing over time. In fact, the ILO data we used shows smaller gender gaps in labor force participation in South Asia than in East Asia in the 1960s and 1970s. If these level differences are to be believed, then South Asia's main problem has been, apart from their stubbornly high gender gaps in education, that female participation and employment has expanded much more slowly than in East Asia, and this is exacting rising growth costs compared to East Asia. This is also consistent with country studies showing that East Asian economies such as China, Vietnam, and Indonesia have benefited particularly from integrating women into the labor market; in South Asia, only Bangladesh has followed such a route and appears to have profited from it.[38]

While these calculations neatly show the particular constraints in different regions, they cannot give clear answers to the question of whether gender gaps in education or employment lead to higher growth costs. This depends to a large degree on the education variable, the time period, and the sample. But we can say with more certainty that, in relative terms, MENA's problems are more on the employment front, while in South Asia they are more on the education front (though rising on the employment front).

CONCLUSIONS AND CAVEATS

The challenge of increasing the economic growth of a country is, as suggested here, to a considerable extent linked to the role played by women in the society. The costs of discrimination toward women in education and employment not only harm the women concerned but also impose a cost for the entire society.

In South Asia, women are still, in the twenty-first century, very much discriminated against in both education level and economic participation. In MENA, the gender gap in education has been reduced from high levels, but gender gaps in employment remain pervasive. In contrast to some Asian countries, where export-oriented industries have led to a reduction of the gender gap in the labor market in the last decades, increased female education in MENA has not translated into higher labor market participation in most countries of that region. Women in this region are encountering structural barriers in employment,[39] but those barriers may also be social, cultural, and ideological (World Bank 2004).

Regarding the growth costs of gender inequality, we find the following. First, gender inequality in education reduced economic growth in the 1990s. The findings from earlier studies that used data until 1990 are largely confirmed through this expanded analysis, although the impact of gender gaps in education in the 1990s in the panel specification is sensitive to the inclusion of specific regions in the 1990s.

Second, gender inequality in education in MENA and the South Asia region continues to harm growth in that region but by decreasing amounts. This is due to the fact that gender gaps in education have been sharply reduced there over the past two decades, with much faster progress in MENA than in South Asia. As a result, we expect the shrinking gender inequality in education to play a decreasing role in harming growth prospects in MENA and South Asia. While this is true in an absolute sense, it is not always true in a relative sense. As East Asia has closed its gender gaps in education much faster than South Asia, the growth differences accounted for by differences in gender gaps between the two regions mounted in past decades.

Third, the panel analysis suggests that gender inequality in labor force participation (as a proxy for gender gaps in employment) has a sizable negative impact on economic growth. Simulations suggest that MENA's and

South Asia's growth prospects, when compared with other regions, are significantly reduced through this effect, as the impact of gender inequality in employment is large and has been falling much more slowly than in other regions.

Thus, an important constraint to higher economic growth in those regions appears to be the substantial gender inequality persisting in education and employment. While these results are suggestive, we want to emphasize that the assessment of the impact of employment gaps is based on data for labor force participation rates that are measured with error and are often not fully comparable internationally. It is highly lamentable that comparable labor force participation and employment data are not available for most developing countries. Despite the fact that increasing numbers of household and labor force surveys are undertaken in these countries, the results are not used by the ILO to generate and publish consistent and comparable data on employment, labor force participation, and pay.[40] This remains a major challenge for the ILO and other international organizations charged with providing such data.

Also, the usual caveats of cross-country regressions apply, including omitted variable bias, model uncertainty, and endogeneity, among others. We have tried to control for some of these issues, but more work will be needed to solidify the findings. In particular, we were only partly able to control for endogeneity in the panel regressions, and further work on identifying suitable instruments is clearly an important area for further research. Lastly, we need to acknowledge that our results concern the impact of gender gaps in education and employment on measured national output. To the extent that higher female labor force participation comes at the expense of reduced household labor, the economic and well-being losses of such a reduction are not included in our assessment.[41] The extent to which this might be a problem is clearly an area of further research.

If our results are confirmed by further studies, this points to an urgent need of increasing women's education level and their participation in the labor force. While our results suggest that changing the composition of the labor force to include more women (and thus fewer men) would have a positive effect on growth, a more realistic policy recommendation would be to develop an employment-intensive growth strategy that makes particular use of women. At the least, the results suggest that current barriers to female employment are not only disadvantageous to women, but also appear to reduce economic growth in developing countries, particularly in MENA and South Asia

One should also bear in mind the findings from a large literature suggesting that gender inequality in education and employment also have a significant negative impact on other development goals such as reductions in fertility, child mortality, and under-nutrition. Thus, reducing existing gender inequality in education and employment will not only promote growth but also further these other valuable development goals.[42]

ACKNOWLEDGMENTS

A version of this contribution was written as a background paper for the World Bank Flagship Report ''Gender and Development in the Middle East and North Africa: Women in the Public Sphere'' (2004). Funding from the World Bank in support of this work is gratefully acknowledged. We would like to thank: Nadereh Chamlou; Susan Razzazz; four anonymous referees and the guest editors of this special issue; participants at the MENA consultative council meeting on gender at the World Bank; Paula Lorgelly; participants at seminars in Munich, IZA in Bonn, Harvard University, and at the 2008 IZA/World Bank Conference on Employment and Development in Rabat; and a workshop dedicated to this volume in New York in 2008 for helpful comments and discussion.

NOTES

1 See Stephan Klasen and Claudia Wink (2003) and Stephan Klasen (2002, 2007) for a discussion of these issues.

2 This literature can be seen as part of a larger literature on the impact of inequality on growth. See, for example, Klaus Deininger and Lyn Squire (1998) and Christiano Perugini and Gaetano Martino (2008).

3 Among the problems in their findings, Barro and Lee (1994) and Barro and Sala-i-Martin (1995) identify the absence of regional dummy variables, particularly for Latin America and East Asia. In the former, low initial gender gaps were accompanied by low growth, while in the latter, relatively high initial gender gaps were accompanied by high subsequent growth. In the absence of regional dummy variables, a causal link is made between these associations. It is quite likely, however, that the growth experiences of these regions were also influenced by other region-specific factors that are largely unrelated to gender gaps. The fact that these regional dummies are (at least jointly) statistically significant and that then the negative effect of female education reverses itself once regional (or country fixed) effects are considered supports this view. Further problems with these studies are the use of initial period education variables, the high collinearity between male and female education, and the endogeneity of these variables. For a discussion of these issues see Dollar and Gatti (1999), Paula Lorgelly and Dorian Owen (1999), Forbes (2000), and Klasen (2002).

4 The reported figures in Klasen (2002) are actually slightly different, as Israel, Sudan, and Turkey were all included in the Middle East region. For the report in the present

study, they were allocated to other regions (Israel to the OECD, Turkey to Eastern Europe, Central Asia and Sudan to Sub-Saharan Africa) and therefore the analysis in Klasen (2002) was redone to reflect this. The figures reported above are based on that analysis.

5 See, for example, Abu-Ghaida and Klasen (2004), Stephan Klasen (2006), Janet Stotsky (2006), and Mark Blackden, Sudharshan Canagarajah, Stephen Klasen, and David Lawson (2007) for a review.

6 See Bloom and Williamson (1998) and Klasen (2002) for a full exposition of these arguments.

7 Klasen (2006) reviews the literature, and also notes that such strategies have now been extended with some success to countries such as Tunisia, Bangladesh, China, and Vietnam.

8 There is also some empirical support for the claim by Seguino (2000a, 2000b) that higher gender wage gaps were a further pre-condition of these export-oriented strategies. There is a related debate as to whether growth has reduced these gender wage gaps, which appears to be the case in many but not all countries; also, they remain large, particularly when controlling for education. For a discussion, see Seguino (2000a, 2000b), Klasen (2002), Busse and Spielmann (2006), and Stotsky (2006), among others.

9 See a related discussion in King, Klasen, and Porter (2008) about the growth and welfare effects of women as policy-makers. The "causes" of these differences in behavior may well be related to the different socialization of girls and boys, a subject that leads beyond the scope of this paper.

10 The exceptions are again the two short-term structuralist models of Blecker and Seguino (2002) where large gender gaps in pay, implicitly combined with no gender gaps in education and employment, can deliver income-enhancing effects.

11 On these issues, see the discussions in Elizabeth M. King and M. Anne Hill (1993), Harold Alderman, Jere R. Behrman, Shahrukh Khan, David R. Ross, and Richard Sabot (1995), Harold Alderman, Jere R. Behrman, David R. Ross, and Richard Sabot (1996), and the World Bank (2001).

12 Also, it is not obvious which factor is the prime cause of gender gaps to be included in a reduced-form estimation.

13 In the case of these papers, the focus on semi-industrialized, export-oriented countries was intended. But therefore, the findings of these papers cannot address the question of whether there is a more general relationship between pay gaps and growth in developing countries that do not belong to this small group.

14 It turns out that, in our total sample, gender gaps in education and employment are not very closely correlated, so it should be possible to separately identify the effects. This overall low correlation is largely driven by a negative correlation between gender gaps in education and employment in Sub-Saharan Africa, and to a lesser extent South Asia, while in the other regions the correlation is positive and usually large and statistically significant. This negative correlation in Sub-Saharan Africa is related to the high female employment in agriculture despite low levels of female education; in this case, low education is not a barrier to high female employment as is the case elsewhere. For Africa's formal sector, see Klasen (2006) and Blackden et al. (2007).

15 See Appendix Table 1 for a list of countries in each region for which we have data availability.

16 Also note that following the World Bank country classification system, Turkey is considered to belong to the Eastern Europe and Central Asia region, and Israel belongs to the OECD.

17 Iran is the only major oil producer included in the sample, but Egypt, Algeria, and Yemen also depend, directly or indirectly (via migration and remittances), on oil production.

18 Sub-Saharan Africa's high female labor-participation rate is largely confined to the agricultural sector, which still employs the majority of workers in most Sub-Saharan African countries. The international comparability of labor force participation data in own-account agriculture is particularly problematic. In formal-sector employment, female employment rates are much lower and the gender gap is significant; but these data are, as discussed, missing for many countries and show consistency and comparability problems.

19 The combination of rapidly shrinking gender gaps in education and large and persistent gender gaps in employment in the MENA region constitutes a major puzzle. See World Bank (2004) for a careful discussion.

20 Unemployment rates for women in Latin America and MENA are several points higher than for men. Thus in these regions, the gender gap in employment is actually slightly larger than in labor force participation. But, as this gender gap in unemployment rates is rather stable over time, it would be absorbed by the country-specific effects in our panel estimation. We also tried to use sectoral employment data available for some countries since the 1980s to adjust our labor force participation data to focus on non-agricultural employment. But there were so many data gaps and measurement errors and the comparability problems were so severe that these data turned out to be unusable.

21 We have also undertaken some further robustness checks with more variables used in standard growth regression analysis. The results are available on request. While the use of regional dummy variables is invariably a measure of our ignorance, in many cross-country regressions they turn out to be significant, pointing to region-specific left-out variables that are hard to capture in standard cross-country regressions.

22 Knowles, Lorgelly, and Owen (2002) suggest that this is the most suitable specification for analyzing gender gaps in education. This specification was also used in Klasen (2002).

23 Note that Equations 3 and 4 contain an additional explanatory variable with respect to Klasen (2002): openness.

24 We use dummy variables for all regions, where the region left out is EAP.

25 In the panel, we use the total years of schooling of the population over 25. We do so because in the panel analysis we only have a 10-year window in which human capital (and gender differences) can have an effect, and thus we want to focus our attention on the human capital of the labor force (rather than also including the 15–24-year-olds, only some of whom are in the labor force). In robustness checks, we also include the years of education of adults 15 or older to particularly capture the effects of young, educated women, who make up a large share of female employment in many developing countries.

26 On the other hand, empirically, male labor force participation rates do not differ much across space and over time, so the growth effects observed are probably due to increased female employment.

27 We have run the regressions for random effect but specification tests (Hausman tests) suggest that the fixed effect specification is superior.

28 The previous version of the Penn World Table 5.6 (Alan Heston, Robert Summers, and Bettina Aten 1998) provided data for the following additional countries: Djibouti; Malta; Oman; Puerto Rico; Saudi Arabia; Somalia; Surinam; Iraq; Liberia; Myanmar; Reunion; Sudan; Swaziland; and Yugoslavia. For the last nine countries, Barro and Lee (2000) data on education were available. In addition, the data for Eastern European countries were not limited to the 1990s. Penn 6.1 (Heston, Summers, and Aten 2002) provides data for the entire sample set only for two Eastern European countries (Romania and Cyprus). Barro and Lee education data are suspicious for Austria and Bolivia, as they suggest stagnating or declining educational attainment despite

substantial increases in enrollment. Hence, we dropped these two countries from our analysis.

29 It is quite difficult to adequately measure trade openness, and the variables we use, export plus imports as a share of GDP, are not free from problems, as these ratios are systematically lower in larger economies despite identical trade policies. Other proxies have different problems. For a discussion, see Jeffrey A. Frankel and David Roemer (1999) and Dani Rodrik and Francisco Rodriguez (2000).

30 The population growth regression does not pass the Reset test, suggesting that omitted variables and/or non-linearities in these regressions might be a problem. This does not affect our main results (including the size of the direct, indirect, and total effects), and could only have a possible (and likely minor) influence on the relative importance of these two indirect effects.

31 But here, endogeneity might be a problem, which will be partially addressed in the panel regressions.

32 While there is a large and conclusive literature that shows that female education reduces fertility (for example, see T. Paul Schultz [1997], Klasen [1999], and World Bank [2001] for a survey), the link between female education and population growth rates is weaker, as population growth is also affected by the age structure of the population. In a population with a large share of women of child-bearing age, even a low total fertility rate for each of them can generate considerable population growth compared with a population where the share of women is lower. Therefore, it is not surprising that the link here is weaker than if one used the total fertility rate as the dependent variable. When we include labor force growth in the population equation to proxy for the effect of the age structure, the effects of the initial female-male ratio of schooling and the ratio of the growth become significant, as expected.

33 This may be related to the fact that the impact of population growth and working-age population growth materializes with some delay and may therefore not be captured well in the 10-year periods considered.

34 It is even larger if we consider the reduced form estimate – that is, if we leave out the investment rate, labor force growth, and population growth. In both cases, they are larger than identical panel regressions in Klasen (2002).

35 We also analyzed the sample where we dropped Sub-Saharan Africa and Latin America in the 1990s and report on the results where appropriate.

36 The regression is not shown but is available on request.

37 This is confirmed by regressions (not shown here) where we replaced the MACT with the total activity rate (TACT) and now find that the impact of the gender gap is larger, while the impact of the total activity rate is now negative. These regressions are available on request.

38 See Klasen (2006) for further discussions on these country studies.

39 Structural barriers, here, are related to the economic reconstruction, recession, and limited domestic and foreign investment.

40 Nevertheless, the World Bank has used these household surveys to generate roughly consistent, comparable, and publicly available poverty statistics for developing countries. With these surveys, one could generate consistent and comparable statistics on labor force participation, employment, unemployment, and pay. The currently available ILO estimates are a poor substitute for such consistently generated survey-based estimates.

41 To the extent that such increased labor force participation would come in addition to non-market work, the double burden this implies for the women concerned is also not considered here but is clearly an issue that is under investigation in the literature.

42 Abu-Ghaida and Klasen (2004) and King, Klasen, and Porter (2008) estimate the magnitude of these effects.

REFERENCES

Abu-Ghaida, Dina and Stephan Klasen. 2004. "The Costs of Missing the Millennium Development Goal on Gender Equity." *World Development* 32(7): 1075–107.

Alderman, Harold, Jere R. Behrman, Shahrukh Khan, David R. Ross, and Richard Sabot. 1995. "Public School Expenditures in Rural Pakistan: Efficiently Targeting Girls and a Lagging Region," in Dominique van de Walle and Kimberly Nead, eds. *Public Spending and the Poor: Theory of Evidence*, pp. 187–221. Baltimore, MD: Johns Hopkins Press.

Alderman, Harold, Jere R. Behrman, David R. Ross, and Richard Sabot. 1996. "Decomposing the Gender Gap in Cognitive Skills in a Poor Rural Economy." *Journal of Human Resources* 31(1): 229–54.

Appiah, Elizabeth N. and Walter W. McMahon. 2002. "The Social Outcomes of Education and Feedbacks on Growth in Africa." *Journal of Development Studies* 38(4): 27–68.

Barro, Robert. 1991. "Economic Growth in a Cross Section of Countries." *Quarterly Journal of Economics* 106(1): 407–43.

Barro, Robert and Jong-Wha Lee. 1994. "Sources of Economic Growth." *Carnegie-Rochester Conference Series on Public Policy* 40: 1–46.

———. 2000. "International Data on Educational Attainment: Updates and Implications." Working Paper 42, Center for International Development, Cambridge, MA.

Barro, Robert and Xavier Sala-i-Martin. 1995. *Economic Growth.* New York: McGraw- Hill.

Blackden, Mark, Sudharshan Canagarajah, Stephan Klasen, and David Lawson. 2007. "Gender and Growth in Africa: Evidence and Issues," in George Mavrotas and Anthony Shorrocks, eds. *Advancing Development: Core Themes in Global Economics*, pp. 349–70. London: Palgrave Macmillan.

Blecker, Robert and Stephanie Seguino. 2002. "Macroeconomic Effects of Reducing Gender Wage Inequality in an Export-Oriented, Semi-Industrialized Economy." *Review of Development Economics* 6(1): 103–19.

Bloom, David E. and Jeffrey G. Williamson. 1998. "Demographic Transition and Economic Miracles in Emerging Asia." *World Bank Economic Review* 12(3): 419–55.

Busse, Matthias and Christian Spielmann. 2006. "Gender Inequality and Trade." *Review of International Economics* 14(3): 362–79.

Cavalcanti, Tiago V. de and José Tavares. 2007. "The Output Costs of Gender Discrimination: A Model-Based Macroeconomic Estimate." Mimeograph, University of Lisbon.

Collier, Paul and Jan Willem Gunning. 1999. "Why Has Africa Grown Slowly?" *Journal of Economic Perspectives* 13(2): 3–22.

Deininger, Klaus and Lyn Squire. 1998. "New Ways of Looking at Old Issues: Inequality and Growth." *Journal of Development Economics* 57(2): 259–87.

Dollar, David and Roberta Gatti. 1999. "Gender Inequality, Income and Growth: Are Good Times Good for Women?" Mimeograph, World Bank, Washington, DC.

Esteve-Volart, Berta. 2004. "Gender Discrimination and Growth: Theory and Evidence from India." STICERD Discussion Papers DEDPS42, London School of Economics.

Forbes, Kristin. 2000. "A Reassessment of the Relationship between Inequality and Growth." *American Economic Review* 90(4): 869–87.

Frankel, Jeffrey A. and David Roemer. 1999. "Does Trade Cause Growth?" *American Economic Review* 89(3): 379–99.

Galor, Oded and David N. Weil. 1996. "The Gender Gap, Fertility, and Growth." *American Economic Review* 86(3): 374–87.

Haddad, Lawrence James, John Hoddinott, and Harold Alderman, eds. 1997. *Intrahousehold Resource Allocation in Developing Countries.* Baltimore: Johns Hopkins University Press.

Heston, Alan, Robert Summers, and Bettina Aten. 1998. Penn World table Version 5.6, Center for International Comparison at the University of Pennsylvania (CICUP). http://pwt.econ.upenn.edu/php_site/pwt_index.php (accessed January 2009).

———. 2002. Penn World table Version 6.1, Center for International Comparison at the University of Pennsylvania (CICUP). http://pwt.econ.upenn.edu/php_site/pwt_index.php (accessed January 2009).

Hill, M. Anne and Elizabeth M. King. 1995. "Women's Education and Economic Well-Being." *Feminist Economics* 1(2): 1–26.

International Labour Organization. 2003. *ILO Report: Key Indicators of the Labor Market,* 5th ed. CD-ROM. Geneva: ILO.

———. 2007. Online database LABORSTA, Bureau of Statistics, Geneva, Switzerland. http://laborsta.ilo.org/ (accessed January 25, 2009).

King, Elizabeth M. and M. Anne Hill. 1993. *Women's Education in Developing Countries: Barriers, Benefits, and Policies.* Baltimore: Johns Hopkins Press.

King, Elizabeth M., Stephan Klasen, and Maria Porter. 2008. "Gender and Development Challenge Paper." Paper prepared for 2008 round of Copenhagen Consensus Project. Mimeographed, Copenhagen Consensus Center.

Klasen, Stephan. 1999. "Does Gender Inequality Reduce Growth and Development?" Policy Research Report Working Paper 7, World Bank, Washington, DC.

———. 2002. "Low Schooling for Girls, Slower Growth for All? Cross-Country Evidence on the Effect of Gender Inequality in Education on Economic Development." *World Bank Economic Review* 16(3): 345–73.

———. 2006. "Gender and Pro-Poor Growth," in Lukas Menkoff, ed. *Pro-Poor Growth: Policy and Evidence,* pp. 151–71. Berlin: Dunker and Humblot.

———. 2007. "Gender-Related Indicators of Well-Being," in Mark McGillivray, ed. *Human Well-Being: Concept and Measurement,* pp. 167–92. London: Palgrave Macmillan.

Klasen, Stephan and Claudia Wink. 2003. "Missing Women: Revisiting the Debate." *Feminist Economics* 9(2/3): 263–99.

Knowles, Stephen, Paula Lorgelly, and Dorian Owen. 2002. "Are Educational Gender Gaps a Brake on Economic Development? Some Cross-Country Empirical Evidence." *Oxford Economic Papers* 54(1): 118–49.

Lagerlöf Nils-Petter. 2003. "Gender Equality and Long-Run Growth." *Journal of Economic Growth* 8(4): 403–26.

Lorgelly, Paula and Dorian Owen. 1999. "The Effect of Female and Male Schooling on Economic Growth in the Barro-Lee Model." *Empirical Economics* 24(3): 537–57.

Perugini, Christiano and Gaetano Martino. 2008. "Income Inequality within European regions: Determinants and effects of growth." *Review of Income and Wealth* 54(3): 373–406.

Rodrik, Dani and Francisco Rodriguez. 2000. "Trade Policy and Economic Growth: A Skeptic's Guide to the Cross-National Evidence," in Ben S. Bernanke and Kenneth S. Rogoff, eds. *NBER Macroeconomics Annual 2000,* pp. 261–324. Cambridge: MIT Press.

Schultz, T. Paul. 1997. "Demand for Children in Low-Income Countries," in Mark Richard Rosenzweig and Oded Stark, eds. *Handbook of Population and Family Economics,* Vol. 1, pp. 1–2. Amsterdam: Elsevier.

Seguino, Stephanie. 2000a. "Accounting for Gender in Asian Economic Growth." *Feminist Economics* 6(3): 27–58.

———. 2000b. "Gender Inequality and Economic Growth: A Cross-Country Analysis." *World Development* 28(7): 1211–30.

Seguino, Stephanie and Maria Sagrario Floro. 2003. "Does Gender Have Any Effect on Aggregate Saving?" *International Review of Applied Economics* 17(2): 147–66.

Sen, Amartya. 1990. "Gender and Cooperative Conflicts," in Irene Tinker, ed. *Persistent Inequalities: Women and World Development,* pp. 123–49. Oxford: Oxford University Press.

Stotsky, Janet. 2006. "Gender and its Relevance to Macroeconomic Policy: A Survey." Working Paper WP/06/233, International Monetary Fund.

Swamy, Anand, Omar Azfar, Stephen Knack, and Young Lee. 2001. "Gender and Corruption." *Journal of Development Economics* 64(1): 25–55.

Thomas, Duncan. 1997. "Incomes, Expenditures and Health Outcomes: Evidence on Intrahousehold Resource Allocation," in Lawrence James Haddad, John Hoddinott, and Harold Alderman, eds. *Intrahousehold Resource Allocation in Developing Countries*, pp. 142–64. Baltimore: Johns Hopkins University Press.

United Nations. 1997. United Nations Women's Indicators and Statistics Database: WISTAT. CD-ROM, Version 3. New York.

World Bank. 2001. *Engendering Development.* Washington, DC: World Bank.

———. 2002. *World Development Indicators (WDI).* CD-ROM. Washington, DC.

———. 2004. *Gender and Development in the Middle East and North Africa.* Washington, DC: World Bank.

———. 2006. *Economic Growth in the 1990s: Learning from a Decade of Reform.* Washington, DC: World Bank.

Yamarik, Steven and Sucharita Ghosh. 2003. "Is Female Education Productive? A Reassessment." Mimeograph, Tufts University, Medford, MA.

APPENDIX

Appendix Table 1 List of countries for our analysis by region

Middle East and North Africa (MENA)	*Sub-Saharan Africa (SSA)*	*Organisation for Economic Co-operation and Development (OECD)*	*Latin American and Caribbean (LAC)*	*Eastern Europe and Central Asia (ECA)*
Algeria	Angola	Australia	Antigua and Barbuda	Albania
Egypt	Benin	Austria	Argentina	Armenia
Iran	Botswana	Belgium	Barbados	Belarus
Jordan	Burkina Faso	Canada	Belize	Bulgaria
Lebanon	Burundi	Czech Republic	Bolivia	Cyprus
Morocco	Cameroon	Denmark	Brazil	Estonia
Syria	Cape Verde	Finland	Chile	Latvia
Tunisia	Central African Republic	France	Colombia	Macedonia^{+}
Yemen	Chad	Germany	Costa Rica	Poland
	Comoros	Greece	Cuba	Romania
East Asia and Pacific (EAP)	Congo, Dem. Rep.	Hungary	Dominica	Russian Federation^{+}
China	Congo, Republic	Iceland	Dominican Republic	Slovak Republic
Fiji	Cote d'Ivoire	Ireland	Ecuador	Slovenia
Hong Kong	Equatorial Guinea	Israel	El Salvador	Turkey
Indonesia	Ethiopia	Italy	Grenada	Ukraine
Korea	Gabon	Japan	Guatemala	
Macao, China	Gambia, The	Luxembourg	Guyana	
Malaysia	Ghana	Netherlands	Haiti	
Papua New Guinea	Guinea	New Zealand	Honduras	
Philippines	Guinea-Bissau	Norway	Jamaica	
Singapore	Kenya	Portugal	Mexico	
Taiwan	Lesotho	Spain	Nicaragua	
Thailand	Madagascar	Sweden	Panama	
South Asia (SA)	Malawi	Switzerland	Paraguay	
Bangladesh	Mali	United Kingdom	Peru	
India	Mauritania	United States	St. Kitts and Nevis	
Nepal	Mauritius		St. Lucia	
Pakistan	Mozambique		St. Vincent and Gren.	
Sri Lanka	Namibia		Trinidad and Tobago	
	Niger		Uruguay	
	Nigeria		Venezuela, RB	
	Rwanda			
	Sao Tome and Principe			
	Senegal			
	Seychelles			
	Sierra Leone			

(*continued*)

Appendix Table 1 (*Continued*)

Middle East and North Africa (MENA)	*Sub-Saharan Africa (SSA)*	*Organisation for Economic Co-operation and Development (OECD)*	*Latin American and Caribbean (LAC)*	*Eastern Europe and Central Asia (ECA)*
	South Africa			
	Tanzania			
	Togo			
	Uganda			
	Zambia			
	Zimbabwe			

Note: + Indicates data were not available for the entire period of analysis.

Appendix Table 2 Annual per capita income and other non-economic indicators by region, 1960–1990

	1960	*1970*	*1980*	*1990*	*2000*
EAP					
Under 5 mortality	138.50	89.63	56.43	42.00	31.59
Total fertility	5.62	4.65	3.39	2.83	2.31
Life expectancy	52.57	59.87	64.94	68.76	71.55
Income per capita	1,813	2,963	5,117	8,930	11,755
SA					
Under 5 mortality	228.00	192.00	154.60	109.40	80.64
Total fertility	6.30	6.02	5.54	4.31	3.45
Life expectancy	45.32	50.02	54.70	59.36	63.80
Income per capita	930	1,099	1,187	1,660	2,186
SSA					
Under 5 mortality	273.89	233.86	182.47	148.96	146.15
Total fertility	6.49	6.53	6.49	5.98	5.13
Life expectancy	40.40	44.30	48.08	51.18	49.06
Income per capita	1,488	1,868	2,087	2,182	2,400
MENA					
Under 5 mortality	233.75	188.13	137.57	68.88	45.14
Total fertility	7.12	6.78	6.13	4.68	3.32
Life expectancy	47.89	53.08	58.55	64.86	68.37
Income per capita	1,968	2,762	3,660	3,499	4,462
ECA					
Under 5 mortality	80.78	55.11	43.20	25.05	16.40
Total fertility	3.24	2.78	2.40	2.14	1.47
Life expectancy	66.15	68.77	69.59	70.79	71.59
Income per capita	2,233	3,650	5,300	9,323	7,346

(*continued*)

Appendix Table 2 (*Continued*)

	1960	*1970*	*1980*	*1990*	*2000*
LAC					
Under 5 mortality	135.58	109.00	70.91	42.65	30.85
Total fertility	6.13	5.37	4.10	3.29	2.69
Life expectancy	57.25	61.64	65.72	69.14	71.56
Income per capita	3,362	4,270	5,072	5,471	7,086
OECD					
Under 5 mortality	37.67	26.05	15.14	9.73	6.61
Total fertility	2.87	2.46	1.93	1.79	1.65
Life expectancy	70.19	71.72	73.80	75.76	77.73
Income per capita	8,386	12,024	15,420	18,875	23,173

Source: Penn World Table 6.1 (Heston, Summers, and Aten 2002) and World Bank (2002).
Notes: The data for ECA refer to only two observations before the 1990s (Cyprus and Romania). All are unweighted averages and might in some cases be affected by compositional changes. The income per capita refers to real GDP per capita in PPP.

Appendix Table 3 Education Indicators by Region, 1960–99

	1960	*1970*	*1980*	*1990*	*1999*
EAP					
Female education 25+ (OFED25+)	2.11	2.71	3.75	5.22	6.55
Male education 25+ (OED25+)	4.11	4.74	5.59	6.81	7.8
Total education 25+ (OTED25+)	3.13	3.73	4.68	6.02	7.18
Ratio female–male education 25+ (ORED25+)	0.5	0.56	0.65	0.75	0.83
Female education 15+ (FED)	2.74	3.53	4.46	5.46	6.7
Male education 15+ (ED)	4.6	5.21	5.9	6.77	7.85
Total education 15+ (TED)	3.68	4.38	5.19	6.12	7.28
Ratio female–male education 15+ (RED)	0.59	0.67	0.7	0.76	0.84
SA					
Female education 25+ (OFED25+)	0.7	1.24	1.51	1.9	2.55
Male education 25+ (OED25+)	1.77	2.37	3.2	3.83	4.49
Total education 25+ (OTED25+)	1.27	1.72	2.39	2.89	3.54
Ratio female–male education 25+ (ORED25+)	0.25	0.34	0.36	0.43	0.51
Female education 15+ (FED)	0.89	1.3	1.86	2.68	3.23
Male education 15+ (ED)	1.9	2.48	3.58	4.5	5.05
Total education 15+ (TED)	1.42	1.91	2.75	3.62	4.16
Ratio female–male education 15+ (RED)	0.29	0.37	0.43	0.54	0.6

(*continued*)

Appendix Table 3 (*Continued*)

	1960	*1970*	*1980*	*1990*	*1999*
SSA					
Female education 25+ (OFED25+)	0.92	0.97	1.37	1.92	2.63
Male education 25+ (OED25+)	1.67	1.80	2.54	3.21	3.92
Total education 25+ (OTED25+)	1.28	1.37	1.93	2.54	3.25
Ratio female–male education 25+ (ORED25+)	0.43	0.45	0.47	0.55	0.62
Female education 15+ (FED)	1.23	1.39	1.73	2.34	2.87
Male education 15+ (ED)	2.05	2.32	2.76	3.52	3.92
Total education 15+ (TED)	1.63	1.84	2.23	2.92	3.38
Ratio female–male education 15+ (RED)	0.48	0.52	0.60	0.62	0.70
MENA					
Female education 25+ (OFED25+)	0.44	0.60	1.25	2.57	4.18
Male education 25+ (OED25+)	1.36	2.10	3.23	4.99	6.39
Total education 25+ (OTED25+)	0.91	1.34	2.24	3.78	5.29
Ratio female–male education 25+ (ORED25+)	0.32	0.28	0.39	0.51	0.65
Female education 15+ (FED)	0.65	1.17	1.86	3.17	4.77
Male education 15+ (ED)	1.76	2.85	3.58	5.11	6.52
Total education 15+ (TED)	1.21	2.01	2.72	4.14	5.65
Ratio female–male education 15+ (RED)	0.38	0.41	0.47	0.58	0.73
ECA					
Female education 25+ (OFED25+)	3.48	4.12	5.20	6.62	7.33
Male education 25+ (OED25+)	5.28	5.66	6.82	8.02	8.32
Total education 25+ (OTED25+)	4.34	4.87	5.99	7.32	7.82
Ratio female–male education 25+ (ORED25+)	0.59	0.66	0.70	0.78	0.85
Female education 15+ (FED)	5.24	5.90	6.56	8.24	7.57
Male education 15+ (ED)	6.13	6.71	7.82	8.92	8.61
Total education 15+ (TED)	5.66	6.29	7.18	8.57	8.09
Ratio female–male education 15+ (RED)	0.82	0.85	0.83	0.91	0.86
LAC					
Female education 25+ (OFED25+)	2.91	3.35	4.2	5.08	5.87
Male education 25+ (OED25+)	3.42	3.93	4.65	5.42	6
Total education 25+ (OTED25+)	3.16	3.63	4.42	5.25	5.94

(*continued*)

Appendix Table 3 (*Continued*)

	1960	*1970*	*1980*	*1990*	*1999*
Ratio female–male education 25+ (ORED25+)	0.83	0.83	0.89	0.93	0.98
Female education 15+ (FED)	3.3	3.88	4.81	5.52	6.08
Male education 15+ (ED)	3.69	4.3	5.09	5.73	6.27
Total education 15+ (TED)	3.49	4.09	4.95	5.62	6.18
Ratio female–male education 15+ (RED)	0.9	0.89	0.94	0.96	0.96
OECD					
Female education 25+ (OFED25+)	6.39	6.91	7.84	8.40	9.12
Male education 25+ (OED25+)	6.98	7.62	8.68	9.30	9.82
Total education 25+ (OTED25+)	6.66	7.25	8.24	8.83	9.46
Ratio female–male education 25+ (ORED25+)	0.91	0.90	0.90	0.90	0.93
Female education 15+ (FED)	6.54	7.13	8.06	8.69	9.30
Male education 15+ (ED)	7.11	7.70	8.66	9.27	9.85
Total education 15+ (TED)	6.81	7.40	8.35	8.97	9.57
Ratio female–male education 15+ (RED)	0.91	0.92	0.93	0.93	0.94

Source: Barro and Lee (2000).
Note: All refer to unweighted averages.

Appendix Table 4 Labor market indicators by region, 1960–2000

	1960	*1970*	*1980*	*1990*	*2000*
EAP					
Male economic activity rate, 15–64 (MACT)	90.69	87.82	86.41	85.71	84.94
Total economic activity rate, 15–64 (TACT)	66.43	67.25	69.84	71.07	72.47
Ratio female–male economic activity rate, 15–64 (RACT)	0.45	0.52	0.61	0.66	0.7
Female economic activity rate, 15–64 (FACT)	41.33	46.25	52.85	56.47	59.67
Female share of labor force, 15–64 (FLFT)	28.52	32.41	36.13	38.66	40.31
Female employee rate (EMPLF)		0.17	0.22	0.29	0.3
Male employee rate (EMPLM)		0.39	0.43	0.46	0.45
Ratio female–male employees (REMPL)		0.4	0.49	0.6	0.66
SA					
Male economic activity rate, 15–64 (MACT)	92.5	90.4	88.6	87.61	86.22
Total economic activity rate, 15–64 (TACT)	71.99	70.31	68.91	68.62	69.1
Ratio female–male economic activity rate, 15–64 (RACT)	0.52	0.53	0.53	0.55	0.59
Female economic activity rate, 15–64 (FACT)	48.61	47.84	47.22	47.88	50.87
Female share of labor force, 15–64 (FLFT)	30.71	31.28	31.82	32.9	35.28

(*continued*)

Appendix Table 4 (*Continued*)

	1960	*1970*	*1980*	*1990*	*2000*
Female employee rate (EMPLF)		0.05	0.06	0.1	0.08
Male employee rate (EMPLM)		0.27	0.3	0.34	0.27
Ratio female–male employees (REMPL)		0.15	0.18	0.27	0.26
SSA					
Male economic activity rate, 15–64 (MACT)	92.65	91.34	89.75	88.59	87.49
Total economic activity rate, 15–64 (TACT)	80.81	79.49	78.13	77.17	76.57
Ratio female–male economic activity rate, 15–64 (RACT)	0.75	0.75	0.75	0.75	0.75
Female economic activity rate, 15–64 (FACT)	69.62	68.59	67.2	66.44	66.1
Female share of labor force, 15–64 (FLFT)	43.45	43.59	43.53	43.56	43.48
Female employee rate (EMPLF)		0.12	0.09	0.09	0.03
Male employee rate (EMPLM)		0.46	0.27	0.26	0.08
Ratio female–male employees (REMPL)		0.2	0.26	0.28	0.34
MENA					
Male economic activity rate, 15–64 (MACT)	88.84	85.39	82.03	81.02	81.21
Total economic activity rate, 15–64 (TACT)	55.44	54.04	53.49	54.34	57.62
Ratio female–male economic activity rate, 15–64 (RACT)	0.24	0.27	0.31	0.34	0.41
Female economic activity rate, 15–64 (FACT)	21.56	23.21	25.54	27.50	33.70
Female share of labor force, 15–64 (FLFT)	19.01	21.45	23.89	25.09	28.94
Female employee rate (EMPLF)		0.07	0.07	0.09	0.11
Male employee rate (EMPLM)		0.56	0.53	0.56	0.58
Ratio female–male employees (REMPL)		0.12	0.13	0.18	0.25
ECA					
Male economic activity rate, 15–64 (MACT)	88.67	84.83	83.76	81.47	80.31
Total economic activity rate, 15–64 (TACT)	73.22	73.12	74.97	73.66	73.65
Ratio female–male economic activity rate, 15–64 (RACT)	0.67	0.73	0.79	0.81	0.84
Female economic activity rate, 15–64 (FACT)	59.42	62.18	66.24	65.85	66.97
Female share of labor force, 15–64 (FLFT)	42.49	43.46	44.74	45.13	46
Female employee rate (EMPLF)		0.25	0.38	0.41	0.31
Male employee rate (EMPLM)		0.51	0.62	0.55	0.44
Ratio female–male employees (REMPL)		0.45	0.57	0.68	0.6
LAC					
Male economic activity rate, 15–64 (MACT)	91.64	88.57	86.34	85.41	84.63
Total economic activity rate, 15–64 (TACT)	59.55	59.45	61.12	63.43	65.78
Ratio female–male economic activity rate, 15–64 (RACT)	0.3	0.34	0.41	0.49	0.56
Female economic activity rate, 15–64 (FACT)	27.91	30.51	35.73	41.77	46.88
Female share of labor force, 15–64 (FLFT)	22.93	25.24	28.87	32.77	35.63
Female employee rate (EMPLF)		0.18	0.21	0.22	0.24
Male employee rate (EMPLM)		0.51	0.48	0.4	0.42
Ratio female–male employees (REMPL)		0.37	0.45	0.56	0.56
OECD					
Male economic activity rate, 15–64 (MACT)	90.28	86.80	84.66	81.55	81.12
Total economic activity rate, 15–64 (TACT)	63.35	64.99	68.64	70.57	72.00

(*continued*)

Appendix Table 4 (Continued)

	1960	*1970*	*1980*	*1990*	*2000*
Ratio female–male economic activity rate, 15–64 (RACT)	0.41	0.50	0.62	0.73	0.77
Female economic activity rate, 15–64 (FACT)	37.32	43.16	52.72	59.36	62.82
Female share of labor force, 15–64 (FLFT)	29.45	33.11	37.96	41.48	43.06
Female employee rate (EMPLF)		0.32	0.41	0.48	0.48
Male employee rate (EMPLM)		0.65	0.64	0.62	0.59
Ratio female–male employees (REMPL)		0.48	0.62	0.75	0.79

Source: WISTAT 3 (United Nations 1997) and ILO LABORSTA (ILO 2007).
Note: All refer to unweighted averages. Employee data only until 1995. The male and female employee rates refer to the numbers of dependently employed as a share of the working-age population. As it excludes self-employment and own-account agriculture, it is therefore an indicator of the formal sector employment rate and has been referred to as such in the text. The female, male, and total economic activity rates refer to the population aged 15–64 and come from the ILO dataset online.

DO GENDER DISPARITIES IN EMPLOYMENT INCREASE PROFITABILITY? EVIDENCE FROM THE UNITED STATES

Ajit Zacharias and Melissa Mahoney

ABSTRACT

This paper investigates whether the contribution of the declining share of wages in national income to the upswing in profitability between 1982 and 1997 in the United States was aided by the growing incorporation of women into employment. The analysis finds that women helped moderate the decline in the aggregate wage share. The reduction in gender pay disparity overwhelmed the negative effect of women's growing share of market work on the wage share. However, in (one-digit) sectors where wage shares fell, women did not contribute to restraining the fall, indicating that the aggregate outcome was the net result of distinct sectoral trends in women's employment conditions. We argue that the perverse process of labor productivity falling faster than the real wage in the service sector may have played a key role in shaping the aggregate outcome. The post-1997 trends in the US are discussed in a postscript.

INTRODUCTION

Gender relations can play a constitutive role in determining the key variables influencing the pace and rhythm of capitalist accumulation. Feminist economists have long recognized the effects of competition between male and female workers on the average level of wages: "Capitalists have indeed used women as unskilled, underpaid labor to undercut male workers, yet this is only a case of the chickens coming home to roost – a case of men's cooptation by and support for patriarchal society, with its hierarchy among men, being turned back on themselves with a vengeance" (Heidi I. Hartmann 1979: 222). However, the effects of such competition on the functional distribution of income or how the accumulation process itself may set the limits to such competition are questions that have not been given sufficient attention. Macrodynamic models that take gender relations explicitly into account are of recent vintage, but they suggest that the secular feminization of market work might boost profitability and growth in high-income countries (Korkut Ertürk and Nilüfer Çağatay 1995; Korkut Ertürk and William Darity, Jr. 2000).

An important strand of the empirical work on the overall dynamics of accumulation in advanced capitalist nations focuses on dissecting the trends in aggregate profitability (Gérard Duménil and Dominique Lévy 1992; Robert Brenner 1998; Ajit Zacharias 2002). However, most of the empirical work on developed capitalist nations does not address the potential effects of gender disparity in pay or the feminization of employment on aggregate profitability. Our main purpose is to make a modest attempt to tackle this much-neglected question in the context of the upward swing of profitability in the United States during the 1980s and 1990s. Economic reasoning suggests that an important channel through which feminization influences profitability is via the wage share, which fell sharply in the US during this period. The conjunction of the three trends – rising feminization, falling wage share, and rising profitability – makes this period interesting from an analytical standpoint.[1]

Recent work has analyzed the contribution of different factors to the rise in profitability in the US. For example, Edward N. Wolff (2003) suggests that the shift in power relations in favor of the capitalist class and structural change, as reflected in the growing share of labor-intensive sectors in total employment, were the main factors behind the US profits boom. Gérard Duménil and Dominique Lévy (2002) also find evidence supporting the existence of the upswing in profitability, utilizing a variety of measures of profitability, and assess the relative importance of technological change and distributional shifts. We begin by briefly recapitulating this familiar ground and showing by means of decomposition analysis that the profits boom was underwritten to a substantial degree by a shift in the functional distribution of national income in favor of capital.

We then turn to examine how the changing functional distribution of income was shaped by the increased integration of women into paid employment in the US at both the aggregate and sectoral levels. Recent work by Kade Finoff and Arjun Jayadev (2006) finds a strong negative correlation between the feminization of the labor force and the labor share of national income in the OECD countries between 1975 and 2000. However, our work differs from their work in two major ways: First, rather than regression analysis, we use a decomposition methodology to separate the effects of the trends in women's employment and wages on the labor share and, in turn, on the general rate of profits. Second, we disaggregate the economy into seven sectors and examine the influence of structural change and distributional shifts within sectors on the movement of the aggregate wage share.

By its very nature, decomposition analysis of the type conducted in this paper (and in other studies of aggregate profitability cited earlier) is descriptive. It does not allow for any direct inference about the causal mechanisms that might have generated the observed outcome. However, the decomposition analysis can shed light on the factual implications of a causal mechanism. Consider, for purely illustrative purposes, a potential causal explanation of the rising profitability of the manufacturing sector sketched as follows. The threat of foreign competition weakened the bargaining power of labor. Consequently, workers could not secure wage gains that kept pace with productivity gains, leading to an increase in the profit-wage ratio. In turn, the rise in the profit-wage ratio contributed to the rising profitability. Now, a decomposition of the manufacturing profit rate can only provide a clue as to whether the last step of the causal story – that is, its observable implication about the effect of a rising profit-wage ratio on the profit rate – was borne out by the data. It cannot tell us about the validity of the postulated causal mechanism – foreign competition weakening the bargaining power of labor.[2]

The focus of the present paper is on the effect of feminization on profitability. Given the well-known inverse relationship between the real wage and the rate of profits in the classical model of prices of production, it is clear that the comparative static effect of a rising share of lower-paid women workers in total employment would be an increase in the long-run profit rate because of its direct effect on lowering the average wage.[3] As already noted above, recent macrodynamic models that explicitly incorporate gender relations have also concluded that, in general, feminization can increase profitability. Decomposition analysis can provide some indication regarding the operation of the effects of feminization during the US profits boom of the 1980s and 1990s. The US experience during this period is analytically interesting because it represents a conjunction of three trends – rising feminization, falling wage share, and rising profitability.

TRENDS IN PROFITABILITY

The economy-wide average profit rate, measured empirically as the ratio of profits to the value of capital stock, is a concise measure that combines information on the functional distribution of national income and technology:

$$\begin{aligned} r &= \frac{Y - W}{K} \\ &= (1 - \omega)\left(\frac{Y_r}{K_r}\right)\left(\frac{p_y}{p_k}\right), \end{aligned} \tag{1}$$

where Y is the amount of value added, W is the wage bill, and K is the value of capital stock. The subscript r indicates real values, and p_y and p_k are the price indexes of value added and capital stock, respectively. (All magnitudes are measured on a per annum basis, with the exception of the capital stock that reflects year-end values.) The profit rate varies inversely with the ratio of the wage bill to value added or wage share (ω). On the other hand, it varies positively with the real output-capital ratio and the ratio of the price index of net output to the price index of capital stock. The first term in the second line of equation (1) reflects the functional distribution of income, while the second is a joint indicator of the technology in use and the rate of capacity utilization. Typically, historical accounts of capitalist dynamics in the classical/Marxian tradition treat technology and distribution as the fundamental variables that determine the long-run trajectory of the profit rate, with the full recognition that the variables in question have reciprocal relations with one another (Gérard Duménil and Dominique Lévy 1990).[4]

There have been recurrent debates about "the" appropriate empirical measure of profit rate (Dennis C. Mueller 1990; Anwar Shaikh 1999). We employed in our analysis two most widely used measures: gross and net profit rates. Both had the same measure of capital stock: current-cost, net stock of private nonresidential fixed capital. The difference between the two is in the measure of profits: Gross profits are the difference between the GDP and employee compensation of private industries. Net profits exclude depreciation and indirect taxes (net of subsidies) from gross profits. The results of our analysis were very similar for both measures and, therefore, we report only the results based on gross profit rates.[5]

Average gross profit rate in the US private sector during the 1947–2005 period is shown in Figure 1. The data suggest that there were two distinct periods of sustained growth in profitability (defined here as a prolonged period of stable or rising annual profit rates). The first phase, occurring toward the end of the so-called "golden age" of US capitalism, lasted from the trough of 1958 to the peak of 1966. The second phase, starting from the depression-like conditions of the early 1980s, lasted from 1982 to 1997.[6] Since 1997, the US profit rate has not displayed any sustained movement in either direction.[7]

Utilizing the standard decomposition technique (see, for example, Wolff [2003: 489]) we can resolve the change in the profit rate between any two years into the contributions made by the profit share ($\pi \equiv 1 - \omega$), real output-capital ratio, and the ratio of the price index of output to that of capital stock.[8] The results from the decomposition analysis indicate that the main driving factor behind the rise in profitability in both periods was the rising real output-capital ratio (Table 1). However, an important difference between the two periods emerges once we examine the behavior of the profit share. During the "golden age," its contribution to the 6.17 percentage points increase in the gross profit rate was a mere 0.03 percentage points (less than one percent of the total increase in the profit

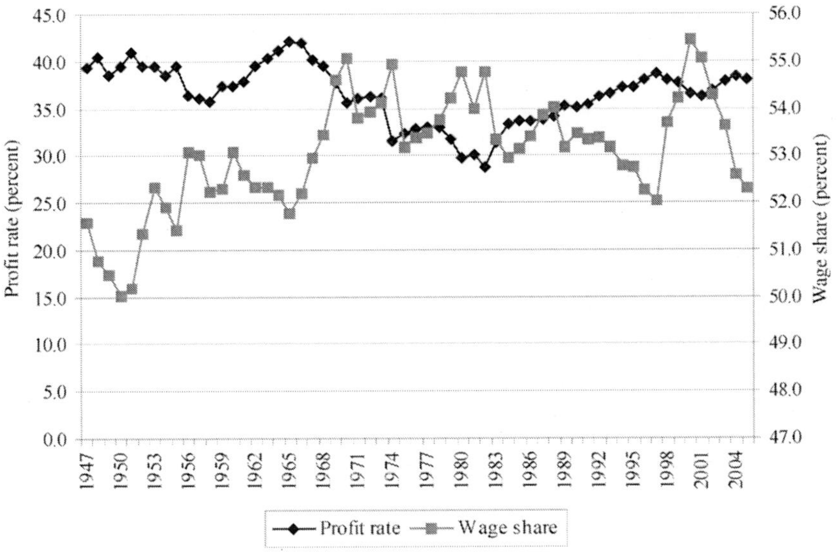

Figure 1 Gross profit rate (left scale) and the wage share (right scale) in the US, 1947–2005 (in percent)

Table 1 Decomposition of the change in gross profit rate in the US (in percentage points)

	"Golden age" 1958–66	*"Leaden age"* 1982–97
Actual change in gross profit rate	6.17	9.92
Contribution of:		
Change in profit share ($\pi \equiv 1 - \omega$)	0.03	1.97
Change in real output-capital ratio (Y_r/K_r)	5.80	5.39
Change in relative price of output (p_y/p_k)	0.34	2.56

rate). In contrast, its contribution to the increase of 9.92 percentage points in the gross profit rate during the recent phase of rising profitability in the US – the "leaden age" – was a substantial 1.97 percentage points (about 20 percent of the total increase in the profit rate).

The accounting separation made between the profit share and output-capital ratio in the decomposition analysis does not imply a causal separation. In fact, they may reflect two interrelated aspects of the same underlying process: a rise in profitability may take place because growth occurs predominantly in labor-intensive activities (which generally have lower output-capital ratios), characterized by labor relations weighed heavily in favor of capital (larger shares of contingent and part-time

Table 2 Decomposition of the change in the US wage share, 1982–97 (in percentage points)

Actual change in wage share (ω)	-2.73
Contribution of:	
Change in male hourly compensation (w_r^m)	4.03
Change in female hourly compensation (w_r^f)	4.41
Change in male labor ratio (λ^m)	-8.59
Change in female labor ratio (λ^f)	-2.59

workers, low levels of unionization, etc.) that helps in keeping wage growth below productivity growth. As noted in the introduction, decomposition analysis cannot tell us whether indeed such a process generated the observed outcomes, yet it does provide some quantitative indication of the relative impact of the characteristics of the underlying accumulation process on the three variables that govern the profit rate: it turns out that the main variable responsible for the changes in the US profit rate during both periods was the change in real output-capital ratio rather than the change in profit share or the relative price of output.[9]

The greater contribution made by the profit share in the latter period is a confirmation that a fundamental shift had occurred in the social and political arrangements governing the distribution of productivity gains between capital and labor between the two periods, apparently in favor of capital (Stephen A. Marglin and Juliet Schor 1991; David M. Gordon 1996). Among the various factors that distinguish the golden and leaden ages, an important difference is the much higher participation rate of women in market work during the leaden age. Given the lower relative wage of women, was the increased role of women in market work related to the considerable deterioration that took place in the US wage share (or alternatively, the increase in the profit share)? As we pointed out in the introduction, theoretical models generally predict that, other things remaining the same, the greater incorporation of women into market work will lower the wage share and boost profitability. However, "other things" that affect the wage share did *not* remain the same in the US during the period under consideration, which makes empirically disentangling the effect of the changes in gendered macroeconomic variables – women's overall average wage and employment – from that of other factors quite a difficult proposition.[10]

Regression analysis with the macroeconomic series is not a feasible option since the number of years in the period under study is quite small. A feasible alternative is an extension of the standard decomposition methodology, and this is the route that we take below. While this is not a substitute for a full-fledged causal analysis, we believe that it can yield some insights into the quantitative significance of the gendered macroeconomic variables on rising profitability during the "leaden age."

WOMEN'S EMPLOYMENT AND FUNCTIONAL DISTRIBUTION

The growth in women's participation in market work – a persistent feature of American economic life since the Second World War – also continued during the period under study here. Between 1982 and 1997, the employment-population ratio for women surged by nearly 10 percentage points (from 47.7 to 56.8 percent) while that for men rose modestly by 2.3 percentage points (from 69.0 to 71.3 percent). The change in the ratio for women was not dramatic compared to the trends in the previous years, but it was so for men. During the 1967–82 period, the employment-population ratio increased by about 9 percentage points for women (from 39.0 to 47.7 percent), while for men it fell by about 9 percentage points (from 78.0 to 69.0 percent).[11]

Some analysts have argued that women in the US have been pulled into market work to maintain family living standards in response to the decline in men's earnings during the 1980s and 1990s. While most scholars recognize that the trend in men's earnings did contribute to the increased labor supply of (married) women, the extent of this contribution is generally considered to be small relative to other relevant factors. For example, Heidi I. Hartmann (2000) argues that in addition to the social and educational forces that changed US women's expectations concerning their economic lives, rising real wages played a crucial role in increasing women's labor-market participation. These insights echo Francine D. Blau (1998), who argues that increased education, which likely resulted from women's increased prospects for continuous attachments to the labor force, contributed to the increasing labor-force participation among women through its impact on wages. Additional explanatory factors include demographic changes (such as decreases in fertility rates, declines in marriage rates, and increases in rates of divorce) and the shifts in the US economy from manufacturing to services (Claudia Goldin 1990; Blau 1998; Deborah Figart and Heidi I. Hartmann 2000).[12]

In addition to women's involvement in market work, the extent of the gender pay disparity will also have an influence on the wage share. For any given increase in women's share of total market work, the potential reduction in the wage share will depend on how much less women are paid, on average, relative to men. A broad measure of gender pay disparity in the US – the ratio of women's mean earnings to men's – showed an improvement of about 6 percentage points between 1982 and 1997 (from 61 to 67 percent). Similar to the trends in the employment-population ratio discussed above, the decline in gender pay disparity in the US during this period was not much different from that observed for the prior fifteen-year period. Compared to 1967, the relative wage of women was also 6 percentage points higher in 1982 (55 versus 61 percent).[13]

Explanations for the improvement in the relative earnings of women in the US during the 1980s and 1990s include reductions in the human capital gap between men and women (in terms of both education and labor-force experience); the decline in unionization, which hurt men more than women; and structural changes that favored economic sectors with relatively high shares of female employment. In addition, gender segregation – by occupation, industry, establishment size, and type of employment contract – while persistent, has also decreased somewhat over time. For example, women are more likely than in the past to be employed in traditionally male and higher-paying jobs, such as managerial and professional positions (Francine D. Blau and Lawrence M. Kahn 1997, 2000; Hartmann 2000).[14] These factors aside, it is important to note that the narrowing of the wage gap, while reflecting absolute improvement in women's wages, has resulted to a large degree from the decline or stagnation in US men's wages over time. The Institute for Women's Policy Research calculated that this accounted for nearly three-fourths of the narrowing of the gap in the US (Hartmann 2000). In spite of the improvements in women's relative wage, a sizable gap still remains between male and female earnings.[15]

The standard decomposition of the wage share does not explicitly take into account the changes in women's market work or wages. Instead, the change in the wage share is resolved into two terms: labor required per unit of net output (the reciprocal of labor productivity) and real wage. While real wages and labor productivity are highly correlated over long periods of time, heterodox economists generally hold that there is no automatic link between productivity growth and real wage growth. Changes in the wage share may then be understood as shaped by the variations in the extent to which social and political arrangements facilitate workers capturing some of the gains in labor productivity in the form of higher wages (Alain Lipietz 2001).[16]

For our purposes here, it is necessary to separate male and female real wages. To capture the effects of the growing involvement of women in market work, it is also necessary to differentiate, by gender, the ratio of net output to labor. While these ratios are not susceptible to technological determination as the average labor productivity is, changes in them may nevertheless be interpreted as reflecting a structural aspect of the accumulation process: the changing division of market work between men and women. Our extension of the standard decomposition represents these variables explicitly:

$$\begin{aligned}\omega &= w^m \frac{L^m}{Y} + w^f \frac{L^f}{Y} \\ &= \left(\frac{w^m}{p_y}\right)\left(\frac{L^m}{Y_r}\right) + \left(\frac{w^f}{p_y}\right)\left(\frac{L^f}{Y_r}\right) = w_r^m \lambda^m + w_r^f \lambda^f\end{aligned} \tag{2}$$

In the above equation, w^m and w^f are, respectively, the male and female nominal average hourly wage rates; L^m and L^f, the male and female hours worked; Y_r, the real gross value added; and λ^m and λ^f, the male and female labor ratios (male and female labor hours per US dollar of real GDP). Real variables, meaning the variables deflated with the price deflator for gross value added (p_y), are subscripted with the letter "*r*." In an accounting sense, the contribution made by women or men to the change in the wage share would depend on the discrepancy between their wage growth and the fall in their labor ratio. In effect, we are taking the changes in the gender labor ratios and compensation rates as given and estimating their impacts on the aggregate wage share.

While the decomposition of the wage share based on equation (2) does not necessarily imply causation, it should be noted that the results derived from it are not tautological. Thus, as discussed above, we know from the relevant data that in the US during the period under study, the wage share fell, women's share of market work grew, and gender pay disparity declined. The conjunction of these facts does not logically imply that the negative effect on the US wage share stemming from the growth in women's market work must have overwhelmed the positive effect due to the reduction in pay disparity. An inspection of the equation would show that the wage share could have fallen even if the net effect of the trends in women's market work and wage on the wage share was positive. This outcome could have emerged solely as a result of the trends in men's real wage and labor ratio. Therefore, we believe that the decomposition can help disentangle the quantitative effects of these different factors on the wage share during the period under study.

The variables required to calculate the wage share as shown in equation (2) are not available directly from the US national income and product accounts (NIPA). Although the NIPA is rich in information, it contains no breakdown of employee compensation or employment by sex. Thus, it is not possible to compute from the NIPA how much of the employee compensation is paid to women or how much of the aggregate hours of market work is performed by women.

Our strategy to disaggregate the NIPA amounts of employee compensation and hours of work by sex was to estimate the male and female components of each of these variables from the Annual Demographic Supplement (ADS) of the Current Population Survey (the March CPS).[17] This estimation process consisted of two steps based on the assumption that the shares of women and men in wages and hours worked observed in the ADS holds for the NIPA aggregates.

In the first step, we calculated hours worked per year for each worker as the product of usual weekly hours and weeks worked per year. Aggregating across all workers, we were able to calculate the total hours worked and the gender composition of employment. We divided the NIPA estimate of hours worked into male and female hours using the proportion calculated from the ADS.

In the second step, we constructed a compensation variable for each worker that corresponds most closely to the NIPA concept of employee compensation. The latter is the sum of wages and salaries, employer contributions for social insurance,[18] and other labor income.[19] In order to approximate this concept, we augmented the wages and salaries received by each worker with the imputed amounts for payroll taxes and employer contributions for health insurance available in the ADS. Aggregating across all workers, we were able to calculate the total "augmented wage bill." Just as in the case of aggregate hours, we split the NIPA estimate of employee compensation into male and female portions using the proportion estimated from the ADS.[20]

We recognize that this method, especially as applied to the compensation data, has several shortcomings (for example, top-coding of the ADS data, differences in the concept of wages and salaries, and reporting errors in the ADS). Most importantly, in this context, the main source of discrepancy between the two sources (at least in terms of concept) is the lack of any estimates in the ADS for components of other labor income, except for health insurance – the single largest component of the NIPA category of "other labor income."[21] Our inclination is to think that using the ADS proportions to split the NIPA compensation data between the sexes may result in overestimating the share of women in total compensation. This is because women's share in jobs with fringe benefits, such as private pension and profit-sharing plans, is generally lower than men's (for example, Melissa A. Hardy and Kim Shuey [2000]). Unfortunately, there exists no comparable alternative to the March CPS for gender-specific information on the value of fringe benefits at the national level.

Once these estimates were obtained, we decomposed the change in the US wage share during the "leaden age" using equation (2). The negative contribution to the change in the wage share from men's labor ratio was much larger than the positive contribution stemming from their hourly wage, with the gap between the two exceeding the overall decline in the wage share. For women, the opposite was true; that is, the negative contribution from the change in their labor ratio was outweighed by the positive contribution from the change in hourly compensation. Our results suggest that, in an accounting sense, the decline in the US wage share was driven primarily by the unfavorable trend in men's wage relative to their labor ratio. The fall in the wage share could have been exacerbated by the decline in women's labor ratio, but this effect was more than offset by the growth in women's wage.

The notable growth in the female share of aggregate hours worked and employment reflects the movements in the US gender labor ratios (Figure 2). Female share in hours grew sharply during 1982–92 and then declined somewhat. Interestingly, the female share in employment grew steadily throughout the period; it was also at relatively higher levels than the

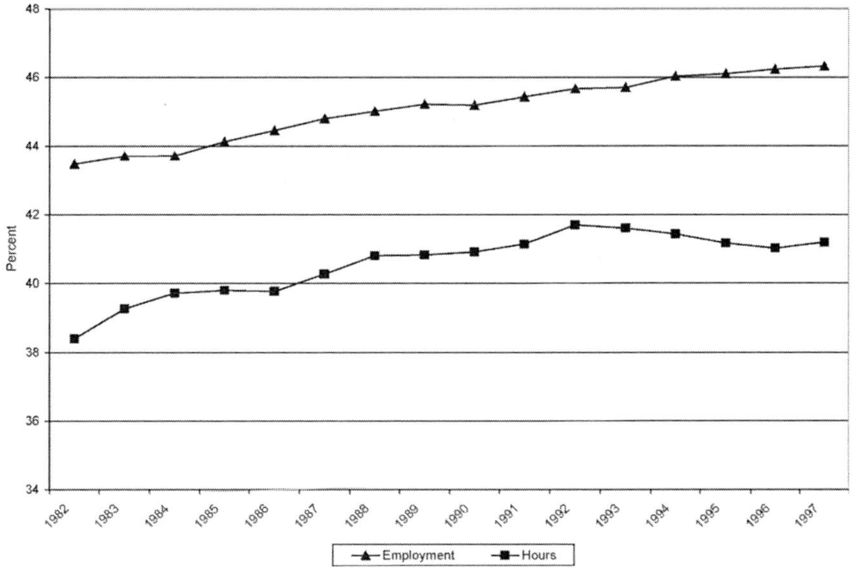

Figure 2 Share of women in total employment and hours worked in the US (in percent), 1982–97

share in hours throughout the period, suggesting that women, on average, had jobs with fewer working hours (for example, part-time and part-year jobs with flexible schedules).

These trends indicate that at the aggregate level, some amount of "substitution" of female for male labor took place during the "leaden age." The substitution that occurred at the aggregate level surely must have been the result of a combination of forces that operated at the disaggregated level: loss of employment in male-dominated occupations and industries, replacement of male by female workers in some occupations and industries, and the faster growth of female-dominated occupations and industries.[22] For our purposes here, the interesting question is the impact of the substitution observed at the aggregate level on the US wage share.[23]

The direct channel of the impact, as noted before, is via the lower relative wage of women and its impact on overall labor costs. Additionally, the growing female share of employment could also be associated with the weakening of labor's bargaining power, and hence on lowering the ability of workers to procure wage gains in tandem with productivity growth. While we do not directly test this hypothesis here, it is useful to note some channels of influence. As Stephanie Seguino argues, women's lower relative wage

> may signal weaker bargaining power on the part of female workers, leading to low unit labor costs, and an assumption on the part of

employers of the reduced cost of extracting labor effort from female workers and limited resistance to poor working conditions. (2000: 1221)

The fact that a substantial share of private-sector women employees are employed in segments of the US labor market that historically have seen a relatively low degree of collective bargaining also contributes to their lower bargaining power. The greater incidence of part-time and part-year work among US women further weakens labor's bargaining power. These difficulties are aggravated by the lack of state support for women workers in the form of public provision of childcare or mandatory maternity and childrearing leave.

While the growing share of women in market work in the US could have the direct and indirect effects discussed above, changes in gender pay disparity also affect the changes in the wage share. Although the gap between female and male hourly compensation rates was still sizeable at the end of the period under study here, it did shrink during the period, as a result of the various factors that were discussed at the beginning of this section. At the aggregate level, two factors emerge as central to this process in terms of mediating the effects on the US wage share (see Figure 3). First, the narrowing of the gender compensation differential took place in an environment of stagnant or slowly growing male hourly compensation.

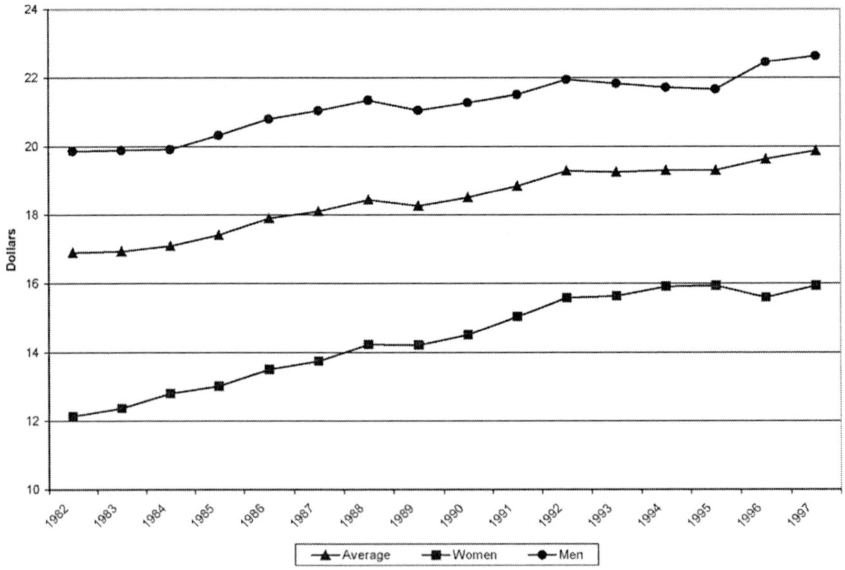

Figure 3 Average real hourly compensation (in 1996 US dollars), 1982–97

Second, the decline was not occurring at a rate sufficient to push overall compensation growth to match or exceed the productivity gains attained during the period. Thus, the rise in gender pay parity could not prevent a decline in the US wage share and did not pose a threat to the overall increase in profitability.

These considerations can be better illustrated by constructing two sets of counterfactual wage shares and profit rates. While the decomposition results are based on a comparison between the starting and ending years of the period under study, the counterfactuals can shed light on the year-to-year changes in the US wage share and profit rate due to the changes in gender pay disparity and female share in total hours of employment. To construct the counterfactuals, it is helpful to express the wage share (see equation (2)) explicitly as a function of the latter:

$$\omega = w_r^m \lambda[(1 - s) + \delta s], \tag{3}$$

where $\lambda = L/Y_r$ is the average labor requirement (the reciprocal of labor productivity), $s = L_f/L$ is the female share in total hours of market work, and $\delta = w_f/w_m$ is the ratio of female to male hourly compensation. The equation clearly implies that, holding everything else constant, the difference between the impact of an infinitesimal change in the female share in market work and a similar change in pay disparity will depend on the difference between the value of the pay gap (δ–1) and the female share in market work, at which the change is evaluated.[24]

In the first counterfactual, we held the pay disparity in the US (δ) at its 1982 level and estimated the wage share and profit rate in each year utilizing the actual annual values for the other variables (w_r^m, λ, s, and v). Similarly, the second counterfactual was constructed by holding women's share in hours of market work (s) at its 1982 level and allowing other variables (w_r^m, λ, δ, and v) to take their actual annual values. Even though women's share of employment grew and gender disparity fell in the US during the period under consideration, these counterfactuals are meaningful to consider because, theoretically, a rising share of female employment need not imply a fall in the gender pay gap. Such an outcome would be inevitable if the trend in women's relative wage was only a function of the forces of (relative) supply and demand. However, as discussed earlier in this section, the reduction in gender pay disparity was driven to a large extent by other factors such as declining gender segregation and improvements in women's educational attainment.[25]

The results of the calculations are displayed in Figures 4 and 5. Since the actual and counterfactual series will have the same values in 1982, we have shown the values for the other years as deviations from the 1982 levels to highlight the potentially divergent behavior of the different series.

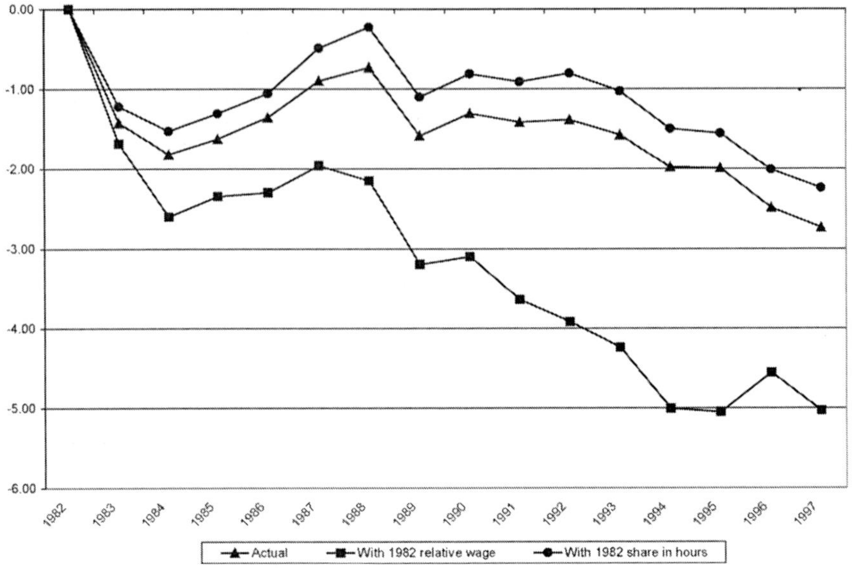

Figure 4 Changes in counterfactual and actual wage shares in the US (in percentage points), 1982–97

If the relative wage of women had remained at its 1982 level, the decline in the US wage share over the 1982–97 period would have been much bigger than what was actually observed (a fall of 5 as opposed to 3 percentage points); correspondingly, the increase in the US profit rate would have been much higher than what was actually observed (a rise of 12 versus 10 percentage points). Conversely, if women's share of market work had remained at its 1982 level, the fall in the US wage share would have been somewhat smaller than actual (2 versus 3 points), and the increase in the profit rate would also have been smaller (9.5 as compared to 10 points). In reality, as discussed above, women's share in total hours did rise and the gender pay differential narrowed, thus resulting in actual wage share and profit rate series that lie between the two counterfactuals. However, the difference in the extent to which the two counterfactual series of changes diverge from the actual series of changes suggests that the narrowing of the gender pay disparity played a substantial role in ameliorating the decline in the wage share and the associated increase in profitability.

Our finding that, in an accounting sense, women contributed to offsetting the loss in the US wage share during 1982 is apparently inconsistent with Jayadev and Finnoff (2006), who find a negative correlation between wage share and female share of the labor force for a panel of OECD countries over the period 1970–2000. While they controlled for a number of factors, such as per capita GDP and unionization, in their regression analysis, our result is derived from decomposition analysis using

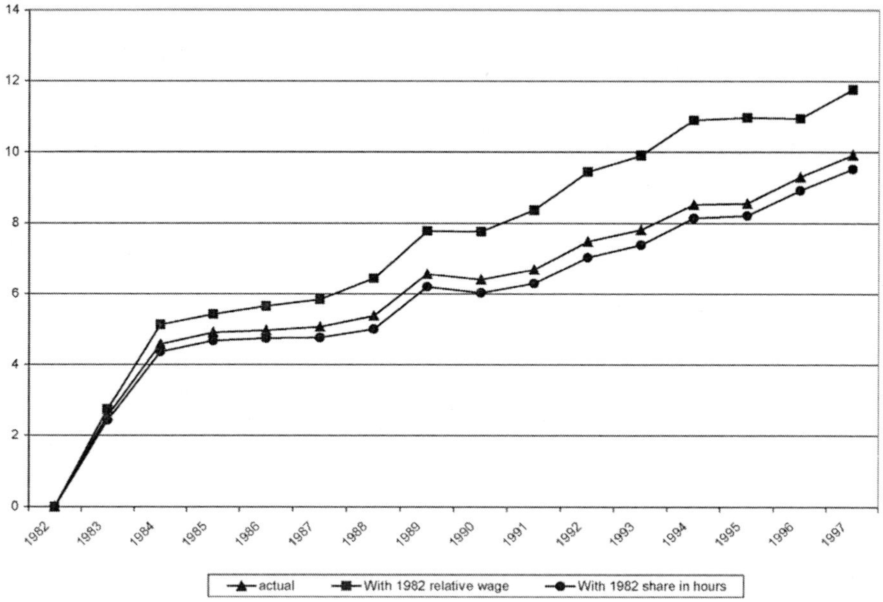

Figure 5 Changes in counterfactual and actual gross profit rates in the US (in percentage points), 1982–97

data for a very specific period for a single country. These differences in data and methods might account for the different findings; yet, it is notable that Jayadev and Finnoff did not control for the differences in the gender pay disparity among countries in their regression models.

DISTRIBUTIONAL SHIFTS AND COMPOSITIONAL SHIFTS

We now turn to examine two issues that are relevant to our findings at the aggregate level. First, the fall in the aggregate wage share could have come about primarily as a result of a shift in the composition of aggregate output in favor of sectors with low wage shares. In such a scenario, the distributional shift that we observed at the aggregate level would appear to be considerably different in its macroeconomic significance from an alternative scenario in which the decline in wage share was primarily due to the changes in social and political environment that prevented employees from securing wage gains in tandem with productivity growth. The second issue relates to the moderating effect that women's employment had on the fall in the aggregate wage share because the contribution from women's rising wage outweighed the contribution from their falling labor ratio. If similar effects could be found in sectors where the wage share fell, we can confirm the existence of palpable sectoral analogs for the observed aggregate outcome. In its absence, the aggregate outcome would confirm the old macroeconomic maxim that the whole is different from the sum of the parts.

Since the aggregate wage share is the weighted sum of sectoral wage shares, we can address the first issue by decomposing the following equation (using the same technique as described before, see note 8):

$$\omega = \sum \kappa_i = \sum \omega_i \gamma_i, \tag{4}$$

where κ_i is the ith sector's contribution to the aggregate wage share, and ω_i and γ_i are, respectively, the ith sector's wage share and share in total nominal value added, Y_i/Y. We separated the private sector into seven broad sectors.[26] While a case for greater disaggregation can be made, we believe that the interesting issue in our context is the impact of the decline of the manufacturing sector and the rise of service-producing sectors (trade, finance, etc.) on the variables of interest.

The results of the decomposition are shown in Table 3. Structural change (as reflected in changing values of γ_i) contributed only about 10 percent of the decline in the aggregate wage share between 1982 and 1997. The contribution of the change in sectoral wage shares was about 90 percent (or 2.45 of the total 2.71 percentage points) of the decline in the aggregate wage share in the US over the period. Thus, while employment shifts in the US during the period had a major positive effect on aggregate profitability via their effects on the organic composition of capital (Wolff 2003), the shifts' effects on profitability via the wage share appear to be rather small. Service-producing sectors that grew in relative importance contributed positively to the aggregate wage share via their own rising wage shares, indicating that the decline at the aggregate level happened in spite of, rather than because of, structural change.

Table 3 Decomposition of the change in the aggregate wage share in the US by sector (in percentage points), 1982–97

		Contribution of the change in the sector's:	
Sector	*Total contribution of the sector to the change in aggregate wage share (κ_i)*	*Wage share (ω_i)*	*Share in value added (γ_i)*
Agriculture, extractive, and construction	-1.18	0.93	-2.11
Durable goods manufacturing	-3.35	-1.51	-1.85
Nondurable goods manufacturing	-1.76	-0.85	-0.92
Transportation and public utilities	-1.48	-0.95	-0.53
Wholesale and retail trade	-0.81	-0.68	-0.13
Finance, insurance, and real estate	1.03	0.15	0.88
Services	4.85	0.46	4.40
All private industries	-2.71	-2.45	-0.26

We now turn to the second issue raised at the beginning of this section, namely, whether the moderating effect that women had on the falling aggregate wage share in the US could be found at the level of the individual sectors where wage shares fell. We addressed this issue by decomposing the sectoral wage shares using the same procedure that we used for the aggregate wage share.[27] The results are shown in Table 4.[28] We have also shown the contribution (the sum of the contributions of labor ratio and hourly compensation) of men and women to the change in sectoral wage shares in Figure 6.

In each of the sectors where a decline in the wage share occurred – manufacturing (durable and nondurable goods), transportation, and trade – the decline was driven primarily by the unfavorable trend in men's wage relative to their labor ratio. Unlike at the aggregate level, women contributed, in an accounting sense, to an exacerbation of the decline in the wage share in these sectors – that is, growth in their wages did not offset the decline in their labor ratio. However, the contribution made by women to the fall in the sectoral wage share was much smaller than men's (as can be seen clearly by a comparison of the heights of the bars in Figure 6). The trade sector constituted a minor exception in the sense that women contributed positively, though a very small amount, to the change in the wage share.

If there were no notable sectoral parallels to the aggregate outcome, how did the aggregate outcome actually come about? This is a question that requires a detailed analysis of sectoral trends, a task that falls beyond the scope of this paper. Our preliminary inspection of the data suggests that there were two distinct factors behind the positive contribution from the

Table 4 Decomposition of the change in sectoral wages shares in the US (in percentage points), 1982–97

	Contribution to the change in wage share from change in:				
	Real hourly compensation		*Labor ratios*		
Sector	*Male*	*Female*	*Male*	*Female*	*Actual change in wage share*
Agriculture, extractive, and construction	14.59	2.34	-7.22	-0.59	9.12
Durable goods manufacturing	28.07	8.11	-40.25	-8.60	-12.68
Nondurable goods manufacturing	3.25	3.69	-10.93	-5.79	-9.76
Transportation and public utilities	3.42	2.12	-10.05	-2.93	-7.44
Wholesale and retail trade	10.54	8.10	-14.63	-7.89	-3.87
Finance, insurance, and real estate	2.62	1.46	-2.31	-0.97	0.80
Services	-1.25	0.33	2.06	1.19	2.33

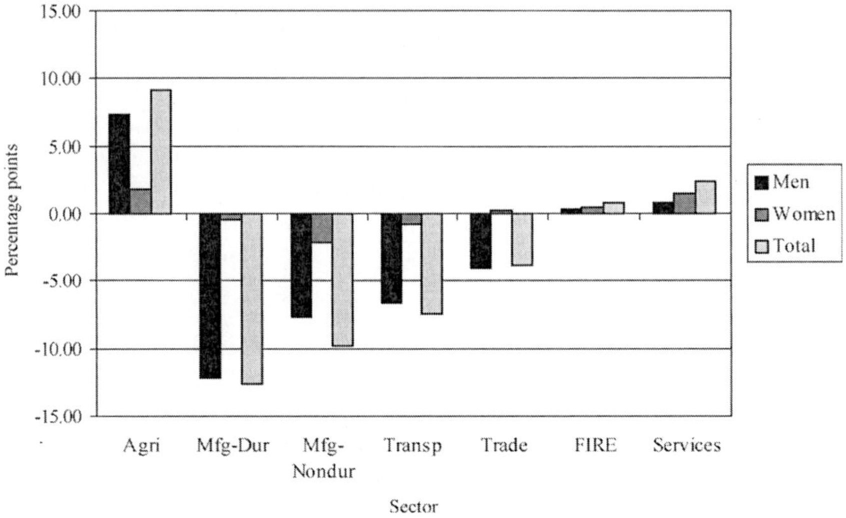

Figure 6 Contribution to the total change in wage share between 1982 and 1997 by men and women in the US, by sector (in percentage points)
Notes: *Agri*=agriculture, mining, and construction; *Mfg-Dur*=durable goods manufacturing; *Mfg-Nondur*=nondurable goods manufacturing; *Transp*=transportation, communication, and public utilities; *Trade*=wholesale and retail trade; *FIRE*=fire, insurance, and real estate.

change in women's wages offsetting the negative contribution from their changing labor ratio at the aggregate level. First, unlike services where there was virtually no growth in female wages, other sectors saw wage gains for women (Figure 7). During this period, the share of services in total US female employment rose rapidly, from 37 to 45 percent, while the share of all other sectors declined (Figure 8). Since services had higher wages than all the other sectors (with the exception of FIRE) in the US in 1982 and higher wages than two sectors in 1997, the shift in favor of services contributed to the growth in female wage rate at the aggregate level. Increasing female wages in all sectors except services as well as the shift of female labor from sectors with wages lower than services toward the services sector were responsible for the overall growth in US women's average wage.

Second, the growth in women's employment in sectors other than services was slower relative to the growth in the respective sectoral GDP, leading to a fall in female labor ratios in these sectors (as shown in Table 4). The combined balance in these sectors between the negative pull from falling labor ratios and the positive push from rising wages would have gone in favor of the labor ratios (as it did for men) resulting in an overall negative contribution of women to the aggregate wage share in the US. But this was offset by the rising labor ratio of women in the services sector. The rising labor ratio of women in this sector coupled with the growth in the

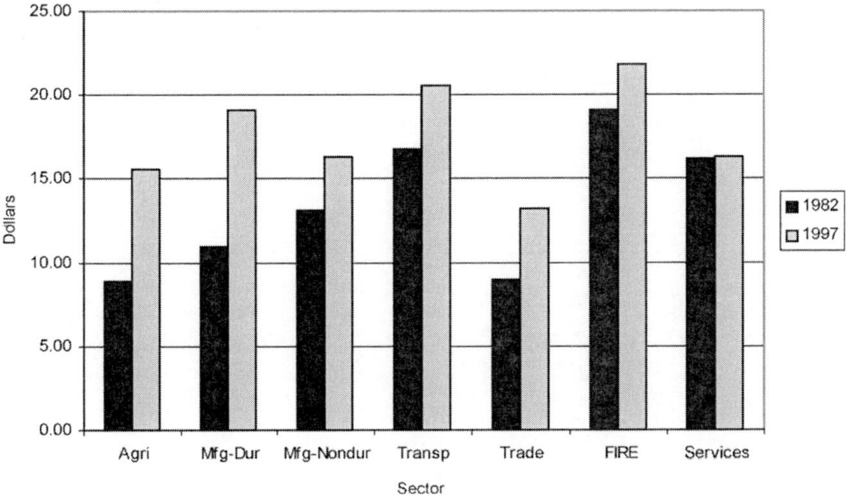

Figure 7 Women's real hourly compensation by sector in the US, 1982 and 1997 (in 1996 US dollars)
Notes: Agri = agriculture, mining, and construction; *Mfg-Dur* = durable goods manufacturing; *Mfg-Nondur* = nondurable goods manufacturing; *Transp* = transportation, communication, and public utilities; Trade = wholesale and retail trade; *FIRE* = fire, insurance, and real estate.

share of this sector in aggregate GDP (from 16 to 23 percent) had the effect of restraining the decline in women's labor ratio at the aggregate level.

The service sector was unique among US sectors. It was the only sector to display rising labor ratios, for both men and women, indicating that average labor productivity was lower in 1997 than in 1982. It was also the only sector in which the average real wage in 1997 turned out to be lower than in 1982 for men (as reflected in the negative contribution of this component in Table 4) and practically unchanged for women.[29] Therefore, the rise in the US wage share of this sector seems to have come about through a perverse process of productivity falling faster than the average wage.[30]

Findings from the sectoral analysis suggest that, at least at the level of disaggregation used here, the aggregate outcome of changes in women's conditions of employment exerting a moderating influence on the falling US wage share had no notable sectoral parallels. In particular, this does not appear to be the result of women being increasingly employed in some dynamic sectors where gains from productivity growth are distributed more in favor of employees than employers. On the contrary, the marked shift in the sectoral distribution of women's working hours in favor of the services sector, a sector in which average labor productivity fell, played a major role in determining the aggregate outcome.

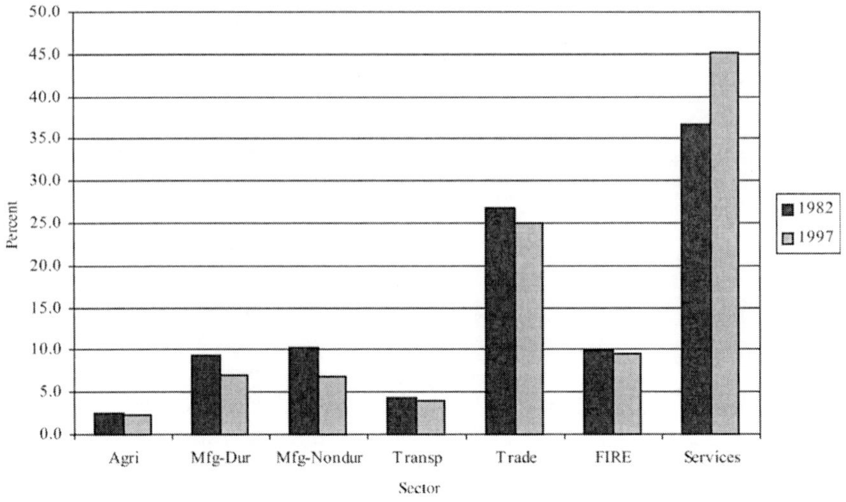

Figure 8 Distribution of women's total hours of market work in the US by sector in 1982 and 1997 (in percent)

Notes: Agri= agriculture, mining, and construction; *Mfg-Dur*= durable goods manufacturing; *Mfg-Nondur*= nondurable goods manufacturing; *Transp*= transportation, communication, and public utilities; *Trade*= wholesale and retail trade; *FIRE* = fire, insurance, and real estate.

CONCLUSION

The US witnessed a sustained rise in aggregate profitability during the 1980s and 1990s. Much of the empirical work on the rise in profitability has neglected the potential effects of trends in women's employment and wages, though theoretical models indicate that such effects could operate via influencing the functional distribution of national income. The aim of this paper is to make a modest contribution to the study of these potential effects. We extended the standard decomposition technique to assess the contribution of women, in an accounting sense, to the decline in the aggregate wage share between 1982 and 1997. The application requires a gender disaggregation of two macroeconomic variables: employee compensation and aggregate hours worked. Our method of circumventing this information gap in the national accounts by utilizing nationally representative household survey data might prove fruitful in other contexts, too, where specific subgroups of the working population need to be identified in analyzing a macroeconomic problem.

In line with the previous literature, we found that the decline in the share of labor in national income played a more important role in the profitability boom of the 1980s and 1990s as compared to the profitability boom of the 1950s and 1960s. Our decomposition method allows us to resolve the change in the wage share into changes in real wages and labor ratios (ratio of hours worked to GDP) differentiated by gender. Results from the decomposition suggest that the decline in the US wage share during the 1982–97 period was driven primarily by the unfavorable trend in men's wage relative to their labor ratio. The fall in the wage share could have been exacerbated by the decline in women's labor ratio, but this effect was offset by the growth in women's wage. We also constructed counterfactual wage shares and profit rates to assess the effects of feminization on yearly changes in these variables. The counterfactuals graphically illustrated that the increasing share of women in hours worked exerted downward pressure on the US wage share because of their lower average wage, but the reduction in the gender wage disparity over time ameliorated this negative effect.

Changes in the sectoral composition of value added in favor of low wage-share sectors could also result in a decline in the aggregate wage share, but our results indicated that the overwhelming bulk of the decline in the US during the 1982–97 period could be attributed to distributional shifts within the goods-producing and trade sectors of the private economy. The decompositions of sectoral wage shares showed that the restraining effect that changes in women's employment had on the fall in the aggregate wage share could not be generally observed among the sectors where wage shares fell. We found that just as at the aggregate level, the principal factor behind the declining US wage shares were the unfavorable trends in men's wages and labor ratios. The restraining effect observed at the aggregate level was not a reflection of women becoming increasingly integrated into some dynamic sectors of the US economy where the distribution of the productivity gains went in favor of employees. It appears to be the net result of distinct sectoral trends in women's employment and wages, with a marked shift to the services sector – a sector where productivity decline outstripped wage decline in the US during the period – playing an important role.

Our analysis provides some quantitative indication of the different aspects of the dynamic relationship between feminization and aggregate wage share. A pure "substitution effect" that stems from women's growing share of market work can lower the wage share. However, the changes in the wage share also depend on the changes in the gender wage disparity. Depending on which of the two effects dominate at the margin, it is quite possible that women's contribution to the change in aggregate wage share can be either positive or negative. The impact of structural change (as reflected in changing shares of major sectors in aggregate output and changing distributions of men and women's employment across sectors) on shaping the aggregate effect of feminization can be complex since wage shares are not necessarily below average in sectors that pay below-average wages. Several countries, with varying historical and institutional backgrounds, have experienced increasing female shares of employment, falling gender pay gaps, and structural changes in the last few decades. Future research on international comparisons are required to place the US experience we have discussed in a comparative context.

The macroeconomic effects of gender relations as well as the impact of macroeconomic conditions on gender relations are areas that require much further study. To approach this issue from the perspective of trends in aggregate profitability is admittedly only one possible approach. A complementary and fruitful approach would be to examine, as has been done in the case of some developing countries (for example, Stephanie Seguino [2000, 2006]), the interrelationships between feminization, gender inequality, and long-run growth.

POSTSCRIPT: WHAT HAS HAPPENED SINCE 1997?

The trajectory of the US profit rate since 1997 has not displayed any sustained movement in either the upward or downward direction (Figure 1). Of course, at the time of writing, the data available is only till 2005, and it is quite possible that the future years might reveal that the US was in the midst of a period of declining profitability and its attendant economic ills. While this limitation prevents us from drawing any definitive conclusions, it may still be worthwhile to briefly describe the pattern of changes in the US during the 1997–2005 period in the major variables analyzed in the main body of the paper.

Two phases can be demarcated in the movement of the US profit rate during the period. From 1997 to 2001, the profit rate fell by 2.46 percentage points. In contrast, it increased by 1.59 percentage points between 2001 and 2005. Decompositions of the change in the profit rate over these two periods are shown in Table 5.

Table 5 Decompositions of the changes in the gross profit rate and the wage share in the US, 1997–2001 and 2001–5 (in percentage points)

	1997–2001	*2001–5*
Actual change in gross profit rate	**-2.46**	**1.59**
Contribution of:		
Change in profit share ($\pi \equiv 1 - \omega$)	-2.43	2.13
Change in real output-capital ratio (Y_r/K_r)	0.78	1.94
Change in relative price of output (p_y/p_k)	-0.80	-2.48
Actual change in wage share (ω)	**3.02**	**-2.66**
Contribution of:		
Change in male hourly compensation (w_r^m)	5.41	1.96
Change in female hourly compensation (w_r^f)	2.94	1.06
Change in male labor ratio (λ^m)	-3.46	-3.68
Change in female labor ratio (λ^f)	-1.88	-2.00

In the first period, the fall in the profit share in the US (or the rise in the wage share) accounted for the bulk of the decline in the profit rate as the contributions made by the real output-capital ratio, and the ratio of the price indexes of output and capital nearly cancelled out each other. The rise in the US wage share was driven by the positive contributions made by male and female real hourly compensation which was offset, though not reversed, by a fall in both labor ratios. The resulting rise in the wage share was quite steep and sufficient to offset the erosion that took place between 1982 and 1997. As is well known, the last years of the "Goldilocks economy" were characterized by exceptionally high employment rates, even among the most marginalized segments of the American labor market.

This state of affairs was, however, short-lived and conditions conducive to rising profitability were soon restored in the US. After peaking in 2001, the wage share fell back gradually almost to its 1997 level. Decomposition results reveal that the contribution to the rise in profit rate made by the increase in profit share far exceeded the actual increase in profit rate. The upward push to the profit rate from the rising real output-capital ratio was more than offset by the downward pull from the falling relative price of output. Thus, the net effect of these two factors on the change in the US profit rate was retarding in the recent past, a sharp contrast to the previous episodes of rising profitability (1959–66 and 1982–97, see Table 1). In the latter instances, the combined effect of the changes in real output-capital ratio and relative price of output contributed positively to the rise in profitability and was much larger than the contribution made by the profit share.[31]

The gender decomposition of the change in the US wage share between 2001 and 2005 also reveals an interesting difference from the 1982–97 period.[32] In the latter period, the unfavorable trend in the male labor ratio relative to their real wages was the main factor behind the decline in the wage share. The male contribution was reversed somewhat, but not offset, by the favorable trend in women's wage relative to their labor ratio. In the recent period, on the contrary, the unfavorable trend in labor ratios relative to real wages for both men and women drove the decline in the wage share. Part of the explanation behind why women failed to provide a moderating effect on the declining wage share in the recent period lies in the fact that their relative pay (measured as a percentage of men's real hourly compensation) remained constant between 2001 and 2005 at about 73 percent.

ACKNOWLEDGMENTS

We are grateful to the anonymous referees and the editors of the Special Issue of *Feminist Economics* for their comments and suggestions. We would also like to thank Korkut Ertürk and Ramaa Vasudevan for their comments on earlier drafts of this paper. We alone remain responsible for any errors and omissions.

NOTES

1 The period since 1997 has not displayed any sustained movement in the US's profit rate till 2005 (the latest year of data that was available at the time of writing); it has also not seen a steady deterioration of the wage share and rising feminization (see the postscript for details).

2 While the empirical validity of the observable implication of a causal mechanism is not the sole criterion by which a theoretical hypothesis is judged in normal scientific practice, it is definitely an important consideration. Regression models are also open to similar caveats regarding causality.

3 The lower average wage could also trigger changes in the methods of production employed in the economy and via that channel influence the rate of profit and relative prices. This effect of the growth in female labor supply, though worthy of study, is probably much harder to quantify than the direct effect on the average wage.

4 The rate of capacity utilization is considered in this tradition as the main determinant of the cyclical fluctuations in the profit rate (Anwar Shaikh 1999).

5 The data on value added and employee compensation in private industries was taken from the "Industry Economic Accounts" section of the website of the US Department of Commerce, Bureau of Economic Analysis (BEA, n.d.a.). Gross value added is the "gross product originating" definition of the US Department of Commerce, BEA. The data on capital stock in private industries was downloaded from the "National Economic Accounts" section of the US Department of Commerce, BEA website (n.d.b.). Capital stock refers to "the current-cost net stock of private nonresidential fixed assets" definition of the US Department of Commerce, BEA.

The US Department of Commerce, BEA does not publish a series for the price deflator of net capital stock. We derived an implicit deflator by converting the current dollar series into a chained-dollar series using the quantity index for net capital stock (available from the BEA, Table 4.2) and then calculating the ratio of the current dollar series to the chained-dollar series. Such a procedure is justified because the percent change in the chained-dollar values will be identical to the percent change in the quantity index. The chain-type price index of value added was taken from the US Department of Commerce, BEA (n.d.a.).

6 The periodization of the upswings in the profit rate was performed by examining the smoothed profit rate series. (The smoothing was done using the standard Hodrick-Prescott filter.) Visual inspection of the filtered series suggested that a sustained upward movement in the profit rate begins from the first year of the chosen period and ends in the last year of the period. That is, for example, 1982 is the year from which the filtered profit rate in every year is higher than the profit rate of the previous year, and 1997 is the last year for which this observation is true. Since the latter period (1982–97) is the focus of this paper, we also conducted a Chow-test to examine whether the two chosen years could be considered as breakpoints in the profit rate series stretching from 1947–2002. The results of the Chow test confirmed the results from the visual inspection. The F-values for 1982 and 1997 were, respectively, 34.38

(0.0001) and 6.38 (0.003), with the numbers in parentheses indicating the p-values. Our periodization also generally accords with that followed in similar studies cited in this paper (Wolff 2003; Duménil and Lévy 2002).

7 We discuss the post-1997 trends in the postscript.

8 Consider the equation $x = yz$. The standard decomposition resolves the change in x between two periods (say 0 and 1) into the weighted sum of changes in the right-hand side variables according to the following equation: $x^1 - x^0 = \bar{z}(y^1 - y^0) + \bar{y}(z^1 - z^0)$, where the bar over a variable indicates that it is the average of the values corresponding to the two periods.

9 The decomposition of the determinants of the profit rate into wage share and output-capital ratio is also not a causal separation because these variables are not independent of each other. Any substantial change in the output-capital ratio due to technological change can be expected to have an effect on the wage share via its effect on labor productivity; while substantial changes in the real wage can influence the kind of methods of production that are employed (as well as the relative prices) and hence have an impact on the output-capital ratio.

10 We borrow the term "gendered macroeconomic variables" from Nilüfer Çağatay, Diane Elson, and Caren Grown (1995: 1830). In a sense, the approach taken in this paper can be viewed as an empirical implementation of the "gendered macroeconomic variable method" that they discuss.

11 The employment-population ratios referred to in this paragraph pertain to individuals who are 16 years and older. They are based on annual household surveys and can be accessed at US Department of Labor, Bureau of Labor Statistics (BLS n.d.b.).

12 Focusing specifically on the labor-supply behavior of married US women, Francine D. Blau and Lawrence M. Kahn (2005: 21–5) find that the elasticity with respect to husband's earnings was small and falling even prior to the 1980s and that the decline continued in the later years (see also Richard Blundell and Thomas MaCurdy [1999] for related analyses and references).

13 The relative wage reported here pertains to full-time, year-around workers. It is based on annual household surveys conducted by the US Census Bureau (n.d.).

14 An interesting issue is the effect of the rise in overall wage inequality on the gender wage gap over the period. One would expect that since women tend to have less marketable skills than men, the factors that aggravated wage inequality – technological change and international competition – would have a negative impact on the gender wage gap. Blau and Kahn (1997) found that over the 1980s the impact of rising inequality and greater returns to skill, while sizeable, was more than offset by improvements in women's measurable qualifications and either a reduction in gender discrimination or an improvement in women's unmeasured labor market skills.

15 Stephen Rose and Heidi I. Hartmann (2004) look at a number of alternative measures of earnings disparity in contrast to the conventional measure that considers only full-time, year-round workers in a given year. They utilized the longitudinal data available from the Panel Study of Income Dynamics to develop their measures and found that the conventional measure may considerably understate the size of the gender wage gap. For example, they found that the gender gap in average annual earnings over the 1983–98 period ranged widely from about 62.1 percent to 36 percent depending on the population for which the earnings were computed. The former figure measured the gender gap in annual earnings calculated over all prime-age workers with reported earnings for *at least one* year between 1983 and 1998, whereas the latter measured the gap computed over all full-time, full-year workers, with earnings reported *each* year over the period. Much of the discrepancy between these measures is due to the fact that women are traditionally less likely to hold full-time, full-year jobs and have continuous work histories. In addition, there is persistent segmentation of

the labor market by sex in which women are more likely to earn less than their male counterparts both within occupations and across traditionally female and male job types.

16 In contrast, in standard marginalist theory, there is not much room for social and political factors to intervene in shaping how effective the workers are in capturing productivity gains because there are strict limits within which the wage share can vary. For example, if the aggregate production function is assumed to be Cobb-Douglas – that is, $Y = AK^{1-\alpha}L^{\alpha}$ – then it is easy to show that under the normal assumptions of perfect competition and homogenous factors of production (K and L represent, respectively, capital and labor), the equilibrium wage share will be equal to the elasticity of output with respect to labor (α). With more general production functions, the constraint on the wage share is still technologically determined (see, for example, Samuel Bentolila and Gilles Saint-Paul [2003]).

17 The ADS (also known as the March CPS) is the source of official data on US household income. For more information about the ADS, please see US Department of Labour, Bureau of Labor Statistics (BLS n.d.a). The calculations described in the text were carried out using the public-use version of the ADS micro-data. Sample sizes for men range from 45,048 in 1982 to 36,583 in 1997 and for women from 36,942 in 1982 to 33,169 in 1997.

18 Employer contributions for social insurance consist mainly of mandatory payments by employers to the government for Social Security, unemployment insurance, and workers' compensation.

19 Other labor income consists of employer contributions to private group health and life insurance, private pension and profit-sharing plans, private supplemental unemployment insurance, private workers' compensation, and publicly administered government employee retirement plans.

20 In both instances, we applied population weights to obtain aggregate estimates.

21 Employer contributions for health insurance amounted to about 55 percent of all other labor income in 1997. Pension and profit-sharing plans accounted for another 40 percent of other labor income in the same year; however, roughly 60 percent of these were publicly administered retirement plans for government employees. The remaining 10 percent was distributed among workers' compensation, life insurance, and supplemental unemployment insurance.

22 A full investigation of the relative importance of these processes in shaping the substitution observed at the aggregate level as well as their relation to the processes of globalization and structural and technological changes is a task that is well beyond the scope of this paper.

23 The increase in US women's share of market work also reflects the growth of, and women's employment in, sectors producing market substitutes for the products of household production (for example, childcare, adult care, and prepared foods). The effect of the latter on the aggregate wage share and profitability would depend on the institutional arrangements under which these substitutes are provided (for example, public provisioning of childcare in the Scandinavian countries versus the predominantly private provisioning in the US) and their conditions of production (for example, the labor intensity of the activities and the presence of collective bargaining).

24 This is because the partial derivatives of the wage share with respect to the female share of employment and wage disparity are, respectively, $\omega_s = w_r^m \lambda(\delta - 1)$ and $\omega_\delta = w_r^m \lambda s$.

25 For example, if the degree of gender segmentation of the labor market had remained unchanged, the growing share of women in employment would occur mostly in the bottom rungs of the wage distribution. Other things remaining the same, such a process can indeed result in a rising, rather than falling, gender pay gap.

26 The data for the value added and employee compensation for the individual sectors were also drawn from the US Department of Commerce, BEA (n.d.a., n.d.b.) as discussed in note 4. A minor point to note regarding the sectoral disaggregation is that the sum of value added of the individual sectors will be different from the aggregate value added because of the very small amount of "statistical discrepancy," the amount of value added that could not be allocated across sectors. As a result, the aggregate wage share reported in this section differs slightly from that reported earlier.

27 As we pointed out in the context of the discussion of the decomposition of the US's aggregate wage share, we are not suggesting that the relationships examined by the decompositions are necessarily causal. We are taking the changes in the sectoral labor ratios and compensation rates as given and then estimating the impacts of these factors on the US's wage share. However, following the same logic as in the instance of aggregate decomposition, this does not mean that the results from the decomposition are purely tautological.

28 The sectoral hourly compensation rates and labor ratios by gender were estimated by utilizing the ADS in conjunction with the US's national accounts. Details about the calculations are available from the authors upon request.

29 The characterization of services sector as a low-wage sector holds only on the average. Several sub-sectors in it include some of the highest-paid occupations, such as legal and health services.

30 The decline in the US service sector's labor productivity appears to fit its frequent characterization as the culprit in the familiar "cost-disease" model originally proposed by William Baumol (William J. Baumol 1967; William J. Baumol, Sue Allen Bateman, and Edward N. Wolff 1987). The poor wage trends in the service sector, however, need not be the effect of low productivity in a causal sense, since the availability of a low-wage labor pool can make the less capital-intensive, low productivity methods of production more profitable to firms (Lester Thurow 2000).

31 Capital-saving technological innovation over the US's "leaden age" is likely to have strengthened the positive contribution to the rise in the profit rate made by real output-capital ratio and the price of output relative to capital stock.

32 Compensation growth for both men and women was notably stronger in the US between 1997 and 2005 than between 1982 and 1997. Between 1982 and 1997, average compensation for men rose at a paltry 0.7 percent per annum and at 1.7 percent for women; in contrast, the annual growth rate was much higher at 2.7 percent for both women and men between 1997 and 2005. However, wage gains were not distributed evenly across the income distribution. Thomas Piketty and Emmanuel Saez (2003), for example, find that the share of wage and salary income going to the top 1 percent of tax filers in the US increased between 1980 and 2005 from 6.4 percent to 11.6 percent. Though a full analysis of the gender dimension of the distribution of wage gains is beyond the scope of this study, findings by Frank Levy and Peter Temin (2007) suggest that women may have contributed considerably to the gains made at the top of the US's wage distribution. They find that between 1980 and 2005, college-educated women in the US were the only major labor market group whose weekly wages kept pace with productivity gains in the US economy.

REFERENCES

Baumol, William J. 1967. "Macroeconomics of Unbalanced Growth: The Anatomy of Urban Crisis." *American Economic Review* 57(3): 415–26.

Baumol, William J., Sue Allen Bateman, and Edward N. Wolff. 1987. *Productivity and American Leadership: The Long View.* Cambridge, MA: MIT Press.

Bentolila, Samuel and Gilles Saint-Paul. 2003. "Explaining Movements in the Labor Share." *Contributions to Macroeconomics* 3(1): Article 9.

Blau, Francine D. 1998. "Trends in the Economic Well-Being of Women, 1970–1995." *Journal of Economic Literature* 36(1): 112–65.

Blau, Francine D. and Lawerence M. Kahn. 1997. "Swimming Upstream: Trends in Gender Wage Differential in the 1980s." *Journal of Labor Economics.* 15(1): 1–42.

———. 2000. "Gender Difference in Pay." *Journal of Economic Perspectives* 14(4): 75–99.

———. 2005. "Changes in the Labor Supply Behavior of Married Women: 1980–2000." Working Paper 11230. National Bureau of Economic Research.

Blundell, Richard and Thomas MaCurdy. 1999. "Labor Supply: A Review of Alternative Approaches," in Orley Ashenfelter and David Card, eds. *Handbook of Labor Economics.* vol. 3A, pp. 1,559–695. Amsterdam: Elsevier.

Brenner, Robert. 1998. "Uneven Development and the Long Downturn: The Advanced Capitalist Economies from Boom to Stagnation, 1950–1998." *New Left Review* (229).

Çağatay, Nilüfer, Diane Elson, and Caren Grown. 1995. "Introduction." *World Development* 23(11): 1827–36.

Duménil, Gérard and Dominique Lévy. 1990. "Post Depression Trends in the Economic Rate of Return for U.S. Manufacturing." *Review of Economics and Statistics* 72(3): 406–13.

———. 1992. *The Economics of the Profit Rate: Competition, Crises, and Historical Tendencies in Capitalism.* Aldershot, Hampshire: Edward Elgar.

———. 2002. "The Profit Rate: Where and How Much Did it Fall? Did It Recover? (USA 1948–2000)" *Review of Radical Political Economics* 34(4): 437–61.

Ertürk, Korkut and Nilüfer Çağatay. 1995. "Macroeconomic Consequences of Cyclical and Secular Changes in Feminization: An Experiment at Gendered Macromodeling." *World Development* 23(11): 1969–77.

Ertürk, Korkut and William Darity, Jr. 2000. "Secular Changes in the Gender Composition of Employment and Growth Dynamics in the North and the South." *World Development* 28(7): 1231–8.

Figart, Deborah and Heidi I. Hartman. 2000. "Broadening the Concept of Pay Equity: Lessons for a Changing Economy," in Ron Baiman, Heather Boushey, and Dawn Saunders, eds. *Political Economy and Contemporary Capitalism: Radical Perspectives on Economic Theory and Policy,* pp. 285–93. Armonk, NY: M.E. Sharpe.

Finoff, Kade and Arjun Jayadev. 2006. "Feminization and the Labor Share." Working Paper 06-4. International Working Group on Gender, Macroeconomics, and International Economics (GEM-IWG).

Goldin, Claudia. 1990. *Understanding the Gender Gap: An Economic History of American Women.* New York: Oxford University Press.

Gordon, David M. 1996. *Fat and Mean: The Corporate Squeeze of Working Americans and the Myth of Managerial "Downsizing".* New York: Martin Kessler Books.

Hardy, Melissa A. and Kim Shuey. 2000. "Pension Decisions in a Changing Economy: Gender, Structure, and Choice." *Journals of Gerontology Series B: Psychological Sciences and Social Sciences* 55(5): S271–7.

Hartmann, Heidi I. 1979. "Capitalism, Patriarchy, and Job Segregation by Sex," in Zilah R. Eisenstern, ed. *Capitalism, Patriarchy, and the Case for Socialist Feminism,* pp. 206–47. New York: Monthly Review Press.

———. 2000. "Closing the Gap: Women's Economic Progress and Future Prospects," in Ray Marshall, ed. *Back to Share Prosperity: The Growing Inequality of Wealth and Income in America,* pp. 119–30. Armonk, NY: M.E. Sharpe.

Levy, Frank and Peter Temin. 2007. "Inequality and Institutions in 20th Century America." Working Paper 13106, National Bureau of Economic Research.

Lipietz, Alain. 2001. "The Fortunes and Misfortunes of Post-Fordism," in Robert Albritton, Makoto Itoh, Richard Westra, and Alan Zuege, eds. *Phases of Capitalist Development: Booms, Crises and Globalizations*, pp. 17–36. Basingstoke, Hampshire: Palgrave.

Marglin, Stephen A. and Juliet Schor, eds. 1991. *The Golden Age of Capitalism: Reinterpreting Postwar Experience.* New York: Oxford University Press.

Mueller, Dennis C. 1990. "Profits and the Process of Competition," in Dennis C. Mueller, ed. *The Dynamics of Company Profits: An International Comparison*, pp. 1–14. Cambridge: Cambridge University Press.

Piketty, Thomas and Emmanuel Saez. 2003. "Income Inequality in the United States." *The Quarterly Journal of Economics* 118(1): 1–39.

Rose, Stephen and Heidi I. Hartmann. 2004. "Still a Man's Labor Market: The Long-Term Earnings Gap." Report C355. Institute for Women's Policy Research.

Seguino, Stephanie 2000. "Gender Inequality and Economic Growth: A Cross-Country Analysis." *World Development* 28(7): 1211–30.

———. 2006. "Gender, Distribution, and Balance of Payments Constrained Growth in Developing Countries." Unpublished manuscript, University of Vermont.

Shaikh, Anwar. 1999. "Explaining the Global Economic Crisis." *Historical Materialism* 5(1): 103–44.

Thurow, Lester. 2000. "Wages and the Service Sector," in Ray Marshall, ed. *Back to Share Prosperity: The Growing Inequality of Wealth and Income in America*, pp. 261–4. Armonk, NY: M. E. Sharpe.

US Census Bureau. n.d. "Historical Income Tables – People." http://www.census.gov/hhes/www/income/histinc/p39ar.html (accessed December 2007).

US Department of Commerce, Bureau of Economic Analysis (BEA). n.d.a. "Industry Economic Accounts." http://www.bea.gov/industry/index.htm (accessed March 2007).

———. n.d.b. "National Economic Accounts." http://www.bea.gov/national/FA2004/index.asp (accessed March 2007).

US Department of Labor, Bureau of Labor Statistics (BLS). n.d.a. "Annual Demographic Survey: Methodology and Documentation." http://www.bls.census.gov/cps/ads/smethdoc.htm (accessed February 2007).

———. n.d.b. "Data Retrieval: Labor Force Statistics (CPS)." http://www.bls.gov/webapps/legacy/cpsatab1.htm (accessed March 2007).

Wolff, Edward N. 2003. "What's Behind the Rise in Profitability in the US in the 1980s and 1990s?" *Cambridge Journal of Economics* 27(4): 479–99.

Zacharias, Ajit. 2002. "Competition and Profitability: A Critique of Robert Brenner." *Review of Radical Political Economics* 34(1): 19–34.

WOMEN'S EMPLOYMENT AND FAMILY INCOME INEQUALITY DURING CHINA'S ECONOMIC TRANSITION

Sai Ding, Xiao-yuan Dong, and Shi Li

ABSTRACT

Economic reforms and trade liberalization have brought profound changes to the Chinese labor market. In this paper, we apply the technique of decomposing the coefficient of variation to examine the impact of changes in married women's employment and earnings on income inequality among Chinese urban households. Using the Chinese Household Income Surveys from 1988, 1995, and 2002, we explore the differences between two phases of economic transition: the gradualist reform period (1988–1995) and the radical reform period (1995–2002). Our analysis shows that the public-sector labor retrenchment of the late 1990s has led to a drastic decline in the employment rates of women, especially those married to low-earning husbands, and the change in women's employment was a major force driving income inequality in post-restructuring urban China.

INTRODUCTION

Over the last two decades, development economics has undergone a paradigm shift from focusing on growth in per capita income to emphasizing provisioning for human development (Michael Todaro and Stephen Smith 2006). The unequal distribution of income, and in particular gender inequality, is a central concern in the quest to improve well-being and fulfill human potential (Amartya Sen 1999). Gender inequality is apparent in the social relations of most societies and more pervasive than other forms of socio-economic disparity. It cuts across other forms of inequality within a society; the interaction of gender and other social markers – such as class, race, age, or education – defines the dynamics of vulnerability (Naila Kabeer 2003). Despite the central importance of gender equality, gender as an analytical category is absent from mainstream macroeconomics, and macroeconomic policies are commonly gender-neutral, as they address women's needs only to the extent to which they conform to traditional gender norms (Lourdes Benería 2003). Drawing lessons from the structural adjustment of the 1980s, feminist economists have established that the seemingly gender-neutral macroeconomic policies implemented through economic institutions that bear and transmit gender biases can impede gender equity, and that gender inequality, in turn, can hinder the attainment of other human development objectives (Diane Elson 1991; Stephanie Seguino and Caren Grown 2006).

In this paper, we apply feminist economic scholarship to analyze the changes in the Chinese urban labor market during China's economic transition.[1] Over the last three decades, China has embarked on the transformation from a centrally planned to a market economy. In contrast to the Central and East European countries, economic reforms in China took place gradually. Until the early 1990s, the reforms sought to improve the performance of central planning and public ownership rather than destroy these defining features of the socialist system. The gradualist reform strategy protected urban workers from the massive open unemployment that had plagued many Central and Eastern European countries, being widely appraised as "a reform with no losers" (Lawrence J. Lau, Yingyi Qian, and Gérard Roland 2001). In the mid-1990s, the pace of urban reforms began to accelerate. Privatization and public-sector labor retrenchment led to large-scale layoffs and a sharp increase in urban unemployment. Women, especially married women, were laid off at higher rates and experienced greater difficulty reentering the labor market.[2] While China's economic transformation has brought about rapid economic growth without fail, the gender and distributional outcomes differed markedly between the two phases of reforms (Xin Meng 2004; Günseli Berik, Xiao-yuan Dong, and Gale Summerfield 2007). In this paper, we analyze the changing patterns of married women's employment and earnings and their impacts on income inequality among urban households, and we compare the differences between the two reform periods.[3]

The relationship between married women's labor-force participation and household income distribution has been the subject of much research in developed countries. Logically speaking, the distributional consequence of wives' labor-force participation is ambiguous: the increase of wives' employment will decrease inequality if it is concentrated in households with low-earning husbands and increase inequality if it is skewed toward households with high-earning husbands. The empirical findings on this issue are mixed. Analyzing different countries, Sheldon Danziger (1980), Reuben Gronau (1982), McKinley Blackburn and David Bloom (1995), and Daniela Del Boca and Silvia Pasqua (2003) find that wives' earnings reduce income inequality in household income in the United States, Israel, Canada, Australia, and Italy. In contrast, Anthony F. Shorrocks (1983), Robert I. Lerman and Shlomo Yitzhaki (1985), and Lynn A. Karoly and Gary Burtless (1995) show that married women's work contributes to family income inequality in the US. Studies on this subject for developing countries are scarce, although the findings are equally controversial. Suet-ling Pong (1991) and Shahina Amin and Julie DaVanzo (2004) find that wives' earnings have an equalizing effect on household income distribution in Hong Kong and Malaysia, whereas Ricardo Paes de Barros and Rosane Silva Pinto Mendonca (1992) find that the distributional effects of women's labor-force participation are negligible in Brazil.[4] Sai Ding (2005) is the first to explore the distributional implications of married women's labor-force participation in a transition country. Decomposing the Theil indexes of income inequality, Ding concludes that wives' market work has an equalizing effect, and this effect is the largest among low-income households in post-reform urban China.

In this paper, we explore the distributional effects of wives' employment and earnings with the technique of decomposing the coefficient of variation (CV). Using data from the Chinese Household Income Survey (CHIS) in 1988, 1995, and 2002, our analysis seeks to shed light on the following questions: (1) How did the patterns of married women's employment and earnings evolve over the two phases of transition: the gradualist reform period (1988–95) and the radical reform period (1995–2002)? (2) What role did married women's labor-force participation play in the distribution of income among Chinese urban households *at a point in time* in each period? (3) How did the changes *over time* in married women's earnings contribute to the rise of income inequality among Chinese urban households in each period? (4) What were the differences between the two phases of transition with respect to the distributional effects of married women's labor market outcomes? By addressing these intriguing issues, our analysis offers new insights into the interplay of macroeconomic policies, gender dynamics, and development outcomes.

WOMEN'S EMPLOYMENT AND EARNINGS AND ECONOMIC TRANSITION IN URBAN CHINA

Under Mao's era, the status of women in China had improved considerably. Much of the progress was attributable to a labor system that was modeled in accordance with the theory of Marx and Engels that social production is an integrated process of the production of material products and the reproduction of human beings themselves under socialism (Frederick Engels 1884/1972; Ulla Grapard 1997). Inspired by the Marxist doctrine that women's emancipation is contingent on women's participation in socialized labor, women's full participation in the labor force played a key role in the leadership's attempt to alleviate discrimination against women (Elisabeth Croll 1983). Most working-age women and men in the cities were employed on a full-time basis in state-owned enterprises (SOEs). The status of state employees entitled women as well as men to lifetime secured employment and a wide range of social services and benefits, from maternity leave, childcare, and healthcare to retirement pensions. While gender segregation remained prevalent and women earned less than men, the gender wage gap in pre-reform China was remarkably small by international standards as a result of the official policy of equal pay for equal work.[5] The socialist norms of a double-income household, full employment, and egalitarian pay scales contributed to exceedingly small income differentials among urban households.

In the late 1970s, China started the transition to a market-oriented economy. In the first fifteen years of reforms, the Chinese government sought reform within the socialist system, directing their efforts primarily to economic decentralization, improving the incentives of state workers and managers, and encouraging the development of non-state sectors. While the entry of rural township village enterprises (TVEs), private firms, and foreign invested firms markedly eroded the share of SOEs and urban collectives in product markets, the two types of public enterprises remained the principal employers of urban workers, accounting for more than three-quarters of total urban employment by 1995 (see Table 1). State enterprises continued to protect workers against open unemployment and shoulder the responsibility of providing social benefits and services to employees. During this period, women's share in total urban employment increased steadily, from 32.9 percent in 1978 to 39.4 percent in 1995, with roughly 70 percent of this increase being created in the state sector (Xiao-yuan Dong, Jianchun Yang, Fenglian Du, and Sai Ding 2006). With respect to gender earnings differentials, Björn Gustafsson and Shi Li (2000) show that the earnings ratio of women to men decreased mildly, from 0.84 in 1988 to 0.82 in 1995.

Although the continuing dominance of public enterprises in the urban labor market played a pivotal role in buffering Chinese workers against the adverse effects of market reforms, the enterprise-based welfare system proved nonviable in an increasingly commercialized environment. The inability of SOEs to adjust labor to changes in demand led to the explosive emergence of a labor surplus,[6] and the responsibility for social-services provision also put huge financial burdens on SOEs. Thus, according to official statistics, about a quarter to half of SOEs were losing money between 1988 and 1995, and subsidies to these enterprises cost the government, on average, 14 percent of its dwindling fiscal revenues during this period (see Table 1). The financial losses of SOEs also resulted in a large amount of non-performing bank loans, threatening the stability of China's financial system (Nicholas R. Lardy 1998).

Table 1 Macroeconomic indicators, China

Year	*Growth rate in real GDP per capita (compared to last year)*	*Fiscal revenue as % of GDP*	*State subsidies to SOEs (billion yuan)*	*Subsidies as % of state fiscal revenue*	*Total urban employment (million)*	*Share of SOEs and collectives in total urban employment (%)*
1978–87[a]	10.2	–	–	–	–	–
1988	11.3	15.8	44.7	18.9	142.7	94.7
1989	4.1	15.8	59.9	22.5	143.9	94.6
1990	3.8	15.8	57.9	19.7	170.4	81.5
1991	9.2	14.6	51.0	16.2	174.7	81.8
1992	14.2	13.1	44.5	12.8	178.6	81.2
1993	13.5	12.6	41.1	9.5	182.6	78.4
1994	12.6	11.2	36.6	7.0	186.5	77.7
1995	10.5	10.7	32.8	5.3	190.4	75.7
1988–95[a]	9.9	–	–	–	–	–
1996	9.6	10.9	33.7	4.6	199.2	71.6
1997	8.8	11.6	36.9	4.3	207.8	67.0
1998	7.8	12.6	33.4	3.4	216.2	51.0
1999	7.1	13.9	29.0	2.5	224.1	45.9
2000	8.0	15.0	27.9	2.1	231.5	41.5
2001	7.5	16.8	30.0	1.8	239.4	37.3
2002	8.3	18.0	26.0	1.4	247.8	33.4
1995–2002[a]	8.5	–	–	–	–	–

Note: [a]average annual rate of growth for the respective period.
Sources: For columns 2 and 3, China's National Bureau of Statistics (NBS) (2000: Tables 5–4); for column 4, NBS (2000: Table 8-3); and for the last two columns, NBS (2005: 18, 21, 66, 67).

Thus, China's economic reform took a sharp turn after Deng Xiaoping's famous southern tour in 1992. In late 1992, China's leaders formally endorsed private-property rights and initiated ownership reforms in public enterprises. In 1994, a new labor law was passed sanctioning the right of employers to dismiss workers. In 1997, Premier Zhu Rongji announced a large-scale labor retrenchment program in an attempt to revitalize the ailing SOE sector. The public-sector restructuring has fundamentally changed the landscape of the urban labor market, as the share of SOEs and urban collectives dropped drastically from 75.7 percent in 1995 to 33.4 percent in 2002 (see Table 1). The public sector restructuring helped reduce the government's budget deficit. Indeed, the share of subsidies paid to SOEs as total fiscal revenues went down from 22.5 percent in 1989 to 1.37 percent in 2002. In the meantime, millions of workers were displaced through mandatory early retirements or layoffs. Analysts estimated that the urban unemployment rate increased from 8 percent to 17 percent over this period (Meng 2004).

As with the macroeconomic policies of structural adjustment in the 1980s, the privatization and public-sector downsizing in China appears to have nothing to do with gender. However, the radical reform measures (unintentionally) destroyed the institutional mechanism that internalized the costs of reproduction and permitted a more equitable gender division of labor under socialism, and no adequate measures were put forth to replace it. In market economies, reproductive activities represent costs to employers as these activities negatively affect the productivity and flexibility of female workers. Subjecting public enterprises to market discipline and removing state protection for female workers, the property rights and labor-market reforms transferred the costs of reproduction that used to be borne partly by the state and employers to women in the forms of more layoffs and lower pay for women. Moreover, under pressure for profits, most urban enterprises ceased to provide subsidized childcare services for employees in the late 1990s. While the employers' duties of providing income security, healthcare, and pensions have been shifted to various newly developed social insurance programs through the welfare reforms,[7] the provision of care and education for preschoolers has turned entirely into the responsibilities of markets and parents. As a result, childcare services became more costly,[8] creating new obstacles to women's labor-force participation, especially women who were married to low-earning husbands.

The declining influence of socialist ideology also led to a re-emergence of traditional patriarchal values, increasing pressures for women to return to the home. The view that is widely shared by Chinese economists is that women's labor-force participation in China is too high to be justified by market forces, and hence their withdrawal from the labor force, permanently or periodically, would be a solution to rising unemployment in the cities (Janet Yee 2001). This sexist attitude is clearly revealed by China's gender-differentiated retirement policy and its implementation during the public-sector downsizing. In accordance with this policy, the retirement age is 60 for men and 55 for women for white-collar employees and 55 for men and 50 for women for blue-collar workers. During the public-sector downsizing, mandatory early retirements were widely applied to employees who were within five years of the legal retirement age.

In short, the radical reform strategies introduced in urban China in the late 1990s bear a resemblance to the structural adjustment policies of the 1980s in that they were formulated based on hidden assumptions that conform to the traditional sex division of labor and failed to acknowledge women's roles in social reproduction. Hence, it is not surprising that women were more likely to be laid off than men and experienced more difficulty finding re-employment in the private sector (Simon Appleton, John Knight, Lina Song, and Quingjie Xia 2002). In consequence, women, especially married women, had higher unemployment rates than men and their spells of unemployment were longer (John Giles, Albert Park, and Fang Cai 2006; Du Fenglian and Xiao-yuan Dong 2008). Women have also withdrawn from the labor force at much higher rates since the 1990s (Dong et al. 2006; Margaret Maurer-Fazio, James Hughes, and Dandan Zhang 2007).

The gender consequences of public-sector restructuring, however, vary across income and social strata. This is not solely due to the fact that rising costs of childcare hurt married women in low-income households more than those in high-income households; it is also a result of the interplay between marriage norms and the role of social networks in the labor market. Economists have long recognized that people tend to mate with those who have similar individual endowments, such as education and other labor market characteristics (Gary S. Becker 1973), and China is no exception. In the post-reform era, the traditional norm of ''assortative mating'' has arguably been strengthened because market reforms intensified economic and social stratification, and the decline of socialist egalitarian ideology discourages selecting partners across classes. As a result of sweeping labor-market reforms, personal connections (*guanxi*) have become increasingly important for advancing individuals' positions in the labor market (Andrew G. Walder 1986; Yanjie Bian 1994), and marriage is known to be one of the most important channels through which people gain access to social networks. Not surprisingly, evidence obtained from ethnographic studies as well as empirical analysis shows invariably that having husbands in powerful positions helped women gain various advantages. Those advantages range from being less vulnerable to redundancy and having easier access to re-employment after their displacement, to obtaining the positions that are less physically demanding, offer higher pay, and have better prospects for career advancement (Lisa Rofel 1999; Yueping Song 2007; Jieyu Liu 2007).[9] Thus, women with husbands occupying the lower social strata tend to be hardest hit by public-sector restructuring.

Moreover, income inequality in urban China has increased markedly in the post-reform period. Increased regional disparities and rising returns to education were among the leading sources of the rise in income inequality during the early years of reforms (Renwei Zhao, Shi Li, and Carl Riskin 1999; Azizur Rahman Khan and Carl Riskin 2005). Meng (2004) compared the patterns of income distribution among urban households in the two phases of reforms. She found that the rise of inequality during the moderate reform period was attributable mainly to the fact that gains of reforms were shared unequally among urban households, whereas the concentration of unemployment and resulting earnings losses (costs of reforms) among low-income households was a major source of rising inequality during the radical phase of reform. In this paper, we study the changing patterns of employment and income distribution in post-reform urban China through a gender lens.

METHODOLOGY

To analyze the impact of the employment and earnings patterns of married women on household income distribution, we use the coefficient of variation (CV) as a summary measure of the level of inequality.[10] The merits of this measure of inequality are widely appreciated: it is scale independent and equally sensitive to changes at all levels of earnings, and can be conveniently decomposed by the sources of income (Stephen Jenkins 1991).[11]

We consider three sources of income: husbands' earnings, wives' earnings, and other sources of income (assets income and social assistance). The decomposition of the squared CV of total household income for the three income sources can be obtained according to the following formulation:

$$CV_{HH}^2 = S_h^2 CV_h^2 + S_w^2 CV_w^2 + S_o^2 CV_o^2 + 2\rho_{hw} S_h S_w CV_h CV_w + 2\rho_{ho} S_h S_o CV_h CV_o + 2\rho_{wo} S_w S_o CV_w CV_o \tag{1}$$

where S_i is the income share of the i-th source of income, CV_i is the CV of the i-th source of income, and ρ_{ij} is the coefficient of correlation between the i-th and the j-th sources of income. Subscript *HH* refers to the household, *h* to the husband, *w* to the wife, and *o* to other sources of income.

We assess the effects of wives' earnings on household income inequality by comparing the actual household distribution to four alternative counterfactual reference distributions, following Maria Cancian and Deborah Reed (1998). The first two are introduced to measure the effects of wives' employment at a point in time, and the last two analyze the impacts of the change over time in the distribution of wives' earnings on the distribution of household income. The first measure is derived by comparing the actual CV of household income (CV_{HH}) to the counterfactual CV under the assumption that all wives had no earnings, which is denoted as CF1. This is the most commonly applied method for evaluating the distributional effects of married women's labor-force participation due to its intuitive clarity. Here, we use this measure to illustrate, in principle, how married women's employment may affect family income distribution.

For the sake of simplicity, we abstract other sources of income from the discussion below,[12] and we write the ratio of the square of actual CV of household income to the counterfactual inequality index of assuming that wives have zero earnings – the square of CV of husbands' earnings, as

$$\frac{CV_{HH}^2}{CV_h^2} = S_h^2(1 + \theta^2 + 2\rho_{wh}\theta) \tag{2}$$

where $\theta = \sigma_w/\sigma_h \geq 0$ is the ratio of the standard deviation of wives' earnings to that of husbands' earnings; $\rho_{wh,}$ which lies between -1 and 1, is the coefficient of correlation between spouses' earnings; and S_h, which takes on values between 0 and 1, is the share of husbands' earnings.[13]

If the ratio on the left-hand side of (2) is greater (smaller) than unity, that is, $CV^2_{HH} > CV^2_h$ ($CV^2_{HH} < CV^2_h$), then household income is more (less) unequally distributed than husband's earnings, and thus the net effect of wives' employment is de-equalizing (equalizing). According to equation (2), wives' *employment* affects household income distribution because it changes the parameters of the distribution of wives' as well as husbands' *earnings* – husbands' share of family earnings (S_h), the relative inequality of wives' and husbands' earnings (θ), and the correlation between the two sources of earnings (ρ_{wh}). Holding husbands' earnings constant, an increase in wives' employment unambiguously decreases S_h by raising the share of wives' earnings and reduces θ by having fewer wives with zero earnings and therefore minimizing wives' earnings dispersion. These changes, in turn, decrease the ratio of CV^2_{HH} to CV^2_h, making income distribution more equitable. The effect of wives' employment on the coefficient of correlation of spousal earnings (ρ_{wh}) is, however, uncertain. While standard microeconomic theory postulates that a wife's labor supply is negatively correlated with her husband's earnings (Mark R. Killingsworth and James J. Heckman 1986), a positive association between employment status and wage rates of wives' and husbands' earnings may arise due to marriage norms of assortative mating and labor-market consequences of social connections. Thus, on the one hand, the growth of wives' labor-market participation would decrease ρ_{wh} and consequently overall inequality if it is concentrated in households that otherwise would have received low earnings. On the other hand, the rise of wives' labor-force participation would increase ρ_{wh} and subsequently overall inequality if it is concentrated in households that would have been well off even without the wives' earnings. However, wives' employment may still reduce income inequality according to (2) even when wives' earnings are positively correlated with husbands' earnings if the correlation is less than perfect, the share of husbands' earnings is low, or the dispersion of wives' earnings is small relative to the dispersion of husbands' earnings. In short, the size of the equalizing (de-equalizing) effect of wives' employment is inversely (directly) correlated with the value of S_h, θ, and ρ_{wh}.

The measure based on a comparison of the observed CV_{HH} to CF1 sheds light on the overall impact of wives' employment and earnings on household income distribution. In the second measure, we compare the observed CV_{HH} with the counterfactual CV_{HH} derived by a small decrease in wives' earnings (S_w), which is denoted as CF2. We illustrate the values of CF2 by plotting the values of CV_{HH} for alternative values of S_w. Cancian and Reed (1998) show that holding constant the values of ρ_{ij} and $CV_{i,}$ the value of CF2 will first decrease and then increase as the share of wives' earnings rises.[14] The CF2 curve offers an assessment of the marginal effect of wives' earnings in the neighborhood of the observed share of wives' earnings, which can be different from the overall effect measured by CF1.

In the last two counterfactual distributions, we compare the distribution of household income in 1995 (2002) with the distribution that would prevail if the mean and dispersion of wives' earnings had not changed since 1988 (1995), which is denoted as CF3, and the distribution if the mean and dispersion of wives' earnings and the correlation of wives' earnings with other sources had not changed since 1988 (1995), CF4. If the observed distribution of household income in the latter year is less equal than the counterfactual distribution CF3, then the changes in the distribution of wives' earnings increased income inequality. Similarly, if the observed inequality of household income in the latter year is greater than the inequality of the counterfactual distribution CF4, then the increase in income inequality can be attributed to the changes in the distribution of wives' earnings as well as the correlation of wives' earnings with other sources. By comparing CF3 and CF4, we can evaluate the extent to which the change in the coefficient of correlation of spouses' earnings may affect household income inequality. In accordance with the decomposition formula (1), an increase in the CV of wives' earnings or an increase in the coefficients of correlation of wives' earnings with other sources of incomes will raise income inequality among households. For the sake of comparison, we also explore how the change in the distribution of husbands' earnings may affect household income inequality with two counterfactuals analogous to CF3 and CF4.

As a partial equilibrium exercise, we do not take into account how husbands may adjust labor supply in response to changes in their wives' earnings in the counterfactual analysis. The impact of this omission should be negligible since a large number of studies have found that the labor supply of husbands is usually not very responsive to income and wage changes (John Pencavel 1986).

DATA AND TRENDS IN EMPLOYMENT, EARNINGS, AND HOUSEHOLD INCOME INEQUALITY

This study uses data obtained from three Chinese Household Income Surveys that were undertaken by the Institute of Economics, Chinese Academy of Social Sciences for the years 1988, 1995, and 1999. One of the authors was involved in carrying out the survey. For 1988, the survey covered ten provinces and province-equivalent municipalities, including Beijing, Shanxi, Jiangsu, Liaoning, Anhui, Henan, Hubei, Guangdong, Yunnan, and Gansu. In 1995 and 2002, Sichuan province was added to the ten provinces in the 1988 sample.[15] The questionnaires were designed in a consistent manner for the three surveys, and hence the data from these surveys are comparable across the three samples. Households in each sample are drawn randomly from China's National Bureau of Statistics' (NBS) annual income and expenditure survey, and NBS enumerators administered the questionnaires.[16]

The sample for our analysis includes only households in which both spouses are present, the wife is aged between 16 and 55, and the husband is between 16 and 60.[17] The sample includes 7,170 households in 1988; 4,886 households in 1995; and 4,728 households in 2002.[18] In the remaining section, we present an overview of the changing patterns of employment and earnings for married men and women in urban China over the sample periods using the data obtained from the three surveys.[19]

Table 2 presents the trends in employment rates of married men and women. We note that in 1988 more than 90 percent of married women were employed, and the gender difference in employment rate was very small. Between 1988 and 1995, little had changed. However, the employment rate fell sharply between 1995 and 2002 – by 6 percentage points for men and 17 for women. Clearly, the public-sector downsizing had led to a drastic increase of gender disparity in employment.

Table 3 presents the employment rates and earnings of wives by quintile of husbands' income distribution. We note that the employment rate of wives in the first (lowest) quintile of husbands' income was slightly higher than that in the last (highest) quintile in 1988, and the between-quintile ratio remained more or less the same in 1995. Between 1995 and 2002, the employment rate of wives fell in all income quintiles but the largest decline occurred in the lowest quintile (by 23 percentage points) and the smallest in the highest quintile (by 10 percentage points). The fall in employment among married women in this period was evidently highest for households with low-earning husbands.

The statistics on earnings of working wives classified by the husbands' earnings quintile reveal a positive association in spouses' earnings. Even in 1988, at the beginning of the reforms, wives in the lowest quintile on average earned only 59 percent of the earnings by wives in the highest

Table 2 Employment rates of husbands and wives, urban China

	1988		*1995*		*2002*	
	Husbands	*Wives*	*Husbands*	*Wives*	*Husbands*	*Wives*
Employment rate (%)						
	96.8	92.3	96.0	91.9	89.6	74.9
Observations	7,170	7,170	4,886	4,886	4,728	4,728

Notes: Earnings are adjusted to 2002 fixed price by urban consumer price index obtained from NBS (2003).
Source: China Household Income Surveys.

quintile, and the earnings ratio fell consistently to 51 percent in 1995 and to 47 percent in 2002. Clearly, the income effect of assortative mating was enhanced by China's transition to a market economy, and the sluggish growth of earnings by working wives in low-income households decreased the equalizing effect of their labor-force participation.

The rise of positive correlation in economic status between husbands and wives in post-reform urban China stemmed partly from the growing importance of social connections in the labor market and partly from the changing pattern of marriage. The latter change can be better illustrated by educational attainments over husbands' earnings distribution in Table 4.[20] In the post-reform period, educational attainment has increased noticeably

Table 3 Employment rates and earnings of wives by quintile of husband income distribution, urban China

	1st	*2nd*	*3rd*	*4th*	*5th*	*1st/5th %*
Employment rates (%)						
1988	93.9	94.5	91.5	90.0	91.7	102.4
1995	91.2	92.3	94.1	90.6	91.3	99.9
2002	71.0	72.8	74.9	74.6	80.3	88.4
Average annual earnings of working wives (*yuan*)						
1988	3696	4124	4475	4944	6290	58.8
1995	4791	5482	6087	7146	9387	51.0
2002	7843	7852	9799	11717	16763	46.8

Source: China Household Income Surveys.

Table 4 Education attainment of husbands and wives by quintile of husband income distribution, urban China

	1st	*2nd*	*3rd*	*4th*	*5th*	*1st: 5th*
1988						
Husbands						
% of college graduates or higher	12.3	15.1	19.3	21.1	25.4	1:2.1
Wives						
% of college graduates or higher	5.1	5.5	7.3	8.6	9.8	1:1.9
1995						
Husbands						
% of college graduates or higher	16.4	27.6	31.8	32.5	38.5	1:2.4
Wives						
% of college graduates or higher	11.2	14.8	17.3	17.6	20.4	1:1.8
2002						
Husbands						
% of college graduates or higher	11.6	21.9	32.8	43.6	52.8	1:4.5
Wives						
% of college graduates or higher	11.5	14.2	22.8	28.7	33.0	1:2.9

Source: China Household Income Surveys.

for both men and women; however, the improvement was spread evenly across husbands' earnings quintiles in 1988 and 1995 but skewed toward the fourth and fifth quintiles in 2002. The ratio of percentage of college graduates or above among wives in the lowest quintile to the highest quintile was 1:1.9 in 1988, fell slightly to 1:1.8 in 1995, but went up sharply to 1:2.9 in 2002. It is evident that the deepening of market reforms in the late 1990s intensified the trend of selecting partners within class, enhancing the positive correlation of spouses' earnings, and this change also curtailed the equalizing effect of wives' labor-force participation.

Table 5 sheds light on the changes in the allocation of working wives and husbands over ownership types, industrial sectors, and occupations. With respect to ownership, women were underrepresented in the SOE sector and overrepresented in the collective sector. A noticeable reallocation from SOEs and collectives to non-public entities occurred between 1995 and 2002. However, sex segregation by ownership appears to have decreased steadily as the Duncan index fell from 0.148 in 1988, to 0.102 in 1995, and to 0.096 in 2002. The Duncan indexes for the industrial sector and occupation unveil a similar trend: the degree of sex segregation fell from 1988 to 1995 and went up from 1995 and 2002, but to levels slightly lower than in 1988. These statistics are consistent with the statistics on earnings for working wives and husbands in Table 7 discussed in the next section, showing that the gender patterns for those still in the labor force were more or less stable over the two reform periods, despite the dramatic changes in employment.

Table 6 presents two measures of income inequality among urban households in the three sample periods. As revealed by these indicators, income dispersion among urban households increased steadily during the period of investigation; for instance, the Gini index rose from a fairly low value of 0.20 in 1988 to 0.25 in 1995 and to 0.31 in 2002. In the next section, we explore the relationship between the employment/earnings of wives and husbands and household income distribution.

DECOMPOSITION AND SIMULATION RESULTS

Main components of household income distribution

We first take a look at how economic transition has affected the main components of household income distribution (see Table 7). Because the market reforms influenced not only the employment status of men and women but also the remuneration of the employed, we present the mean, standard deviation, and CV of earnings for working wives and husbands as well as for all wives and husbands. The differences between the two sets of measures cast light on the extent to which the changes in the distribution of

Table 5 Distribution of working husbands and wives by ownership, industry, and occupation, urban China

	1988		*1995*		*2002*	
	Husband	*Wife*	*Husband*	*Wife*	*Husband*	*Wife*
Ownership (%)						
SOEs	86.7	71.8	86.4	76.1	57.5	47.8
Collectives	12.6	26.4	11.4	21.1	19.2	26.1
Other types	0.7	1.8	2.2	2.8	23.4	26.1
Total	100.0	100.0	100.0	100.0	100.0	100.0
Duncan index	0.148		0.102		0.096	
Sector (%)						
Agriculture, forestry, animal husbandry, fishing, or water conservancy	1.1	0.83	2.01	1.37	1.26	1.08
Industry	40.0	44.6	41.8	43.1	27.3	25.2
Mining and geological survey and prospecting	4.9	2.9	1.2	1.0	6.8	4.5
Construction	4.0	3.0	3.4	2.7	4.3	2.1
Transportation, communications, and telecommunications	8.8	4.8	6.2	3.6	9.4	4.8
Commerce and trade, restaurants and catering, materials supply, marketing, and warehousing	10.7	17.4	11.8	17.2	9.2	14.3
Real estate, public utilities, personal, and consulting services	2.0	2.8	3.1	4.3	8.0	14.7
Health, physical culture, and social welfare	3.7	6.7	3.8	5.5	3.9	6.7
Education, culture, arts, and broadcasting	7.3	8.1	6.7	7.5	8.6	9.4
Scientific research and technical services	2.6	1.6	2.8	2.0	1.9	1.5
Finance, insurance	1.4	1.2	1.5	1.6	2.5	2.7
Government and party organs, social organizations	13.0	5.3	14.8	9.4	14.1	10.2
Other	0.6	1.0	0.9	0.8	2.8	2.9
Total	100.0	100.0	100.0	100.0	100.0	100.0
Duncan index	0.163		0.106		0.156	
Occupation (%)						
Owner of private enterprises	0.7	0.7	1.4	1.5	0.3	0.5

(*continued*)

Table 5 (Continued)

	1988		1995		2002	
	Husband	*Wife*	*Husband*	*Wife*	*Husband*	*Wife*
Managerial personnel	0.2	0.1	0.2	0.2	4.6	4.6
Mid-rank managerial personnel	2.2	12.5	5.8	18.2	5.1	16.2
Technicians and engineers	17.3	17.5	21.9	22.6	22.1	20.5
Administrative personnel	22.1	28.3	22.3	19.9	23.6	16.9
Workers in manufacturing sector	34.5	24.1	26.6	22.3	14.7	15.7
Workers in service sector	17.6	10.4	11.0	7.7	16.6	6.3
Total	100.0	100.0	100.0	100.0	100.0	100.0
Duncan index	0.171		0.116		0.156	
No. observations	7170	7170	4886	4886	4728	4728

Source: China Household Income Surveys.

Table 6 Inequality Measures of Household Income, Urban China

	1988	*1995*	*2002*
Gini coefficient	0.20	0.25	0.31
CV	0.42	0.48	0.62
No. households	7,170	4,886	4,728

Source: China Household Income Surveys.

earnings for all wives and husbands are attributable to the change in employment status or to the change in earnings for those still in the labor force. According to the statistics in Table 7, average real household income for all married couples grew rapidly, by 47.4 percent between 1988 and 1995 and 56.1 percent between 1995 and 2002. Disaggregated by gender, the estimates show that average earnings of husbands (working and non-working combined) grew at a lower rate than that of wives (42.8 versus 44.7 percent) between 1988 and 1995 but at a noticeably higher rate (62.1 versus 46.3 percent) between 1995 and 2002. As a consequence, the share of wives' earnings in household income rose from 39.8 percent in 1988 to 40.8 percent in 1995, and then fell to 36.9 percent in 2002. Given that the difference in the rate of earnings growth between working husbands and wives was much smaller (68.5 versus 66.2 percent) between 1995 and 2002, the decline of wives' share in total household income in this period was primarily attributable to the widening gender gap in employment.[21]

Table 7 Main components of CV^2_{HH} decomposition, urban China

	1988			*1995*			*2002*		
	All	*h*	*w*	*All*	*h*	*w*	*All*	*h*	*w*
μ_{all}	10535	5589	4313	15530	7983	6242	24236	12944	9131
μ_{working}	–	5629	4694	–	8064	6572	–	13595	10926
σ_{all}	4407	2657	2342	7496	4148	3520	15038	8770	7401
σ_{working}	–	2574	2254	–	4134	3299	–	8759	7354
CV_{all}	0.418	0.475	0.543	0.483	0.519	0.564	0.620	0.677	0.811
CV_{working}	–	0.457	0.480	–	0.510	0.500	–	0.644	0.673
S_i	–	54.68	39.75	–	52.95	40.81	–	55.37	36.85
$\rho_{hw\ all}$			0.369			0.407			0.434
$\rho_{hw\ working}$			0.427			0.491			0.529
$\rho_{hw\ all}/\rho_{hw\ working}$ (%)		86.42			82.89			82.04	

Notes: Statistics for other sources of income are omitted to streamline the exposition. All, h, and w stand for all observations, husbands, and wives, respectively.
Source: China Household Income Surveys.

The rapid growth in earnings was associated with rising earnings inequality, as evidenced by the steady increase in the values of CV for wives and husbands in each reform period. The CV for all wives or husbands is greater than the respective CV for working wives or working husbands alone, indicating that variation in employment status is an importance source of earnings inequality. Noticeably, the difference in earnings dispersion between wives and husbands in China is conspicuously small compared with market economies.[22] This may be due to gender differentials in labor-force participation as well as the patterns of employment (part-time versus full-time), which are small in China relative to established market economies even in the later phase of reforms. While income dispersion grew for both wives and husbands, the rate of growth (in CV) was lower for wives than husbands (by 3.9 and 9.3 percent respectively) between 1988 and 1995 but much higher (43.8 versus 30.4 percent) between 1995 and 2002. Comparing the patterns of changing earnings inequality among working wives and husbands with the patterns of all wives and husbands, we note that the difference in the change in CV between all wives and working wives (7.4 percentage points) is greater than the difference between all husbands and working husbands (3 percentage point) in the period from 1995 to 2002. Evidently, while the radical labor-market reforms in that period markedly increased earnings dispersion among employed men and women and consequently contributed to the rise of earnings inequality for all wives and husbands, the main factor accounting for the increased *relative* earnings dispersion of wives to husbands in that period was the fact that more women than men were out of the labor force.

Turning to the coefficients of correlation of spouses' earnings, we find that spouses' earnings (by both measures) were positively correlated with each other, and the positive correlation grew steadily over time as we expected. The degree of spousal earnings correlation (between 0.37 and 0.43 for all couples) appears much stronger in China than in market economies. For instance, the coefficient of correlation of spousal earnings is between 0.135 and 0.214 in Italy (Del Boca and Pasqua 2003), 0.01 and 0.113 in the US (Cancian and Reed 1998), and 0.13 and 0.25 in Malaysia (Amin and Da Vanzo 2004). This is not surprising given that married women's labor-force participation rates are lower in market economies than in China, and their labor hour supplies are also more diverse. Hence, the effect of negative correlation between wives' labor supply and husbands' earnings is greater for the former than for the latter. Indeed, the coefficients of earnings correlation for all couples in China are smaller than the coefficients for working couples alone, and the ratio of the two indicators decreased by an appreciable margin between 1988 and 1995, from 86.4 percent to 82.9 percent, but did not change much between 1995 and 2002. This result is congruent with the interpretation that married women's labor-force participation became more responsive to economic incentives in the course of market reforms. However, the growth of the "incentive-induced labor supply effect" stalled in the radical phase of reforms, perhaps due to the fact that the decline of women's employment was concentrated in low-income households, as demonstrated in the previous section.

In summary, the statistics in Table 7 demonstrate that the deteriorating employment status of married women in the post-restructuring period played a major role in explaining the changing gender patterns of earnings distribution. It has reduced the share of wives' earnings in household income, increased the relative variation of wives' earnings to husbands, and offset the mitigating effect of incentive-induced married women's labor supply on the positive correlation of spousal earnings. We next examine how these changes have contributed to income inequality among urban households.

How did wives' employment contribute to household income inequality at a point in time?

We first measure the impact of women's employment on income inequality in each period by comparing the inequality indexes of the actual income distribution with inequality calculated on the income distribution less wives' earnings (Table 8, CF1). This implies the calculation of the inequality in household income that would occur if wives had no earnings. We find that wives' employment reduced inequality because the CVs of total income are lower than the counterfactual CF1s, which are calculated using total income less women's earnings in all years considered. Including wives' earnings reduced the coefficient of variation of household income by 14.8 percent in 1988, 19.7 percent in 1995, and 11.5 percent in 2002, which indicates that wives' employment had an equalizing effect, and this effect increased in the moderate reform period but decreased in the radical reform period. The equalizing effect of wives' labor-force participation in urban China in relative terms is greater compared with the estimates obtained from some market economies. For instance, Cancian and Reed

Table 8 Inequality in counterfactual distributions, urban China

	True	*Counterfactual if wives' earnings = 0*	
	CV_{HH} (1)	*CF_1* (2)	*Impact of wives' earnings* (3)
1988	0.418	0.480	-14.8%
1995	0.483	0.578	-19.7%
2002	0.620	0.691	-11.5%

Note: (3) is calculated as ((2)/(1) -1) multiplied by 100.
Source: China Household Income Surveys.

(1998) find an equalizing effect of about 10 to 12 percent in the US, and the estimates of Del Boca and Pasqua (2003) imply an equalizing effect of between 3.6 and 5.8 percent in Italy. The higher share of wives' earnings and a smaller relative dispersion of wives' earnings to husbands' are the main factors contributing to the relatively large equalizing effect of wives' earnings in China, in spite of the country's comparatively strong positive correlation of spouses' earnings.

Figure 1 shows the values of the coefficient of variation of household income (CF2) for the alternative values of the share of wives' earnings (S_w). For all three periods, the CV curves are downwardly sloping in the neighborhood of the actual values of S_w, indicating that had the share of wives' earnings been marginally lower, the inequality in household income distribution would have been greater. Numerically, our estimates show that if S_w declined from the observed value by 5 percentage points, the CV_{HH} would have increased from 0.418 to 0.420 in 1988, from 0.483 to 0.484 in 1995, and from 0.620 to 0.623 in 2002. Thus, both measures (CF1 and CF2) show consistently that wives' labor supply has led to less inequality in the

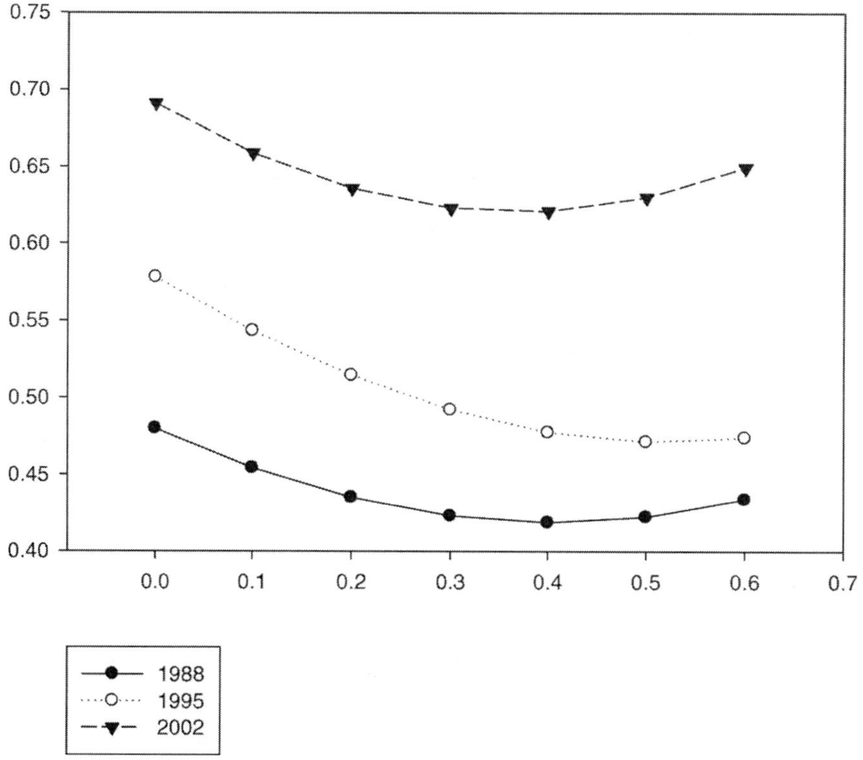

Figure 1 Coefficient of variation and wives' share of household income

distribution of household income, and therefore the decline of women's employment in the late 1990s would contribute to increased income inequality among urban households.

How did changes over time in the distribution of wives' earnings contribute to the change in the inequality of household income distribution?

We pointed out earlier that the average earnings and earnings dispersion of wives and husbands were all on the increase in the two reform periods. However, compared with husbands, the rate of growth in earnings for wives was higher, and the rate of growth in earnings dispersion for wives was lower during the moderate reform period. The converse patterns of comparison were observed in the radical reform period. We now take a look at how these changes shaped the dynamics of income inequality among urban households. The two counterfactual measures of CF3 and CF4 are presented in Table 9. In 1995, the coefficient of variation of household income was 0.483. If the mean and the CV of wives' earnings had not changed between 1988 and 1995, the coefficient of variation of household income in 1995 would have been 0.476. In this sense, the change in wives' earnings dispersion increased inequality, accounting for about 11 percent of the rise in inequality of

Table 9 Decomposition of change in inequality of household income

		1988–95			
	True CV_{hh}	CV_{hh} *if* (μ_w, CV_w) *at 1988 level*	CV_{hh} *if* $(\mu_w, CV_w, \rho_{hw}, \rho_{wo})$ *at 1988 level*	CV_{hh} *if* (μ_h, CV_h) *at 1988 level*	CV_{hh} *if* $(\mu_h, CV_h, \rho_{hw}, \rho_{ho})$ *at 1988 level*
1988	0.418				
1995	0.483	0.476	0.472	0.464	0.452
Change	0.065	0.007	0.011	0.019	0.031
% of actual change	100.0	10.9	17.2	29.7	48.4
		1995–2002			
	True CV_{hh}	CV_{hh} *if* (μ_w, CV_w) *at 1995 level*	CV_{hh} *if* $(\mu_w, CV_w, \rho_{hw}, \rho_{wo})$ *at 1995 level*	CV_{hh} *if* (μ_h, CV_h) *at 1995 level*	CV_{hh} *if* $(\mu_h, CV_h, \rho_{hw}, \rho_{ho})$ *at 1995 level*
1995	0.483				
2002	0.620	0.554	0.551	0.550	0.560
Change	0.137	0.066	0.069	0.071	0.060
% of actual change	100.0	48.2	50.4	51.8	43.8

Source: China Household Income Surveys.

total household income. During this period, the correlation between wives' earnings and other sources of income also increased. If the mean, the CV, and the correlations of wives' earnings had not changed from 1988, the coefficient of variation of household income would have decreased further to 0.472. The difference between the two counterfactual measures implies that the change in the correlation of wives' earnings alone contributed to 6.3 percent of the increase in inequality of household income during this period. To assess the importance of the changes in wives' earnings relative to husbands' earnings, we compute the two counterfactual measures for husbands' earnings. The parallel calculation shows that the change in husbands' earnings explained about 29.7 percent and 48.4 percent of the change in household income inequality. Thus, the de-equalizing effect of the change in wives' earnings was much smaller than the effect of increased inequality in husbands' earnings during the moderate reform period.

Turning to the simulation results for the radical reform period, we see that the observed CV_{HH} went up 13.7 percentage points during this period, from 0.483 in 1995 to 0.620 in 2002. Had the mean and variance of wives' earnings remained at 1995 levels while the distribution of husbands' and other sources of income changed to 2002 levels, the CV_{HH} in 2002 would have been 0.554, lower than the observed CV_{HH} by 6.6 percentage points. That is, the change in wives earnings accounted for 48.2 percent of the increase in overall inequality. Holding constant the correlation of wives' earnings with husbands' earnings and with other sources of income at 1995 levels, in addition to the mean and variance of wives' earnings, we obtain a slightly smaller estimate of 0.551. A comparison of the two counterfactual measures suggests that the change in the correlation of wives' earnings with other sources of income also increased inequality, but the effect (0.3 percentage points) was tiny.[23] Compared to the results for the early reform period, the de-equalizing effects of the change in wives' earnings went up considerably during the radical reform period, becoming quantitatively comparable to or greater than the impact of the changes in husbands' earnings obtained from a parallel calculation of the two counterfactual measures for husbands. The increased contribution of the change in wives' earnings to household income inequality can be attributed to the larger increase in earnings disparity for wives than for husbands, and this change, to a large extent, was a consequence of women's disproportionate withdrawal from the labor force in the post-restructuring period as we underscored at the beginning of this section.

CONCLUSIONS

In this paper, we analyzed the changing patterns of married women's employment and earnings and their impact on household income distribution during China's economic transition, and compared the contrasts between two phases of the transition: the gradualist phase of the reforms (1988–95) and the period of radical reforms (1995–2002). We found that wives' employment and earnings equalized the distribution of household income in urban China at all three points in time we investigated. The relative size of the equalizing effect based on the discrete counterfactual measure increased over the moderate reform period but decreased over the radical phase of reforms. We also found that earnings inequality among wives as well as husbands increased in both reform periods, and the changes in earnings dispersion, in turn, contributed to rising inequality in the distribution of household income. However, the changes in the distribution of wives' earnings played only a minor role in driving up household income inequality, compared with the impact of husbands' earnings, over the moderate reform period; in contrast, the de-equalizing effect of wives' earnings increased by an appreciable margin, accounting for increased overall inequality as much as the effect of husbands' earnings in the radical period of reforms.

Our analysis indicates that the changing gender pattern of employment plays a major role in explaining the contrasts in the distributional consequences of wives earnings between the two reform periods. In the gradualist phase of transition, the traditional functions of state enterprises as job security guarantors and social services providers remained intact despite transformations in other areas. The continuing dominance of public enterprises in the urban labor market cushioned workers against open unemployment, thereby minimizing the undesirable gender impact of market reforms. During this period, the prospect of wage employment for urban women continued to improve. Consequently, the share of wives' earnings in household income increased and the relative variation of wives' earnings to husbands' earnings decreased. These trends amplified the equalizing effect of wives' labor-force participation and dampened the relative contribution of rising earnings inequality among wives to increased income inequality among urban households. However, public-sector restructuring introduced in the late 1990s dismantled the institutional mechanisms that protected workers in general, and women in particular, under socialism. From a gender perspective, the radical reform strategy resembled the structural adjustment policies of the 1980s, which emphasized the efficiency of production and overlooked women's roles in social reproduction. This gender insensitive reform strategy has led to a drastic increase in gender disparity in employment rates, which decreased the share of wives' earnings and augmented the relative earnings dispersion of wives to husbands. As a consequence, the equalizing effect of wives' labor-force participation was lessened, and the change in the distribution of wives' earnings became a major force driving up household income inequality in post-restructuring urban China.

We also found evidence that the gender outcomes of reforms varied with class and social connections. China's economic transition has enhanced the prominence of marriage as a means for advancing labor-market positions and reinforced the traditional norm of assortative mating, as made evident by the rising positive correlation between spouses' earnings. As a consequence, women in households with low-earning husbands assumed a disproportionately large share of lay-offs and unemployment, contributing to the increased polarization of household income distribution and rising urban poverty.

Our analysis demonstrates that macroeconomic policies can reinforce or help reduce gender inequality, and this change in gender inequality, in turn, can promote or impede the achievement of other development objectives. To tackle rising income inequality and social tensions, the Chinese government introduced a new human-centered development program (*yi-ren-wei-ben*) that aims to transform China into a harmonious, well-off society (*hexie, xiaokang*) at the Sixteenth Chinese Communist Party Congress in 2002. To achieve the agenda of growth with equity, Chinese policy-makers can draw lessons from the country's transition experience and take adequate measures to address the unequal gender division of domestic responsibilities and its adverse effect on women in the labor market. Key among these initiatives is to incorporate the provision of care and education of preschoolers into China's emerging social welfare programs. Likewise, gender inequality can be addressed by changing the gender-differentiated retirement policy, which disadvantages women, to one that gives men and women an equal right to decide their retirement age. The government could also implement and monitor labor programs to promote gender equity in hiring/firing and programs to encourage an equal sharing of domestic responsibilities and care between men and women. In addition, policy-makers and development practitioners who design poverty alleviation programs could address gender equity by paying attention to the interplay between gender and traditional norms of marriage and social connections and providing special assistance to households where both wives and husbands are in vulnerable situations to ease the pain borne by these workers in the face of labor-market turbulence.

While illustrating that gender equality in wage employment is instrumental for achieving growth with equity in China, we concede that creating a level playing field for women and men in the paid sector is also intrinsically imperative for the well-being and agency of women themselves as well as their families. Studies have provided indisputable evidence from a diverse set of countries, including China, that an increase in a woman's share in household income raises the share of the household budget (monetary as well as non-monetary) allocated to children's education, health, and nutrition-related expenditures, and other activities essential for human development (Elizabeth M. King and Andrew D. Mason 2001; Fiona MacPhail and Xiao-yuan Dong 2007). Gender equality in the paid sector is, however, not sufficient for the quest to improve well-being; in the absence of affordable, high-quality substitutes for out of home care services, women's full labor-force participation may come at the expense of time poverty and inadequate provisioning for human reproduction, as feminist economists have long been arguing (Benería 2003). Hence, any assessment of the welfare implications of economic transition is incomplete without a proper understanding of its impact on the interaction of paid and unpaid sectors.

ACKNOWLEDGMENTS

We are grateful for the comments and suggestions of guest editors, style editors, and three anonymous referees. We also thank the Ford Foundation for its support for the postgraduate economic research and mentoring program for young Chinese women economists.

NOTES

1 While rural–urban disparity is an important source of income inequality in China, our analysis is confined to the urban sector. The data we used provide no information on earnings of wives and husbands in rural households. While farming is the dominant form of economic activity for the majority of married women in rural areas, the contributions of individual members to household production are unobservable in monetary terms.

2 For China's labor-market reforms in the late 1990s and its gender outcomes, see Simon Appleton, John Knight, Lina Song, and Qingjie Xia (2002); Xiao-yuan Dong, Jianchun Yang, Fenglian Du, and Sai Ding (2006); John Giles, Albert Park, and Fang Cai (2006); and Margaret Maurer-Fazio, James Hughes, and Dandan Zhang (2007).

3 Due to data limitations, our analysis is confined to the financial aspect of women's labor-force participation, while recognizing the importance of unpaid activities for human well-being.

4 Amin and DaVanzo (2004) provide a summary of the empirical findings of studies on this subject.

5 Michael M. Kidd and Xin Meng (2001) find that female workers in Chinese state enterprises earned around 86 percent of the average wage received by men in 1981, and the ratio rose slightly to 87 percent in 1987. As a point of reference, the average nonagricultural earnings ratio of female to male is 76 percent in the US, 57 percent in South Korea, and 51 percent in Japan (Joyce P. Jacobsen 1998: 350).

6 Xiao-yuan Dong and Louis Putterman (2003) estimate that 20 to 40 percent of workers in state firms were redundant in the early 1990s.

7 For the welfare reforms, see Gang Fan, Maria Rosa Lunati, and David O'Connor (1998).

8 According to official statistics, the number of childcare centers and kindergartens fell by 14 percent in the urban sector between 1995 and 2003 (China's Ministry of Education 2005).

9 Investigating the causes of unemployment in post-restructuring urban China, Du and Dong (2008) find that a person is more likely to be unemployed when one or more other family members (primarily spouse) are also unemployed.

10 CV is defined as the standard deviation of income divided by the arithmetic mean.

11 While Gini coefficients have most of the desirable properties of CV, they cannot be conveniently decomposed (Maria Cancian and Deborah Reed 1998).

12 The inclusion of other sources of income should not alter the main results presented below since income from sources other than husbands' and wives' earnings only accounts for a small proportion of total household income in our sample.

13 The original decomposition formula is in Reuben Gronau (1982), and the discussion for equation (2) is from Cal R. Winegarden (1987).

14 Mathematically, the second derivative of CV_{HH}^2 in (1) is greater than zero, indicating that the CF2 is a U-shaped curve.

15 Sichuan province has a per capita income close to the national average, and hence adding this province to the samples of 1995 and 2002 should not bias the comparison.

16 Because the CHIS samples are drawn from the NBS's parent sample, they inherit some of the problems of the NBS sample (see Shaohua Chen and Martin Ravallion [1996]). One limitation for our purposes is that the sample over-represents the public sector and excludes migrant workers, creating a downward bias in the estimate of income inequality.

17 The upper limits of age are set in conformity with China's gender-differentiated retirement policy that we explained earlier. As a sensitivity check, we also performed the decomposition analysis to a sample with husbands and wives both aged between 16 and 60, and the results are substantively similar to those reported in Tables 8 and 9.

18 The sample for 1988 is larger than those for 1995 and 2002 due to funding cuts in the later years.

19 A person is considered employed if he/she selects the category of "have a job" in the question regarding employment status in the survey. Earnings of husbands and wives are defined as the sum of wages (or salaries), non-wage compensation, net income of self-employment, and non-monetary benefits minus income tax. Other sources of income include the earnings of other family members, assets income (rent, interests, and dividends), and transfer income. All income measures are discounted by urban consumer price indexes with 2002 as base year. It is noteworthy that we omit outlying observations in earnings that are likely attributable to recalling errors or data-entering mistakes. Because the mistakes are random, the omission of those outlying observations should not bias inequality estimates (Jeffrey M. Wooldridge 2005).

20 The pattern of educational attainment is more indicative of the change in marriage norms than that in spousal earnings since the majority of urban Chinese people entered the labor market and got married only after completing education.

21 The stable earnings differentials between working wives and husbands are in line with the trends in sex segregation presented in Table 5. Using data derived from two urban labor-force surveys in 1997 and 2002, Dong et al. (2006) find that public-sector downsizing has led to a dramatic shift of employment from the formal sector to the informal sector. In contrast to the trends of the feminization of informality following structural adjustments in many developing countries, this study shows that the gender effect of informalization in urban China was small, and full-time positions (defined as forty hours or more work per week) were still the predominant mode of employment for both men and women in 2002. We are unable to examine the changing patterns of employment in this paper because the CHIS provides no information on working hours or informality.

22 For instance, the CV of wives' earnings is about twice that of husbands' in Italy (0.80 versus 1.96) (Del Boca and Pasqua 2003) and in the US (0.65 versus 1.27) (Cancian and Reed 1998).

23 In the face of the rising positive correlation of spouses' earnings in this period, why was the effect of correlation changes so miniscule? This is because the Chinese government increased transfer payments to mitigate the income losses of laid-off workers after public-sector downsizing, which weakened the correlation of wives' earnings with other sources of income, offsetting the impact of the rising positive correlation between spouses' earnings.

REFERENCES

Amin, Shahina and Julie DaVanzo. 2004. "The Impact of Wives' Earnings Inequality among Married-Couple Households in Malaysia." *Journal of Asian Economics* 15(1): 49–70.

Appleton, Simon, John Knight, Lina Song, and Qingjie Xia. 2002. "Labor Retrenchment in China: Determinants and Consequences." *China Economic Review* 13(2–3): 252–75.

Barros, Ricardo Paes de, and Rosane Silva Pinto Mendonca. 1992. "A Research Note on Family and Income Distribution: The Equalizing Impact of Married Women's Earnings in Metropolitan Brazil." *Sociological Inquiry* 62(2): 208–19.

Becker, Gary S. 1973. "A Theory of Marriage: Part 1." *Journal of Political Economy* 81(4): 813–46.

Benería, Lourdes. 2003. *Gender, Development, and Globalization.* New York: Routledge.

Berik, Günseli, Xiao-yuan Dong, and Gale Summerfield. 2007. "China's Transition and Feminist Economics." *Feminist Economics* 13(3–4): 1–33.

Bian, Yanjie. 1994. *Work and Inequality in Urban China.* Albany: State University of New York.

Blackburn, McKinley and David Bloom. 1995. "Changes in the Structure of Family Income Inequality in the United States and Other Industrialized Nations during the 1980s." *Research in Labor Economics* 14: 141–70.

Cancian, Maria and Deborah Reed. 1998. "Assessing the Effect of Wives' Earnings on Family Income Inequality." *Review of Economics and Statistics* 80(1): 73–9.

Chen, Shaohua and Martin Ravallion. 1996. "Data in Transition: Assessing Rural Living Standards in Southern China." *China Economic Review* 7(1): 23–56.

China's Ministry of Education. 2005. *China's Educational Statistic Yearbook,* 2005. Beijing: People's Education Press.

China's National Bureau of Statistics (NBS). 2000. *China Statistical Yearbook,* 2000. Beijing: China Statistics Press.

———. 2003. *China Statistical Yearbook,* 2003. Beijing: China Statistics Press.

———. 2005. *China Statistical Abstract,* 2005. Beijing: China Statistics Press.

Croll, Elisabeth. 1983. *Chinese Women Since Mao.* London: Zed Books.

Danziger, Sheldon. 1980. "Do Working Wives Increase Family Income Inequality?" *Journal of Human Resources* 15(3): 444–51.

Del Boca, Daniela and Silvia Pasqua. 2003. "Employment Patterns of Husbands and Wives and Family Income Distribution in Italy (1997–98)." *Review of Income and Wealth* 49(2): 221–45.

Ding, Sai. 2005. "The Impact of Married Women's Labor Force Participation on Household Income Inequality in Urban China." *China Labor Economics* 2(2): 75–87.

Dong, Xiao-yuan and Louis Putterman. 2003. "Soft Budget Constraints, Social Burdens, and Labor Redundancy in China's State Industry." *Journal of Comparative Economics* 31(1): 110–33.

Dong, Xiao-yuan, Jianchun Yang, Fenglian Du, and Sai Ding. 2006. "Women's Employment and Public-Sector Restructuring: The Case of Urban China," in Grace O. M. Lee and Malcolm Warner, eds. *Unemployment in China: Economy, Human Resources and Labour Markets*, pp. 87–107. London and New York: Routledge Contemporary China Series.

Du, Fenglian and Xiao-yuan Dong. 2008. "Why Do Women Have Longer Durations of Employment than Men in Post-Restructuring Urban China?" *Cambridge Journal of Economics* Advance Access Published October 7, 2008. DOI: 10.1093/cje/ben034.

Elson, Diane. 1991. *Male Bias in the Development Process*. Manchester: Manchester University Press.

Engels, Frederick. 1884/1972. *The Origin of the Family, Private Property and the State*. New York: International Publishers.

Fan, Gang, Maria Rosa Lunati, and David O'Connor. 1998. "Labor Market Aspects of State Enterprise Reform in China." Technical Paper 141. OECD Development Center.

Giles, John, Albert Park, and Fang Cai. 2006. "Reemployment of Dislocated Workers in Urban China: The Roles of Information and Incentives." *Journal of Comparative Economics* 34(3): 582–607.

Grapard, Ulla. 1997. "Theoretical Issues of Gender in the Transition from Socialist Regimes." *Journal of Economic Issues* 31(3): 665–86.

Gronau, Reuben. 1982. "Inequality of Family Income: Do Wives' Earnings Matter?" *Population and Development Review* 8(Supp): 119–36.

Gustafsson, Björn and Shi Li. 2000. "Economic Transformation and the Gender Earnings Gap in Urban China." *Journal of Population Economics* 13(2): 305–29.

Jacobsen, Joyce P. 1998. *The Economics of Gender*, 2nd ed. Malden, MA: Blackwell.

Jenkins, Stephen. 1991. "The Measurement of Income Inequality," in Lars Osberg, ed. *Economic Inequality and Poverty: International Perspectives*, pp. 3–38. New York: M. E. Sharpe.

Kabeer, Naila. 2003. *Gender Mainstreaming in Poverty Reduction and the Millennium Development Goals: A Handbook for Policy-Makers and Other Stakeholders*. Ottawa: Canadian International Development Agency, Commonwealth Secretariat, International Development Research Centre.

Karoly, Lynn A. and Gary Burtless. 1995. "Demographic Change, Rising Earnings Inequality, and the Distribution of Personal Well-Being, 1959–1989." *Demography* 32(3): 379–406.

Khan, Azizur Rahman and Carl Riskin. 2005. "China's Household Income and Its Distribution, 1995 and 2002." *China Quarterly* 182: 356–84.

Kidd. Michael M. and Xin Meng. 2001. "The Chinese State Enterprise Sector: Labour Market Reform and the Impact on Male–Female Wage Structure." *Asian Economic Journal* 15(4): 405–25.

Killingsworth, Mark R. and James J. Heckman. 1986. "Female Labor Supply: A Survey," in Orley C. Ashenfelter and Richard Layard, eds. *Handbook of Labor Economics*, vol. 1, pp. 103–204. Amsterdam: Elsevier/North Holland.

King, Elizabeth M. and Andrew D. Mason. 2001. *Engendering Development: Through Gender Equality in Rights, Resources, and Voice*. New York: World Bank and Oxford University Press.

Lardy, Nicholas R. 1998. *China's Unfinished Economic Revolution.* Washington, DC: Brookings Institution Press.

Lau, Lawrence J., Yingyi Qian, and Gérard Roland. 2001. "Reform without Losers: An Interpretation of China's Dual-Track Approach to Transition." *Journal of Political Economy* 101(1): 120–43.

Lerman, Robert I. and Shlomo Yitzhaki. 1985. "Income Inequality Effects by Income Sources: A new Approach and Applications to the United States." *Review of Economics and Statistics* 67(1): 151–56.

Liu, Jieyu. 2007. "Gender Dynamics and Redundancy in Urban China." *Feminist Economics* 13(3–4): 125–58.

MacPhail, Fiona and Xiao-yuan Dong. 2007. "Market Labor and Women's Household Status in Rural China." *Feminist Economics* 13(3–4): 91–122.

Maurer-Fazio, Margaret, James Hughes, and Dandan Zhang. 2007. "Gender, Ethnicity, and Labor Force Participation in Post-reform Urban China." *Feminist Economics* 13(3–4): 189–212.

Meng, Xin. 2004. "Economic Restructuring and Income Inequality in Urban China." *Review of Income and Wealth* 50(3): 357–79.

Pencavel, John. 1986. "Labor Supply of Men: A Survey," in Orley C. Ashenfelter and Richard Layard, eds. *Handbook of Labor Economics,* vol. 1, pp. 3–102. Amsterdam: Elsevier/North Holland.

Pong, Suet-ling. 1991. "The Effect of Women's Labor on Household Income Inequality: The Case of Hong Kong." *Economic Development and Cultural Change* 40(1): 131–52.

Rofel, Lisa. 1999. *Other Modernities: Gendered Yearnings in China after Socialism.* Berkeley: University of California Press.

Seguino, Stephanie and Caren Grown. 2006. "Gender Equity and Globalization: Macroeconomic Policy for Developing Countries." *Journal of International Development* 18(8): 1081–104.

Sen, Amartya. 1999. *Development as Freedom.* New York: Alfred A. Knopf.

Shorrocks, Anthony F. 1983. "The Impact of Income Components on the Distribution of Family Incomes." *Quarterly Journal of Economics* 98(2): 311–31.

Song, Yueping. 2007. "Does Gender Make a Difference? Career Mobility in Urban China." *China Economic Quarterly* 6(2): 629–54.

Todaro, Michael and Stephen Smith. 2006. *Economic Development,* 9th ed. New York: Addison-Wesley Publishing Company.

Walder, Andrew G. 1986. *Communist Neo-Traditionalism: Work and Authority in Chinese Industry.* Berkeley: University of California Press.

Winegarden, Cal R. 1987. "Women's Labor Force Participation and the Distribution of Household Incomes: Evidence from Cross-National Data." *Economica* 54(214): 223–36.

Wooldridge, Jeffrey M. 2005. *Introductory Econometrics: A Modern Approach,* 3rd ed. Boston: South-Western College.

Yee, Janet. 2001. "Women's Changing Roles in the Chinese Economy." *Journal of Economics* 27(2): 55–67.

Zhao, Renwei, Shi Li, and Carl Riskin. 1999. *Analysis of Chinese Household Income Re-Distribution: Income Distribution in the process of Economic Transition and Development.* Beijing: China's Finance and Economic Press.

Do Economic Reforms Influence Home-Based Work? Evidence from India

Uma Rani and Jeemol Unni[1]

ABSTRACT

This paper analyzes the factors that influence the conditions under which a woman in India participates as a home-based worker using secondary level data at the micro level. At the macro level, the paper analyzes whether trade and industrial liberalization in India led to an increase in subcontracted work, of the home-based variety. The results show a historically high share of women in home-based work, which implies that female participation in such work was more likely to be determined by their cultural milieu than by the recent liberalization process. Further, while the micro model of social determinants appears to fit the female home-based work equation, the macro model is found to be insignificant. The lower but increasing share of male home-based work and the statistical significance of the macro model as a determinant of such work lead us to conclude that the economic reforms in India had a statistically significant impact on this form of production organization among men.

HOME-BASED WORK: A CONCEPTUAL OVERVIEW

Recent decades have seen particularly dynamic changes in the Indian economy due to economic reforms. Some of these changes have been largely a result of the changing global economic environment, which has led to increased competition, the introduction of new forms of technology, global production chains, a reorganization of work, and some restricted labor mobility. The efforts of multinational corporations (MNCs) and governments worldwide that are undergoing restructuring have led to the proliferation of irregular forms of employment and increased outsourcing to the informal sector. While MNCs have contributed to this process by quickening the relocation of labor-intensive production processes to low-wage sites in developing economies, at the macro level, governments especially in developing countries have implemented a drive to deregulate labor markets. This has led to a decrease in the size and proportion of core formal-sector jobs with job security, opportunities to advance, and social security. Besides increasing flexibility in wage jobs, the new form of work organization includes subcontracting to smaller informal enterprises and home-based producers.

These new forms of work opportunities that are created could be a major source of income inequality in developing countries as wage differentials widen between formal- and informal-sector workers. Income inequalities arise either due to structural changes in the labor market or access to certain segments of the labor market. Structural change could be a shift from manufacturing to services or a move to more flexible forms of paid work. Increase in precarious, irregular work, particularly for women, might have an impact on household income inequalities. Further, only a few jobs of good quality are created. The majority of the workforce with low human capital endowments is sorted into informal low-paid work without social protection, due to rationing of good jobs. In the absence of unemployment benefits, these changes could lead to labor-market segmentation and rising inequalities in income.

The economic reforms in India occurred in phases. The industrial policies of the early 1990s intended to remove the shackles on industry through abolishing investment licensing, simplifying rules, and reducing the exclusive monopolies of the public sector. The trade liberalization policies dismantled quantitative restriction and reduced tariff and non-tariff barriers (NTBs) (Deb Kusum Das 2003). All these early policies appeared to have helped the growth of the organized/formal sector in India. The rapid reforms of the mid-1990s, such as the de-reservation of products and raising the limits of investment in plant and machinery, allowed India's small-scale industries to expand. The trade liberalization measures also allowed technology inflow (often secondhand technology) into the small-scale industries, which encouraged productivity growth. The period after the mid-1990s saw rapid growth in the unorganized/informal sector in India (Uma Rani and Jeemol Unni 2004). Through the adoption of flexible production processes, large firms subcontracted to small firms, leading to the high growth of the informal segment in output, employment, and capital (Jeemol Unni and Uma Rani 2008). The early empirical literature on India argued that the subcontracting inter-firm linkages were exploitative: the workers were paid low wages, did not receive any benefits, and the nature of work did not allow them to organize themselves, thus reducing their bargaining power (Amitav N. Bose 1978; John Harriss 1982; Nirmala Banerjee 1988). However, the more recent literature on subcontracting in India argues that this is an efficient form of production organization, though there is an implicit mention of the attendant exploitation of labor (Rakesh Basant and Pankaj Chandra 2002; Sebastian Morris and Rakesh Basant 2004). The exploitative nature of work within the subcontracting chain is more likely to occur in informal enterprises and home-based situations.

There are a number of empirical studies on home-based work from both definitional and analytical angles. This paper makes a contribution to the existing literature at two levels. At the micro level, much of the empirical work consists of case studies and focuses on one or more occupational categories, providing valuable insights on the working conditions, nature of work, and production relations. This paper analyzes the factors that influence the conditions under which a woman in India participates as a home-based worker using secondary level data. Further, it differs from earlier empirical work as it adopts a much more comprehensive definition of home-based work and takes into consideration all the industrial groups in India's manufacturing sector. At the macro level, India has witnessed dynamic changes due to economic reforms – trade and industrial liberalization. This paper adds to the macro debate with regard to whether trade and industrial liberalization lead to an increase in subcontracted home-based work and analyzes the factors that might lead to the growth of such work.

In this context, the paper analyzes the growth of home-based workers in the new policy environment in India where the economy has been opened to the forces of globalization. We adopt a micro perspective to understand why women undertake home-based work or what characteristics determine home-based work. To examine this, we consider the individual or micro decision to participate and the macroeconomic factors that might have led to the increase in such work. Finally, we test the "efficiency" argument to see whether the easing of licenses and trade liberalization in India (through proxy variables) led to the growth of home-based work, as large firms sought to reduce the transaction costs of coordination. There seems to be a thin line between "efficiency" and "exploitation" as the firms that adopt cost-cutting strategies actually cut labor costs by subcontracting out, thus exploiting labor.

Theoretical framework

The process of liberalization underway has led to changes in the way production is organized in India. The production process has been decentralized most in the industrial sector, with a wide range of activities subcontracted to small firms and home-based workers, in an attempt to increase profits and marketability. Firms in India are pushed into outsourcing or subcontracting because of increasing economic costs, heavy competition, and efforts to circumvent labor legislation. Some economic literature argues that subcontracting is the most "efficient" form of production organization (Ronald H. Coase 1937; Oliver E. Williamson 1975), while empirical studies have very clearly shown such relationships to be exploitative (Bose 1978; Harriss 1982; Emmanuel Romatet 1983;

Banerjee 1988).[2] Women as home workers become one of the main targets in the restructuring of production, as they get low wages and remain outside the realm of unions, social security, labor standards, and other state guarantees. Outsourced work is actually the least skill intensive and involves minimal capital, and the labor process is generally repetitive and monotonous.

Arguing from a micro efficiency point of view, the neoclassical model puts forward two reasons to explain the existence of home-based work: First, there are fixed costs of working on-site such as the time and financial costs of travel and providing alternative arrangements for caring for the young and sick. These are greatly reduced by home-based work. Second, with home-based work it is possible to engage in the joint production of income and household commodities, such as cooking and looking after children. The flexibility of home-based work enables women to better integrate their family and work roles (Linda N. Edwards and Elizabeth Field-Hendrey 2002).

From a Marxist perspective, home-based work is seen as part of a global capitalist system of exploitation and dependent relations (Isa Baud 1987). Karl Marx (1977) referred to home workers as an invisible thread and an outside department of the factory, the manufactory or the warehouse, who were part and parcel of the production of consumer goods during the industrial revolution of Western economies. Marx argued that, "piece wage is a form of wage in harmony with the capitalist mode of production" and is most favorable for its own development (1977: 521). The piece rate system reduces the need for supervision, reduces monitoring costs, and improves the workers' "self-control." Such a hierarchically organized system of exploitation facilitates the intensification of exploitation and the extension of the working day (as discussed in Peter Custers [1997]). Romatet argued: "The daily working time is regulated by the owner and by the product, that is, the time required to complete a piece" ([1983], as quoted in Custers 1997: 126).

Claudia von Werlhof analyzes the position of home workers differently by taking "the present-day reality in terms of the dichotomy between the 'free wage labor' on the one hand, and the 'housewife' on the other" ([1988], quoted in Custers 1997: 127). She argues that the ever-increasing expansion of the informal sector leads to the abolition of the first type of worker. The conditions of the increasing number of home workers approximate those of the housewife, the individualized, atomized worker whose labor is not regulated by a wage. Maria Mies (1982) refers to home workers as "semi-domesticated," which means that in their social appearances they are housewives. But in reality, they are wage laborers fully integrated into a world market-oriented production system (Custers 1997: 186). The social definition of home workers as housewives has economic consequences in the sense that it facilitates the ruthless exploitation of labor in terms of the underpayment of wages and denial of any benefits that a factory worker (salaried or casual) might receive.

Martha A. Chen, Jennefer Sebstad, and Lesley O'Connell (1999) argue that home-based work does not emerge simply because women prefer to work at home (that is, the "housewife theory") but also because employers prefer to subcontract work to home-based workers as a cost-reducing strategy. This apart, falling male wages or employment reduces female and household welfare, forcing women's participation in paid work, especially home-based work (L. Alan Winters 2000). This is, in turn, grounded by and affected by macroeconomic and sectoral policies and regulations. Custers (1997) also points out that although the housewife theory might explain workers' sociological conditions, it fails to define the economic or production relations under which they work. Home-based work in Marxist-Feminist theory is seen as an extreme form and consequence of an unequal sexual division of labor, which manifests to a large extent in many consumer goods industries (Andrea M. Singh and Anita Keller-Viitanen 1987; Custers 1997).

There is no doubt that the exploitative elements discussed in the Marxian framework are prevalent in the present day reality of home-based work and have relevance even today. However, by emphasizing wage labor and its exploitative elements alone, the Marxian understanding of the complex reality is very narrow in scope. Marx in his analysis of home workers does not take into consideration the sexual division of labor, and thus fails to take into account the double task of self-/wage-employed work and domestic work undertaken especially by female home-based workers.

Definition

The traditional sources of data on employment, the population censuses and India's national labor force surveys, classify workers according to three international classification schemes – industry, occupation, and status – but none of them capture home-based work as a category. Empirical micro studies over the last two decades have tried to capture this set of invisible home-based workers, with each adopting a different definition depending upon the sector or region, making comparisons difficult (Mies 1982; Romatet 1983; Singh and Keller-Viitanen 1987; Banerjee 1988; Paula Kantor 2000; Jeemol Unni and Namrata Bali 2002). These studies fail to give us any reasonable estimates of such work even in a particular activity. As these studies cover a wide range of productive activities in home-based work, they have allowed researchers to explore the definitional ramifications. The definitional issue assumes importance both from a conceptual perspective and because of the need to evolve an operational definition that could be incorporated into standard national data-gathering exercises for undertaking meaningful empirical analysis and policy intervention.

The 1993 International Classification of Status in Employment (ICSE) followed a dichotomous system in which workers were classified as either self-employed or wageworkers. This classification system is unable to represent the realities of home-based workers and producers due to two reasons: First, the dichotomy is a reductionist categorization of the complex relations of production and distribution characterizing home-based work, where many producers are neither wageworkers nor self-employed but something in-between (Kantor 2000). Second, the dichotomy is based on legal definitions of the wageworker and the self-employed person, drawn from Western liberal assumptions of autonomous and self-contained individuals, which cannot be applied to home-based producers (Elisabeth Prügl and Irene Tinker 1997).

The International Labour Organization (ILO) adopted a Convention of Home Work in 1996, Number 177, which refers exclusively to home workers, a category not included in the ICSE 1993. It defined a home worker as a person who carries out work for remuneration in premises of his/her own choice, other than the workplace of the employer, resulting in a product or service as specified by the employer, irrespective of who provides the equipment, materials, or inputs used (ILO 1996). This is a subcategory of a broader category of home-based workers. Marilyn Carr, Martha Alter Chen, and Jane Tate (2000) distinguish between "home workers" and "home-based workers," the latter including own-account workers. They emphasize the broader usage of the term "home-based workers," which refers to both independent own-account producers and dependent subcontract workers in the analysis of global values chains, as they are the most dominant forms of employment in developing economies.

The Ministry of Statistics and Programme Implementation, Government of India, constituted an Independent Group on Home-Based Workers in India to suggest a definition, identify data needs, and recommend pilot data collection for filling the gap in statistics related to this group of workers (Government of India [GOI] 2008). The group submitted its report in March 2008 and recommended the following definition: home-based workers are (1) own-account workers and contributing family workers helping own-account workers involved in the production of goods and services in their homes, for the market, and (2) workers carrying out work in their homes for remuneration, resulting in a product or service as specified by the employer(s), irrespective of who provides the equipment, materials, or other inputs used, and those contributing family workers helping such workers.

In our view, home-based workers form a broader category of workers within which home workers are included. Besides home workers, home-based workers also include those own-account workers and unpaid family helpers who pursue economic activity within their homes, that is, their place of work. Wageworkers employed in the homes of employers also constitute part of the production organization of home-based work.

Home-based workers fall into a continuum of production systems with varying relationships of dependence along the following lines:

(1) Own-account worker/employer: persons working on household premises, having a relatively independent status.
(2) Home worker: outworkers who work at home, or in another home other than the employer/contractor's premises under subcontracting arrangements, having a dependent status.
(3) Wageworker: persons working for wages or salaries in enterprises located in the employer's home.

This classification is much more comprehensive and allows us to capture a larger number of home-based workers, who would otherwise be invisible. We realize that this varies from the international literature reviewed earlier, including ILO (1996), in which home work is considered synonymous with home-based work, and the definition of GOI (2006), since it includes wageworkers working in enterprises located at home. But we use this more comprehensive definition as the dependent variable in the macro model since we are attempting to understand the determinants of a form of production organization in that model. The micro model focuses only on the first two categories since it attempts to understand the individual's choice with regard to the location of her work at home.

DESCRIPTION OF DATA AND THE DEPENDENT VARIABLES

The database used in this study is obtained from the National Sample Survey Organisation (NSSO), part of the Central Statistical Organisation of India. We use two separate data-sets for the micro and macro models. The micro model is estimated on the individual level records of the NSSO's Fifty-fifth and Sixty-first Round Survey of Employment and Unemployment, 1999–2000 and 2004–5 (NSSO 2001a, 2001b, 2006a 2006b). This national labor force survey for the first time included a question on "place of work" in 1999–2000 that helped identify workers who undertook their economic activity at home (NSSO 2001a). The dependent variable in the micro model is persons undertaking home-based work in the manufacturing sector. Since this model tries to explain why individuals choose to work at their own homes as opposed to outside the home, we take into consideration own-account workers and home workers for the analysis. For the micro model, the only selection criterion is age, and we have included all persons aged 15–64 years in the sample.

The macro model was estimated on a separate survey of the NSSO, the Survey of Unorganized Manufacture, Fifty-first Round, 1994–5

(NSSO 1998a, 1998b) and the Fifty-sixth Round, 2000–1 (NSSO 2002a, 2002b, 2002c). The data on the unorganized manufacturing sector for these two years – 1994–5 and 2000–1 – have a location code that helped us to identify home-based enterprises, coded as ''premises same as household's residence'' in 1994–5 and ''within household premises'' in 2000–1 (NSSO 1998a, 2002a: 4). Data on enterprises and workers in them located in the household premises allowed us to estimate the change in this form of work organization for total workers over this period.[3]

From a macro perspective, home-based work is a particular form of work organization in which the costs of production are quite low. Hence, industries and large enterprises that engage in cost-cutting strategies could undertake production in home-based situations. Such home-based units could also hire wageworkers, and in general such employees would be paid comparatively low wages, helping in the cost-cutting strategies of the industry. The dependent variable in the macro model is the percentage point increase in the share of persons engaged in home-based enterprises and includes hired or wageworkers in enterprises that may be engaging in own-account work or subcontracted home work. Family and hired workers constitute this particular form of production organization. The model attempts to understand the phenomenon of work moving from the factory to the home from a macro perspective.

TRENDS IN HOME-BASED WORK IN INDIA

The economic reform policies of the Indian government since 1991, including the liberalization of trade and deregulation of industries (documented in Rani and Unni [2004]), affected the manufacturing sector to a large extent by, among other things, allowing the inflow of technology into the country. These measures made technology transfer easier and facilitated alliances with foreign firms and the inflow of foreign direct investment (FDI). The economic reforms were seen to have a positive impact on the unorganized (informal) manufacturing sector in the 1990s (Rani and Unni 2004), leading to growth of value added and employment.

To study the impact of trade liberalization on specific industries in the manufacturing sector in India, we have categorized the industries into trade categories: export oriented and import penetration. This is based on the value of export and import in the two years 1993–4 and 1999–2000.

Trade categories

The following five trade groups were distinguished:

Category I: Export oriented – If the value of export was greater than the value of import in both years.

Category II: Import penetrating – If the value of import was greater than the value of export in both years.

Category III: Import penetrating to export oriented – If the value of import was greater in the first year and the value of export was greater in the last year.

Category IV: Export oriented to import penetrating – If the value of export was greater in the first year and the value of import was greater in the last year.

Category V: No trade category – Neither export nor import in the industry group.

Home-based production workers

The share of home-based work among production workers in India, including family and hired workers in the unorganized manufacturing sector, is rather high. Home-based workers constituted about 81 percent of all female workers and about 46 percent of male workers in 2000–1 (Table 1). This tells us that a large part of India's unorganized manufacturing was undertaken as part of household industry and was obviously of a smaller scale and used more primitive technology.

Home-based production workers grew at a much faster rate during the phase of India's recent reforms (1994–5 to 2000–1), 6.5 percent (Table 1) compared to only 1.1 percent for all workers (Jeemol Unni and Uma Rani 2005). The gender differentials in the growth of home-based workers are rather striking and contrary to expectations. There was a sharp growth in male home-based workers, about 13 percent per year, while there was a decrease of 0.4 percent in female home-based workers. Given the high share of home-based women workers, this form of work was perhaps part of the cultural milieu and not really affected by India's new economic reform policies. Also, given the high level of female home-based work, we can expect low percentage change over time. Further, while there was a small increase in the share of male home-based workers, there was actually a decline in the share of female home-based workers (Table 1). This gender differential has important implications for the strategy adopted by Indian firms, where we expected that home-based women production workers would grow and replace the more expensive male workers. The strategy instead appeared to be one of replacing male factory workers with male home-based workers.

There were, however, major differences in the change in the share of home-based workers among India's trade categories of industries. Predominantly export-oriented industries had a decline in the share of male home-based workers, while the industries with major import

Table 1 Percentage and growth rate of production workers in enterprises located at home in select three-digit export categories[a]

		Men		*Women*		*Total*		*Growth rate (1994–2001)*		
		1994–5	*2000–1*	*1994–5*	*2000–1*	*1994–5*	*2000–1*	*Male*	*Female*	*Total*
CAT I: export-oriented industries										
151	Meat, fish, fruit, and vegetables	39	36	50	69	43	41	13	4	10
155	Beverages	63	63	85	69	75	65	17	-7	6
160	Tobacco products	79	85	93	94	90	91	20	12	14
171	Spinning, weaving, and finishing	62	66	84	82	73	71	7	-8	-0.4
172	Other textiles	71	69	91	91	81	78	7	1	4
181	Wearing apparel except fur	42	40	59	89	45	54	37	56	44
182	Fur products	45	29	67	63	47	36	8	25	12
191	Tanning and dressing	50	40	85	38	59	40	7	-28	0.4
192	Footwear	51	51	81	62	55	51	2	-13	0
242	Other chemical products	36	21	65	81	53	52	9	17	15
251	Rubber products	18	21	66	29	22	22	7	2	6
252	Plastic products	16	23	39	53	19	29	11	19	14
281	Structural metal products	17	17	44	80	17	20	25	66	28
289	Other fabricated metal products not elsewhere classified	33	39	73	54	38	40	9	-16	6
319	Other electric equipment	1	16	2	8	1	14	87	62	81
333	Watches and clocks	5	11	0.3	96	2	23	8	44	21
341	Motor vehicles	–	–	–	–	–	–	–	–	–
342	Bodies, coach, and other parts	49	6	68	0	49	6	-23	–	-23
359	Transport not elsewhere classified	34	27	96	71	39	28	-0.4	-30	-3
361	Furniture	48	29	94	69	57	30	0.2	-32	-5
369	Manufacturing not elsewhere classified (jewellery, sports, and music)	27	32	95	79	58	41	11	-16	-4
	Subtotal	48	47	87	87	66	60	13	4	8

(*continued*)

Table 1 (Continued)

		Men		Women		Total		Growth rate (1994–2001)		
		1994–5	2000–1	1994–5	2000–1	1994–5	2000–1	Male	Female	Total
CAT II: import-penetrating industries										
202	Wood products	69	66	93	92	84	72	20	-7	7
210	Paper products	51	34	93	83	68	50	4	3	3
222	Publishing and printing	17	21	42	32	20	22	12	-4	9
231	Coke oven products	18	6	17	37	18	7	-7	-13	-8
232	Refined petroleum	39	31	77	0	50	31	-14	–	-24
241	Basic chemicals	4	3	28	5	5	3	-7	-4	-7
272	Non-ferrous metal	23	22	29	38	24	23	7	-7	6
291	General purpose machinery	8	11	7	17	8	11	35	54	35
292	Special purpose machinery	23	32	69	13	24	32	15	-21	13
300	Office accounting	4	0.4	0	3	3	1	-61	–	-56
311	Electric motor, generator, transmission, and distribution	46	28	44	1	46	28	26	-66	23
312	Generators	15	5	15	7	15	5	-12	5	-7
314	Accumulators, cells, and batteries	19	21	86	36	20	22	10	27	12
321	Electric values and tubes	20	7	45	6	23	7	-9	-2	-7
322	TV/radio transmitters	48	50	82	3	54	49	39	-51	33
323	TV/radio receivers	35	44	17	19	34	41	-1	23	-0.1
332	Optical	66	13	94	7	73	13	-30	-79	-37
351	Ships and boats	21	2	–	–	21	2	-8	–	-8
352	Railways and tramway	0	0.5	50	24	1	1	–	-26	4
353	Space craft and aircraft	0	0	–	–	0	0	–	–	–
	Subtotal	48	53	91	86	69	59	18	-7	7

(*continued*)

Table 1 (Continued)

		Men		Women		Total		Growth rate (1994–2001)		
		1994–5	*2000–1*	*1994–5*	*2000–1*	*1994–5*	*2000–1*	*Male*	*Female*	*Total*
CAT III: import penetrating to export oriented										
153	Grain mill production	45	50	88	77	61	55	18	-3	10
154	Other food	33	34	72	58	50	39	5	-18	-6
243	Man-made fibers	100	0			100	0	–	–	–
261	Glass and glass products	60	56	60	92	60	62	-2	11	1
269	Other non-metallic	45	38	62	32	54	36	9	-18	-2
271	Basic iron and steel	35	20	24	51	35	20	-4	21	-4
313	Insulated wire and cables	17	0	0	0	16	0	-88	–	-88
343	Parts and accessories	19	9	21	16	19	10	10	-4	8
	Subtotal	41	41	71	53	54	44	11	-12	2
CAT IV: export oriented to import penetrating										
152	Dairy products	71	77	96	98	85	83	22	-0.2	12
173	Knitted and crocheted	42	29	51	70	44	47	-2	21	9
201	Saw milling of wood	16	12	38	18	16	13	-4	-3	-4
293	Domestic appliances	25	9	20	7	24	9	-2	-24	-4
315	Electric lamps	27	26	8	36	23	27	10	21	11
331	Medical instruments	19	14	15	3	19	14	14	-13	12
	Subtotal	32	42	83	83	45	51	13	4	9
CAT V: no trade industries										
273	Casting metals	15	13	64	17	23	13	5	-51	-5
All	*Total*	46	46	83	81	62	56	13	-0.4	7

Note: [a]Production workers include family and hired workers.

Source: National Sample Survey Organisation (NSSO 1994a, 1994b, 1998a, 1998b, 2002a, 2002b, 2002c).

penetration actually registered an increase in the share by nearly 5 percentage points (Table 1). The opposite was true of the share of female home-based workers, with import penetration industries showing a decline and export-oriented industries retaining their high share at 87 percent.

While it is difficult to arrive at any conclusion from such aggregate data, we hazard an explanation. With the relaxation of India's trade barriers, it is likely that the export-oriented industries were able to upgrade their technologies and adopt a productivity-increasing strategy rather than a cost-cutting strategy of engaging home-based workers. The industries that faced import competition, however, marginally increased their share of male home-based workers perhaps in an effort to remain in the market.

The opposite strategy with regard to the share of women home-based workers among India's export-oriented industries can be explained by the fast expansion of two industry groups, garment and chemical industries, which engaged a large and increasing share of women workers. Among industries with import penetration, those with an increase in the share of male home-based workers were publishing and printing, general and special purpose machinery, and TV and radio equipment. With a large number of printing and publishing houses shifting their operation to India and major import competition in the machinery industries, these industries appeared to adopt the cost-cutting strategy of engaging a larger share of male home-based workers.

MICRO DETERMINANTS OF HOME-BASED WORK

The neoclassical models of participation in the labor market assume that the workers are able to choose the status of their employment given their individual and regional characteristics. These models put forward two reasons to explain the existence of home-based work. First, the fixed costs of working on-site such as travel costs, both time and financial, are greatly reduced by home-based work. Second, it is possible to engage in joint-production of income and household commodities, such as cooking, looking after children and other household chores with home-based work. Both these reasons lead to the conclusion that women will have a lower reservation wage for home-based work than for on-site work, which would be beneficial for the employer as production costs are reduced. This is the efficiency argument of the neoclassical model, as home-based work helps to reduce production costs, while it enables women the flexibility to integrate better their family and work lives. In this context, we predict whether women in India participate in home-based work due to different wage offers and joint production possibilities.

In this section, we present a very simple model of the participation in home-based work that consists of a set of variables to determine the causes for the rise in the reservation wage or to proxy for the fixed costs of working on-site, and to predict the wages of home-based work. The explanatory variables are exogenous factors that affect the supply of labor to all labor-market statuses, particularly home-based work. The empirical model employed here is the multinomial choice model with four choices open to the population in the 15–64 age group. The multinomial model involves one categorical dependent variable Y and a set of explanatory variables. The four choices are: to work as a home-based worker in the manufacturing sector, to work as a home-based worker in the non-manufacturing sector, to work outside the home, or to be outside the labor force. The dependent variable is the choice of undertaking home-based work or working outside the home as opposed to not working. The dependent variable takes the value 1 for undertaking home-based work in manufacturing, the value 2 for undertaking home-based work in other than manufacturing, the value 3 for working outside the home, and the value 0 for not working. Table 2 presents a list of variable names, definitions, and data sources.

Table 2 Variable names, definitions, and data sources

Variable name	*Definition*	*Data source*
Micro model		
Age	Age of the individual	Raw data from Employment Unemployment Survey CD, 2004–5, NSSO
Age squared	Square of age	
Illiterate	Dummy variable for an individual having reported being illiterate	
Literate	Dummy variable for an individual not having attended school but reporting being literate	
Primary school	Dummy variable for an individual having attended primary school	
Middle school	Dummy variable for an individual having attended middle school	
Secondary school	Dummy variable for an individual having attended secondary school	
Scheduled castes	Dummy variable for an individual belonging to a scheduled caste family	
Scheduled tribes	Dummy variable for an individual belonging to a scheduled tribe family	
Other backward castes	Dummy variable for an individual belonging to other backward caste family	
Muslim	Dummy variable for an individual belonging to a Muslim family	

(*continued*)

Table 2 (Continued)

Variable name	*Definition*	*Data source*
Christian	Dummy variable for an individual belonging to a Christian family	
Other religions	Dummy variable for an individual belonging to other religions	
Living in rural areas	Dummy variable for an individual living in rural area	
Aged 0–6 years	Number of children in the household aged 0–6 years	
Aged 7–15 years	Number of children in the household aged 7–15 years	
More than 65 years	Number of persons in the household above the age of 65 years	
Married	Status of being married	
Female	Female head of the household	
Medium-growth states	Dummy variable for medium-growth states	
Low-growth states	Dummy variable for low-growth states	
Macro model		
Gross value added	Growth of gross value added (in Rs.)	(NSSO 1994a, 1994b, 1998a, 1998b, 2002a, 2002b, 2002c)
Capital labor intensity	Growth of capital labor intensity (ratio of fixed capital to number of workers)	
Wage rate	Growth of wage earnings per worker in the unorganized sector	
Weighted applied tariff 1997	This is the import weighted average applied tariff rate applied on goods entering the country and is reported in percentage points. It takes into consideration the available data for preferential schemes.	Nicita and Olarreaga (2006) database
Non-tariff barrier (NTB) 1997	This is simple average of ad-valorem equivalent of core NTB from HS 6-digit level data. The NTB includes price-control measures, finance-control measures, and quantity-control measures.	
Share of value added in reserved industries 2001	Percentage of value added of the items that were reserved in 2001 at national industrial classification three-digit level	(NSSO 1994a, 1994b, 1998a, 1998b, 2002a, 2002b, 2002c)

Wage offer variables

The variables we use to predict the wage offers are age and square of age, dummy variables for levels of education, social groups, and residence in a rural area. Since we are using the same predictors to estimate the two wage offers, the effect of different wage offers on the labor supply decisions cannot be distinguished. The opposite effects are more or less assumed for the wage offers at home and outside the home. Age and the square of age are expected to test for non-linearity of the relationship. For the education variable we have constructed dummies for persons who are illiterate; are literate without formal schooling; have passed primary, middle, or secondary school; and have completed higher secondary school. Education above higher secondary was considered the reference category for the education variable. We expect illiterate persons and persons with lower levels of schooling to have lower wage offers of outside work and hence to be more likely to be engaged in home-based work. The proxy constructed for social groups were dummy variables representing scheduled castes (SC), scheduled tribes (ST), and other backward castes (OBC).[4] For religion, dummy variables were constructed for Muslim, Christian, and other religious groups. We expect the lower social groups, SC, ST, and OBC, which more often have lower educational status, to also have lower wage offers both at home and outside the home. With social restriction on their mobility, poor Muslim women were also expected to be more often in home-based work. For region, dummy variables were constructed for persons residing in rural areas, and urban areas were used as a reference category. The wage offer for persons residing in rural areas was expected to be lower for both home-based and non-home-based work compared to those residing in urban areas. Living in rural areas was expected to increase commuting cost for an on-site job; hence, a positive association with home-based work is expected.

Fixed cost variables

The set of variables we use to proxy for fixed costs for working on-site is having a child below 6 years of age, children between 7 and 15 years of age, and persons over 65 years of age in the household. We expected all these variables to be positively related to the fixed costs of working outside the home and therefore to increase the probability of undertaking home-based work. The household responsibilities of being married were also proxy measures of the value of women's household productivity while being engaged in market work at home, the joint-production function. These variables reflect women's potential demand for care-taking services at home, which they would provide if working at home. They can be understood to raise the chances of home-based work, as such work would imply a joint production of household and economic goods. Female members in a female-headed household were less likely to be home-based since the need for better incomes would override the positive impact of working at home in the joint-production function.

Macro variables

In the micro model it is difficult to construct a proxy variable for the macro scenario of growing opportunities for work. So, we constructed a simple dummy variable taking the level of growth of state domestic product into consideration. High-growth states are those growing at more than 6 percent, medium-growth states are those growing between 4.5 and 6 percent, and low growth states are those growing below 4.5 percent per annum during the 2000–5 period. We have taken the high-growth states as the reference category. The economic reforms are expected to have a greater positive impact on industries in the more developed and better-performing states. We expect that home-based work would not be high in states that are growing rapidly.

The hypothesis is that there is a likelihood that women would choose home-based work in manufacturing or other sectors if the wage offer for outside work is lower than the home-based work, if the fixed costs of working outside are high, or if they are not in economically better-performing states. The first two hypotheses are individual choices, while the third hypothesis is macro determined.

EMPIRICAL RESULTS OF MICRO MODEL

We estimate the multinomial model for male and female workers separately, with the entire set of explanatory variables representing the wage offers, fixed costs, and macro variables for the four work states. We use the individual-worker-level data of the NSSO Employment Unemployment Survey for both 1999–2000 and 2004–5, but we only present results for 2004–5. To find out whether the two work states, home-based and non-home-based, are statistically distinct or not, we conducted the chi-square test, which was statistically significant. This means that the two equations are statistically distinct, and we reject the hypothesis of equality. The equations were found to be quite robust based on the log likelihood ratios. Two descriptive measures of goodness of fit, Cox and Snell and Nagelkerke, show 12.6 and 27.3 percent of the variances for women, and 58.2 and 73.0 percent for men (Tables 3 and 4). The individual ß coefficients were tested using the Wald chi-square statistic. All variables except for having children in the 7–15 age group were statistically significant predictors for women choosing home-based work. In the case of men, all variables except for being in rural areas and having children in the 7–15 age group were statistically significant predictors for choosing home-based work. The Hausman-McFadden test for the independence of irrelevance alternatives (IIRA) shows that the estimated coefficients for both male and female micro models are independent of the omitted outcomes.

Table 3 Multinomial logit regression coefficients of participation in home-based work, women aged 16–64 years in India, 2004–5

	Home-based manufacturing vs. not in labor force		*Home-based non-manufacturing vs. not in labor force*		*Not home-based vs. not in labor force*	
	Coeff (β_1)	*SE of* β_1	*Coeff* (β_2)	*SE of* β_2	*Coeff* (β_2)	*SE of* β_2
Intercept	-7.173***	0.088	-7.871***	0.131	-5.4839***	0.0556
Age	0.190***	0.005	0.198***	0.007	0.2149***	0.0032
Age squared	-0.003***	0.000	-0.002***	0.0001	-0.0026***	0.0000
Level of education (above secondary school)						
Illiterate	1.549***	0.075	0.773***	0.053	0.623***	0.021
Literate	1.288***	0.083	0.279***	0.063	0.114***	0.025
Primary school	1.223***	0.079	0.474***	0.058	-0.028	0.024
Middle school	0.839***	0.078	0.090	0.059	-0.381***	0.024
Secondary school	0.294***	0.091	-0.049	0.066	-0.607***	0.028
Caste/religion (forward castes)						
Scheduled castes	0.481***	0.052	-0.225***	0.039	0.297***	0.018
Scheduled tribes	0.170***	0.074	-0.724***	0.055	0.942***	0.021
Other backward castes	0.744***	0.038	0.055**	0.029	0.320***	0.015
Muslim	0.488***	0.040	-1.074***	0.050	-0.823***	0.021
Christian	-0.312***	0.097	0.135**	0.065	0.235***	0.024
Other religions	-0.299***	0.096	0.765***	0.045	-0.210***	0.028
Living in rural areas	0.086***	0.034	1.256***	0.034	0.958***	0.014
Number of children aged 0–6 years	-0.097***	0.012	0.011	0.009	-0.025***	0.004
Aged 7–15 years	0.004	0.010	0.020***	0.007	-0.009***	0.004
Number of persons more than 65 years	-0.112***	0.027	-0.013	0.018	-0.023***	0.009
Married	-0.778***	0.043	0.158***	0.040	-0.170***	0.017
Household head (male)						
Female	0.312***	0.047	0.534***	0.041	0.745***	0.018
Regional characteristics (high growth states)						
Medium-growth states	0.251***	-0.195	0.030***	0.015	0.117***	0.013
Low-growth states	-0.499***	-0.443	0.032***	0.016	-0.696***	0.017
Number of observations				187,074		
Likelihood ratio chi-square (df)				40,614.37 (63)		
Pseudo R^2				0.1256		
Cox and Snell				0.273		
Nagelkerke				0.363		

Notes: Text in parenthesis is reference category. ***Denotes significance at the 1 percent level; **denotes significance at the 5 percent level; *denotes significance at the 10 percent level.

Tables 3 and 5 present hypotheses with regard to the probability of participation in home-based work. The coefficients indicate the direction and strength of the relationships between the independent and dependent

Table 4 Marginal effects of participation in home-based work, women aged 16–64 years in India, 2004–5

	Home-based manufacture		*Home-based non-manufacture*		*Not-home-based*		*Out of labor force*	
	Marginal effects		*Marginal effects*		*Marginal effects*		*Marginal effects*	
Predicted outcome	0.021		0.032		0.263		0.683	
Age	0.003***	(.0002)	0.004***	(.0002)	0.039***	(0.001)	-0.046***	(0.001)
Age squared	-.00004***	(0.000)	-.0001***	(0.000)	-.0005***	(0.000)	0.001***	(0.000)
Level of education (above secondary school)								
Illiterate	0.034**	(0.002)	0.018***	(0.002)	0.105	(0.004)	-0.157	(0.005)
Literate	0.043**	(0.004)	0.007***	(0.002)	0.007	(0.005)	-0.057	(0.006)
Primary school	0.040**	(0.004)	0.016***	(0.002)	-0.021**	(0.004)	-0.035**	(0.005)
Middle school	0.027**	(0.003)	0.005***	(0.002)	-0.075	(0.004)	0.043**	(0.005)
Secondary school	0.011***	(0.003)	0.003	(0.002)	-0.105	(0.004)	0.092	(0.005)
Caste/religion (forward castes/Hindus)								
Scheduled castes	0.009**	(0.001)	-0.009***	(0.001)	0.059**	(0.004)	-0.059	(0.004)
Scheduled tribes	-0.003**	(0.001)	-0.024**	(0.001)	0.212	(0.005)	-0.186	(0.005)
Other backward castes	0.015***	(0.001)	-0.002	(0.001)	0.058**	(0.003)	-0.071	(0.003)
Muslim	0.018***	(0.001)	-0.021**	(0.001)	-0.133	(0.003)	0.136	(0.003)
Christian	-0.007***	(0.001)	0.002	(0.002)	0.048	(0.005)	-0.044**	(0.005)
Other religions	-0.005***	(0.002)	0.037**	(0.003)	-0.046**	(0.005)	0.014***	(0.005)
Living in rural areas	-0.004***	(0.001)	0.028**	(0.001)	0.163**	(0.002)	-0.187	(0.002)
Number of children aged 0–6 years	-0.002***	(.0003)	0.001**	(0.0003)	-0.004**	(0.001)	0.006	(0.001)
Aged 7–15 years	0.0001	(.0002)	0.001***	(0.0002)	-0.002**	(0.001)	0.001	(0.001)
Number of persons more than 65 years	-0.002***	(0.001)	-0.0001	(0.001)	-0.004	(0.002)	0.006***	(0.002)
Married	-0.018**	(0.001)	0.007***	(0.001)	-0.029**	(0.003)	0.041**	(0.004)
Household head (male)								
Female	0.001	(0.001)	0.010***	(0.002)	0.152	(0.004)	-0.163	(0.004)
Regional characteristics (high growth states)								
Medium-growth states	0.005***	(0.001)	-0.007***	(0.001)	0.023**	(0.003)	-0.021**	(0.003)
Low-growth states	-0.006***	(0.001)	-0.008***	(0.001)	-0.117	(0.003)	0.131	(0.003)

Notes: Text in parentheses is reference category. Figures in parentheses are standard errors. ***Denotes significance at the 1 percent level; **denotes significance at the 5 percent level; *denotes significance at the 10 percent level.

Table 5 Multinomial logit regression coefficients of participation in home-based work, men aged 16–64 years in India, 2004–5

	Home-based manufacturing vs. not in labor force		*Home-based non-manufacturing vs. not in labor force*		*Not home-based vs. not in labor force*	
	Coeff (β_1)	*SE of* β_1	*Coeff* (β_2)	*SE of* β_2	*Coeff* (β_2)	*SE of* β_2
Intercept	-15.191***	0.175	-13.063***	0.142	-10.551***	0.082
Age	0.638***	0.010	0.609***	0.008	0.633***	0.005
Age squared	-0.008***	0.0001	-0.008***	0.0001	-0.008***	0.0001
Level of education (above secondary school)						
Illiterate	3.016***	0.069	1.722***	0.050	1.990***	0.032
Literate	3.437***	0.074	2.061***	0.058	2.263***	0.038
Primary school	3.124***	0.068	1.849***	0.049	1.971***	0.030
Middle school	2.005***	0.066	1.196***	0.042	1.206***	0.024
Secondary school	1.051***	0.074	0.489***	0.045	0.468***	0.024
Caste/religion (forward castes)						
Scheduled castes	0.333***	0.055	-0.383***	0.046	-0.029	0.026
Scheduled tribes	-0.274***	0.078	-0.718***	0.060	-0.050	0.031
Other backward castes	0.670***	0.041	0.067**	0.032	0.041**	0.019
Muslim	0.519***	0.046	-0.235***	0.045	-0.034	0.025
Christian	-0.831***	0.112	-0.288***	0.071	-0.242***	0.036
Other religions	-0.700***	0.099	-0.101	0.061	-0.152***	0.036
Living in rural areas	0.373***	0.037	0.446***	0.031	0.422***	0.018
Number of children aged 0–6 years	-0.026**	0.013	0.027***	0.011	0.026***	0.007
Aged 7–15 years	-0.009	0.011	-0.017**	0.009	-0.008	0.006
Number of persons more than 65 years	-0.173***	0.028	-0.073***	0.022	-0.101***	0.013
Married	1.471***	0.054	1.401***	0.045	1.460***	0.027
Household head (male)						
Female	-0.550***	0.088	-0.169***	0.062	-0.051	0.029
Regional characteristics (high growth states)						
Medium-growth states	0.335***	0.039	0.269***	0.033	0.209***	0.019
Low-growth states	0.415***	0.043	0.402***	0.036	0.108***	0.022
Number of observations				192,125		
Likelihood ratio chi-square (df)				81,384.05		
Pseudo R^2				0.2836		
Cox and Snell				0.582		
Nagelkerke				0.703		

Notes: Text in parentheses is reference category. ***Denotes significance at the 1 percent level; **denotes significance at the 5 percent level; *denotes significance at the 10 percent level.

variables. The marginal effect reports the effect of a unit change in a variable on the probability of work participation holding all other variables constant at their mean values. (It is the derivative or the slope of the prediction function.) The odds ratio is defined as the ratio of the odds of an event occurring in one group to the odds of it occurring in another group. In this paper, we present the marginal effect of variable on the probability of selecting each labor market status in Tables 4 and 6.

Marginal Effects of Wage offer variables

For women in India, we predicted a positive impact on participation in home-based work on all the variables that could have a positive impact on the wage offer for that work status, such as age, illiterate and lower levels of education, lower social status, and rural residence. Rising at first and declining later, age was found to have a non-linear relationship with the probability of labor-force participation in both statuses of work. The dummy variables for education at all levels showed a positive impact on the participation of women in home-based work but a negative effect on non-home-based work at higher levels of education, perhaps due to the income effect. These effects declined marginally in 2004–5 compared to 1999–2000. Women belonging to lower castes SC, ST, and OBC, and the Muslim community had a higher positive impact on participation in home-based manufacturing compared with other work. Women in rural areas had very low participation in home-based work compared with not home-based (Table 3).

The marginal effects for participating in home-based manufacturing work for illiterate women was 3.3 and for just literate 4.3 percent (Table 4). The marginal effect of being in such employment decreases consistently thereafter with each higher level of education, being only 1 percent for women with secondary school education. The marginal effect of women working in home-based, non-manufacturing work is lower than in manufacturing but also declines systematically with higher levels of education. The marginal effect of women working outside the home is not statistically significant with level of education. The well-known effects of income and social prestige are the declining participation of women in home-based work with increasing levels of education and not enough statistically significant impact on work outside the home. The better-educated women also belong to higher-income households, and social norms tend to reduce their participation outside the home.

The marginal effects of SC, ST, and OBC women participating in home-based manufacturing work was 1 and 1.5 percent respectively, while it was nearly 6 percent in work outside the home compared with forward castes (Table 4). These women coming from lower social, and perhaps economic, households have fewer restrictions on their participation in work outside their homes. The marginal effect of Muslim women in home-based manufacturing work was about 2 percent and had no statistically significant effect on participation in work outside the home. Due to social restrictions on their mobility outside the home, Muslim women tend to find such work

Table 6 Marginal effects of participation in home-based work, men aged 16–64 years in India, 2004–5

	Home-based manufacturing		*Home-based non-manufacture*		*Not home-based*		*Out of labor force*	
	Marginal effects		*Marginal effects*		*Marginal effects*		*Marginal effects*	
Predicted Outcome	0.023		0.046		0.874		0.057	
Age	0.001***	(0.0002)	.0006***	(0.0003)	0.032**	(.0005)	-0.034**	(0.0004)
Age squared	-.00001***	(0.000)	-.0001***	(0.000)	-0.0004	(0.000)	0.0004***	(0.000)
Level of education (above secondary school)								
Illiterate	0.036**	(0.003)	-0.009***	(0.002)	0.042**	(0.003)	-0.069**	(0.001)
Literate	0.047**	(0.004)	-0.007***	(0.002)	0.024**	(0.004)	-0.063**	(0.001)
Primary school	0.044**	(0.003)	-0.004***	(0.002)	0.024**	(0.003)	-0.064**	(0.001)
Middle school	0.025**	(0.002)	0.001	(0.002)	0.025**	(0.003)	-0.050**	(0.001)
Secondary school	0.0170***	(0.002)	0.001	(0.002)	0.004	(0.003)	-0.023**	(0.001)
Caste/religion (forward castes/Hindus)								
Scheduled castes	0.010***	(0.001)	-0.014**	(0.001)	0.003	(0.002)	0.002	(0.001)
Scheduled tribes	-0.004***	(0.001)	-0.023**	(0.001)	0.023**	(0.003)	0.004***	(0.002)
Other backward castes	0.016***	(0.001)	0.0005	(0.001)	-0.013**	(0.002)	-0.003***	(0.001)
Muslim	0.016***	(0.001)	-0.009**	(0.001)	-0.008***	(0.002)	0.001	(0.001)
Christian	-0.011***	(0.001)	-0.002	(0.003)	-0.002	(0.004)	0.015***	(0.002)
Other religions	-0.010***	(0.001)	0.002	(0.002)	-0.001	(0.003)	0.009***	(0.002)
Living in rural areas	-0.0005	(0.001)	0.002**	(0.001)	0.022**	(0.002)	-0.024**	(0.001)
Number of children aged 0–6 years	-0.001***	(0.0003)	0.0001	(0.0004)	0.002**	(0.001)	-0.001***	(0.0004)
Aged 7–15 years	-0.00002	(0.0002)	-0.0004	(0.0003)	-.00002	(.0005)	0.0004	(0.0003)
Number of persons more than 65 years	-0.002***	(0.001)	0.001	(0.001)	-0.005**	(0.001)	0.005**	(0.001)
Married	0.003***	(0.001)	0.002	(0.002)	0.0943	(0.003)	-0.099	(0.002)
Household head (male)								
Female	-0.009***	(0.001)	-0.005**	(0.002)	0.010***	(0.003)	0.004**	(0.002)
Regional characteristics (high growth states)								
Medium-growth states	0.003***	(0.001)	0.003**	(0.001)	0.005***	(0.002)	-0.011***	(0.001)
Low-growth states	0.007***	(0.001)	0.014	(0.002)	-0.014**	(0.002)	-0.007***	(0.001)

Note: Text in parentheses is reference category. Figures in parentheses are standard errors. ***Denotes significance at the 1 percent level; **denotes significance at the 5 percent level; *denotes significance at the 10 percent level.

through social networks. Micro studies also show that due to social restrictions home-based work provided an important avenue of work for Muslim women and a means for them to improve their status within the family (Zarina Bhatty 1987).

Women living in India's rural areas had a negative marginal effect of participation in home-based manufacturing work. The marginal effect of participating in non-home-based work was 16 percent, largely because women in rural areas undertake economic activities either on their own farms or others' farms (Table 4).

There was a positive and increasing impact of men participating in home-based manufacturing work at all levels of education in 2004–5 compared with 1999–2000. The effects were much higher for men than women in both years (Table 5). There was also a positive impact of men participating in home-based manufacturing among the lower caste groups (SC, ST, and OBC) and those belonging to the Muslim community.

The marginal effect of participating in home-based manufacturing work for illiterate men was 3.6 percent, and it increased to 4.7 percent with just literacy before declining with higher levels of education (Table 6). The marginal effect of men participating in home-based manufacturing was higher than women in all education groups except middle school. Further, the marginal effect of men participating in home-based work in India's non-manufacturing sectors was negative for men in the lower educational groups. The marginal effect of men participating in non-home-based work was much higher than that of women, while it was strongly negative for being outside the labor force at all levels of education, which probably simply reflects the social milieu.

The marginal effect of men participating in home-based manufacturing among India's lower caste groups was similar to that of women participating in home-manufacture, but much lower than women participating in work outside the home. This is difficult to explain, except to say that it is likely that the male participation in home-based work is mainly from these lower caste groups rather than the forward castes, who probably have better options. The marginal effects of ST participating in home-based manufacturing work was negative, indicating that such work has not yet penetrated into tribal areas (Table 6).

The marginal effect for Muslim men participating in home-based manufacturing work was 1.6 percent compared with Hindu men. The marginal effect of participating in non-home-based work for Muslim men was negative. The participation of Muslims in home-based work could be a reflection of the high proportion of self-employment among them and the traditional industries they are engaged in (Government of India [GOI] 2006). Christians and other religious groups did not participate in home-based manufacturing work (Table 6). This in some sense indicates that better education does provide access to better opportunities to work outside the home even if certain jobs are rationed for workers belonging to certain religious groups. The marginal effect for men participating in home-based manufacturing work in rural areas was positive because of the predominance of agricultural activity undertaken outside the homes in India's rural areas (Table 6).

Marginal Effects of Fixed cost variables

All the variables related to household responsibilities that raised the fixed costs of working on site were expected to have a positive effect on working at home. These variables were the household composition in terms of children and old people. The results showed that having children below the age of 6 and elderly persons reduced the participation of women in home-based manufacturing work or made them withdraw from the labor market (Table 3). The participation of women who had children in the 7–15 age group and were married in home-based manufacturing was positive (Table 3). Women in female-headed households participated in home-based and non-home-based work as hypothesized.

The marginal effect of women with children in the 0–6 age group, women with elderly persons in the household, and married women on participating in home-based-work was negative. This could be due to their added responsibility of care for children and elderly, which would not allow them much time to engage in productive work. Having children between 7 and 15 years old marginally increased the probability of their participation in home-based manufacturing work as expected. It is possible that women begin home-based work after the children reach school-going age or are able to care for their younger siblings. The marginal effect of being married (3 percent), and having children between 0 and 15 years old (less than 1 percent) was negative for participation in work outside the home. This supports the hypothesis that as the fixed costs increase, women either participate in home-based work or withdraw from the labor market, meaning they do not participate in home-based or non-home-based work (Table 4).

The marginal effect of women belonging to households with a female head engaged in home-based non-manufacturing activity was 1 percent (Table 4). This probably reflects the need for female heads of household, who are the main earners of the household, to earn more income, as home-based manufacturing among women is one of the lowest-paid activities (Unni and Rani 2005).

Marginal Effects of Macro variables

We did not expect the high-growth states to follow a cost-cutting strategy involving engaging home-based workers, since the opportunities for growth in these states would be many-fold. The results showed that for women, there was a positive impact of home-based manufacturing and non-manufacturing in medium-growth states. In low-growth states, the impact was negative in home-based manufacturing (Table 3). The marginal effect of being engaged in home-based manufacturing work for women was 0.5 percent in medium-growth states while it was negative in low-growth states. The marginal effect was 2.3 percent for non-home-based work in the medium-growth states (Table 4).

For men, participation in all kinds of work, home-based or non-home-based, was positive in both medium- and low-growth states (Table 5). The marginal effects were also positive though below 1 percent in all types of work except non-home-based work in low-growth states. This clearly indicated that high growth and predominantly developed regions meant more opportunities for non-home-based work for men (Table 6). High-growth states did not follow cost-cutting strategies as such, but work opportunities increased for both men and women. In some sense, these results do show a shift of work from factory to home for men in India's medium- and less-developed states.

The micro model thus provides evidence for India's increase in participation of men in the home-based manufacturing sector compared with women over the five-year period, as was observed earlier. It appeared that the probability of such participation of men was higher among the illiterate and poorly educated and in the manufacturing sector, rather than in the services sector. The probability of participation of the illiterate and women with low levels of education in home-based work was found in both the manufacturing and the non-manufacturing sectors.

It is difficult to explain this partial reversal of India's gender roles. Why would men opt for home-based work in manufacturing when it is really the women who are constrained in mobility by the social norms? We have to move out of the micro explanation of these choices and to a macro view to understand this phenomenon. As we argued earlier, home-based work is not an individual choice alone but is instead dictated by the exigencies of the market where, in the face of competition, certain industry groups are engaging in cost-cutting strategies. We observed that it was mainly the import-competing manufacturing industries that showed an increase in the share of male home-based work. Within this group, all machine-related industries – including those engaged in the manufacture of special and general machinery (increased share and growth) and the manufacture of electrical motors and television/radio transmitters (increased growth) – showed an increase in male home-based work (Table 1).

Researchers often argue that men's jobs are associated with working with certain tools and machines. The argument begins with supposed biological differences between men and women – such as women do not have the strength to operate some machines or a woman's monthly cycle is polluting and therefore she cannot work during that time – rather than any proven ability or inability (Naila Kabeer 1999). When the biological differences are not translated into the social organization of production and labor, then the discourse shifts to "culture" based on social norms, and these are used to justify certain social sanctions. Most of India's import-competing industries noted above that engaged in the cost-cutting strategy of contracting to home-based work were manufacturing machinery. It is likely that these activities were socially and culturally more acceptable as men's work, and therefore when the opportunity arose or when the industry outsourced, they preferred male workers even when the activity was home-based.

MACRO DETERMINANTS OF SHIFT TO HOME-BASED WORK

The micro determinants of home-based work correspond to the choice of the individual, though we have tried to show (by introducing region dummies) that this choice is mediated through what is occurring in the economy at the macro level. Our argument is that home-based work in India does not emerge simply because women prefer to work at home, but because the economics of production necessitates forms of organization that are cheaper for firms to remain competitive in the new fast changing economy. In fact, as we noted earlier, there is an increase in men engaged in home-based work as well.

The Western literature presented in the conceptual framework mainly addresses the issue of home-based work as being synonymous with "home work" or subcontracted work at home. However, we have emphasized the need to broaden the definition of home-based work to include own-account work in the context of India and other developing countries. In the macro model, we consider home-based work as an organization of production and include hired and family workers participating in enterprises located at home within the definition of home-based work. The logic of such home-based work is not simply determined by the microeconomics of the worker's choice, though to a large extent women in India, dominated by the patriarchal systems, appear overwhelmingly to work at home. The micro model fits well.

India's economic reforms of the 1990s had very specific trade and industry policies that led to the growth of manufacturing industries. Given the limitations of addressing the determinants of home-based work from a purely micro perspective, we present below a simple macro model to analyze to what extent the economic policies led to a shift toward home-based work. The dependent variable in our regression equation is measured as a percentage point increase in the share of home-based workers in the unorganized manufacturing sector during the recent rapid phase of economic reforms, 1994–5 to 2000–1. The dependent variable is constructed separately for total, male, and female home-based workers. As discussed above, workers include family and hired production workers as well as owner proprietors and managerial and supervisory staff. The analysis is undertaken for a cross-section of fifty-four industry groups at the three-digit industry level. Independent variables are constructed to proxy for the growth of value added and capital intensity of the industry, and the growth of wage rates, trade policy, and industrial policy.

Growth of value added

The growth of the industry is measured by the annual percentage growth of value added computed for each three-digit industry group. The growth of value added in an industry could lead to an increase in total employment, but the rate of growth of home-based work could be faster or slower than that of all workers. If the industry followed a cost-cutting strategy to employ home-based workers, the change in the share of home-based workers would be positively related to the growth of value added. A negative relationship would then mean that the industries do not follow cost-cutting strategies involving the use of home-based workers but rather follow a technology strategy to enhance productivity per worker.

Capital intensity

The growth of employment in India's industry and consequently home-based workers is mediated by whether the growth of the industry is labor intensive or capital intensive. We computed the growth of the ratio of fixed capital to number of workers to proxy for growth of capital intensity in an industry group. We hypothesize that a more capital-intensive industry would not increase its share of home-based workers, and hence, we expect a negative relationship between growing capital-intensity and a change in the share of home-based work.

Growth of wage rates

We have computed the growth of wage earnings per worker in the unorganized manufacturing sector. We hypothesize a positive relationship between the rise in wage earnings per worker and a change in the share of home-based work, through the substitution of the cheaper source of labor for more expensive labor.

Trade policy

A number of changes occurred in trade policy in recent years, mainly reducing the tariff barriers and also some NTBs. Ideally, we should depict trade policy through an index of reduction in such barriers. However, it is difficult to construct a variable for a reduction in trade barriers. We have obtained proxies for the tariff barrier and NTB from the World Bank data set (Alessandro Nicita and Marcelo Olarreaga 2006). The tariff barrier for 1997 is the import-weighted, average tariff rate applied on goods entering the country, which takes into consideration the available (not complete) data for preferential schemes. In constructing the average, the applied average tariff takes the tariff rates for each partner that exports to the market country. The NTB represents the simple average of ad-valorem equivalent of core NTB for HS 6-digit-level data in 1997. The core NTB includes price-control measures, finance-control measures, and quantity-control measures.

The tariff barrier is a measure of the additional cost of importing commodities or the protection given to the industry that manufactures those products. If an industry group has a higher tariff barrier, then there are greater chances of growth of the industry. A higher tariff barrier could imply lower home-based work since the industry would be more protected from foreign competition. A higher NTB would also mean more protection for the industry and hence less need for the cost-cutting strategy of home-based work. Both trade variables can be hypothesized to have a negative effect on growth in the share of home-based work.

Industry policy

The industry policy reforms were largely geared toward relaxing controls on the manufacturing industry through licenses and the reservation of products for public-sector or small-scale industry. The policy reforms included the de-licensing of certain industries, removal of restrictions on private sector entry into specified industries, and changes in the list of industries reserved for the small-scale sector. It is difficult to construct one indicator for all these policies. We have constructed a proxy variable by taking into consideration the value added of the industries in the manufacturing sector that the government added to the reserve list in 2001.[5] We created the industry policy variable by identifying the industries that were reserved in 2001 at five-digit level. Then, we calculated the percentage share of value added in these industries at the three-digit level (for the fifty-four industry groups used in the macro model). Reservation in an industry group implies more protection to small-scale industries, and since we assume that these industries are less likely to subcontract to home-based workers, we expect a negative relationship.

EMPIRICAL RESULTS OF MACRO MODEL

We have estimated simple OLS regression equations for the change in the share of home-based workers in India among all workers separately for male, female, and total home-based workers.

Change in the share of home-based work among production workers

The regression equations for the determinants of a shift toward (or away from) home-based work in India are statistically significant for total and male workers but not for female workers (Table 7). The variables included explain about 30 percent of the variance for total home-based workers and 24 percent for male home-based workers. The significance of the independent variables was assessed based on the standard errors. As we discussed earlier, the micro model appears to explain the choice of home-based work for women, while the macro model is not statistically significant. Further, the historically high level of women home-based workers indicates that India's economic reforms did not really affect their size or their share. The macro model estimated here further confirms that the macro indicators considered, including the trade and industry policy variables, do not have a statistically significant impact on women home-based workers.

Growth in value added was not a statistically significant determinant of the shift toward home-based work in India's manufacturing industry. However, the growth in capital intensity had a significant negative impact on male and total home-based workers. A 1 percent growth of capital intensity resulted in a 7.6 and 6.6 percentage point decline in the share of total and male home-based work. This implies that the industries following a technology-intensive strategy relied on increasing productivity per worker

Table 7 Determinants of change in share of home-based work among all workers, 1994–5 to 2000–1

	Total		*Male*		*Female*	
	Coefficients	*SE*[a]	*Coefficients*	*SE*	*Coefficients*	*SE*
Intercept	-9.316**	4.662	-8.839*	4.698	-7.890	10.000
Growth of gross value added	-0.204	0.145	-0.153	0.146	-0.385	0.312
Growth of capital labor intensity	-0.761***	0.155	-0.661***	0.156	-0.556*	0.332
Growth of wage rate	1.479***	0.484	1.406***	0.488	0.810	1.038
Weighted applied tariff 1997	0.037	0.082	0.046	0.083	0.078	0.176
Non-tariff barrier 1997	-5.714	17.999	5.943	18.139	-13.376	38.609
Share of value added in reserved industries 2001	0.008	0.059	-0.042	0.059	0.015	0.127
Adjusted R square	0.308		0.243		-0.034	
F statistic	4.939		3.839		0.712	
Number of observations	54					

Notes: ***Denotes significance at the 1 percent level; **denotes significance at the 5 percent level; *denotes significance at the 10 percent level. [a]Figures in SE columns denote standard error.

and not on the cost-cutting strategy of outsourcing work to home-based workers. Further, as hypothesized, an increase in the cost of hired labor in the industry had a positive and statistically significant impact on the shift toward male and total home-based workers. A 1 percent increase in the growth of real wage rates led to a more than 14 percentage point statistically significant increase in the share of total and male home-based work. That is, the shift to home-based work was used as a cost-cutting strategy, given the capital intensity and growth of the industry in certain industry groups. The industry groups faced with a rise in the wage earnings of hired labor were substituting cheap home-based workers for expensive labor.

The proxies for trade and industry policy were not statistically significant determinants of total and male home-based workers. The industries with no protection through tariff and NTBs or the reservation policy had to maintain the quality of the products and also perhaps were more technology intensive and therefore did not resort to subcontracting to home-based workers.

As noted earlier, female home-based workers in India were not statistically significantly affected by the macro determinants, including trade and industry policy variables. It is therefore an economically statistically significant result that total and male home-based workers were more likely to be affected by the macro determinants resulting from economic reforms, while the already high proportion of female home-based work remained more or less unaffected. Even if our proxies for trade and industry policies were not statistically significant, these policies' indirect impact on growth of capital intensity may have led to the significant negative impact on total and male home-based work.

CONCLUSION

The economic reforms in India have led to an expansion of markets and the entry of globally competitive conditions. The easing of licenses and trade liberalization brought in better technology and increased capacities for production. We see the growth of home-based work within this context of changing macroeconomic policies. The organized sector output and employment grew during the late 1980s and early 1990s and tapered down in the late 1990s, largely due to recession. A number of policies that apparently did not favor small-scale industries, such as a reduction in tariff barriers and de-reservation, were introduced during the late 1990s. These policies actually enabled the inflow of technology and brought about a growth of small-scale enterprises in the informal sector, which resulted in growth of output and employment in the unorganized manufacturing sector.

India's trade policy reforms had an impact on industries, and they could be divided into export-promoting and import-penetrating industries. Overall, India's export-promoting industries showed a decline in the share of home-based work, and the absolute number of home-based workers grew due to the overall growth in the sector. The reforms had a direct, positive impact on the apparel and chemical-products industries, which had a large share of women in general and home-based work in particular. An increase in male home-based work was observed in import-penetrating industries. Industries engaged in the manufacture of general purpose machinery, special purpose machinery, and TV and radio equipment perhaps faced severe competition from imports and engaged in the cost-cutting strategy of increasing the share of male home-based workers.

At the micro level, the decision to participate in home-based activities was determined by illiteracy and low levels of education. It was also largely influenced by the households' socioeconomic situation, such as belonging to lower castes and Muslim households. The fixed cost effects showed that the participation of women in home-based work was higher among women with children of school-going age (7–15 years), as compared with women who had younger children and were more likely to remain outside the labor force. Married women's participation in home-based work was lower perhaps due to the income effect, but women belonging to female-headed households had higher participation rates. The micro determinants of home-based work better explains women's participation in such work. Also, women's home-based work was of a very high proportion over a long period and was less affected by the macro variables capturing economic-reform measures.

A simple macro model to analyze the determinants of the increase in the share of home-based work in India showed a positive impact of growth in wage rates, implying that the shift to this form of production organization could be a cost-cutting strategy. Increase in capital intensity had the opposite or a negative impact on home-based work. The proxies for trade and industry policies did not affect total or male home-based work.

The gender differential in the determinants of home-based work in India is brought out clearly in this paper. The historically higher share of women in home-based work, which did not show much increase in the period of reforms, implies that female participation in such work was more likely to be determined by the cultural milieu than by the recent liberalization process. Further, while the micro model of social determinants appear to fit the female home-based work equation, coefficient estimates were statistically insignificant for female home-based workers in the macro model. For male home-based work the coefficient estimates of most of the determinants of such work were statistically significant in the macro model, which leads us to conclude that the economic reforms had an impact on this form of production organization among men.

The importance of the macro determinants of home-based work among men explains the paradox of why only men's home-based work increased when we expected women's home-based work to increase, given that women were constrained by immobility. The conclusion is that while women may individually choose home-based work in India due to social compulsions, men did not choose but were chosen for home-based work by the larger economic exigencies played out at the macro and industry levels. The increase in male home-based work with rising economic growth could also be a reason for increasing income inequalities, as the incomes earned through such activities are substantially lower than in the new on-site jobs that are created in the highly productive services. This lower wage of home-based work would have an impact on household income and also on women, who would have to participate in the labor market due to low household incomes.

ACKNOWLEDGMENTS

This is part of a larger study that we undertook, and we would like to thank the Human Development Resource Center, United Nations Development Programme, New Delhi for funding and support. We would specially like to thank Professor Seeta Prabhu for her insightful comments on the earlier draft. We would also like to thank Ms. Kalyani Menon-Sen, Ms. Meenakshi Kathel, Ms. Alka, and many others at the HDRC-UNDP for their constant support. We particularly benefited from the discussions at the workshops and would like to thank all the participants. Ms. Arti Oza provided painstaking statistical assistance and catered to our continuous demands of tabulations and re-tabulations. We gratefully acknowledge the inputs and services of all these organizations and individuals. We are, however, responsible for any errors in the analysis and interpretation.

NOTES

1 The names of the authors are in alphabetical order.

2 The relationships are argued to be exploitative as the wages paid are very low, sometimes half that of a regular wage, and they do not receive social security or any other benefits, such as sick leave, paid leave, medical insurance, old age pension, and provident funds. These workers are not well organized, which weakens their bargaining power. The wages paid to these workers are piece-rated and not on fixed time, which allows for further exploitation compared to those hired on a regular or casual basis.

3 There is a small probability that since the codes devised in the two surveys were different, the data were not perfectly comparable. However, given the lack of any other source of data on home-based workers for more than one time point, we analyze these estimates with caution.

4 Scheduled Castes (SC) are the former untouchable castes. They are economically the weakest and historically subjected to discrimination and deprivation. In addition to the caste system, India has been home to several tribes that have been similarly designated (Scheduled Tribes). The Other Backward Castes (OBC) are the erstwhile Sudra jatis, who were not targets of untouchability, but their social and economic position was close to that of dalits (Untouchable Castes). OBC are supposed to capture the jatis that have been described in the constitution as "socially and educationally backward classes" (Ashwini Deshpande 2005: 3). The use of the word "backward" is a hangover from the British period, when terms such as "backward classes" or "depressed classes" were used. There has been considerable debate, even during the British period, whether reservations (preferential treatment) should be extended to the OBC as they have not suffered the stigma of untouchability. In a number of states in British India, education benefits were given to OBC and in some of the major states, such as Madras, Bombay, and Mysore, preferential treatment was given to OBC that included reservations and welfare schemes (Ashwini Deshpande 2005: 11). The preferential treatment during the British period was extended to low castes as well as classes, indicating their low social and economic situation. Since independence, caste groups have been clustered in broad categories and identified in a government schedule as beneficiaries of affirmative action – Scheduled Castes (SC), Scheduled Tribes (ST), Other Backward Castes (OBC), and Others (Forward Castes) (Ashwini Deshpande 2007: 739).

5 The products under the "reserved list" are for the exclusive production of small-scale industries, and they get complete support for raw materials and subsidized finance from the government.

REFERENCES

Banerjee, Nirmala. 1988. "Small and Large Units: Symbiosis or Matsyanyaya?" in Kul Bhushan Suri, ed. *Small Scale Enterprises in Industrial Development*, pp. 184–202. New Delhi: Sage Publications.

Basant, Rakesh and Pankaj Chandra. 2002. "Building Technological Capabilities in a Liberalising Developing Economy: Firm Strategies and Public Policies." *Economics of Innovation and New Technology* 11(4/5): 399–421.

Baud, Isa. 1987. "Industrial Subcontracting: The Effects of the Putting Out System on Poor Working Women in India," in Andrea M. Singh and Anita Keller-Viitanen, eds. *Invisible Hands: Women in Home Based Production*, pp. 69–91. New Delhi: Sage Publications.

Bhatty, Zarina. 1987. "Economic Contribution of Women to the Household Budget: A Case Study of the Beedi Industry," in Andrea M. Singh and Anita Keller-Viitanen, eds. *Invisible Hands: Women in Home Based Production*, pp. 35–50. New Delhi: Sage Publications.

Bose, Amitav N. 1978. *Calcutta and Rural Bengal: Small Sector Symbiosis.* Calcutta: Minerva Associates.

Carr, Marilyn, Martha Alter Chen, and Jane Tate. 2000. "Globalization and Home-Based Workers." *Feminist Economics* 6(3): 123–42.

Chen, Martha A., Jennefer Sebstad, and Lesley O'Connell. 1999. "Counting the Invisible Workforce: The Case of Homebased Workers." *World Development* 27(3): 603–10.

Coase, Ronald H. 1937. "The Nature of the Firm." *Economica* 4(16): 386–405.

Custers, Peter. 1997. *Capital Accumulation and Women's Labour in Asian Economies.* New Delhi: Vistaar Publications.

Das, Deb Kusum. 2003. "Manufacturing Productivity under Varying Trade Regimes: India in the 1980s and 1990s." Working Paper 107, Indian Council for Research on International Economic Relations, New Delhi.

Deshpande, Ashwini. 2005. "Affirmative Action in India and the United States." Background paper for *World Development Report 2006. Equity and Development.*

———. 2007. "Overlapping Identities under Liberalization: Gender and Caste in India." *Economic Development and Cultural Change* 55(4): 735–60.

Edwards, Linda N. and Elizabeth Field-Hendrey. 2002. "Home-Based Work and Women's Labor Force Decisions." *Journal of Labor Economics* 20(1): 170–200.

Government of India (GOI). 2006. *Social, Economic and Educational Status of the Muslim Community of India.* New Delhi: Prime Minister's High Level Committee (Sachar Committee), Government of India.

———. 2008. *Report of the Independent Group on Home-based Workers.* New Delhi: Ministry of Statistics and Programme Implementation, Government of India. http://www.unifem.org.in/PDF/HBWReport.pdf (accessed September 2008).

Harriss, John. 1982. "Character of an Urban Economy: 'Small Scale' Production and Labour Markets in Coimbatore." *Economic and Political Weekly* 17(24): 993–1002.

International Labour Organization. 1996. "Home Work Convention." No. 177. http://www.ilo.org/ilolex/cgi-lex/convde.pl?c177 (accessed April 2007).

Kabeer, Naila. 1999. "From Feminist Insights to an Analytical Framework: An Institutional Perspective on Gender Inequality," in Naila Kabeer and Ramya Subrahmanian, eds. *Institutions, Relations and Outcomes: A Framework and Case Studies for Gender-Aware Planning,* pp. 3–48. New Delhi: Kali for Women.

Kantor, Paula. 2000. "Gender Differentials in Microenterprise Success for Homebased Garment Makers in Ahmedabad, India." PhD diss., University of North Carolina at Chapel Hill.

Marx, Karl. 1977. *Capital: A Critique of Political Economy,* Vol. 1. Moscow: Progress Publishers.

Mies, Maria. 1982. *The Lacemakers of Narsapur: Indian Housewives Produce for the World Market.* London: Zed Books.

Morris, Sebastian and Rakesh Basant. 2004. "Role of Small Scale Industries in the Age of Liberalisation." Paper presented at the first Technical Workshop of the ADB Policy Networking Project, New Delhi.

National Sample Survey Organisation. 1994a. *Tables with Notes on the Survey of Unorganized Manufacture: Non-Directory Establishments and Own Account Enterprises, Part-I (All India).* NSS 45 Round (July 1989–June 1990), No. 396/1. New Delhi: Department of Statistics, Government of India.

———. 1994b. *Tables with Notes on the Survey of Unorganized Manufacture: Non-Directory Establishments and Own Account Enterprises, Part-II (States),* vols. 1 and 2. NSS 45 Round (July 1989–June 1990), No. 396/2. New Delhi: Department of Statistics, Government of India.

———. 1998a. *Unorganized Manufacturing Sector in India: Its Size, Employment and Some Key Estimates, Directory Establishments and Own Account Enterprises.* NSS 51 Round (July 1994–June 1995), No. 433 (51/2.2/1). New Delhi: Department of Statistics, Government of India.

———. 1998b. *Unorganized Manufacturing Sector in India: Salient Features.* NSS 51 Round (July 1994–June 1995), No.434 (51/2.2/2). New Delhi: Department of Statistics, Government of India.

———. 2001a. *Employment and Unemployment Situation in India 1999–2000 (Part-I).* NSS 55 Round (July 1999–June 2000), No.458 (55/10/2). New Delhi: Ministry of Statistics and Programme Implementation, Government of India. (Raw data from this survey was used.)

———. 2001b. *Employment and Unemployment Situation in India 1999–2000 (Part-II).* NSS 55 Round (July 1999–June 2000), No. 458 (55/10/2). New Delhi: Ministry of Statistics and Programme Implementation, Government of India. (Raw data from this survey was used.)

———. 2002a. *Unorganised Manufacturing Sector in India: Characteristics of Enterprises.* NSS 56 Round (July 2000–June 2001), No. 478 (56/2.2/2). New Delhi: Ministry of Statistics and Programme Implementation, Government of India.

———. 2002b. *Unorganised Manufacturing Sector in India: Employment, Assets and Borrowings.* NSS 56 Round (July 2000–June 2001), No. 479 (56/2.2/3). New Delhi: Ministry of Statistics and Programme Implementation, Government of India.

———. 2002c. *Unorganised Manufacturing Sector in India: Input, Output and Value Added.* NSS 56 Round (July 2000–June 2001), No. 480 (56/2.2/4). New Delhi: Ministry of Statistics and Programme Implementation, Government of India.

———. 2006a. *Employment and Unemployment Situation in India 2004–5(Part-I).* NSS 55 Round (July 2004–June 2005), No. 515(61/10/1). New Delhi: Ministry of Statistics and Programme Implementation, Government of India. (Raw data from this survey was used)

———. 2006b. *Employment and Unemployment Situation in India 2004–5(Part-II).* NSS 55 Round (July 2004–June 2005), No. 515 (61/10/1). New Delhi: Ministry of Statistics and Programme Implementation, Government of India. (Raw data from this survey was used)

Nicita, Alessandro and Marcelo Olarreaga. 2006. "Trade, Production and Protection 1976–2004." World Bank. http://econ.worldbank.org/WBSITE/EXTERNAL/EXTDEC/EXTRESEARCH/0,,contentMDK:21085384~pagePK:64214825~piPK:64214943~theSitePK:469382,00.html (accessed June 2008).

Prügl, Elisabeth and Irene Tinker. 1997. "Microentrepreneurs and Homeworkers: Convergent Categories." *World Development* 25(9): 1471–82.

Rani, Uma and Jeemol Unni. 2004. "Unorganised and Organised Manufacturing in India: Potential for Employment Generating Growth." *Economic and Political Weekly* 39(41): 4568–80.

Romatet, Emmanuel. 1983. "Calcutta's Informal Sector – Theory and Reality." *Economic and Political Weekly* 18(50): 2115–28.

Singh, Andrea M. and Anita Keller-Viitanen, eds. 1987. *Invisible Hands: Women in Home Based Production.* New Delhi: Sage Publications.

Unni, Jeemol and Namrata Bali. 2002. "Subcontracted Women Workers in the Garment Industry in India," in Radhika Balakrishnan, ed. *The Hidden Assembly Line: Gender Dynamics of Subcontracted Work in a Global Economy*, pp. 115–44. Connecticut: Kumarian Press.

Unni, Jeemol and Uma Rani. 2005. "Impact of Recent Policies on Home-Based Work in India." Discussion Paper Series 10. UNDP Human Development Resource Centre, New Delhi.

———. 2008. *Flexibility of Labour in Globalizing India: The Challenge of Skills and Technology.* New Delhi: Tulika.

Von Werlhof, Claudia. 1988. "Women's Work: The Blind Spot in the Critique of the Political Economy," in Maria Mies, Veronika Bennholdt-Thomsen, and Claudia von Werlhof, eds. *Women: The Last Colony*, pp. 13–26. London: Zed Books.

Williamson, Oliver E. 1975. *Markets and Hierarchies: Analysis and Antitrust Implications.* New York: Free Press.

Winters, L. Alan. 2000. "Trade Liberalisation and Poverty." PRUS Working Paper 7. Poverty Research Unit, University of Sussex, Brighton.

GENDER DISPARITIES AND ECONOMIC GROWTH IN KENYA: A SOCIAL ACCOUNTING MATRIX APPROACH

Bernadette Mukhwana Wanjala and Maureen Were

ABSTRACT

Realizing high economic growth and generating gainful employment present major challenges for Kenya. This paper analyzes the gendered employment outcomes of various investment options in Kenya using Social Accounting Matrix multiplier analysis. Results reveal that Kenya's agriculture sector accounts for the highest increase in employee compensation (mainly benefiting skilled labor and disproportionately benefiting men), while its manufacturing sector accounts for the largest share of job creation. Although women stand to benefit more from employment creation, most of these new jobs are informal with low wages. Kenya's gender disparities are a reflection of existing disparities in its labor market and socioeconomic structure. Therefore, policies aimed at addressing the constraints that limit women's effective participation in the Kenyan labor market, including increasing productivity and raising women's skills, are important for allowing men and women to benefit equally from employment and growth-promoting opportunities.

INTRODUCTION

Since Kenya's independence in 1963, the government has identified employment creation as a central objective. In the post-independence years (1960s and 1970s), the state played a major role in driving economic growth and providing employment. By the early 1980s, however, economic management had begun to weaken as fiscal indiscipline intensified. Faced with budgetary constraints, the government reluctantly started to liberalize the economy through structural adjustment programs under pressure from multilateral financial institutions. Since the early 1990s, the government has focused on creating a conducive environment for the private sector to play a leading role in economic growth and employment generation. However, sustaining high economic growth while simultaneously generating gainful employment remains one of Kenya's greatest challenges. The growth in employment has fallen short of the growth in the labor force, leading to high unemployment rates. While Kenya's development policy emphasizes investments in priority areas to realize key development objectives, such as achieving high economic growth and employment creation, this paper seeks to address whether Kenya's growth-promoting investments generate equal employment opportunities for men and women. Arguably, this depends on the gender and institutional structure of the labor market and the economy as a whole.[1]

Considerable gender disparities exist in the Kenyan labor market. Although women constitute about 50 percent of Kenya's total population, they account for only about 30 percent of the total formal-sector wage employment and earn less than men, even after making adjustments for the type of employment, occupation, and hours of work (Jane Kabubo-Mariara 2003). The gender gap in Kenya's overall labor force participation rates seems to be narrowing (74.7 percent for men and 72.6 percent for women [Republic of Kenya 1999]). However, women's participation rates are higher (compared to men's) in rural areas, where they are actively involved in subsistence activities and agricultural production in addition to unpaid domestic work. Along with their expanding labor participation, Kenyan women have experienced a higher unemployment rate compared to Kenyan men. Estimates for the late 1990s show that Kenya's overall urban unemployment rate was about 25 percent, with female unemployment at 38 percent compared to male unemployment at 12.5 percent (Damiano Kulundu Manda 2002). Although estimates for 2005–6 show a decline in the urban unemployment rate to 19.9 percent, female unemployment is still higher at 25.9 percent compared to male unemployment at 15 percent (Republic of Kenya 2008). Kenyan women also spend less time in wage employment and devote more time to household production than Kenyan men.[2] Given Kenyan women's less favorable terms in the labor market, a high dependency ratio, and existing gender disparities, the gender-blind implementation of growth and employment policies can perpetuate gender inequalities in development.

Despite gender imbalances, analyses of growth and employment outcomes in Kenya have largely been gender blind (see, for instance, Damiano Kulundu Manda [2004], Damiano Kulundu Manda and Kunal Sen [2004], and Maureen Were [2007]). The limited research that explores gender and employment outcomes in Kenya has shown that increased access to education can increase equality of outcomes only in the public-sector labor market (Kabubo-Mariara 2003; Rosemary Atieno and Francis Teal 2006). Given that Kenya's policy reforms aim to increase the private sector's role, the challenge is in reducing the gender differentials in the private sector, which are largely informal. Using Social Accounting Matrix (SAM) multiplier analysis that draws from a 2003 disaggregated SAM with a sectoral employment extension, this paper analyzes the effects of Kenya's different sectoral investment policy options (simulations) on employment generation in terms of gender, skill levels, and broad employment sectors (formal and informal). This paper attempts to illustrate how gender disparities in Kenya's labor market and economic structure largely determine the differential employment outcomes for men and women. Strategies and policies aimed at addressing gender-based constraints are, thus, critical if both men and women in Kenya are to benefit equally from employment and growth-promoting opportunities. This is the first attempt to generate an employment satellite account for Kenya and link it with the production sectors.[3]

ECONOMIC GROWTH AND EMPLOYMENT TRENDS IN KENYA

Economic structure and growth trends

Since independence, Kenya's development agenda has emphasized the role of agriculture and manufacturing as twin engines of economic growth. Although Kenya has transformed from a broadly agriculture-based to a service-based economy, agriculture still accounts for about 25 percent of Gross Domestic Product (GDP). Agricultural production in Kenya consists of both large-scale (mainly commercial) and small-scale farming. Overall, Kenya's economic growth history, like many African economies, has been episodic. The country's growth can be subdivided into three major broad phases: a period of rapid growth after independence (1964–73); an era of external shocks dominated by oil price shocks and structural adjustment (1974–89); and an era of liberalization, inconsistent donor inflows, and economic stagnation (1990–2002), which led to recovery beginning in 2003.

Kenya witnessed rapid economic growth between 1964 and 1973, with an annual average real GDP growth rate of 6.6 percent, which was mainly promoted through public investment, the encouragement of smallholder agricultural production, and incentives for private industrial investment under the import-substitution industrialization strategy. However, the oil crises of the 1970s led to severe balance of payments problems, exposing the country's vulnerability to external shocks and the inefficiency and inadequacy of the import-substitution policy. By the early 1980s, economic management had begun to weaken, fiscal discipline was rising, and the public sector was over-extended (Maureen Were, Rose Ngugi, and Phyllis Makau 2006). The first half of the 1980s (1980–4) performed poorly, with an average real GDP growth rate of 3.4 percent. Although the economic performance in the second half of the 1980s was better, real GDP growth rate declined from 5 percent in 1989 to 2.1 percent in 1991. Between 1991 and 1993, economic growth stagnated, and agricultural production shrank at an annual rate of 3.9 percent.

As the economic crisis deepened, Kenya's government, under pressure from the Bretton Woods financial institutions, began implementing a major program of market-oriented reforms and economic liberalization in 1993. Reforms were initiated (or rapidly progressed) in key sectors, including trade, the social sector (health and education), agriculture, and the public sector (Were, Ngugi, and Makau 2006). These included trade liberalization, the downsizing of the public sector, and a reduction in the state's role in the economy, with greater emphasis on the private sector's role. The 1990s were also characterized by the curtailment of external aid inflows as a basis for more reforms. In 2000, the economy recorded a negative real GDP growth rate, but the economy showed remarkable recovery, beginning in 2004, until the post-election violence in December 2007, which reversed some of the economic gains. The average real GDP growth rate for 2004–6 was 5.6 percent. However, no marked employment gains were witnessed in the recent economic recovery period. After nearly two decades of reforms since 1990, sustainable growth and employment creation have remained elusive. Despite the abundant available labor, the economy has become more capital-intensive. The manufacturing sector's contribution to GDP has stagnated at about 10 percent.

The reforms and the associated obstacles to sustainable growth and employment creation have had a particular impact on women in Kenya, who contribute substantially to the national economy. Women's contribution is particularly large in the agricultural and informal business sectors, while men tend to dominate the formal sector. It is estimated that 85 percent of female-owned businesses are in the informal sector, and women make up 48 percent of micro, small, and medium enterprises (Amanda Ellis, Jozefina Cutura, Nouma Dione, Ian Gillson, Clare Manuel, and Judy Thongori 2007). However, the progress toward reform has not assuaged the existing gender inequalities that still constrain women's ability to effectively participate in and benefit from economic development. Notwithstanding the limited gender impact analysis, there is no doubt that the donor-driven reforms implemented since the early 1990s had disproportionately negative effects for women. The retrenchment programs cut down many jobs predominantly filled by women in the public sector's lower cadres (International Labour Organization [ILO] 1999; Maureen Were and Jane Kiringai 2003). In the health sector, the introduction of cost sharing passed the burden of care from public healthcare providers to women, and the HIV/AIDS pandemic has exerted an immeasurable toll on women (Pamella A. Opiyo, Takashi Yamano, and T.S. Jayne 2008; United States Agency for International Development [USAID] 2002). These factors have increased women's workloads and financial burdens, with implications for women's productivity and time availability for economic activities (Were and Kiringai 2003; Opiyo, Yamano, and Jayne 2008).

Moreover, the reforms did not address some of the more critical limitations that curtail women's effective contribution, including their ability to own property, their insecure land-use rights, and their limited access to agricultural inputs and credit.[4] Although women in Kenya supply 70 percent of labor in the agricultural sector, they hold only about 1 percent of registered land titles, with 5–6 percent of registered titles in joint names (World Bank 2004). In Kenya, land is vital both because of the predominance of agriculture and because of its use as collateral for business finance. Thus, their lack of land ownership restricts Kenyan women's access to formal financial services and hence hinders business growth. Other broader challenges such as poor rural infrastructure, environmental degradation, low agricultural productivity, and lack of access to markets and market information also affect gender equality and development.

These obstacles to women's contribution to the Kenyan economy reinforce gender disparities in the labor market and hinder gender equality, with implications for Kenya's economic development. For instance, it has been estimated that eliminating gender-based inequalities in education and access to agricultural inputs could result in a one-time increase of as much as 4.3 percent in GDP growth, followed by a sustained year-on-year increase of 2.0–3.5 percent in GDP growth (Ellis et al. 2007).

General employment structure and gender composition

In order to more fully explore the gender-based inequalities in Kenya's labor market, one must first understand the nature of the country's fragmented labor market in which the formal and informal sectors coexist. The formal sector consists of employment in both the private and public sectors. Informal-sector jobs tend to be labor intensive and have modest skill requirements, and are often characterized by lower wages and little or no job security.[5] The sector covers a wide range of (small-scale) activities that are generally not registered with the registrar of companies.

Kenya has experienced a general decline in the growth of formal-sector employment since the early 1990s, particularly in the public sector, which declined from an annual average of 6.2 percent for 1964–73 to -0.5 percent for 1990–2000 and -1.1 percent for 2001–5. Public-sector reforms in the 1990s led to retrenchment and an employment freeze for some categories of professionals, such as teachers. Since many Kenyan women train as teachers, this increased the unemployment rate for women. In the private sector, the decline was attributed to various factors such as the collapse of private firms, retrenchment due to stiff competition from imports following trade liberalization, and the poor economic performance in the 1990s (Manda 2002). Figure 1 shows that growth in Kenya's formal-sector employment has largely followed the decline in economic growth, particularly since the mid-1980s.

Kenya's informal-sector employment has grown rapidly, particularly since the early 1990s, mainly as a counterweight to the formal sector's failure to create sufficient jobs. Most of the workers retrenched from the formal sector ended up in the informal sector. Informal-sector employment surged in the 1990s, with an estimated average growth of 26 percent during 1990–2000 and 8.8 percent during 2001–5.[6] Table 1 shows total employment excluding employment in small-scale agriculture. Whereas the share of formal-wage employment declined from 76.2 percent in 1989 to 21.9

percent in 2005, the informal sector's share increased from 21.3 percent to 77.3 percent over the same period. The majority of Kenyan women are engaged in informal-sector activities since the flexible nature of work in the informal sector enables women to balance work and their additional domestic and reproductive roles. It should be noted however, that informal-sector jobs are precarious: they offer little or no security, have no statutory entitlements, and have a high risk of occupational accidents.

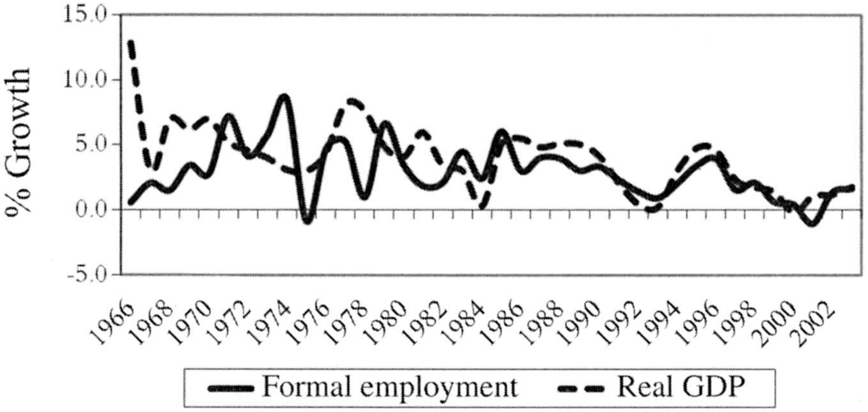

Figure 1 Growth in real GDP and formal employment, 1966–2003
Source: Authors' computations from various economic surveys.

Table 1 Total employment excluding small-scale agriculture

Year	*Total ("000")*	*Formal wage employment (percent)*	*Self-employed & unpaid family workers (percent)*	*Informal sector (percent)*	*Total (percent)*
1989	1,796.2	76.2	2.5	21.3	100
1990	2,395.0	58.8	2.0	39.3	100
1991	2,557.1	56.4	2.0	41.6	100
1992	2,753.2	53.1	2.0	44.9	100
1993	2,998.2	49.2	1.9	48.9	100
1994	3,356.2	44.8	1.4	53.4	100
1995	3,858.6	40.4	1.6	58.0	100
1996	4,325.8	37.4	1.5	61.1	100
1997	4,698.4	35.1	1.3	63.6	100
1998	5,083.2	32.8	1.2	66.0	100
1999	5,492.6	30.7	1.2	68.1	100
2000	5,911.6	32.1	1.1	70.2	100
2001	6,366.9	26.3	1.0	72.6	100
2002	6,851.6	24.8	1.0	74.2	100
2003	7,325.7	23.6	0.9	75.5	100
2004	7,800.1	22.6	0.9	76.5	100
2005	8,271.4	21.9	0.8	77.3	100

Source: Republic of Kenya (1993, 1998, 2003b, 2007).

In terms of sectoral contribution to employment, the service sub-sector accounts for over 50 percent of Kenya's total formal wage employment. In the informal sector in 2006, hotels, restaurants, and wholesale and retail trade accounted for 58.6 percent of informal-sector employment, followed by the manufacturing sector at 22 percent.

Formal-sector employment in Kenya is dominated by men with women constituting slightly less than a third of the workforce (see Figure 2). Furthermore, approximately 70 percent of these women are in the lower income bracket, receiving 8,000–25,000 Kenyan shillings (US $103–321) per month. Education services, followed by agricultural and forestry industries, are the major employers of women in the formal sector. The gender composition of employment by occupational categories has remained fairly static over time – on average, about 58 percent of women employed in the formal sector work in the services industry (community, social, and personal services). In general, women engage mostly in traditionally female-dominated activities, while men are relatively evenly distributed across sectors. Women are least represented in sectors such as building and construction, manufacturing, electricity, and water. Further analysis also shows that in all jobs, including the services industry, especially in the public sector, men outnumber women at the top, whereas women occupy the lower cadres.

Women account for about 14 percent of Kenya's formal manufacturing employment, mainly in the export-oriented textile and garment industries under the Export Processing Zones and in the food and agro-processing industries (Were 2007). In sectors that predominantly employ women, such as the horticultural industry,[7] women are concentrated in "flexible" and seasonal forms of labor that are associated with income and employment insecurities (Catherine Dolan and Kirsty Sutherland 2002). They are largely employed as unskilled or less-skilled casual labor with low pay, long working hours, and exposure to occupational health risks. Overall, there has been a

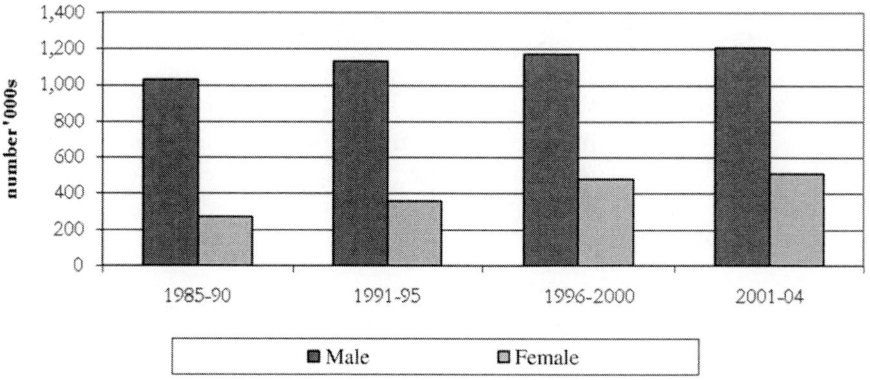

Figure 2 Distribution of wage employment by gender
Source: Republic of Kenya (1983, 1988, 1993, 1998, 2003b, 2007).

remarkable improvement in Kenyan women's labor force participation rates, but their limited access to formal employment is reflected in higher unemployment rates and lower earnings compared to men's. Thus, trade has increased women's economic vulnerability (Ellis et al. 2007).

The employment structure reflects the traditional gender division of labor and the wider gender inequalities in Kenyan society. In the agricultural sector, for instance, women are predominantly engaged in small-scale and subsistence agricultural activities, while men dominate large-scale commercial farming. The commercialization of agriculture has greatly affected women's role in food provision, since land has been increasingly dedicated to producing cash crops and men control cash-crop earnings (Helen Ruth Aspaas 1998). As a result, more Kenyan women are pushed into informal-sector activities.[8]

Women find it difficult to obtain employment outside the informal sector because of their difficulty in accessing education and training. Although the gender gaps in Kenya's primary and secondary education enrollment have decreased, gender disparities persist in tertiary education, including technical training and university education (Institute of Economic Affairs 2008). In 2005–6, the gender parity index for primary school enrollment was 95 percent, but women constituted only about 37.5 percent of the enrollment in Kenya's universities. Moreover, there are considerable gender disparities in the selection of programs, with arts-based courses consistently having high female representation. In Kenya, the widely held notion that girls do not have an aptitude for sciences contributes to girls' low enrollment and poor performance in these subjects (Elizabeth Orchardson-Mazrui 2006). In some communities, girls are viewed as economic resources (for their bride price and child labor) and boys as economic investments. Consequently, some girls end up in early marriages. Education for girls, particularly in Kenya's rural areas, is also affected by gender roles that require them to perform domestic chores (Orchardson-Mazrui 2006). In rural area schools, the percentage of boys is higher than that of girls (Jacqueline Agesa and Richard U. Agesa 1999).

In general, limited access to relevant skills, negative cultural perceptions about women's aptitudes, dispositions, reproductive and domestic responsibilities, and gender inequalities in the acquisition of human capital constrain women's ability to effectively participate in productive activities and economic development, relegating them to low-skilled, low-paying informal-sector activities.[9]

THE SOCIAL ACCOUNTING MATRIX FRAMEWORK

The Social Accounting Matrix (SAM) is a particular representation of the macro and meso economic accounts of a socioeconomic system that captures the transactions and transfers between all economic agents in the system (Graham Pyatt and Jeffery I. Round 1985; Kenneth A. Reinert and David Roland-Holst 1997). The SAM captures an economic system's circular interdependence characteristics between production, the distribution of the value added to various factors, and income distribution among institutions, particularly for different socioeconomic household groups (Jacques Defourny and Erik Thorbecke 1984). It provides a framework for studying the link between the macro and the micro and can therefore shed some light on the impact of the different policy options on employment creation.[10] The SAM has increasingly become a basis for simple modeling, more specifically through multiplier analysis, with the SAM multipliers reflecting the strength of the linkages among different sectors of an economy (Alka Parikh and Erik Thorbecke 1996).

The 2003 social accounting matrix for Kenya

The 2003 Kenya SAM includes the six standard accounts: the production account (activities and commodities), the factors of production (land, labor, and capital), institutions (households and enterprises), the government (including taxes), capital account (savings-investments), and the rest of the world.[11] The SAM distinguishes between "activities" (the entities that carry out production) and "commodities" (representing markets for goods and non-factor services). SAM flows are valued at producers' prices in the activity accounts and at market prices (including indirect commodity taxes and transactions costs) in the commodity accounts. Similarly, the SAM distinguishes between own-production, own-consumption output and marketed consumption because own-production, own-consumption output is valued at producer prices, while marketed consumption is valued at market prices. For the purposes of this paper, we disaggregated the government into a core government account and different tax collection accounts.

We further disaggregated the production account (activities and commodities) into twenty-seven sectors each as defined in national accounts.[12] Ideally, it would have been interesting to disaggregate the agricultural sector into various sub-sectors or crops. However, the lack of corresponding disaggregated employment data for the different agricultural sectors meant that it was not possible to map the production account with the employment data (satellite account) at a disaggregated sector level. Consequently, we aggregated and retained the agricultural sector as a whole to ensure consistency in the aggregates.[13]

Under factors of production accounts, we did not disaggregate land and gross operating surplus. We disaggregated compensation of employees into sixteen categories according to gender (male/female); region (rural/urban); sector (formal/informal); and skill level (skilled/unskilled). The labor force survey questionnaire did not explicitly capture skill levels, so we derived them using education qualifications.[14] In the case of institution accounts (households and enterprises), we did not disaggregate enterprises, but we did disaggregate households according to region (rural/urban) and expenditure deciles (lower/upper).[15] For the government account, we disaggregated taxes into commodity and direct and trade taxes, plus a core government account. We did not disaggregate capital (savings-investments) and the rest of the world accounts.

The employment satellite account

The construction of an employment satellite account was mainly motivated by the need to analyze employment outcomes (in numbers) in a SAM framework, given a conventional SAM framework presents labor in monetary terms (Jorge Alarcon, Jan Van Heemst, and Nick de Jong 1997). Given the different nature of such an extension, the interpretation of multipliers therefore does not refer to average propensities but instead refers to employment ratios.

We developed the 2003 Kenya SAM employment satellite account using national accounts employment data, which we supplemented with national household survey data. The former provided national aggregates on employment (disaggregated into formal [public and private] and informal), from which we further disaggregated formal employment into various sectors and also by gender. We found that total employment in Kenya in 2003 was 7,325,700, of which 1,727,300 was formal employment and 5,598,400 was informal employment (representing about 76 percent of Kenya's total employment in 2003). Women accounted for 30 percent of total formal employment, predominantly in education, agriculture, and public administration sectors, while men were predominantly employed in agriculture, manufacturing, and education.

We then further disaggregated formal employment into various labor categories: gender (male/female), region (rural/urban), sector (formal/informal), and skill level (skilled/unskilled), using the respective (employment) ratios derived from the national labor force survey (Republic of Kenya 1999). We included only individuals' earnings and income in the sample (as we did for the derivation of wage categories under compensation of employees). Unfortunately, only paid employees, representing about 25 percent of the total sample, reported their incomes; that is, no income was reported for the other employment categories such as employers, own-account workers, and unpaid family workers. Given that a large percentage of women in Kenya engage in unpaid activities, such as unpaid work, the proportion of women in the sample was small. Statistics from the labor force survey revealed that only 13.3 percent of women were paid employees (compared to 35.9 percent of men), while 62.7 percent were unpaid family workers (compared to 35.9 percent of men). To increase the sample size, the data set was merged with the *Welfare Monitoring Survey 1997* (Republic of

Kenya 1997), which contained information on non-wage income.[16] The resultant sample was 66 percent men and 34 percent women, which is a close approximation of the national employment statistics.

Highly disaggregated employment data for the informal sector were not available, so we derived ratios of the different labor categories from the labor force survey (Republic of Kenya 1999). For example, if male rural skilled labor in the informal sector accounted for 1 percent of total employment as per the labor force survey, then it would similarly account for 1 percent of total employment (at the national level) in the national accounts. Thus, for consistency, the disaggregation ensured that the aggregate figure from national accounts was maintained.

The SAM model

In developing a simple multiplier model, the first step is to decide which accounts should be exogenous and which should be endogenous. It is customary to regard transactions in the government account, the capital account, and the rest of the world account as exogenous (Defourny and Thorbecke 1984; Jeffrey I. Round 2003). This is because government outlays are essentially policy determined, and the external sector is outside domestic control. Moreover, since the model has no dynamic features, investment is exogenously determined. The corporate enterprise outlays (for example, distributed profits and property incomes) are treated as either exogenously or endogenously determined. The endogenous accounts are therefore usually limited to production (activities and commodities), factors of production, and households (private institutions). Defining the endogenous transactions in this way helps focus on the relationship between two sets of agents (production activities and households) interacting through two sets of markets (factors and commodities). Table 2 shows the endogenous and exogenous accounts for this particular analysis. The production account, factors of production, and households are endogenous, while other institutions, the government, savings-investment, and rest of the world are exogenous.

Derivation of SAM multipliers

Following Round (2003), the SAM multipliers are derived as follows. Like an input–output model, the matrix of endogenous transactions, represented in summary form by the matrix T, can be used to define a matrix A of column shares by dividing elements in each column of T by its column total Y:

$$T = AY \qquad (1)$$

where T and A have the partitioned structure shown in Table 4. The component sub-matrices of A show, for example, that A_{21} is the matrix of

Table 2 The SAM endogenous and exogenous accounts

Account	*Endogenous*		*Exogenous*		*Total*
Products	Intermediate consumption		Household consumption expenditures	Other final demands	Total demand for products
Factors	Value added			Factor income from abroad	Total factor income receipts
Households		Factor income to households	Inter-household transfers	Non-factor income receipts	Total household incomes
Other accounts (Exogenous)	Imports, indirect taxes	Other factor payments	Savings, etc.		Total exogenous receipts
Total	Total activity outputs	Total factor income payments	Total household outlays	Total exogenous payments	

Source: Adopted from Round (2003).

value-added shares of factor incomes generated by activities; A_{32} is the shares of factor incomes distributed across households; and A_{13} shows the pattern of expenditures by household group.

X and Y are, respectively, the vectors of exogenous injections and account totals, where, for example, X_1 is the vector of final demand for goods and services other than those by households, and Y_1 is the total supply of products. An increase in final demand is equated with an increase in production, which also implies an increase in intermediate inputs. The endogenous row accounts can then be written as a series of linear identities, and the system can be solved to give:

$$Y = AY + X => Y = (I - A)^{-1}X = M_aX \qquad (2)$$

where M_a is the SAM multiplier of "accounting" multipliers. If A represents the pattern of outlays (that is, expenditure and distribution coefficients) and is assumed to be fixed, then M_a is fixed, and Equation (2) determines the equilibrium total outputs and incomes Y consistent with any set of injections X. While the input-output multipliers only capture inter-industry effects, SAM-based multipliers account not only for the direct and indirect effects but also for the induced effects on factor and household incomes and activity outputs due to the (Keynesian) income–expenditure multipliers (Sherman Robinson 1989; Irma Adelman and Sherman Robinson 1989).

Multiplier analysis

In most cases, multiplier analysis aims to examine the nature of an income injection's multiplier effects in one part of an economic system on the functional and institutional distribution in general, and on the incomes of socioeconomic groups of households in particular (Graham Pyatt and Jeffery I. Round 1979; Round 2003). In this study, we also use multiplier analysis to analyze the effect of external injections into the key growth-priority sectors on gendered employment outcomes.

A SAM framework assumes that excess final demand exists, so any increase in demand can be met by increasing supply. It also assumes that there is excess production capacity, so any increase in output can be met by increasing the capacity of the existing factors of production.[17] But intermediate consumption can mainly be increased through an exogenous injection (investment). The question therefore is what the likely impact of this additional investment in employee compensation and gendered employment outcomes would be. The starting point is to determine a target growth rate in output and then derive the level of exogenous investment that is required to achieve that growth in output. In this case, we used the actual growth in GDP at factor cost (valued at the cost of factors of production, excluding taxes) between 2003 and 2004 (in nominal terms) as the target growth rate, that is, 13 percent nominal growth in GDP. The questions were: What was the level of exogenous injection required to achieve that target growth rate?[18] What would be the resulting gendered impact of this injection on employee compensation (wage income), the distribution of factor incomes across households, and employment creation? Among the priority sectors, which sector or combination of sectors would yield the best gender outcomes in terms of compensating employees and employment? Given that $Y = (I\text{-}A)^{-1}X$ as shown above, then the level of injection (X^*) is given by $X^* = ((I\text{-}A)^{-1})^{-1}Y$. The resulting impact of the exogenous injection on endogenous accounts is then given by $(I\text{-}A)^{-1}X$, while the impact on exogenous accounts and employment is given by $L(I\text{-}A)^{-1}X$ and $E(I\text{-}A)^{-1}X$, where L and E are shares of exogenous accounts and employment categories respectively; that is, L is as defined in Table 3.

Policy simulations

The government of Kenya's blueprint for economic recovery (Republic of Kenya 2003a) recognizes agriculture, industry, and services as the major sources of growth. The Kenyan government envisages that investing in these sectors would not only spur growth but also generate gainful employment. To carry out simulations using multiplier analysis, we chose the sub-sectors with the most backward and forward linkages because they would generate greater synergies and consequently higher growth in other sectors as well. We selected meat, dairy, grain milling, beverages, tobacco, textiles, and footwear for manufacturing, and trade, hotels, restaurants, transport, communication, and financial services for services. We opted for five different types of simulations targeting different combinations of sectors: (1) agriculture, (2) manufacturing, (3) private services, (4) agriculture and manufacturing, and (5) agriculture, manufacturing, and private services. The different combinations of simulations facilitate an assessment of the individual, broad, sector-specific effects of exogenous injections compared to a combination of sectors, as has been the practice in the Kenyan policy framework. The sectors have different structures (such as

Table 3 Derivation of SAM multipliers matrix

ACCOUNT	*Endogenous*			*Exogenous*	*Total*
	Products	Factors	Households		
Products	T_{11}		T_{13}	X_1	Y_1
Factors	T_{21}			X_2	Y_2
Households		T_{32}	T_{33}	X_3	Y_3
Other accounts (exogenous)	L_1	L_2	L_3		ΣL
Total	Y_1	Y_2	Y_3	ΣX	

the male-female employment ratio) and levels of formality (some are more informal than others), among other differences, and are therefore expected to contribute differently to growth and have different impacts on value added and employment generation.

From the simulations, it is expected that more jobs will be created in the informal sector than the formal sector, reflecting trends in the employment structure. In addition, female job creation is expected to be more predominant in the informal sector. Below, we discuss the simulation results of the impact of the exogenous injections on compensation of employees, distribution of factor incomes across households, and employment creation.

SIMULATION RESULTS

Impact of exogenous injections on compensation of employees

The analysis of the injections' impact on compensation of employees reveals that targeting Kenya's agricultural sector results in the highest increase in employee compensation (14.1 percent compared to an 8.5 percent increase when the injection is put into services, see Table 4). This is mainly because agriculture is more labor-intensive than private services, which are more capital intensive. Kenya's agriculture sector also has low labor ratios, which have mainly been attributed to the sector's prevailing low wages, as well as the dominance of self-employment and unpaid family workers (Republic of Kenya 1996). The 2003 SAM shows that while labor costs accounted for about 47 percent of total production costs in agriculture, they only accounted for 37 percent of production costs in private services. Private services have become more capital intensive over time, with increased automation, especially in financial services, and rapid growth in the information and communication technologies.

In agriculture, the increase in labor costs is higher in Kenya's informal sector, which is anticipated because employment trends reveal that employment creation has largely occurred in the informal sector. Further sectoral analysis shows that private services accounted for the highest proportion of the increase in formal-sector labor costs, accounting for 61 percent compared to 50 percent in manufacturing and 42 percent in agriculture. This is to be expected given that financial services, transport, communication, hotels, and restaurants are largely formal, while agriculture is largely informal and characterized by small-holder subsistence farming and unpaid family labor. In terms of gender, the private services sector is likely to employ high-skilled labor, which largely benefits men. For instance, in Kenya's formal services sector, men accounted for 54 percent of the total increase in compensation of employees compared to only 8 percent for women. In general, the increase in labor costs in the formal sector disproportionately benefits men.

Table 4 Impact of exogenous injections on compensation of employees (percentages)

	Baseline	*Agriculture*	*Manufacturing*	*Services*	*Agriculture and manufacturing*	*Agriculture, manufacturing, and services*
Total increase in cost		14.1	9.5	8.5	10.0	6.9
Formal	63.4	42.2	49.6	61.2	44.3	52.0
Of which:						
male	54.0	35.2	42.6	53.5	37.3	44.6
female	9.4	7.0	7.1	7.8	7.0	7.4
Informal	36.6	57.8	50.4	38.8	55.7	48.0
Of which:						
male	29.6	46.6	40.4	31.5	44.8	38.8
female	7.0	11.2	10.0	7.3	10.9	9.2
Skilled	65.9	86.1	79.3	73.6	84.1	79.9
Of which:						
male	55.4	70.7	66.1	63.0	69.4	67.0
female	10.5	15.4	13.2	10.6	14.7	12.9
Unskilled	34.1	13.9	20.7	26.4	15.9	20.1
Of which:						
male	28.1	11.1	16.8	21.9	12.7	16.4
female	5.9	2.9	3.9	4.5	3.1	3.7

Notes: This table shows the impact of injections on compensation of employees (COE), considering the different combinations of simulations compared to the baseline proportions. The results indicate that investing in agriculture results in the highest increase in COE (14.1 percent), mainly in the informal sector (57.8 percent), benefiting skilled labor (86.1 percent) and mainly men (about 70.7 percent).

In terms of skill level, skilled labor accounted for over 70 percent of the increase in labor costs in all sectors. This finding supports evidence of earning disparities between skilled and unskilled workers, with higher returns to education (see Were 2007). Overall, men account for a larger proportion of trained and skilled workers than women, as evidenced by the higher proportion of men in Kenya's higher education institutions. In the sample used, about 65.9 percent of the labor force was skilled, of which 55 percent were men and 11 percent were women. The analysis reveals that the increase in the labor costs was higher for skilled labor than unskilled, and consequently higher for men. At the sector level, investing in agriculture results in an 86 percent increase in the cost of skilled labor compared to only 14 percent for unskilled labor. The same trend applies to the other sectors. The increase from the baseline is higher for men than for women, which implies that male wages would increase more than female wages. This can be attributed to the existing socioeconomic structure and the gender inequalities in education and human capital development that are reflected in the labor market.

Impact of exogenous injections on distribution of wage income across households

The increase in compensation of employees is further distributed across households in the form of wage income. This analysis reveals that investing in Kenya's agriculture results in the highest increase in wage incomes for households, 26 percent, compared to 19 percent for a combination of agriculture and manufacturing and 18 percent for manufacturing alone (Table 5). The increase benefits rural households more than urban households and households that are in upper deciles more than lower deciles. This is mainly because agriculture is predominantly a rural activity in Kenya, with about 70 percent of the population deriving their livelihood from agriculture. As indicated earlier, the majority of poor women are based in rural areas. Thus, efforts to reduce poverty and raise rural incomes must take into consideration the role of agriculture.

Investing in services results in the lowest wage-income increase for households, averaging about 6.2 percent and mainly benefiting urban households. Services have weaker linkages with households through wage income compared to agriculture mainly because services are more capital intensive, implying that they use less labor, which is supplied by households. Investing in manufacturing also benefits the urban population more than the rural population because the industry sector is predominantly urban in Kenya.

Due to data limitations, the income or wage analysis could not incorporate gender characteristics within the household. Nonetheless, it can be inferred, for instance, that women are likely to benefit from investing in agriculture since the majority of women are engaged in the agricultural sector. However, for such investments to fully benefit women, policy-makers have to consider the gender relations in the sector. For example, as mentioned previously, women are largely engaged in subsistence farming, and they have limited land ownership. Thus focusing on subsistence activities would greatly benefit women, as compared to activities that involve landowners, such as large-scale farming.

Impact of exogenous injections on gendered employment creation

In contrast to employee compensation, investing in manufacturing results in the highest increase in employment, generating about 17 percent additional jobs, compared to 14 percent for agriculture and 12 percent for services (Table 6). However, the jobs created are largely informal, casual, precarious, and low-paying. Investing in the manufacturing sector accounts for the highest increase in informal-sector jobs (85.8 percent compared to 79.6 percent in the case of agriculture, for example), which disproportionately affects women, who account for a larger proportion of informal-sector employment.

Table 5 Impact of exogenous injections on distribution of wage incomes across households (percentages)

	Baseline	*Agriculture*	*Manufacturing*	*Services*	*Agriculture and manufacturing*	*Agriculture, manufacturing, and services*
Total increase		26.4	18.4	16.2	18.9	13.1
Rural households	43.6	14.8	7.9	5.4	9.8	5.8
Of which: rural lower decile	16.1	6.0	3.2	2.2	4.0	2.4
rural upper decile	27.6	8.8	4.7	3.2	5.8	3.4
Urban households	56.4	11.6	10.5	10.8	9.0	7.3
Of which: urban lower decile[a]	1.4	0.3	0.3	0.3	0.3	0.2
urban upper decile	55.0	11.3	10.2	10.5	8.8	7.1

Notes: [a]The low percentages for urban lower decile could be attributed to a sampling bias. This category accounted for a very small proportion of the total population.

This table shows the impact of injections on distribution of wage incomes across households, considering the different combinations of simulations compared to the baseline proportions. The results indicate that investing in agriculture results in highest increase in incomes (26.4 percent), mainly benefiting rural households (14.8 percent) and the upper decile (8.8 percent).

Table 6 Impact of exogenous injections on gendered employment creation

	Baseline	*Agriculture*	*Manufacturing*	*Services*	*Agriculture and manufacturing*	*Agriculture, manufacturing, and services*
Total employment creation		14.1	17.0	11.6	12.4	8.5
Formal	23.6	20.4	14.2	15.6	17.6	17.5
Of which:						
male	17.2	14.5	10.9	11.7	12.9	12.9
female	6.4	5.9	3.3	3.9	4.8	4.6
Informal	76.4	79.6	85.8	84.4	82.4	82.5
Of which:						
male	43.2	45.5	45.0	44.6	45.3	44.9
female	33.2	34.1	40.8	39.8	37.1	37.7
Skilled	37.6	28.9	32.0	35.9	30.1	32.7
Of which:						
male	25.9	19.5	20.7	24.3	19.9	22.0
female	11.7	9.4	11.2	11.6	10.1	10.7
Unskilled	62.4	71.1	68.0	64.1	69.9	67.3
Of which:						
male	34.5	40.5	35.1	31.9	38.3	35.8
female	27.9	30.6	32.9	32.2	31.7	31.5

Notes: This table shows the impact of injections on gendered employment creation, considering the different combinations of simulations compared to the baseline proportions. The results indicate that investing in manufacturing results in the highest job creation (17 percent increase), mainly in the informal sector (85.8 percent), in unskilled labor (68 percent), and mainly for men (about 35.1 percent). The proportion of females is higher in informal and unskilled labor compared to the formal skilled categories.

Unskilled labor accounts for the highest increase in employment, with agriculture accounting for the highest increase (71.1 percent, compared to 68 percent and 64.1 percent for manufacturing and services respectively). Yet, as previous analysis has shown, unskilled labor accounts for less than 30 percent of labor costs. This evidence supports the concern over the rising trends in income and employment insecurities. The proportion of employment for skilled labor declines for both men and women (from the baseline), while women benefit slightly more from the increase in unskilled labor, in part because their lower level of skills make them cheaper. The manufacturing sector accounts for a slightly higher proportion of increase in female employment (32.9 percent compared to 32.2 percent for services and 30.6 percent for agriculture). Though women still constitute a small proportion of manufacturing-sector employees, the numbers are gradually rising, especially in casual employment (Were 2007).

Overall, it is unlikely that investment opportunities will automatically generate equal employment opportunities for men and women unless policies are put in place to address the existing gender inequalities in the labor market and economic structure.

CONCLUSION AND POLICY INSIGHTS

This study has analyzed the impact of Kenya's investment in key sectoral priorities – agriculture, manufacturing, and services – on gendered employment outcomes. We used the SAM multiplier analysis to analyze the employment and income effects in Kenya by gender, region (rural/urban), skill level, and sector (formal/informal). Using a 2003 SAM for Kenya, we selected the actual growth rate in GDP between 2003 and 2004 as the target growth rate to carry out policy simulations on a combination of sectors with the most linkages within the economy. These included agriculture, manufacturing (meat, dairy, grain milling, beverages, tobacco, textiles, and footwear), and services (trade, hotels, restaurants, transport, communications, and financial services).

Simulation results revealed that investing in Kenya's agriculture resulted in the highest increases in compensation of employees, which benefited rural households more than urban households. A gender analysis of increases in compensation of employees also showed that the proportion of women was higher in the informal sector than in the formal sector. Since women are largely engaged in agricultural activities, it can be inferred that, if well designed, investments in agriculture could help boost the incomes of rural women.

On the other hand, investing in the manufacturing sector resulted in the highest employment increase, with 86 percent of that increase being in the informal sector. Thus, although women benefited relatively more from the employment creation in the manufacturing sector, they had to take precarious, informal, or casual jobs with lower wages. Unskilled labor accounted for the highest proportion of the increase in employment creation; yet, it accounted for less than 30 percent of the increase in compensation of employees. Since the majority of women are unskilled, the increase in wage income disproportionately benefited men. Thus, gender disparities in the labor market are a reflection of the gender inequalities in human capital development and economic structure, which ensure that women remain unskilled and work in the informal sector.

Overall, the results of this analysis point to a need to rethink the Kenyan policy agenda of growth and employment policies by considering not only the number of jobs created but also the quality of jobs. Although the manufacturing sector holds great employment potential for women through the export-based processing industries, the precariousness of most of the jobs created is of concern and raises the need for appropriate policy actions. Also of policy concern is the need to address the constraints that inhibit or limit women's effective participation in productive sectors in the labor market and economic development. These constraints include women's limited access to higher education and training opportunities that would enable them to acquire skills for higher-skilled jobs with higher earnings. Overall, policies aimed at promoting growth and employment should be gender aware; otherwise, there is no guarantee that they will result in equal opportunities for men and women.

However, a more detailed sectoral analysis of the gendered employment outcomes was limited by the lack of highly disaggregated employment data, particularly for the agricultural sector. Also, the lack of time use data limited the development and use of a gendered SAM, as documented in Marzia Fontana and Peter Wobst (2001). This is therefore an area for further research. It should also be noted that SAM multipliers provide a first-cut estimate of the effects of a policy or external shock, which only rely on the SAM structure. Further analysis would require the development of a computable general equilibrium model that interconnects the general equilibrium effects of different policy options.

ACKNOWLEDGMENTS

We would like to thank Michael Lahr for his useful comments on an earlier version of this piece. We are also grateful to the participants of the Inequality, Development and Growth Workshop held on May 19–20, 2008 in New York for the general comments raised on the version that was presented. We also received valuable comments during the IAFFE 2008 annual conference in Turin, and are grateful to the organizers of the conference. Lastly, we thank the three anonymous reviewers for their critical comments on earlier versions of this contribution. We are responsible for any errors and omissions

NOTES

[1] Empirical evidence indicates that there may be an unemployment-growth trade-off in the long run (Robert J. Gordon 1995; Martin Zagler 2000; Patrick Toche 2001). If economic growth is driven by structural change, which could entail a shift toward capital-intensive production as the Kenyan experience demonstrates, then a social cost of unemployment is expected.

2 For instance, an analysis based on the Kenyan Urban Labour Force Survey in 1986 revealed that when combining domestic chores with economic activities, women of working age worked 50.9 hours per week, compared to only 33.2 hours for men (Kabubo-Mariara 2003).

3 Conventionally, the labor sector in the SAM is captured in monetary values, but an employment satellite account presents employment data in numbers and links it with the production account.

4 For details, see Ellis et al. (2007).

5 The contrast between formal and informal sectors is no longer as straightforward as it seemed in the 1970s and 1980s, since the formal sector (particularly the private sector) also utilizes informal labor arrangements such as reliance on casual or high turnover workers. ''Employment in the informal sector'' and ''informal employment'' are concepts that are now recognized as different aspects of the normalization of employment (see Ralf Hussmanns 2005).

6 It is difficult to get precise estimates of the size of the informal sector, given the diversity. The numbers reported for the latter years are projections as given annually by Kenya National Bureau of Statistics. Additionally, definitions and coverage of the informal sector have changed over time.

7 Women constitute between 65 and 75 percent of workers in the cut-flower sector (Ellis et al. 2007).

8 Intrahousehold patterns are characterized by ''separate purses'' whereby men and women maintain a certain level of independent control over their earnings and resources while adhering to gender-specific expenditure patterns (Aspaas 1998).

9 Outdated labor laws have also affected women's ability to fully benefit from employment opportunities.

10 The absence of appropriate, gender-related macroeconomic analytical tools has penalized quantitative analyses of gender issues, especially for Kenya (Anushree Sinha and Haider Khan 2008). Notwithstanding the restrictive assumption of fixed prices, the incorporation of gender in a SAM-based multiplier models facilitates analyses of the impact of various macro policies by gender, thus making the effects more visible to policy-makers.

11 For details on SAM construction, see Jane Kiringai, Bernadette Wanjala, James Thurlow, Nicholas Waiyaki, Clive Mutunga, Moses Njenga, Nancy Nafula, and John Mutua (2007).

12 These are agriculture, fishing, forestry, mining and quarrying, meat and dairy processing, milling, bakery and confectionary, beverages and tobacco, other food manufactures, textiles and footwear, wood and paper, printing and publishing, petroleum, chemicals, metals and machinery, non-metallic manufactures, other manufactures, electricity and water, building and construction, trade, hotels and restaurants, transport and communication, financial services, other services, education, health, and public administration.

Note that even though tourism is an important source of growth for the Kenyan economy, the sector is not explicitly captured in national accounts. It is captured within the service sectors, which mainly include hotels and restaurants, trade, and transport and communication. Therefore, the tourism sector is similarly captured through these service sectors in the 2003 SAM for Kenya.

A more highly disaggregated micro SAM is available with fifty activities and fifty commodities (twenty-two agriculture, eighteen industry, and ten services), three transaction costs (domestic, import, and export), twelve labor categories (by gender and skill level), twenty household categories (by region and per capita expenditure), capital (by region and formal/informal), enterprises (region and formal/informal), and three taxes (direct, commodity, and trade taxes).

[13] The problem of data constraints in SAM frameworks is not uncommon given the detailed data requirements and the fact that relevant data has to be extracted from various available sources (for example, see Parikh and Thorbecke [1996]; Sinha and Khan [2008]).

[14] The unskilled included those with no education and those with only nursery and primary education but with no vocational/professional training. The skilled included those (1) who did not have a formal education, but did have trade tests, or who had nursery and primary education, trade tests, and an ordinary diploma; (2) who had a secondary education, with/without trade tests, and an ordinary diploma; (3) who had a secondary education, a higher national diploma, and professional training, such as the Certified Public Accountants or Certified Public Secretaries; (4) who had a bachelor's degree, with/without an ordinary diploma; and (5) who were postgraduates, with/without additional professional training.

[15] It was not possible to disaggregate households by gender because of complications related to the definition of gender and household head in the household survey. Eighty-four percent of the respondents were in rural areas, which could have an impact on the definition of male- or female-headed households. For instance, in some households, the male head resided in an urban area and transferred income to a rural home headed by his wife. Such households were probably termed female-headed; thus classifying households by gender could result in biased estimates that overestimated the proportion of female-headed households.

[16] Additional data were obtained only when the same households could be identified.

[17] This assumption makes sense for the Kenyan economy given the high unemployment rate and the high incremental capital output ratio, which implies that output can be increased through increasing production efficiency.

[18] As previously stated, several assumptions hold in multiplier analysis, such as excess production capacity, which implies that increasing production in the productive sectors will not have an impact on prices.

REFERENCES

Adelman Irma and Sherman Robinson. 1989. ''Income Distribution and Development,'' in Hollis Chenery and T.N. Srinivasan, eds. *Handbook of Development Economics, Vol II*, pp. 949–1003. Amsterdam: North-Holland.

Agesa, Jacqueline and Richard U. Agesa. 1999. ''Gender Differences in the Incidence of Rural to Urban Migration: Evidence from Kenya.'' *Journal of Development Studies* 35(6): 36–58.

Alarcon, Jorge, Jan Van Heemst, and Nick de Jong. 1997. ''Extending the SAM with Social and Environmental Indicators: An Application to Bolivia.'' Working Paper Series 256, Institute of Social Studies, the Hague, the Netherlands.

Aspaas, Helen Ruth. 1998. ''Heading Households and Heading Businesses: Rural Kenyan Women in the Informal Sector.'' *Professional Geographer* 50(2): 192–204.

Atieno, Rosemary and Francis Teal. 2006. ''Gender, Education and Occupational Outcomes: Kenya's Informal Sector in the 1990s.'' Working Paper GPRG-WPS-050, Global Poverty Research Group.

Defourny, Jacques and Erik Thorbecke. 1984. ''Structural Path Analysis and Multiplier Decomposition within a Social Accounting Matrix Framework.'' *Economic Journal* 94(373): 111–36.

Dolan, Catherine and Kirsty Sutherland. 2002. ''Gender and Employment in the Kenya Horticulture Value Chain.'' Discussion Paper 8, School of Development Studies and Overseas Development, University of East Anglia, Norwich.

Ellis, Amanda, Jozefina Cutura, Nouma Dione, Ian Gillson, Clare Manuel, and Judy Thongori. 2007. *Gender and Economic Growth in Kenya: Unleashing the Power of Women.* Washington, DC: World Bank.

Fontana, Marzia and Peter Wobst. 2001. "A Gendered 1993–94 Social Accounting Matrix for Bangladesh." TMD Discussion Papers 74, International Food Policy Research Institute.

Gordon, Robert J. 1995. "Is There a Trade-Off between Unemployment and Productivity Growth?" Working Paper 5081, National Bureau of Economic Research.

Hussmanns, Ralf. 2005. "Measuring the Informal Economy: From Employment in the Informal Sector to Informal Employment." Working Paper 53, International Labour Organization (ILO).

Institute of Economic Affairs. 2008. *Profile of Women's Socio-Economic Status in Kenya,* Nairobi: Institute of Economic Affairs.

International Labour Organization (ILO). 1999. "Employment Creation in Eastern and Southern African Sub-regions." Paper presented at the East and Southern Africa Sub-regional Follow-up Conference to the World Social Summit, Nairobi, Kenya.

Kabubo-Mariara, Jane. 2003. "Wage Determination and the Gender Wage Gap in Kenya: Any Evidence of Gender Discrimination?" Research Paper 132, African Economic Research Consortium (AERC).

Kiringai, Jane, Bernadette Wanjala, James Thurlow, Nicholas Waiyaki, Clive Mutunga, Moses Njenga, Nancy Nafula, and John Mutua. 2007. "A 2003 Social Accounting Matrix (SAM) for Kenya." Discussion Paper DP/72/2007, Kenya Institute for Public Policy Research and Analysis and International Food Policy Research Institute.

Manda, Damiano Kulundu. 2002. "Globalisation and the Labour Market in Kenya." Discussion Paper 6, Kenya Institute for Public Policy Research and Analysis (KIPPRA) and Department for International Development (DFID).

———. 2004. "Globalisation and the Labour Market in Kenya." Discussion Paper DP/31/2004, Kenya Institute for Public Policy Research and Analysis (KIPPRA).

Manda, Damiano Kulundu and Kunal Sen. 2004. "The Labour Market Effects of Globalization in Kenya." *Journal of International Development* 16(1): 29–43.

Opiyo, Pamella A., Takashi Yamano, and T.S. Jayne. 2008. "HIV/AIDS and Home-based Health Care." *International Journal for Equity in Health* 7(8): 1–4.

Orchardson-Mazrui, Elizabeth. 2006. "The Impact of Cultural Perspectives on Gender Issues," in Colin Creighton, Felicia Yieke, and Eunice Smith, eds. *Gender Inequalities in Kenya,* pp. 144–65. Paris: United Nations Educational, Scientific and Cultural Organization (UNESCO).

Parikh, Alka and Erik Thorbecke. 1996. "Impact of Rural Industrialization on Village Life and Economy: A Social Accounting Matrix Approach." *Economic Development and Cultural Change* 44(2): 351–77.

Pyatt, Graham and Jeffery I. Round. 1979. "Accounting and Fixed Price Multipliers in a SAM Framework." *Economic Journal* 89(356): 850–73.

———. 1985. *Social Accounting Matrices: A Basis for Planning.* Washington, DC: World Bank.

Reinert, Kenneth A. and David Roland-Holst. 1997. "Social Accounting Matrices," in Joseph F. Francois and Kenneth A. Reinert, eds. *Applied Methods for Trade Policy Analysis: A Handbook,* pp. 94–121. Cambridge: Cambridge University Press.

Republic of Kenya. 1983. *Economic Survey,* Nairobi: Central Bureau of Statistics, Ministry of Planning and National Development.

———. 1988. *Economic Survey.* Nairobi: Central Bureau of Statistics, Ministry of Planning and National Development.

———. 1993. *Economic Survey.* Nairobi: Central Bureau of Statistics, Ministry of Planning and National Development.

———. 1996. *Economic Survey*. Nairobi: Central Bureau of Statistics, Ministry of Planning and National Development.

———. 1997. *Welfare Monitoring Survey 1997*. Nairobi: Central Bureau of Statistics, Ministry of Planning and National Development.

———. 1998. *Economic Survey*. Nairobi: Central Bureau of Statistics, Ministry of Planning and National Development.

———. 1999. *Labor Force Survey of 1998/99*. Nairobi: Central Bureau of Statistics, Ministry of Planning and National Development.

———. 2003a. *The Economic Recovery Strategy for Employment and Wealth Creation (2003–2007)*. Nairobi: Central Bureau of Statistics, Ministry of Planning and National Development.

———. 2003b. *Economic Survey*. Nairobi: Central Bureau of Statistics, Ministry of Planning and National Development.

———. 2007. *Economic Survey*. Nairobi: Central Bureau of Statistics, Ministry of Planning and National Development.

———. 2008. *Labor Force Analytical Report*. Nairobi: Central Bureau of Statistics, Ministry of Planning and National Development.

Robinson, Sherman. 1989. "Multisectoral Models," in Hollis Chenery and T.N. Srinivasan, eds. *Handbook of Development Economics, Vol II*, pp. 885–947. Amsterdam: North-Holland.

Round, Jeffery I. 2003. "Social Accounting Matrices and SAM-Based Multiplier Analysis," in François Bourguignon and Luiz A. Pereira da Silva, eds. *The Impact of Economic Policies on Poverty and Income Distribution: Evaluation Techniques and Tools*, pp. 301–24. Washington, DC: World Bank.

Sinha, Anushree and Haider Khan. 2008. "Gender and Informal Sector Analysis in India: Economy Wide Approaches." Research Paper 2008/65, United Nations University World Institute for Development of Economic Research.

Toche, Patrick. 2001. "Is There a Growth–Employment Trade-off?" Discussion Paper 62, Department of Economics, University of Oxford.

United States Agency for International Development (USAID). 2002. "Review of Gender Issues in the USAID/Kenya Integrated Strategic Plan (ISP) 2001–2005." Unpublished Report, Women in Development Technical Assistance Project, USAID, Washington, DC. http://www.usaid.gov/our_work/cross-cutting_programs/wid/pubs/kenya_gi_0900.pdf (accessed February 2009).

Were, Maureen. 2007. "Employment Outcomes and Earnings during Trade Liberalisation in Kenya: The Case of the Manufacturing Sector in Kenya." PhD diss., University of Dar es Salaam.

Were, Maureen and Jane Kiringai. 2003. *Gender Mainstreaming in Macroeconomic Policies and Poverty Reduction Strategy in Kenya*. Nairobi: African Women's Development and Communication Network (FEMNET).

Were, Maureen, Rose Ngugi, and Phyllis Makau. 2006. "Understanding Reforms in Kenya," in Joseph Mensah, ed. *Understanding Reforms in Africa, A Tale of Seven Nations*, pp. 22–56. New York: Palgrave Macmillan.

World Bank. 2004. *From Periphery to Center: A Strategic Country Gender Assessment*. Washington, DC: World Bank.

Zagler, Martin. 2000. "Economic Growth, Structural Change and Search Unemployment." Working Paper ECO 00/16, European University Institute, Florence.

GLOBALIZATION, GENDER, AND POVERTY IN THE SENEGAL RIVER VALLEY

Jeanne E. Koopman

ABSTRACT

In an impressive attempt to guarantee food security, well over two billion dollars have been invested in the modernization of the agrarian economy in the Senegal River Valley. But, even though two huge dams and thousands of village-based irrigation schemes have been constructed since the late 1970s, food security is still as illusive as ever. This study attempts to explain why. In doing so it focuses on the impact of donor-dominated macro-structural change on gender and class relations. This analytical perspective has two benefits: First, it reveals the risks posed by foreign domination of development programs for different segments of the rural population. Second, it points to a critical element in a new approach to improving farm productivity and food security – improving women's access to land and technology.

INTRODUCTION

The history of agricultural modernization in the Senegal River Valley can be read as a precautionary tale. It shows how contradictory Northern-dominated policies badly damaged both the traditional *and* the modern livelihood systems of over a million farmers, fishers, and pastoralists. Modernization policies also brought substantive changes in class and gender relations that will be highlighted in this study.

The externally driven investments and changing policies that resulted in dramatic macro-structural changes in the valley followed a well-known and widespread trajectory. During the twenty years after African independence (achieved for most countries in the early 1960s), international donors offered huge loans for investments like the dams and irrigation schemes discussed in this study. Loans were offered on attractive terms as Northern banks sought to invest the enormous deposits generated by the Organization of Petroleum Exporting Countries (OPEC) during the late 1970s. When African debts soared, donors began to fear repayment problems and abruptly reversed course. From the mid-1980s, in order to get new credit African governments had to accept World Bank-crafted structural adjustment policies that forced large cutbacks in government budgets, including the elimination of agricultural input subsidies for small farmers.[1] In the 1990s, loan conditionalities included the reduction or elimination of protective tariffs, government credit, and crop-marketing assistance. While donors have often defended these policies as essential to raising the productivity and global competitiveness of African agriculture, many analysts contend that they have been a major factor in the decline in African food production (Marjorie Mbilinyi 1997; Philip Raikes 2000; Demba Moussa Dembele 2003).[2]

My objectives in this paper are three: (1) to demonstrate how foreign-financed investments and foreign-dominated policy-making have affected men and women of different ages and caste positions in the Senegal River Valley; (2) to describe household and gender-specific coping strategies in the face of declining food security; and (3) to provide evidence to support the argument that women's land rights must be a key element in any growth strategy whose goal is to overcome food insecurity and poverty.

The Senegal River Valley was known for centuries as the breadbasket of the Sahel, the broad band of semi-arid land that forms the southern border of the Sahara Desert (Philippe Lavigne Delville 1991). The vibrancy of its rural economy depended on the annual flooding of the Senegal River's 15–20 mile wide floodplain (the shaded portion of the map in Figure 1). The floods allowed farmers to cultivate not only in the single rainy season, but also during the dry season when flood-recession fields retained enough moisture to produce a large crop of sorghum, the region's staple grain. The floods also revived pastures and forests, allowing pastoralists to keep their animals in the valley all year round, and filled the fish spawning ponds that are critical to the productivity of river fishing. In short, the floods were the lynchpin of an intensive, multi-season, and multi-caste land-use system that had provided food security in the valley for centuries.

From the late 1960s through the early 1980s, several years of severe droughts badly damaged flood dependent traditional livelihoods. As the droughts worsened in the 1970s, ambitious modernization plans were drawn up for the valley by European consultants hired by the Senegalese government with the financial backing of the World Bank and the United Nations Development Programme (Groupement d'Etudes et des Réalisations de Sociétés d'Aménagement Régional [GERSAR] 1980; Groupement d'Etudes et des Réalisations de Sociétés d'Aménagement Régional and Commonwealth Association of Corporate Governance [GERSAR-CACG], Euroconsult, Sir Alexander Gibb and Partners, and SONED-AFRIQUE 1988, 1991). The plans promised to ensure food security by constructing two massive dams (the Manantali and the Diama) and thousands of irrigation schemes. The flood water collected in the Manantali's huge

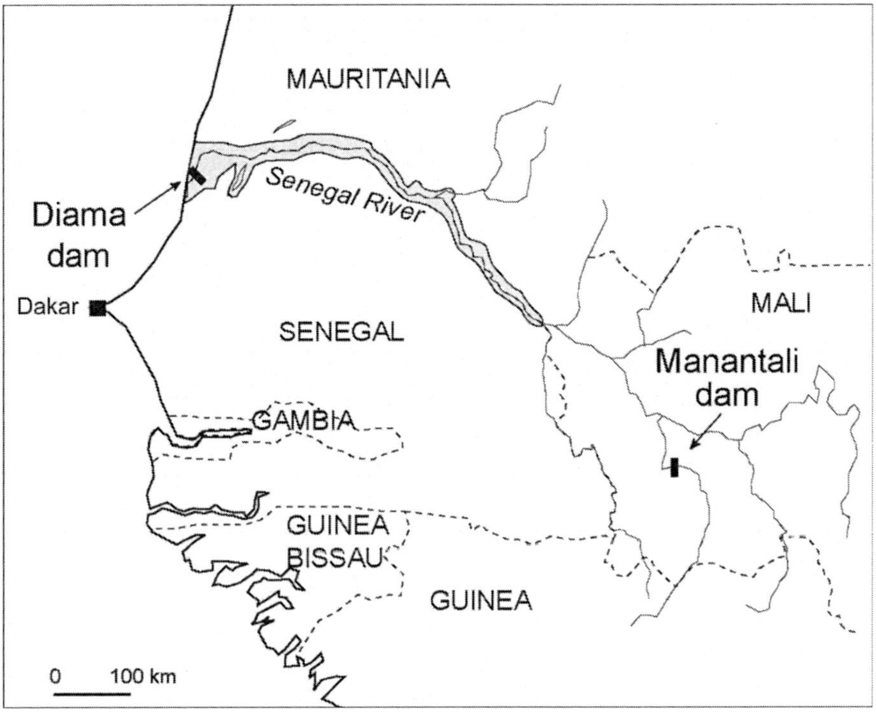

Figure 1 The Senegal River Valley and its floodplain
Source: Map courtesy of Stephanie Duvail.

reservoir would be released during the dry season to prevent a seasonal drop in the river's water level, allowing river water to be pumped all year round to a vast network of village-based irrigation schemes. The irrigation schemes would produce rice, a crop widely imported and consumed in Senegal since colonial times. The farmers of the Senegal River Valley, however, had never before produced rice.

This extremely ambitious modernization program had barely started when the World Bank and IMF initiated Senegal's structural adjustment program in 1985 (Gilles Duruflé 1995; Dembele 2003). At that time, the dams were nearly finished, but the network of irrigation schemes had reached less than a quarter of the population. Since the dams had already seriously reduced flood-dependent grain production, to terminate the construction of irrigation schemes in the name of structural adjustment was out of the question. Instead, the World Bank did not object to the continuation of the expensive irrigation scheme construction program, but it did force the government to reduce spending on the support systems that had been set up to make capital-intensive irrigated rice production economically viable for peasants. From 1985 to 2000, input subsidies, credit, and marketing assistance were all gradually eliminated, even though the prices of imported inputs were rising faster than the local producer price for rice. By the late 1990s, the cost of production was higher than the producer price for local rice. Most farmers had to abandon their irrigation schemes. Furthermore, as irrigation floundered, so did traditional farming. By limiting the natural flooding of the Senegal River valley when the rains were above normal so that only half the flood-recession fields were watered and by failing to provide adequate flood support in dry years, water management policies at the dams both reduced farmers' access to viable flood-recession fields in good years and failed to protect them against drought in bad ones. Thus, in the end, the modernization of the Senegal River Valley did not reduce the rural population's risks, it *increased* them – adding to the ancient risk of drought water, distribution policies that were not favorable to rural livelihoods, and the risk of rapid global price changes in the irrigated rice sector (Jeanne Koopman 2007).[3]

This story has much to say about the impact of policy on gender and class relations. Irrigation had an equity-increasing impact on class relations (in this case, caste relations) because the government distributed equal-sized plots to all household heads, regardless of caste.[4] In contrast, the impact of irrigation on gender was to intensify male bias because irrigated plots were distributed only to heads of households, over 90 percent of whom were male. Inequalities in the gender distribution of labor time also increased because the heavy emigration of younger men prompted household heads to draw more women into the labor-intensive tasks of rice production.

As male-controlled irrigated rice production as well as traditional flood-recession farming began to flounder in the 1980s, women's groups, with the support of international and local NGOs, sought and received small amounts of land from large landholders for vegetable gardens. Plots in these gardens were usually distributed equally to all women in the village. Individual plots were very small, but by giving women access to land that did not depend on their marital or caste status, the gardens provided all women with a resource that allowed them to farm on their own account.

This study is based on a wide reading of the literature on the Senegal River Valley, which includes comparable data from 1958 and 1991–2 that demonstrate the combined impact of the dams and the irrigation schemes on men's, women's, and children's labor time. My own 2003 random sample survey of 100 male and female farmers in the village I will call Wouromayo (see map in Figure 1) provides data on the costs of and returns to women's irrigated vegetable farming and male-controlled rice production. (The major surveys used in this analysis are described in the Appendix.) The village data support my argument that reducing the constraints to women's land rights can have an important positive impact on household livelihoods. The next section links this argument to the global feminist economics literature on gender and land, the Africanist-feminist literature on rights to labor and rights to land, and the recent debates on land reform in Africa.

THE FEMINIST LITERATURE ON LAND AND LABOR

Gender inequalities in land rights and why they matter

Carmen Diana Deere and Cheryl R. Doss's (2006) comprehensive assessment of global gender asset gaps shows that on all continents, women control far less land than men. In Latin America women account for just a quarter of all landowners (Carmen Diana Deere and Magdalena Leon 2003), in Asia even fewer women own land (Bina Agarwal 1994), and in Africa, where private ownership itself is rare, it is *extremely* rare for women to own land in their own right (Sandra Fullerton Joireman 2008).

More than three quarters of total farmland in Africa is held under customary tenure (Joireman 2008: 1235). African women's customary land rights depend on their marital status, a circumstance that makes women's rights to land far less secure than men's (Fatou Sow 1993; Susana Lastarria-Cornhiel 1997; Thea Hilhorst 2000; Ann Whitehead and Dzodzi Tsikata 2003). Women almost always lose their farms when they are divorced and sometimes even when they are widowed (Joireman 2008). By contrast, in Latin America women can expect an equal division of property in cases of separation, divorce, or the death of their husband (Deere and Leone 2003).

And why does women's access to land in their own right matter? There are at least three reasons: First, there is considerable evidence that women with independent land rights and access to technology can substantially raise their productivity and output (Jean Davison 1988; Jeanne Koopman Henn 1988; Judith A. Carney and Michael J. Watts 1991). Part of the evidence comes from studies of women farmers who are responsible for providing most, if not all, family food (Jeanne Koopman Henn 1983; Jane I. Guyer 1984). These women also produce substantial market surpluses in good years. Furthermore, as the present study shows, even women who rarely farmed in the past can make substantial contributions to household incomes with improved access to land and technology.

Second, women's access to land is important because women use their food products and cash incomes to improve household nutrition and child welfare to a greater extent than men (Kofi Owusu-Bempah 1988; Mary N. Tembo and Elizabeth Chola Phiri 1988; Ellen Bortei-Doku Aryeetey 2002). In Africa, men and women have gender-specific responsibilities for household provisioning that they are expected to fulfill with their individual earnings (Eleanor R. Fapohunda 1988). At a minimum, women are responsible for growing and/or purchasing the ingredients for the sauce that is customarily served with sorghum, rice, or tubers like manioc. A woman must use whatever resources she has to earn the income she needs to fulfill her responsibilities – land (if she has access to a plot that she can farm on her own account) or some combination of trading, micro-enterprise, and day labor. If husbands fail to provide adequate support to their wives and children, women with access to land are able to improve family welfare on their own.

Women's household provisioning responsibilities differ by farming system and change over time depending on changing intra-household power relations and the robustness of male versus female farming (Jane I. Guyer 1988). While rural women's cash earnings from farming have rarely been more than a fraction of men's (Guyer 1988), when self-consumed agricultural production is accounted for, African women's total contributions to household food provisioning have been shown to be far more robust.[5]

Third, women's independent control over land empowers them in ways that have positive personal and social consequences. Women with land have a better chance of resisting men's demands on their labor time. This is important since male mobilization of women's labor reduces the time women have to earn income they can control and spend according to their own assessment of their children's and their own needs (Whitehead 1981; Diane Elson 1997). Further, as Pradeep Panda and Bina Agarwal (2005) have argued for India, Deere and Leon (2003) for Latin America, and Joireman (2008) for Africa, women with independent access to land can support themselves outside marriage, a situation that not only contributes greatly to the welfare of divorcees and widows but also makes it economically possible for women to leave violent marriages. Lastly, more secure land rights also encourage women to lobby collectively for their interests as farmers and increase the probability that they will get the support they need to raise their productivity (Agarwal 1994; Muneera Salem-Murdock 1995; Ruth S. Meinzen-Dick, Lynn R. Brown, Hilary Sims Feldstein, and Agnes R. Quisumbing 1997; Michael Kevane and Leslie C. Gray 1999).

Gender, land, and labor in African agrarian households

The overlapping of class and gender disparities in African agriculture creates a wide variation in women's access to land and to household labor. Women from landless households, for example, often have to work harder and longer than women from landholding households simply because their households have the additional costs of renting or sharecropping the land they farm. With respect to gender, men's control over household land supports their customary power to mobilize family labor. The conjugal contract often requires women to work on the fields that their husbands control before they can work on their self-controlled enterprises (Guyer 1984; Sow 1993). Similar customary rules govern the labor of junior, unmarried men who are commonly required to work on their father's fields without any remuneration. But when a young man marries, he begins to have access to family land in his own right and can thereby command the labor of his own dependents. This is a fundamental difference from the evolution of women's situation upon marriage (Jeanne Koopman 1991).

Many married women have customary use rights to land that allow them to produce some output they can control. Social recognition of women's customary use rights does not mean, however, that they cannot be withdrawn, especially under the pressure of labor-intensive agrarian modernization (Judith A. Carney 1988; Leslie Gray and Michael Kevane 1999; Pauline E. Peters 2004; Joireman 2008). Furthermore, in almost all cases a woman's use rights to land depend on her marital status; if she is divorced she loses her land.

Men's control of the great bulk of household land limits married women's control over their own labor time. When agricultural modernization projects require more of what planners commonly refer to as ''family labor,'' senior men's control of household land enables them to shift more work onto women (Henn 1978; Janet M. Bujra 1986; Lila E. Engberg, Jean H. Sabry, and Susan A. Beckerson 1988). This exacerbates what are often considerable gender inequalities in the distribution of total household labor hours since when domestic labor is taken into account, women's total labor times often exceed men's by a considerable margin (Henn 1978; Han Bantje 1995). Men are usually aware of women's heavy labor burden, but when agricultural development projects make no provision for compensating household laborers, household heads tend to mobilize family labor as a free resource, a situation that reduces women's time to produce crops they control (Carney and Watts 1991; Koopman 1991).

The almost universal failure of development projects to grant women equal rights when land is being distributed can be linked to contemporary pressures to liberalize global markets. The recent European push for free trade in agriculture at a time when Northern farmers are still heavily subsidized but African farmers are not is not only fundamentally unfair, it also puts great pressure on African governments to try to improve the global competitiveness of African crops. Since African farmers often depend on expensive imported Northern inputs, one of the few ways of reducing their costs of production is to keep labor costs extremely low. In this context, it becomes evident that depriving women of enough land to make their own farming decisions, thereby forcing them to work for their husbands for a lower return than they would probably earn on land of their own, contributes to reducing the cost of African exports.

Gender and the land reform debate in Africa

All participants in the African land reform debate want to increase the security of land tenure in order to raise farmers' productivity. The question is how. In the 1990s, the debate was between advocates of privatization via registration of both traditional holdings and purchased land, and advocates of allowing customary land tenure systems to evolve under market pressure (John W. Bruce and Shem E. Migot-Adholla 1994; Jean-Philippe Platteau 1996; Pauline Peters 2004). A major problem with the arguments on both sides was their tendency to reason from an exclusively male perspective. They assumed that male control over land maximizes household utility and assures intra-household equity, an assumption that does not square with the African custom of separate gender responsibilities for household provisioning, separate budgets, and the evidence that women dedicate more of their incomes to household welfare than men.

Since 2000, a new group of participants in the debate have argued that privatization and customary tenure systems both pose serious dangers to non-dominant groups (Whitehead and Tsikata 2003; Peters 2004). Rising land values tempt people with power in either system to deprive lower-class households, migrants, unmarried men, and women of their land rights. Peters (2004) makes the important point that the intertwining of government and customary leadership makes it imperative to look at who is winning and who is losing in African land disputes, and why.

There is a great deal of evidence that both customary and state-sponsored land redistribution mechanisms are biased against women (Gray and Kevane 1999). State agencies almost always distribute land by household, a procedure that increases the power senior men have under customary land tenure (Camilla Toulmin, Philippe Lavigne Delville, and Samba Traore 2002). Furthermore, while women who head their own households *in principle* have the right to receive land in state-sponsored land distribution programs, in fact they are often deprived of their plots when local leaders redefine them as dependents of their fathers or fathers-in-law (Carney 1988; Margreet Z. Zwarteveen 1997).

But if women have thus far failed to obtain individual rights to own or co-own family or household land in most villages, especially in patrilineal societies, since the early 1980s women's *groups* have been gaining state-sanctioned rights to farm and manage collective gardens. Most often, individual plots are established on the group-managed or group-owned land. Women can count on keeping this land as long as they live in the village (Meinzen-Dick, et al. 1997; Gray and Kevane 1999). The problem is that these individual plots are usually tiny – far below women's pent-up demand for land. On the other hand, because land rights based on group membership are residence-based rather than family-based, they are more secure in the event of divorce or widowhood. Furthermore, it is far easier for women to register claims to group-held land in state land agencies than it is for an individual woman to secure an officially registered right to land that is customarily controlled by her father or by her husband's family. The challenge is to extend secure land rights for women to larger parcels.

THE TRADITIONAL LIVELIHOOD SYSTEM IN THE SENEGAL RIVER VALLEY

The traditional Halpulaar agrarian system, which prevailed until the mid-1980s when a decade of repetitive droughts and the damming of the Senegal River deprived it of adequate water, consisted of inter-dependent livelihoods in farming, livestock rearing, fishing, and micro-enterprise. Except for farming, each livelihood was carried out by a single caste. All depended on the annual flooding of the Senegal River. The flood allowed farmers to cultivate two crops a year: millet during the rainy season and sorghum during the early dry season when flood-recession fields retained enough moisture to support a second crop. Sorghum cultivation was highly productive because the flood-recession fields were both watered and fertilized by the floodwaters. Fish were plentiful because the flood regularly filled the spawning ponds. Cattle and small ruminate rearing was prosperous because the flood regenerated pastures and forests, allowing pastoralists to avoid a long transhumance during the dry season. Communities were self-reliant because women from all castes bartered surplus grain, milk, fish, and artisans' products with one another.

This complex Halpulaar livelihood system coped with occasional droughts with a system of grain storage and distribution that provided basic food security for all castes. In normal years it provided plentiful food and excellent nutrition for all castes. A 1958 nutrition study found that protein intake was twice the level of international nutrition standards (J. L. Boutillier, P. Cantrell, J. Caussé. C. Laurent, Th. N'Doye 1962).

From the sixteenth through the nineteenth centuries, the Halpulaar economy was based on the labor of slaves captured during wars of conquest and in slave raids fostered by the Atlantic slave trade (Thomas K. Park, Mamadou Baro, and Tidiane Ngaido 1993). Slavery made it possible for the landholding castes to avoid most agricultural fieldwork and domestic labor (Yaye Wane 1969). The French colonial government, which controlled Senegal from about 1830 to 1960, abolished slavery in 1903. This legally freed former slaves to leave their masters' farms, but as a landless caste, most could only survive by sharecropping land from the free castes. Sharecropping had onerous terms – half or more of the harvest had to be paid to the landholder. Almost a century later, studies found that most people in what was still considered an ex-slave caste were sharecroppers on flood-recession fields although some had received land as a gift or had managed to purchase it (Wane 1969; Thomas K. Park 1993; Muneera Salem-Murdock and Madiodio Niasse 1993).

In contrast to other male farming systems in the Sahel and with the exception of a few women from the most elite landholding castes, Halpulaar women did not have customary use rights to plots of land that they could farm in their own right (Kate Cloud 1986; Tidiane Ngaido 1993). This changed only in the 1980s when women's groups obtained land rights that were not based on family affiliation (Sow 1993).

STAGES IN THE MODERNIZATION OF POVERTY

The 1970s: Droughts, dams, irrigation, and migration

With the advent of the repetitive Sahelian droughts that began in the late 1960s, worsened in the 1970s, and did not end until the early 1980s, traditional rain-fed and flood-recession farming, livestock rearing, and fishing were all badly damaged. During the droughts, Northern donors and the Senegalese government argued that only irrigation could provide reliable food security in the valley. A modernization program was proposed that would *replace* the flood-dependent farming system with capital- and labor-intensive irrigated rice farming (GERSAR 1980). By building pump-fed irrigation perimeters in all villages in the floodplain, the government hoped to accomplish two objectives: (1) to assure food security and (2) to produce enough rice to replace the 500,000 tons Senegal imported each year to feed its cities (Sidy Mohamed Seck 1991). The proponents of the modernization plan argued that in order to provide adequate amounts of water to the irrigation schemes, the water level of the Senegal River needed to be controlled by two dams – the first, the Manantali, to capture the water of the annual flood in a huge reservoir and to release it during the dry season, and the second, the Diama, to prevent the loss of river water and to prevent sea water from entering the river bed (see map in Figure 1). Keeping the water level relatively high would permit irrigation pumps placed on the edge of the river to draw water to the fields all year round, thereby facilitating (at least technically) the cultivation of two crops of rice per year. The planners recognized that capturing most of the natural flood water in the Manantali Dam reservoir meant that the area of flood-recession farming would be reduced by at least half, but they insisted that intensive cultivation of rice during both the rainy and dry seasons would make up for the losses to the flood-recession economy.

The plan also included a hydroelectric plant at the Manantali dam, financed and built only fifteen years after the dam itself was completed, and a separate project, never fully implemented, to permit year-round navigation of the river by ocean going vessels (Koopman 2007). The plan also included a hydroelectric plant at the Manantali dam, which was financed and built only fifteen years after the dam itself was complete, and a separate project, never fully implemented, to permit year-round navigation of the river by ocean-going vessels (Koopman 2007). Altogether, well over two billion dollars have been spent on the dams, hydroelectric plants, and irrigation schemes.[6]

Local activists had two objections to this vast and expensive modernization plan. First, they questioned the economic feasibility of replacing flood-recession food production that requires little labor and no capital with capital- and labor-intensive irrigated rice production. Second, the critics pointed out that by drastically reducing the natural flood, the dams would not only weaken flood-recession agriculture but would also badly damage both wetlands and pastures, potentially decimating fishing and milk production (Christophe Nuttall 1991; Adrian Adams 2000). Subsequent studies showed that the critics were correct about the decimation of fishing and milk production (Koopman 2007), but nutrition studies from 1958 and 1990–1 show that protein consumption may not have fallen as much as one might expect (Boutillier et al. 1962: 175; Eric Bénéfice and Kristen Simondon 1993: 57). This is probably because local fisherwomen turned to importing frozen fish from the ocean and pastoralist women began making their popular curdled milk from imported dry milk.[7]

As the droughts worsened in the mid-1970s, the concerns of the local activists were brushed aside. The government began a vast irrigation construction program that was expected eventually to provide every household, regardless of caste, with an irrigated plot (Paul Mathieu 1991). The policy of distributing equal-sized plots to every household presaged a substantive change in caste relations. Gender relations, however, did not move in a more equitable direction. By 1990, only 6 percent of irrigated plots were attributed to women, all of whom were household heads (Salem-Murdock 1995). Furthermore, as noted in analyses of irrigation projects in other areas (Zwarteveen 1997), many younger widows and divorcees who actually headed their own households were being denied land because during the distribution process, which was dominated by elite men, these women were socially defined as dependents of a male relative. No married women were listed as co-owners of the plots they would farm with their husbands. At the time, however, with the traditional economy reeling under the impact of drought, the gender inequities and the caste implications of the modernization program were overshadowed by the promise that irrigation would restore food security.

In the late 1970s and early 1980s, Halpulaar households took up irrigated rice production with considerable enthusiasm (Philippe Lavigne Delville 1995). It was not, however, an easy transition (Jean-Louis Boutillier and Jean Schmitz 1987). Both irrigation and rice production were entirely new to the farmers of the valley. Since modern rice production required farmers to purchase fuel, seeds, and fertilizer, farmers had to sell over a quarter of their harvest to pay off their seasonal debts even though their inputs had been subsidized. Worst of all, after paying their debts, farmers rarely had enough rice left to feed their families for the whole year. The planners had assumed that farmers would cultivate a second season during the dry season, thereby doubling their annual rice production. In fact, however, the high cost of pumping the large amount of water needed in the dry season meant that farmers could not afford to buy the inputs for a second season. This is still a fundamental problem.

The construction of small-scale irrigation schemes in all villages of the valley was expected to take less than 20 years. In fact, although much progress was made during the first 20 years (1975 to 1995), construction still continues in 2009, much of it rehabilitating schemes that had been abandoned for reasons that will become clear shortly. By the late 1970s, only a small minority of villages had access to irrigated rice plots. When the droughts kept recurring right into the mid-1980s, all families without irrigated land had to send sons to seek work outside the villages. During the 1970s and 1980s, three quarters of all households had at least one migrant (Delville 1995: 99), and migrants' remittances often provided the bulk of household food (Delville 1991).

Household heads preferred to send their sons to areas from which they could return seasonally to help with farming if there was adequate rain, but migration to other African countries and to Europe also increased in this period (Cheikh Oumar Ba 1996). French demand for both skilled and unskilled labor was strong during the 1960s and 1970s, such that some Halpulaar migrants, in addition to sending remittances, were able to save enough to build a large house in the village (Aly Tandian 2003). The extreme disparities in household income distribution that emerged as a result of migration to Europe are visible in the startling contrast between the beautiful modern houses of a few very successful migrants and the small mud-brick houses of mostly everyone else.

Even as migration was dramatically increasing inter-household wealth disparities, it was having an equalizing effect on wealth differences by caste. A 1990 study found that artisans' household incomes, two thirds of which came from remittances, were 35 percent higher than incomes in an elite landholding caste (Salem-Murdock and Niasse 1993: 364). Wealthy migrants from the ex-slave caste could also sometimes translate their economic power and technical knowledge into influence on village decision making (Ba 1996; Fatou Sow 2006).

The 1980s: All livelihood strategies become more difficult

The 1980s began with great hope and ended in great deception. By the end of the decade, a survey of 3,405 households in thirty-two villages found that only 30 percent had an irrigated plot (Salem-Murdock and Niasse 1993: 13–4). More ominously, during the 1980s it became clear that the entire irrigated rice edifice was being built on a very shaky foundation: without subsidies, pump-dependent irrigated rice cultivation was not economically sustainable. To compensate for this fundamental problem, the state agency that was supervising the building of the irrigation plots also purchased the expensive, imported pumps used on the schemes and delivered subsidized fuel, seeds, and fertilizers to the farmers on credit. After the harvest, the same state agency purchased enough of the crop to cover the amount farmers owed for their inputs. From 1975 to 1985 farmer's input costs were subsidized, ostensibly by the government agencies, but these agencies were relying on loans from foreign donors. These subsidies were not to last.

In 1985, Senegal signed a structural adjustment agreement with the World Bank that compelled the government to cut back on services to small farmers (Duruflé 1995; Dembele 2003). In 1986, the government stopped subsidizing fertilizer and fuel for irrigated rice production. Farmers' input costs jumped from a quarter to a third of the harvest (Seck 1991; Delville 1991). In 1987, the government stopped providing seasonal credit. This forced plot owners to send more male dependents out of the villages so that non-farm earnings could help pay the rising cost of inputs. By 1989, two thirds of these costs were being paid with remittances (Michael Horowitz, Muneera Salem-Murdock, Curt Grimm, Oumar Kane, André Lericollais, John Magistro, Madiodio Niasse, Christophe Nuttal, Thayer Scudder, and Monica Sella 1990: 259). By 1990, over 48 percent of male household members aged 15–60, including many household heads, were absent from the villages (Salem-Murdock and Niasse 1993: 110–1). Even 14 percent of women aged 15–45 had migrated (Salem-Murdock 1995: 8).

Irrigated rice production is far more labor-intensive than flood-recession farming. Indeed, it requires *twice as much work* to produce the same amount of grain (Delville 1991: 66). As male emigration intensified over the course of the 1980s, women and girls, who had done less than a third of the work on traditional fields in the 1950s, were obliged to increase their work on irrigation schemes to make up for the absence of half the adult male labor force (Fatou Sow 1990; Ba 1996).

Table 1 compares the proportion of total household agricultural labor time carried out by men, women, and children, first in 1958, then in 1990-91.[8] It illustrates the shift in the gender and age distribution of household agricultural labor from men to women and children that took place as

Table 1 Percentage distribution of total household agricultural labor time by sex and age 1958 & 1991–92

	Men	*Boys (under 15)*	*Women*	*Girls (under 15)*
Traditional fields 1958	51.2%	18.3%	21.6%	8.9%
Traditional and irrigated fields 1991–92	42.4%	21.3%	26.6%	9.7%

Note: Traditional fields include rain-fed and flood-recession fields as well as some smaller fields that only a small minority of households farm.
Sources: Boutillier et al. 1962: 110; Salem-Murdock and Niasse 1993: 223.

household heads added labor-intensive irrigated rice cultivation to the traditional flood-recession farming system.

This shift of an important share of total household labor in agricultural production onto women and children when a new crop is introduced is consistent with the pattern observed when colonial governments imposed export crops on African farming systems (Henn 1978; Bujra 1986; Engberg, Sabry, and Beckerson 1988). But while the gender story is familiar, the larger story of the changes in labor times as irrigation was introduced in the Senegal River Valley has a surprising and very important twist. When actual labor *time* is examined we find that the average household's agricultural labor days *declined* from 1958 to 1990.

Adult men's labor days declined by 46 percent, reflecting the high rates of migration for men over 15. The decline in women's annual labor days was only 20 percent, reflecting the observation in Table 1 about the shift in household agricultural labor time from men onto women. Children's share declined by 25–30 percent.[9]

At first, it seems incredible that total household labor days in agriculture could decline by 35 percent during a period (1958 to 1990) in which a very labor-intensive form of farming – irrigated rice production – had been *added* to the traditional agricultural system. This counterintuitive result is not only surprising but also alarming. It reflects the severity of the damage to the traditional farming system from both the 1970s and early 1980s droughts and the subsequent water management policy at the dams, which, from the mid-1980s, never authorized the release of enough water to properly soak more than half the existing flood-recession fields. The decline in agricultural labor days in Table 2 also picks up the fact that by 1991–2 irrigated agriculture had reached only about 30 percent of the valley's households (Salem-Murdock and Niasse 1993:198). What is worse, however, is that the outlook for the irrigated rice sector was already dire. The prevailing input-output price relationships meant that by 1990, after paying for inputs, many rice farmers had less than 40 percent of their harvest to feed their families (Seck 1991). The sector had become economically unsustainable.

Table 2 Agricultural household labor days per year by gender and age group

	Men	*Boys (under 15)*	*Women*	*Girls (under 15)*	*Total household labor days*
Traditional fields 1958	215	77	91	37	420
Traditional field and rice fields 1991–2	116	58	73	26	273
Percentage decline from 1958 to 1991–2	46%	25%	20%	30%	35%

Note: Labor days are calculated as 8 hours of work. They are reported per household, not per person.
Sources: Boutillier et al. 1962: 110; Salem-Murdock and Niasse 1993: 223.

To cope with these enormous difficulties, farmers without access to irrigated plots had to depend on migrants' remittances to purchase much of their food. Those farmers who did have access to irrigation had to use remittances to purchase inputs, in effect replacing the subsidies that the donors and the state had withdrawn in 1986. But in some areas, irrigation schemes had to close down anyway because too many farmers did not receive enough remittance income to continue purchasing fuel and fertilizer. By 1989, a quarter of the village irrigation schemes constructed since 1975 had been abandoned (Delville 1991:140). Some of the many farmers who had to abandon their irrigated plots could not return to their flood-recession fields because those fields did not receive enough water to sustain a crop (Park 1993).

In response to the declining ability of male-controlled agriculture to meet household consumption needs, village women began to seek access to land through their traditional women's groups. From the early 1980s, foreign-funded NGOs began promoting women's gardens as drought relief projects (Fatou Sow 2007). The promise of outside assistance helped women's groups obtain gifts or loans of a few acres of land from male customary landowners. Here the women's groups established collective women's gardens, usually giving each woman in the village a tiny plot to farm in her own right. Until the mid-1990s, women's vegetable gardens were watered by hand using buckets to carry water from the river. The work was onerous and yields were limited, but the women, most of whom had never before farmed on their own account, soldiered on, motivated by the need to feed their families.

The 1990s to the present

The high cost of inputs and the lack of seasonal credit led to a 36 percent decline in rice production between 1990 and 1994 (Adams 2000: 25). In 1994, a 100 percent devaluation of Senegal's currency should have helped rice farmers by doubling the price of imported rice, but instead it actually worsened their situation.[10] This happened because the Senegalese government, fearing urban unrest if it allowed the consumer price of rice to rise substantially, subsidized the price of imported rice. But because the government did not similarly subsidize the prices of the imported inputs (fuel, fertilizer, and seeds), farmers' costs of production rose while the prices they received stayed the same. As a result, many more rice farmers had to give up their struggle to produce food for their families. By 1995, of the 72,000 hectares of irrigated land that had been developed in Senegal, less than 30,000 hectares were cultivated (Adams 2000). The rate of abandonment had begun to outstrip the rate of construction.

There was worse to come. In 1996, when global rice prices were falling, the United States Agency for International Development (USAID) convinced a highly debt-burdened and aid-dependent Senegalese government to undertake what was called the "total liberalization" of the rice sector (David Tardif-Douglin, Jeffrey Metzel, and Thomas Randolph 1998). The government agency that had supported the establishment of irrigated rice production in the valley suddenly had to stop all purchases of small farmers' rice in order to make way for private traders. But with Asian ships arriving in Senegalese ports loaded with hundreds of tons of cheap rice from Thailand and India, traders had no incentive to come to the valley so farmers themselves had to scramble to find buyers, often outside the country. Worst of all, in 1997, prices for imported rice actually dropped *below* the cost of production in Senegal (Tardif-Douglin, Metzel, and Randolph 1998).[11] The fact that international rice prices could fall below the cost of production in Senegal is all the more shocking because the standard way of estimating the cost of production for peasant rice producers does not include the unpaid labor of women and children or even the labor of the plot owner. People's response to this impossible situation was predictable. By 2002 only 20,000 hectares of the 80,000 hectares of irrigation schemes constructed since the 1970s were cultivated. In 2003 and 2004, the cultivated area dropped to 15,000 hectares (Fara Sambe 2007). The smallholder irrigated rice sector had imploded.

The situation of traditional flood-recession agriculture has also remained dire. In the 1990s, the Organisation Pour la Mise en Valeur du Fleuve Sénégal (OMVS), the international organization that manages the dams according to the water allocation policies agreed to by its member governments (Senegal, Mauritania, Mali, and Guinea), rarely provided environmental flows to support the natural flood coming from the river's un-dammed tributaries. Despite pleas from experts on the livestock, fishing, and agricultural economies in the valley for a more balanced water distribution policy (P. Fraval, J. C. Bader, L. K. Mané, H. David-Benz, J. P. Lamagat, O. Diop Diagne 2002), ever since the hydroelectric plant at the Manantali dam came on line in 2002, the OMVS has followed a policy of maximal electricity production. This policy has not changed even in dry years, making it impossible to provide an environmental flow when the lack of rain makes flood support essential for even a minimum of flood-recession agriculture as well as for the preservation of the wetlands and pastures upon which fishing and livestock rearing depend.

The OMVS policy is shaped by the fact that electricity, unlike flood support, is a priority for all its members. The OMVS has spent millions of dollars on high voltage lines to transfer electricity to the capital cities of its member countries, all of which have experienced electrical outages as industrial and household demand for electricity has grown. The World Bank is the lead donor for the OMVS multi-year project to build several new hydroelectric plants on the tributaries of the Senegal River (Koopman 2007). These small hydroelectric dams will make it even more difficult to provide adequate flood support to the rural residents of the valley. Absent a great deal of pressure, however, the OMVS is unlikely to change its absolute priority to hydroelectricity in water management policy because a tax on the electricity the organization sells to its member countries services the international loans that it continues to take for new investments and for its own administration costs. Clearly these are formidable obstacles to the more balanced water control policy needed to preserve flood-recession farming, fishing, livestock-rearing, and environmental health in the valley.

What then are the prospects for migration as a bulwark against food deficits in the valley? Anyone who has followed the tragic losses of young lives as thousands of Africans tried to enter an increasingly barricaded Europe in 2006 and 2007 has seen how determined Europeans are to stop the flow of unskilled African youth desperate to support their families. Militarized European ships and planes constantly patrol the borders of West Africa searching for "clandestine" migrants. Senegal has criminalized young people's attempts to emigrate without a visa and signed repatriation agreements allowing European countries to expel undocumented immigrants (Aly Tandian 2006). These developments have caused much anguish in the valley, but I have not yet heard of an organized response.

In Senegal, as in other parts of Africa, 2008 was a year of food deficits. Since Senegal still imports 80 percent of the rice it consumes, the government was extremely worried by the soaring world price of rice in 2007–8. It therefore turned its attention to the valley, where it has begun to take a few tentative steps to change some of the structural adjustment policies adopted in the 1980s and 1990s. For the 2008 dry season (the season that is most costly for farmers), fuel and fertilizer for rice were subsidized by 70 percent (Gabriel Barbier 2008). The resulting 60 percent increase in production shows the power of protecting the economic viability of local rice production (Amadou Diagne Niang 2009; Agence de

Presse Sénégalaise 2008). The government has not, however, publicly cited the subsidies as even one of the reasons for the increase in production. Indeed, as of early 2009, there is no indication that the subsidies will be extended to the main production season. Furthermore, since global rice prices have been falling in the wake of the global economic crisis, creating an expectation that imported rice will once again be cheaper than local rice, it is unlikely that the Senegalese government will continue to provide the level of subsidies that small farmers need to make rice cultivation economically sustainable much less profitable. The lower costs of production in the countries from which Senegal imports most of its rice (Thailand and India) in conjunction with the Northern countries' push for free trade bode ill for Senegalese rice producers.

A 2003 CASE STUDY OF WOMEN'S VEGETABLES AND MEN'S RICE

In this last section, I reduce the scope of the analysis to a single village, Wouromayo, and I focus on a single issue, the impact of women's independent land rights on household food supplies and incomes. I argue that Wouromayo's women's gardens provide a compelling example of how women's contributions to household livelihoods can increase substantially when gender-specific constraints on their access to land and technology are loosened and when women have both the right and the incentives to farm on their own account.

Wouromayo's male farmers have been forced to invest heavily in rice production because as soon as the dams came on line in the mid-1980s, Wouromayo's unusual topography meant that the reduced natural flood could no longer provide *any* of its flood-recession fields with adequate water to sustain a crop. Rice farmers finance most of their inputs with migrants' remittances. This inevitably means that much of the work on the rice schemes is done by women. Indeed several women told me that they do as much work on the rice plots as men.[12] Women have also taken up vegetable farming in irrigated women's gardens to support household livelihoods.

Wouromayo's women's gardens were established in the mid-1980s with support from an international NGO. With the promise of support for the establishment of two gardens, the presidents of Wouromayo's two women's groups convinced their fathers, both of whom were large landowners, to give them some unused land near the river.[13] Each president then established a garden – one of 12 acres and one of 25 acres – and gave every woman in her group a plot. All the women in the village over the age of fifteen received an equal sized plot, regardless of caste.[14] The problems with the gardens were threefold: (1) productivity was low because the plots had to be watered by hand; (2) individual plots were very small; and

(3) women's land rights to their individual plots were tenuous. These problems were not addressed for the first ten years the gardens were operating.

In 1995, a development project began rehabilitating Wouromayo's badly deteriorated irrigated rice schemes and building new ones. Once the irrigation schemes were rehabilitated, village leaders allocated a one-hectare rice plot to all household heads, again regardless of caste. Many women who were de facto household heads, however, did not receive a plot, in large part because village elders managed to redefine widows, divorcees, and wives of long-term migrants as dependents of their sons, brothers, or fathers-in-law.[15] Elite male privilege was again asserted when the irrigation scheme management committees were formed; neither women nor men from the non-dominant castes were represented.[16]

As it became clear that men would not share control of either the irrigation schemes or the 'household' rice plot, the women's garden groups tried another tactic – increasing the productivity of the women's gardens. In 1997, they asked the project that was rehabilitating the rice schemes to provide irrigation pumps for the gardens. The women's groups also took two important steps: (1) to register their groups as official economic entities and (2) to register the land on which they had established gardens with the Rural Councils, the elected bodies that are responsible for rural land allocation in Senegal. These steps secured a new form of land rights for women, that is, group-based, state-sanctioned *ownership* rights on a collective basis. While an individual woman's rights to her own plot are likely to be withdrawn if she or her children can no longer cultivate it, her land rights cannot be withdrawn simply because she is widowed or divorced.

Women's registration of the land in their collective gardens has, to my knowledge, not been contested – a fact that I think is related to the fact that the gardens are relatively small (only 37 acres for over 700 women). Each woman's plot is a mere 10 by 20 meters, which is only 5 percent the size of the male-controlled household rice plots. This amount of officially recognized "women's land" does not effectively threaten men's ability to mobilize individual women's labor on the rice plots.

As small as their individual plots remain, however, nearly all women have made maximal use of their collective gardens. Pump irrigation allows each woman to plant three crops a year. The number of times a woman actually cultivates her plot depends, in part, on how much other work she has, and this depends on the cultural constraints of gender, age, and household status. Women and girls are responsible for providing the household with water for drinking and washing, for providing firewood, and for cooking two meals a day. My 2003 one-off random sample survey of 100 villagers, including sixty-seven women, did not attempt to record labor times, but there is little reason to think that domestic labor is much less time consuming today than it was in 1991–2, when Salem-Murdock and Niasse

(1993: 295) found that the average woman worked the equivalent of 200 eight-hour days a year on domestic tasks.

The combined labor demands of domestic work and rice farming leave little time for women to cultivate their vegetable plots, especially from June through October when rice is cultivated. Nonetheless, motivated by their need to contribute to household food supplies and their ability to sell their surplus garden crops on their own account, most women *make* time for their garden plots. In June and August 2003, I observed many women working in their gardens both before sunrise and well into the night.

On the negative side, women have not been able to secure access to more land so that their daughters can obtain plots without reducing the size of their mothers' plots. The women's groups have continually sought new land from the male landowners who control most areas near the river, but in 2008, they had not succeeded either in extending their current gardens or in establishing new ones.

Finally, I worry about the economic sustainability of women's irrigated gardens. As is true for the male-controlled rice schemes, the profitability of women's gardening has been reduced by the rising costs of fuel, seeds, and fertilizer. Even more ominously, women onion growers have been increasingly hurt by competition from subsidized European onions. In August 2003 one woman told me that she can tell exactly when the onions from Holland hit the market. The fact that there is already competition from European onions in a remote area like the Senegal River Valley provides a preview of the widespread damage to African family farming that can be expected if the Economic Partnership Agreements (EPAs) that the European Union is currently seeking are ratified. The EPAs are, in fact, free trade agreements.

Neoliberal economists argue that free trade bolsters food security because when imported food crops are cheaper than locally produced food crops, food security is increased. The problem with this argument is that it abstracts from the real world factors that bias the competition in local as well as world markets: Northern subsidies, access to technology at affordable prices, and the risks associated with high price volatility on world markets, among others. When world food crop prices are, for whatever reason, lower than the cost of producing food locally, African family farmers, who make up well over 70 percent the population in most countries, are driven out of local markets, thereby losing both income and their own food security. Free trade is a serious threat to African farmers, including women gardeners.

Women's gardens and household welfare

In studying the gardens of especially successful women farmers, I was struck by the complexity of their enterprises. Most women have developed strategies to cultivate food for household consumption while at the same time selling surpluses of subsistence food crops and planting other crops mainly for the market. The most successful farmer in our study cultivated onions in one season and sorrel, eggplant, hot pepper, and black-eyed peas in another. After paying for inputs, her 2002–3 annual income in cash and in kind was US$900, three times the average household's net return to rice. A woman from a nine-person household produced vegetables and sweet potatoes whose value, about US$360, was almost evenly split between products sold at local markets and products consumed in the household.[17]

In 2003 the average contribution of women's vegetable production to household income was US$130 a year – 42 percent of average household rice earnings in a village where rice production was still seriously pursued. Women's average contribution to livelihoods in *poor* households (US$125) was over half a poor household's average rice earnings. These are, of course, very low incomes, but they are critical contributions to household food supplies in a poor rural area where food security is highly precarious.

Women's earnings from vegetable gardening are all the more impressive because they are generated from plots that are only 5 percent as large as the household irrigated rice plot. Most women I interviewed in 2003 wanted to cultivate a plot two or three times larger. The challenge is to better understand and assist women in removing the obstacles to their access to land.

The way forward: Reducing gender bias to promote small farm prosperity

As the African food crisis has deepened and spread, women have increasingly taken up farming as a means of shoring up household food supplies (Mbilinyi 1997). As women increase their economic contributions to household welfare, they are increasingly challenging the patriarchal and caste constraints that limit their access to land. The recent intensification of the long-standing African food crisis suggests that women are unlikely to give up this struggle any time soon.

There are many possibilities for improving women farmers' access to resources and women's representation in the institutions that affect their economic and social interests. The case study highlights two critical contributions that development projects, international and local non-governmental organizations, and progressive politicians, among others, can make. These are: (1) to support rural women's own activism and priorities, and (2) to work to change what Fatou Sow has called "the sex of the state" (1997: 127).

On the first issue, no matter how good outsiders' ideas for improving women's farming seem, all efforts to promote women's access to improved technology and/or land must be planned and implemented with the active and continual participation of the rural women whose lives and livelihoods will be affected. Only women themselves can fully understand the complexities of local culture and politics that affect the pros and cons of a particular policy change or technology in their villages.

Secondly, Sow's concept of "the sex of the state" reminds us that women are seriously underrepresented in the institutions that affect their access to land and technology. By working with local women to identify these institutions, progressive groups can find plenty of opportunities to work with women to improve the gender equity of village, regional, state and even international institutions. In the Senegal River Valley, for example, women's representation on the male-controlled committees that manage the village irrigation schemes would allow women to lobby more effectively for permission to use the scheme to cultivate women's crops. At the regional level, women's election to Rural Councils, which have the authority to allocate and register land, can improve their chances of obtaining formal land rights. Nationally, a better gender balance in agencies that promote irrigation development could improve the chances of breaking down the obstacles that constrain women farmers' independent or joint ownership of irrigated plots and their access to inputs and markets. Finally, at the international level, women's representation at the OMVS would provide women farmers with information on how the water of the Senegal River is controlled. It might also provide opportunities to develop cross-gender coalitions to magnify farmers', pastoralists', and fishers' demands for a more balanced water policy. It is highly important that gender-sensitive male farmers, progressive politicians, civil servants, NGOs, and even international financial institutions argue for more democratic and gender-balanced governance structures in the institutions on which they have some influence.

CONCLUSION

A collective understanding of how global economic change is managed is critical to changing the current global trajectory toward extreme inequality and extreme rural poverty in Africa and elsewhere. Having described how major foreign-financed investments in dams and irrigation schemes in conjunction with Northern-influenced (or imposed) policies have had serious negative effects on the livelihoods and welfare of family farmers, fishers, and pastoralists in the Senegal River Valley, I will end with what I see as some of the necessary changes in the Northern-dominated policies if the objectives of food security and poverty alleviation are to be achieved rather than simply and interminably invoked.

First, free trade policies must be rethought from the perspective of the family farmers who make up 50–80 percent of the population in most African countries. African farmers, be they male or female, are under continual threat of bankruptcy when they must compete in their own markets with European and US-based farmers, many of whom are heavily subsidized. Government subsidies permit the North's high tech corporate and family farmers to "compete" in world markets with extraordinarily unfair advantage, even as international financial institutions like the World Bank try to prevent African governments from subsidizing their far poorer farmers. When African farmers lose local as well as international markets as a result of this distorted competition, they can lose their entire livelihoods, putting not only their food security but even their very survival in jeopardy. Agricultural subsidies for Northern corporate and family farmers who export their output must be eliminated.

Second, if food security and poverty alleviation are major objectives of international aid, agricultural development projects should learn from the multiple failures of foreign-influenced agricultural modernization projects that have damaged traditional livelihoods. Most agricultural projects should focus on improvements in existing agrarian systems and/or on modernization proposals that have been thoroughly vetted with both male and female farmers from various social strata. Special attention needs to be paid to alleviating the specific social, political, and economic constraints faced by women and poor men.

Finally, we need to recognize that improving the security of women's land rights is critical to African food security and poverty alleviation. When government agencies allocate land, they must recognize that distributing land by household is a male-biased policy that can eliminate women's ability to use that land for their own food crops. Furthermore, when women farmers and agricultural projects increase the productivity of land that women farm under customary tenure, strenuous efforts must be made to prevent local men or powerful groups of outsiders from taking over women's land. While the issue of male encroachment has not emerged in the case of the very small plots women farmers control in women's gardens, it is a well-known problem almost anywhere that African women have begun to control enough land and technology to make substantial profits.

ACKNOWLEDGMENTS

Many people have helped me with this study, but I owe the greatest debts to my friends and colleagues from the Senegal River Valley, all of whom provided invaluable insights and generous hospitality. I would like to thank them individually, but since I don't want to link them to the criticisms or errors for which only I bear the responsibility, I have reluctantly decided to forego naming names. Among those to whom I owe the most are the people who shared their homes with me, members of the village research team, the villagers who attended open meetings, the people who responded to our questionnaire, and my research assistant, who contributed ideas and masterful interpretation.

My second set of debts is to the extremely helpful and patient guest editors of this special issue (especially Günseli Berik), three anonymous reviewers, the discussants at the *Feminist Economics* workshop on this volume, and the *Feminist Economics* style editors. Finally, I thank the many long-suffering friends who read and offered advice on the paper's many drafts.

NOTES

[1] Structural adjustment policies included fiscal and monetary policies designed to reduce government spending and to increase exports and reduce imports so that governments would have the foreign exchange needed to service their international debts. For an overview of the impact of these policies in rural Africa, see Philip Raikes (2000). For Senegal, see Gilles Duruflé (1995), Demba Moussa Dembele (2003), and Jeanne Koopman (2007). For case studies of the impact on African women farmers, see Christina Gladwin (1990).

[2] In emphasizing the dominance of Northern power in negotiations over national investment and agrarian policies, I do not mean to imply that national leaders were powerless to defend the interests of their rural populations. Rather, I think they have reacted to tremendous pressure to go along with World Bank/IMF demands, knowing that most Northern donors required compliance as a prerequisite to obtaining new loans. Nonetheless, by accepting structural adjustment, both socialist and liberal governments in Senegal bear considerable responsibility for the policies and practices that have badly damaged peasant livelihoods in the Senegal River Valley.

[3] These issues will be discussed and the assertions supported in subsequent sections.

[4] See Aly Tandian (2003) for an epistemological justification for the use of the term caste in socioeconomic analyses of Halpulaar society. See Yaya Wane (1969) for an extensive description of specific castes and a discussion of salience of caste relations in the 1960s.

[5] Data from 1974 showed that in southern Cameroon, where women have extensive responsibility for growing nearly all the household food, the average woman's contribution to household cash earnings was only 28 percent, but her contribution to cash *and* subsistence income combined was over 47 percent (Jeanne Koopman Henn 1978: 165).

[6] The hydroelectric plant was finally built in 2002, over fifteen years after the dams were completed. Since its completion, electricity generation has become the number one priority in the water management system. It has also become the major source of funding for servicing the international debts incurred by the dams and for running the international agency that controls the dam's water policy (Koopman 2007).

[7] The impact of the dams and irrigation schemes on nutrition has not been adequately studied. The nutrition studies conducted in 1958 (when the traditional system was still strong) and in 1990–1 (when the dams had badly damaged flood-dependent livelihoods) are unfortunately not comparable. The 1958 nutrition study was conducted in three villages spread throughout the valley (Boutillier et al. 1962: 173). It found that caloric intake surpassed WHO standards and that protein intake was 230 percent of these standards, even for the ex-slave caste (Boutillier et al. 1962:

191). The 1990–1 nutrition study was conducted in a single area where all households farmed a newly renovated mid-sized irrigation scheme (Bénéfice and Simondon 1993: 50). It found adequate caloric and protein consumption on average, but it also found that 35 percent of households did not meet their energy requirements (Bénéfice and Simondon 1993: 58). The Bénéfice and Simondon results can obviously not be generalized. They show only that when irrigation is widely accessible, nutrition can be adequate on average, but that it will probably not be adequate for a third of irrigated rice farmers. The fact that the great majority of households in the valley have not had sustained access to viable irrigation schemes due to the inability of the state to construct enough village irrigation schemes and even more importantly, to the economic crisis in the rice sector since the beginning of structural adjustment in the 1980s. To assess the nutritional results of thirty years of modernization in the valley, a truly comprehensive nutrition study is sorely needed.

8 See the Appendix for a fuller description of the studies on which the comparisons in Table 1 and Table 2 are based.

9 While all household members also worked on domestic tasks, such as cooking, firewood collection, and house repair, the gender distribution of domestic labor was extremely skewed. The 1991–2 labor time survey found that the average woman spent the equivalent of 200 eight-hour labor days on domestic tasks, the average girl 125 days, a boy 23 days, and a man less than 16 (Salem-Murdock and Niasse 1993: 293, 295).

10 The devaluation was engineered by France, which has controlled the CFA franc, the currency of most West and Central African francophone countries, since the colonial period. By 1994, France considered the CFA franc overvalued compared to the French franc to which it was pegged, so it proceeded to devalue the CFA by 100 percent. Instead of 50 CFA per French franc, importers now had to pay 100 CFA per franc.

11 World rice prices are highly volatile because the international rice market is small relative to the amounts of rice produced and consumed globally. Production changes in Thailand, India, and the US can drastically affect world prices. Large subsidies to American rice exporters also have an important effect on world prices.

12 We did not conduct a labor time survey. Information about annual hours of work done on the valley's the irrigation schemes by gender and age has not been systematically gathered since 1991–2.

13 I use the term "give" somewhat loosely, although that is the term that was used in my notes of conversations about the origins of the women's gardens. It may be that the male landowners considered the land as a long-term loan, but the fact that they did not formally contest the registration of this land as the property of the women's groups supports the characterization of this land by both presidents of the women's groups as gifts from their fathers. These women transferred the land to their women's groups.

14 The caste inclusiveness of women's gardens supports Agarwal's (1994) argument for India that women are generally more willing to cross caste boundaries than men.

15 The option of registering the so-called household plots in both men's and women's names was not considered.

16 There is no doubt that women were interested in gaining access to the rehabilitated irrigation plots, but they have been continually frustrated. Even after the women's gardens had been irrigated, women who found their plots too small formally petitioned the all-male (indeed all *elite* male) management committees to allow them to cultivate women's crops during the dry season when rice was not cultivated. They were denied.

17 Because the village research team was able to gather complex production and cost data from women vegetable producers as well as from both men and women whose households produce rice, I was able to compare the contributions to household income of average net incomes from women's gardens and average net incomes from

rice production. For women's garden plots, data were gathered on the quantities of all crops produced over the course of a year. These data were valued at market prices and reduced to a net value by deducting input costs. This calculation of net earnings follows the method generally used for irrigated rice, taking into account cash payments for inputs and credit as well as wages to non-household workers (often paid in kind), but not calculating an implicit payment for unpaid family labor.

REFERENCES

Adams, Adrian. 2000. *Quel avenir pour la vallée?* [What future for the valley?] Dakar: International Institute for Environment and Development.

Agence de Presse Sénégalaise [Senegal Press Agency]. 2008. "Sénégal: La campagne de commercialization du riz lancée à Saint-Louis" [Senegal: The rice marketing campaign launched in St. Louis]. *Agence de Presse Sénégalaise,* December 4.

Agarwal, Bina. 1994. "Gender and Command Over Property: A Critical Gap in Economic Analysis and Policy in South Asia." *World Development* 22(10): 1455–78.

Aryeetey, Ellen Bortei-Doku. 2002. "Behind the Norms: Women's Access to Land in Ghana," in Camilla Toulmin, Philippe Lavigne Delville, and Samba Traore, eds. *The Dynamics of Resource Tenure in West Africa,* pp. 86–97. Portsmouth, NH: Heinemann.

Ba, Cheikh Oumar. 1996. "Dynamiques migratoires et changements sociaux au sein des relations de genre et des rapports jeunes/vieux des originaires de la moyenne vallée du fleuve Sénégal" [Migratory dynamics and social change in gender and age relations of the people of the middle valley of the Senegal River]. PhD diss., Université Cheikh Anta Diop, Dakar.

Bantje, Han. 1995. "Women's Workload and Reproductive Stress," in Deborah Bryceson, ed. *Women Wielding the Hoe,* pp. 111–30. Washington, D.C.: Berg Publishers.

Barbier, Gabriel. 2008. "Programme d'autosuffisance en riz à l'horizon 2015" [Program for rice self-sufficiency by 2015]. *Wal Fadjri (Dakar),* April 14.

Bénéfice, Eric and Kristin Simondon. 1993. "Agricultural Development and Nutrition among Rural Populations: A Case Study of the Middle Valley in Senegal." *Ecology of Food and Nutrition* 31(1/2): 45–66.

Boutillier, J. L., P. Cantrelle, J. Caussé, C. Laurent, Th. N'Doye. 1962. *La moyenne vallée du Sénégal* [The middle valley of the Senegal River]. Paris: Presses Universitaires de France.

Boutillier, Jean-Louis and Jean Schmitz. 1987. "Gestion traditionnelle des terres (système de décrue/système pluvial) et transition vers l'irrigation: Le cas de la vallée du Sénégal" [Traditional land management (flood-recession system/rainfed system) and the transition toward irrigation: The case of the Senegal River Valley]. *Cahiers des Sciences de l'Humanité* 23(3–4): 533–54.

Bruce, John W. and Shem E. Migot-Adholla, eds. 1994. *Searching for Land Tenure Security in Africa.* Washington, DC: World Bank.

Bujra, Janet M. 1986. "Urging Women to Redouble their Efforts: Class, Gender, and Capitalist Transformation in Africa," in Claire Robertson and Iris Berger, eds. *Women and Class in Africa,* pp. 117–40. New York: Africana Publishing.

Carney, Judith A. 1988. "Struggles Over Land and Crops on an Irrigated Rice Scheme: The Gambia," in Jean Davison, ed. *Agriculture, Women and Land: the African Experience,* pp. 59–78. Boulder, CO: Westview Press.

Carney, Judith A. and Michael J. Watts. 1991. "Disciplining Women: Rice, Mechanization, and the Evolution of Mandinka Gender Relations in Senegambia." *Signs: Journal of Women in Culture and Society* 16(4): 651–81.

Cloud, Kate. 1986. "Sex Roles in Food Production and Distribution in the Sahel," in Lucy E. Creevey, ed. *Women Farmers in Africa: Rural Development in Mali and the Sahel,* pp. 19–49. Syracuse: Syracuse University Press.

Davison, Jean, ed. 1988. *Agriculture, Women and Land: the African Experience*. Boulder, CO: Westview Press.

Deere, Carmen Diana and Magdalena Leon. 2003. "The Gender Asset Gap: Land in Latin America." *World Development* 31(6): 925–47.

Deere, Carmen Diana and Cheryl R. Doss. 2006. "The Gender Asset Gap: What Do We Know and Why Does It Matter?" *Feminist Economics* 12(1/2): 1–50.

Delville, Philippe Lavigne. 1991. *La rizière et la valise: Irrigation, migration et stratégies paysannes dans la vallée du fleuve Sénégal* [The rice field and the suitcase: Irrigation, migration, and strategies in the Senegal River Valley]. Paris: Syros-Alternatives.

———. 1995. "Introduction: Irrigation et activités extra-agricoles: Les mutations de l'économie familiale" [Introduction: Irrigation and non-agricultural activities: Changes in the family economy] in P. Boivin, I. Dia, A. Lericollais, J.C. Poussin, C. Santoir and S. M. Seck, eds. *Nianga, Laboratoire de l'agriculture irriguée en moyenne vallée du Sénégal* [Nianga, laboratory of irrigated agriculture in the middle valley of the Senegal River], pp. 303–18. Paris: Éditions de l'Orstom.

Dembele, Demba Moussa. 2003. *Debt and Destruction in Senegal: A Study of Twenty Years of IMF and World Bank Policies*. London: World Development Movement. www.wdm.org.uk/resources/reports/debt/senegal01112003.pdf (accessed January 2007).

Duruflé, Gilles. 1995. "Bilan de la nouvelle politique agricole au Sénégal" [Appraisal of the new agricultural policy in Senegal]. *Review of African Political Economy* 22(63): 73–84.

Elson, Diane. 1997. "Gender Analysis and Economics in the Context of Africa," in Ayesha Imam, Amina Mama, and Fatou Sow, eds. *Engendering African Social Sciences*. pp. 153–89. Dakar, Senegal: Council for the Development of Social Sciences in Africa (CODESRIA).

Engberg, Lila E., Jean H. Sabry, and Susan A. Beckerson. 1988. "A Comparison of Rural Women's Time Use and Nutritional Consequences in Two Villages in Malawi," in Susan V. Poats, Marianne Schmink, and Anita Spring, eds. *Gender Issues in Farming Systems Research and Extension*, pp. 99–110. Boulder, CO: Westview Press.

Fapohunda, Eleanor R. 1988. "The Nonpooling Household: A Challenge to Theory," in Daisy Dwyer and Judith Bruce, eds. *A Home Divided: Women and Income in the Third World*, pp. 143–54. Stanford, CA: Stanford University Press.

Fraval, P., J. C. Bader, L. K. Mané, H. David-Benz, J. P. Lamagat, and O. Diop Diagne. 2002. "The Quest for Integrated and Sustainable Water Management in the Senegal River Valley." Paper presented at the 5th Inter-Regional Conference on the Environment and Water, Ouagadougou, Burkina Faso.

Gladwin, Christina, ed. 1990. *Structural Adjustment and African Women Farmers*. Gainesville, FL: University of Florida Press.

Gray, Leslie and Michael Kevane. 1999. "Diminished Access, Diverted Exclusion: Women and Land Tenure in Sub-Saharan Africa." *African Studies Review* 42(2): 15–39.

Groupement d'Etudes et des Réalisations de Sociétés d'Aménagement Régional [Group for Studies and Implementation of Regional Development Organizations] (GERSAR). 1980. Senegal River Left Bank Irrigation Projects: Rehabilitation, Feasibility, and Detailed Draft Studies, Irrigation Master Plan. Paris: GERSAR.

Groupement d'Etudes et des Réalisations de Sociétés d'Aménagement Régional [Group for Studies and Implementation of Regional Development Organizations and Commonwealth Association of Corporate Governance] (GERSAR-CACG), Euroconsult, Sir Alexander Gibb and Partners, and SONED-AFRIQUE. 1988. "Plan directeur de développement intégré pour la rive gauche de la vallée du fleuve Sénégal: Schema directeur de Matam – rapport" [Integrated development plan for the left bank of the Senegal River Valley: Planning schema for Matam – report]. New York: PNUD/BIRD/République de Sénégal [United Nations Development Program/World Bank/Republic of Senegal].

———. 1991. "Plan directeur de développement intégré pour la rive gauche de la vallée du fleuve Sénégal – Rapport finale et annexes. [Integrated development plan for the left bank of the Senegal River Valley – Final report and annexes]". New York, NY: PNUD/BIRD/République de Sénégal [United Nations Development Program/World Bank/Republic of Senegal].

Guyer, Jane I. 1984. *Family and Farm in Southern Cameroon.* Boston: Boston University African Studies Center.

———. 1988. "Dynamic Approaches to Domestic Budgeting: Cases and Methods from Africa," in Daisy Dwyer and Judith Bruce, eds. *A Home Divided: Women and Income in the Third World,* pp. 155–72. Stanford, CA: Stanford University Press.

Henn, Jeanne Koopman. 1978. "Peasants, Workers, and Capital: The Political Economy of Labor and Incomes in Cameroon." PhD diss., Harvard University.

———. 1983. "Feeding the Cities and Feeding the Peasants: What Role for Africa's Women Farmers?" *World Development* 11(12): 1043–55.

———. 1988. "Intra-Household Dynamics and State Policies as Constraints on Food Production: Results of a 1985 Agro-economic Survey in Cameroon," in Susan V. Poats, Marianne Schmink, and Anita Spring, eds. *Gender Issues in Farming Systems Research and Extension,* pp. 315–30. Boulder, CO: Westview Press.

Hilhorst, Thea. 2000. "Women's Land Rights: Current Development in Sub-Saharan Africa," in Camilla Toulmin and Julian Quan, eds. *Evolving Land Rights, Policy and Tenure in Africa,* pp. 181–96. Portsmouth, NH: Heinemann.

Horowitz, Michael, Muneera Salem-Murdock, Curt Grimm, Oumar Kane, André Lericollais, John Magistro, Madiodo Niasse, Christophe Nuttall, Thayer Scudder, Monica Sella. 1990. *Suivi des activités du bassin du fleuve Sénégal: rapport final intégré* [The Senegal River Basin Monitoring Activity I: Final Report]. Binghampton, New York: Institute for Development.

Joireman, Sandra Fullerton. 2008. "The Mystery of Capital Formation in Sub-Saharan Africa: Women, Property Rights and Customary Law." *World Development* 36(7): 1233–46.

Kevane, Michael and Leslie C. Gray. 1999. "A Woman's Field is Made at Night: Gendered Land Rights and Norms in Burkina Faso." *Feminist Economics* 5(3): 1–26.

Koopman, Jeanne. 1992. "Neoclassical Household Models and Modes of Household Production: Problems in the Analysis of African Agricultural Households." *Review of Radical Political Economics* 23(3–4): 148–73.

———. 2007. "The Challenges of Post-Dam Environmental and Economic Rehabilitation in the Senegal River Valley." Program for the Study of the African Environment Research Series, 1. African Studies Center, Boston University.

Lastarria-Cornhiel, Susana. 1997. "Impact of Privatization on Gender and Property Rights in Africa." *World Development* 25(8): 1317–33.

Mathieu, Paul. 1991. "Irrigation, transformation économique et enjeux fonciers: Le cas des perimeters villageois" [Irrigation, economic transformation and the challenges of property rights: The case of village irrigation schemes], in Bernard Crouse, Paul Mathieu, and Sidy M. Seck, eds. *La vallée du fleuve Sénégal: Evaluations et perspectives d'une décennie d'aménagements (1980–1990)* [The Senegal River Valley: Evaluations and perspectives from a decade of development projects (1980–1990)], pp. 197–214. Paris: Karthala.

Mbilinyi, Marjorie. 1997. "Beyond Oppression and Crisis: A Gendered Analysis of Agrarian Structure and Change in Tanzania," in Ayesha Imam, Amina Mama, and Fatou Sow, eds. *Engendering African Social Sciences,* pp. 317–64. Dakar, Senegal: Council for the Development of Social Sciences in Africa (CODESRIA).

Meinzen-Dick, Ruth S., Lynn R. Brown, Hilary Sims Feldstein, and Agnes R. Quisumbing. 1997. "Gender, Property Rights, and Natural Resources." *World Development* 25(8): 1303–15.

Ngaido, Tidiane. 1993. "Land Tenure and Social Structure of the Halaybé," in Thomas K. Park, ed. *Risk and Tenure in Arid Lands: The Political Ecology of Development in the Senegal River Basin*, pp. 145–82. Tuscon: University of Arizona Press.

Niang, Amadou Diagne. 2009. "Sénégal: Campagne 2008 à Podor – Le riz irrigué est très prometteur" [Senegal: 2008 sales in Podor – Irrigated rice is very promising]. *Le Soleil*, January 5.

Nuttall, Christophe. 1991. "Quels types d'aménagement du territoire?" [What types of land management?], in Bernard Crouse, Paul Mathieu, and Sidy M. Seck, eds. La vallée du fleuve Sénégal: Evaluations et perspectives d'une décennie d'aménagements *(1980–1990)* [The Senegal River Valley: Evaluations and perspectives from a decade of development projects (1980–1990)], pp. 83–96. Paris: Karthala.

Owusu-Bempah, Kofi. 1988. "The Role of Women Farmers in Choosing Species for Agroforestry Farming Systems in Rural Areas of Ghana," in Susan V. Poats, Marianne Schmink, and Anita Spring, eds. *Gender Issues in Farming Systems Research and Extension*, pp. 427–43. Boulder, CO: Westview Press.

Panda, Pradeep and Bina Agarwal. 2005. "Marital Violence, Human Development and Women's Property Status in India." *World Development* 33(5): 823–50.

Park, Thomas K. 1993. "Arid Lands and the Political Economy of Flood-Recession in Fuuta Tooro," in Thomas K. Park, ed. *Risk and Tenure in Arid Lands: The Political Ecology of Development in the Senegal River Basin*, pp. 1–30. Tucson: University of Arizona Press.

Park, Thomas K., Mamadou Baro, and Tidiane Ngaido. 1993. "Crisis of Nationalism in Mauritania," in Thomas K. Park, ed. *Risk and Tenure in Arid Lands: The Political Ecology of Development in the Senegal River Basin*, pp. 1–30. Tucson: University of Arizona Press.

Peters, Pauline E. 2004. "Inequality and Social Conflict Over Land in Africa," *Journal of Agrarian Change* 4(3): 269–314.

Platteau, Jean-Philippe. 1996. "The Evolutionary Theory of Land Rights as Applied to Sub-Saharan Africa: A Critical Assessment." *Development and Change* 27(1): 29–86.

Raikes, Philip. 2000. "Modernization and Adjustment in Peasant Agriculture," in Deborah Fahy Bryceson, Cristobal Kay, and Jos Mooij, eds. *Disappearing Peasantries? Rural Labour in Africa, Asia and Latin America*, pp. 64–80. London: Intermediate Technology Publications.

Salem-Murdock, Muneera. 1995. "Gender Bias in Development Projects: A Question of Empowerment," Working Paper 97, Institute for Development Anthropology.

Salem-Murdock, Muneera and Madiodio Niasse. 1993. "Landuse, Labor Dynamics, and Household Production Strategies: The Senegal River Valley." Working Paper 94, Institute for Development Anthropology.

Sambe, Fara. 2007. "Production de riz dans le nord, les acteurs de Dagana diagnostiquent les causes du marasme" [Rice production in the north, Dagana farmers diagnose the causes of the marasmus]. *Le Soleil*, March 12.

Seck, Sidy Mohamed. 1991. "La dynamique de l'irrigation dans la vallée du fleuve [The dynamic of irrigation in the river valley]," in Bernard Crouse, Paul Mathieu, and Sidy M. Seck, eds. *La vallée du fleuve Sénégal: Evaluations et perspectives d'une décennie d'aménagements (1980–1990)* [The Senegal River Valley: Evaluations and perspectives from a decade of development projects (1980–1990)], pp. 17–43. Paris: Karthala.

Sow, Fatou. 1990. "Le pouvoir économique des femmes dans le Département de Podor: Rapport Provisoire" [The economic power of women in the Department of Podor]. Manuscript, available from Widener Library, Harvard University.

———. 1993. "Les Femmes et la Terre: Étude sur la Tenure Foncière au Sénégal." [Women and Land: A study of land tenure in Senegal]. Manuscript, abridged version of a study on Women and Land Tenure in Senegal conducted for WEDNET, York University, Toronto, Canada and the Environmental Liaison Center-ELCI, Nairobi, Kenya, available from Boston University Library.

———. 1997. "Les femmes, le sexe de l'Etat et les enjeux du politique: l'exemple de la régionalisation au Sénégal" [Women, the sex of the state and policy challenges: the example of regionalization in Senegal]. *Femme d'Afrique* 6: 127–44.

———. 2006. "Genre, droits humains et migrations en Afrique subsaharienne" [Gender, human rights, and migration in Sub-Saharan Africa]. Paper presented at the International Colloquium on Migration and Development, Rome.

———. 2007. "Politiques néolibérales et alternatives feministes: l'apport des mouvements des femmes en Afrique" [Neo-liberal policies and feminist alternatives: the contribution of African women's movements]. Laboratoire SEDET-CNRS, Paris. www.gtm.cnrs-bellevue.fr/site-gtm/Clq%20Mond%2007/Sow.pdf (accessed February, 2009).

Tandian, Aly. 2003. "Des migrations internationales à la question identitaire. Redéfinition des status des migrants et évolution des identitiés féminines dans la moyenne vallée du fleuve Sénégal" [From international migration to the identity question: Redefinition of the status of migrants and the evolution of female identities in the middle Senegal River Valley]. Lille: Atelier National de la Reproduction des Thèses.

———. 2006. "Barça ou Barsaax: aller à Barcelone ou mourir: Le désenchantement des familles et des candidates Sénégalais à la migration" [Barcelona or death: Go to Barcelona or die: The disenchantment of families and Senegalese candidates for migration]. *Diasporas* 9: 124–37.

Tardif-Douglin, David, Jeffrey Metzel, and Thomas Randolph. 1998. "Programme de reforme de la politique du riz au Sénégal: Troisième rapport de situation et rapport final" [Program for the reform of rice policy in Senegal: third and final situation report]. Unité de politique agricole, Ministère de l'agricultue, République de Sénégal et Projet d'analyse de la politique agricole, USAID/Dakar.

Tembo, Mary N. and Elizabeth Chola Phiri. 1988. "The Impact of Modern Changes in the Chitemene Farming System in the Northern Province of Zambia," in Susan V. Poats, Marianne Schmink, and Anita Spring, eds. *Gender Issues in Farming Systems Research and Extension*, pp. 361–72. Boulder, CO: Westview Press.

Toulmin, Camilla, Philippe Lavigne Delville, and Samba Traore. 2002. "Introduction," in Camilla Toulmin, Philippe Lavigne Delville, and Samba Traore, eds. *The Dynamics of Resource Tenure in West Africa*, pp. 1–24. Portsmouth, NH: Heinemann.

Wane, Yaya. 1969. *Les Toucouleur du Fouta Tooro (Sénégal): Stratification sociale et structure familiale* [The Toucouleur of the Fouta Tooro (Senegal): Social stratification and family structure]. Dakar, Senegal: Institut Fondamental d'Afrique Noire, Université de Dakar.

Whitehead, Ann and Dzodzi Tsikata. 2003. "Policy Discourses on Women's Land Rights in Sub-Saharan Africa: The Implications of the Re-turn to the Customary," in Shahra Razavi, ed. *Agrarian Change, Gender and Land Rights*, pp. 67–112. Oxford, UK: Blackwell.

Zwarteveen, Margreet Z. 1997. "Water: From Basic Need to Commodity: A Discussion on Gender and Water Rights in the Context of Irrigation." *World Development* 25(8): 1335–49.

APPENDIX

Surveys used in this study

This study compares the results of two major agricultural household surveys in the Senegal River Valley. The first was from the late colonial period – 1958 – when traditional flood-recession farming, fishing, and herding were all relatively prosperous. The second was conducted in 1991–2, five years after the dams had come on line. Flood-recession activities had begun to decline, but only a third of agricultural households had access to irrigated rice plots. Both studies provide comparable data on labor hours by gender and age collected over the course of a full year. The 1958 survey recorded the major agricultural task of every member of thirty households daily for the entire year of 1958. The 1991–2 survey used a twenty-four-hour recall procedure to record agricultural, non-agricultural, and domestic labor times for all members of 331 households, each of which was visited on a monthly basis for an entire year.

The 1958 data was collected by the *Mission Socio-Economique du Fleuve Sénégal* [The Socio-Economic Mission of the Senegal River] (MISOES) financed by the French colonial government. The demographic and household agricultural data are derived from a survey of 100 villages throughout the valley. The labor time data were collected in only three villages. These data are presented by Boutillier, Cantrell, Caussé, Laurent, and N'Doye (1962).

The 1991–92 data were collected by a large research team directed by Muneera Salem-Murdock and Madiodio Niasse working under the auspices of the Institute for Development Anthropology (IDA) at the State University of New York, Binghamton and funded by the US Agency for International Development. These data were collected in two surveys conducted in 1991–92, one of 3,405 households and a more intensive yearlong labor time survey of 331 households. The survey results are presented in a 468-page report by Muneera Salem-Murdock and Madiodio Niasse (1993).

My own 2003 random sample survey of 100 respondents in the village provides data on irrigated rice farming for ninety households and on women's vegetable garden production for sixty-seven individual women. The data was collected by means of a one-off questionnaire that focused on output and incomes, but did not attempt to collect annual labor time data. The survey of women's vegetable production collected detailed information on the annual output and market prices of seven different vegetables commonly grown for both household consumption and sale (onions, *niebe* beans and leaves, *osseille* leaves, gombo, piment, eggplant, and tomatoes). I have not seen this type of data reported in any other research reports on African women's farming.

Prior to drafting the survey questionnaire, my research assistant and I invited villagers from different socioeconomic groups (male rice farmers from each of five village irrigation schemes, female vegetable farmers from each of two women's gardens, men fishers, women fishers, men herders, women herders, and so forth) to open-ended discussions. Once drafted, the survey questionnaire was translated into Pulaar and refined by a team of twenty young men and women from the village who subsequently acted as enumerators. As the data came in, two villagers (one man and one woman) and I checked it for validity and consistency. I was highly impressed with the minimal number of errors, which each enumerator corrected immediately by seeking clarification from the respondent. The excellent quality of the data collected was especially striking since most young women on the village research team were not literate in French and had only recently become literate in Pulaar after taking a six-month course.

Appendix Table 1 Summary characteristics of the surveys

Survey and reference	*Year*	*Location*	*Number of observations*	*Method of data collection*
MISOES survey of agricultural households (Boutillier et al. 1962: 67–105; 111–34)	1958	100 villages located throughout the valley	680 households	One-off questionnaire with data differentiated by gender, age, and caste
MISOES survey of annual labor days (Boutillier et al. 1962: 106–10)	1958	Three villages (all near Podor)	30 households; labor time survey of all household members over age 10	Daily observations; only the major agricultural activity of day was recorded
IDA survey of agricultural households (Salem-Murdock and Niasse 1993)	1991–2	32 villages located throughout the valley	3405 households	One-off questionnaire with data differentiated by gender age, and caste
IDA survey of labor times (Salem-Murdock and Niasse 1993: 221–300)	Aug 1991–July 1992	32 villages located throughout the valley	331 households; each household visited monthly	Twenty-four-hour recall data on labor times in agriculture, non-agriculture, and domestic work
Koopman survey of irrigated rice and vegetable production and incomes	Aug 2003	One village in the middle valley	100 randomly selected households	One-off questionnaire

MODELING GENDER EFFECTS OF PAKISTAN'S TRADE LIBERALIZATION

Rizwana Siddiqui

ABSTRACT

This study uses a computable general equilibrium (CGE) model specially constructed for investigating gender dimensions of the effects of trade liberalization in Pakistan in both production and consumption. The model employs various indicators to measure the gendered impacts, including income poverty (Foster-Greer-Thorbecke [FGT] Indices), time poverty (leisure), capability poverty (literacy and infant mortality), and welfare (Equivalent Variation [EV]). The simulation results show that revenue-neutral trade liberalization in Pakistan increased women's employment in unskilled jobs and increased women's real wage income more than men's for all types of labor, but kept the division of labor biased against women. The study finds that Pakistan's trade liberalization adversely affected women in relatively poor households by increasing their workload, deteriorating capabilities, and increasing relative income poverty. However, the effects remained gender neutral or favored women in the richest group of households.

INTRODUCTION

Many developing countries have benefited from trade liberalization for two main reasons. First, lower import tariffs in developing countries have reduced the prices of consumer goods as well as the prices of producer inputs. Second, lower tariffs in developed country destination markets have raised the demand for developing country exports. However, some developing countries have gained relatively little or made no gain from trade liberalization (reducing tariff and quota restrictions) because developed countries restrict market access and show preferential treatment to least developed countries, giving these few countries greater access to their markets (Thomas W. Hertel and L. Alan Winters 2005; Rizwana Siddiqui 2008c). For instance, Bangladesh reaps the benefits of this preferential treatment by increasing its trade in textiles, while other developing countries face quota restrictions on their textile exports under the multi-fiber agreement (MFA) that was put in place before 2005.

Under the structural adjustment program recommended by World Bank, Pakistan has also undertaken extensive trade liberalization during the last three decades. Quotas were replaced with tariffs in the 1980s and the tariff structure rationalized in the 1990s.[1] This benefited Pakistan by accelerating growth, increasing share of industrial goods in both exports and imports with the former mainly driven by an increase in textile exports, reducing income poverty, and improving welfare at the national level, as shown in numerous studies (for example, see Rizwana Siddiqui and Abdur-Razzaque Kemal [2006], Rizwana Siddiqui [2008b, 2009], and Rizwana Siddiqui et al. [2008]). However, these studies do not measure effects by gender. This study fills this gap and measures the impact of trade liberalization by gender.

The major factor that determines gender differences in economic and social roles is the difference in the division of labor. Reproductive tasks are predominantly considered women's responsibilities in the majority of developing countries. In addition, in Pakistan low literacy rates and low health status due to bias in resource allocation make women more vulnerable to the change in policies. The relationship to the means of production is also highly gendered, and women bear a disproportionate responsibility for unpaid household work, whereas men are largely engaged in paid market work (Rizwana Siddiqui 2005). Women are also engaged in market work but generally have low-paying jobs. Within industry, women's labor at all skill levels is concentrated in Pakistan's export-oriented industries. On average, women earn less than men.[2]

Hence, I expect differential effects from liberalization on time allocation for market and nonmarket activities, income, income poverty, welfare, and capability poverty. For instance, the expansion of export-oriented industries could impinge on women's leisure time if a rise in women's employment is not accompanied by a reduction in their unpaid household work. Similarly, if economic reforms increased the prices of goods largely consumed by women and/or reduced real income, there would be an adverse effect on consumption by women compared to men. The study measured this effect through the capability indicator infant mortality rate (IMR), which reveals the most basic dimensions of deprivation, in nutrition intake, education, and health, and can be defined on the basis of gender.

Using Pakistan as a case study, I explore the major research question of whether or not women and men share equally in the effects (positive or negative) of trade liberalization using a computable general equilibrium (CGE) framework, which is widely used for trade policy analysis in both developed and developing countries.[3] A CGE model can capture gender effects if it includes the linkages between market and nonmarket economies – domestic activities and leisure (see Marzia Fontana and Adrian Wood [2000]; World Bank [2001]; Ismail Fofana, John Cockburn, and Bernard Decaluwé [2003]; Naila Kabeer [2003]; Ismail Fofana, John Cockburn, and Bernard Decaluwé [2005]; and Siddiqui [2005]). This study presents a gender-aware CGE model for analyzing revenue-neutral trade liberalization policies in Pakistan.[4] In my review of the literature, I identify previous models that have adopted a similar approach to mine in this study. However, my contribution extends the analysis by incorporating consumption and poverty indicators by gender. I also measure impact at the household welfare level in two ways: using consumption of market goods only and using consumption of both market and nonmarket goods. This study uses three indicators of poverty – capability,[5] income, and time – to measure gender-specific impacts and welfare indicators EV1 and EV2 (Equivalent Variation). I also highlight gender features of the model, discuss simulation results, and draw conclusions about the differential effects of trade liberalization in Pakistan on women and men. The results of this study will also help other developing countries in general and South Asian countries in particular to minimize gender biases.

REVIEW OF LITERATURE

I group studies of gender inequalities into the following categories: (1) Studies that explore the micro–macro linkages using household survey data focused on market economy or subsectors of the economy (Zeba Sathar and Shahnaz Kazi 1997; Rehana Siddiqui et al. 2003; Rehana Siddiqui et al. 2006); (2) Economy-wide CGE models that only introduce gender into the labor market (Channing Arndt and Finn Tarp 2003; Jeevika Weerahewa 2002; Anushree Sinha and N. Sangita 2003; Channing Arndt, Sherman Robinson, and Finn Tarp 2006); (3) Studies that integrate nonmarket activities into the above-mentioned CGE framework (Fontana and Wood 2000; Marzia Fontana 2001, 2002; Fofana, Cockburn, and Decaluwé 2003, 2005; Siddiqui 2005).

Since they exclude the household unpaid economy, studies in the first two categories cannot capture all gender effects. The group of studies in category (C) overcomes this problem. The first such study, Fontana and Wood (2000), focuses on technical issues such as how distinctions are made between household, market, and leisure activities, and how rigidities in social reproduction and market production can be introduced.[6] In a later study, Fontana (2001, 2002) develops detailed gendered CGE models for Bangladesh and Zambia respectively. Subsequently, Fofana, Cockburn, and Decaluwé (2003, 2005) and Siddiqui (2005) develop gender-aware CGE models for Nepal, South Africa, and Pakistan, respectively.[7] All of these studies introduce gender-related rigidities by assuming low elasticities of substitution between the labor of men and women. They show that explicitly modeling leisure and the household economy changes findings regarding the impact of trade liberalization policies such as tariff reduction on women's employment and wages. The increase in women's employment reduces women's leisure time. Fontana and Wood (2000) suggest that greater flexibility in gender roles in the nonmarket sphere reduces the negative impact on women. Similarly, Fofana, Cockburn, and Decaluwé (2003) demonstrate that an increased role for men in household production reduces the adverse impact of trade liberalization on women. This type of counterfactual analysis is very important for building a gender-aware policy framework. All of these studies focus on the production side of the economy and ignore consumption effects.

On the consumption side the increase in prices not only reduces consumption at the household level and changes the structure of demand by shifting toward cheaper goods, it also changes intrahousehold allocation of resources. Various studies show that price changes due to reduction in tariffs reallocate resources within a household,[8] which may affect men and women in different ways (Lawrence Haddad and Ravi Kanbur 1990; Lawrence Haddad, John Hoddinott, and Harold Alderman 1994; Angus Deaton 1997; Martin Browning, Pierri-Andre Chiappori, and Arthur Lewbel 2003; Jeremy Lise and Shannon Seitz 2004). For instance, Deaton (1997) and Howard White and Edoardo Masset (2002) both analyze intrahousehold allocation estimating Engles and Rothbarth models and demand systems using micro household survey data but arrive at different conclusions. Deaton (1997) finds no evidence of discrimination in allocation of resources between boys and girls within households, while White and Masset (2002) find positive discrimination in consumption against female children in rural, male-headed households. Therefore, analysis of intrahousehold allocation of resources would improve our understanding of the mechanisms through which macroeconomic policies such as trade liberalization affect different dimensions of poverty, income poverty, capability poverty, and time poverty, by gender.

Income poverty is measured by Foster-Grear-Thorbecke (FGT) indices, which are gender neutral, but relative income poverty is measured by gender – the change in the share of poor women relative to poor men. The study measures capability poverty through literacy rates and infant mortality rates, which can be defined by gender. These indicators have not been included in the earlier analysis. These indicators are included particularly to measure the impact of bias in intrahousehold allocation of resources. Time poverty is measured by change in leisure time by gender.

TRADE LIBERALIZATION IN PAKISTAN

Since independence, Pakistan has adopted an import substitution strategy to protect its infant industries. In 1980, under the recommendation of the World Bank, a structural adjustment program was implemented to correct imbalances in the economy and improve the level of efficiency to achieve accelerated growth. Pakistan implemented trade liberalization in 1980–1 by reducing non-tariff barriers (quota and licensing) and replaced them with tariffs. In the 1990s, Pakistan adopted a more open and liberal trade policy. During liberalization, bans on imports into the country were removed except those restricting items for religious or health purposes. Import duties were also reduced, as were the number of duty rates. As a result, the effective rate of protection (ERP) in Pakistan was reduced from 42.5 to 27.4 percent during the 1990–2002 period (Rizwana Siddiqui et al. 2008).

Tariff reduction has enormously reduced government revenue. To compensate for this, Pakistan introduced a general sales tax (GST) of 12 percent on both imports and domestic products in 1989–90. In the subsequent years, government broadened the GST basis and adopted a uniform rate of 15 percent, but a large number of commodities and services are still exempted from the sales tax, thus reducing the average sales tax on imports to 5.6 percent and on domestic production to 5 percent (Rizwana Siddiqui et al. 2008). On average, tariff revenue as a percentage of GDP fell from 4.5 percent to 1.7 percent, whereas the share of sales tax revenue went up to compensate for losses in revenue from international trade. We disaggregate consumption by gender to measure the impact on consumption of men and women.

INTRAHOUSEHOLD ALLOCATION OF RESOURCES

The literature documents that the allocation of household resources in South Asia is generally biased against women (White and Masset 2002; Sunny Jose 2003). This inequality is also reflected in the low female literacy rate and child mortality rate. The Pakistan Human Condition Report shows that the female literacy rate was 32.6 percent for 1999, and the female child and maternal mortality rates were 24.3 per 1,000 live births for 1997–2000 and 300–400 per 100,000 live births for 1998 respectively (Centre for Research on Poverty Reduction and Income Distribution [CRPRID] 2002). Therefore, the estimation of the aggregate consumption function may generate biased results and hide the costs (such as the reduction of meals in response to price increases) borne by women (Diane Elson 1995; Kabeer 2003).

The Federal Bureau of Statistics (1993a) conducted the Household Integrated Economic Surveys (HIES) to collect data on consumption expenditure at the household level. This study uses HIES data to test a number of hypotheses for differences between the consumption of women and men in Pakistan. To calculate the share of women's and men's consumption in total household consumption, I define first an equation in Working-Lesser form linking expenditure to household income and demographic characteristics in the following way:

$$W_i = \beta_o + \beta_m M_{ades} + \beta_f F_{ades} + \beta_y Ln(Y_{ades}) + \sum_k \beta_s S \tag{1}$$

where W= Household consumption share of ith commodity in total expenditure,
Y_{ades} = Household income per adult equivalent,[9]
M_{ades} = Number of adult equivalent males,
F_{ades} = Number of adult equivalent females,
S = is a vector of socioeconomic characteristics such as occupation and education level.

Although it is an oversimplification to assume that all individuals behave in a similar fashion, I have aggregated households by the education and employment status of the head of household. In urban areas, households are categorized on the basis of the education of the head of the household. In rural areas households are first categorized by gender as female- and male-headed households, and then male-headed households are further distinguished by the employment status of the head of the household – employee, employer, self-employed, and "others," which contains miscellaneous households. I estimated the consumption function for each representative household assuming that all households in a group are normally distributed and, on average, behave homogenously. Therefore, I dropped the last term in Equation (1) in the actual estimation. I estimated this equation for each commodity and for each type of household separately using data from the HIES (Federal Bureau of Statistics 1993a). The coefficients β_f and β_m, represent the change in the share of household consumption of good i with an increase in one adult man and one adult woman holding all other things constant.

I tested the following hypotheses:

$$H_O : \beta_f = \beta_m \text{ against } H_1 = \beta_f \neq \beta_m$$

If the null hypothesis is rejected, this means that the share of good i in total expenditure rises by a different amount for an increase of one adult equivalent female as compared to one adult equivalent male. I calculated the share of women's consumption in household expenditure on i^{th} good by normalizing the coefficients by one of the coefficients; for β_f, I got:

$$\beta_f / \beta_f = 1 \tag{2}$$

and

$$\beta_m / \beta_f = Z \tag{3}$$

If Z > 1, then the male consumption share of good i is greater than that of women and vice versa. I broke down a household's total consumption of commodity i (C_i) for women (C_i^F) and men (C_i^M) as:

$$C_i^F = (\frac{1}{1+Z}) * C_i * F_{ades} \tag{4}$$

$$C_i^M = (\frac{Z}{1+Z}) * C_i * M_{ades} \tag{5}$$

The following ratios determine the share of women (a_f) and men (a_m) in household consumption:

$$a_f = \frac{C_i^F}{C_i^F + C_i^M} \text{ and } a_m = \frac{C_i^M}{C_i^F + C_i^M} \text{ where } a_f + a_m = 1$$

Table 1 reports findings based on regression results for basic needs expenditures (food items, clothing, education, and health).[10] The values in the upper part of the table show that the share of consumption of these items is greater in poorer households in Pakistan.[11] The results also show that male consumption of these items is uniformly greater than that of females (except in rural female-headed households), a finding captured in the ratio in the bottom row of Table 1. Finally, the consumption differences by gender tend to be greater among poorer households.

Similar gender differences are shown in capability indicators, such as the literacy rate and the infant mortality rate, which are strongly associated with intrahousehold allocation of resources. For example, the female literacy rate in 1999 in Pakistan is less than two-thirds the male rate (32.6 to 56.5 percent), and the female child mortality rate in the 1997–2000 was 24.3 per 1,000 compared to 15.4 per 1,000 for male child mortality (CRPRID 2002).

TIME ALLOCATION BY GENDER

In organizing the data set to operationalize the CGE, I introduced gender in social accounting matrix (SAM) for the year 1990 by integrating market,[12] household, and leisure activities (for details see Rizwana Siddiqui [2007]). First, I compiled a matrix of time allocation between market, household (social reproduction), and leisure activities for the eight labor types in each of the nine representative households following the standard system of national accounts (SNA). The SNA considers activities as either productive (market) or non-productive (social reproduction and leisure). I deducted ten hours (minimum time used for self-care) from twenty-four hours to calculate fourteen hours available for market work, household

Table 1 Consumption by gender for basic needs goods

Goods	*Urban households by education of the head of household*				*Rural households*				
						Male-headed households by employment status			
	Illiterate	*Low education*	*Medium education*	*High education*	*Female-headed households*	*Employee*	*Self-employed*	*Others*	*Employe*
Percentage share of expenditure on basic needs goods in total household expenditure									
Men	34.0	34.3	32.2	28.2	24.0	36.7	39.6	38.2	34.2
Women	25.0	23.1	25.3	23.8	41.1	29.7	28.1	24.8	28.7
Total	59.0	57.4	57.5	52.0	65.1	66.4	67.7	63.0	62.9
Ratio of per adult equivalent expenditure									
Women/men	0.84	0.82	0.90	0.93	1.49	0.89	0.76	0.81	0.92

Notes: Low education = less than five years of education; medium education = five to nine years of education; high education = more than nine years of education work, and leisure.[13] I assumed these activities are separable.[14] Therefore, I calculated leisure by subtracting working hours (market and household) from fourteen hours. I valued the nonmarket activities at the weighted average wage of the labor used in these activities.

The results for Pakistan in Table 2 show that men allocate approximately half of their time to market work, and about 40 percent to leisure, usually spending 10 percent or less on domestic activities. Women spend less time on market activities, but market work still takes up about one-third of their total time, with a larger share going to domestic activities, leaving less than 20 percent of their time for leisure, that is, less than half that taken by men. The results at the disaggregated level show that, irrespective of the type of household and skill level, all women have more working hours than men.[15]

GENDER FEATURES OF THE CGE MODEL FOR PAKISTAN

The CGE model combines market, household, and leisure activities, and is a disaggregated version of that presented in Siddiqui (2005). In addition, it incorporates consumption and poverty indicators by gender.

The model is neoclassical in nature, assuming: (1) people with rational preferences; (2) full employment of factors of production; and (3) optimizing behavior: households maximize utility and firms maximize profit.[16] From a gender point of view, the limitation of the neoclassical model is that it does not allow for differences among the preferences of household members. While assuming rational utility-maximizing behavior, this study takes into account differences in consumption by men and women in Pakistan. Men and women derive maximum utility subject to the resources they receive, which depend upon total household income, total available time, and distribution factors.

Table 2 Time allocation of households between market and non-market activities (percentages)

	Women		*Men*	
	Minimum	*Maximum*	*Minimum*	*Maximum*
Urban				
Market	26.5	40.0	50.6	57.4
Social reproduction	34.1	45.3	2.9	10.7
Leisure	10.0	20.0	40.0	Above 40
Rural				
Market	34.1	45.3	47.5	53.3
Social reproduction	35.9	47.3	1.6	16.8
Leisure	10.0	20.0	40.0	About 40

Notes: Minimum–maximum is the range of time allocation of representative households among market, social reproduction, and leisure, so it does not total 100.

The model employs six blocks of equations: income and savings, production, demand, prices, trade, and equilibrium. Gender rigidities appear by assuming a low elasticity of substitution (0.3) between the labor of men and women. Nonmarket sectors (social reproduction and leisure) behave like market sectors and produce goods that are consumed by the households themselves. Social reproduction and leisure are joint products of all types of labor of both women and men in each representative household. I defined their production using a Constant Elasticity of Substitution (CES) technology. I derived the demand for labor in market and nonmarket sectors from the first order condition. The price of nonmarket goods (Ph) is the weighted average of the wages of the labor used in production.

I defined total income of a household (Y_T) as the sum of receipts from the market economy and the nonmarket economy. Maximizing a Stone-Geary utility function of market goods (C_i), home produced goods (C_H), and leisure (C_L) subject to total income and time constraints, I derived household demand for goods and services.

Model closure and calibration

The total supply of each type of labor is fixed, and the wage rate is adjusted to maintain labor market equilibrium for each type of labor. Capital stock is sector specific (that is, capital cannot move from one sector to the other) so returns to capital (profit) adjust in each sector to equalize supply and demand for capital at the sectoral level.[17]

The three blocks, savings-investment, government, and the rest of the world, are associated with the macro constraints of the model. Savings from domestic institutions and the rest of the world finance total investment. Household savings adjust to equilibrate investment and savings. The nominal exchange rate acts as the numeraire and the real exchange rate varies in order to keep the current account balance (CAB) fixed.[18] An increase in imports leads to a depreciation of the real exchange rate, which stimulates exports. This closure eliminates the possibility that external resources would finance domestic policies.

Given that Pakistan has a small open economy, world export prices and world import prices are exogenous. Loss in tariff revenue is compensated for by domestic tax, which adjusts uniformly on all commodities. Government consumption and investment are fixed in real terms, so an increase of household consumption is not at the expense of domestic investment or government consumption. The price indices for government consumption and investment adjust in response to a policy shock. The model is homogeneous of degree zero in volumes and degree one in prices. An exogenous increase in prices increases all nominal variables by the same percentage but does not increase the volumes.

First, I constructed the benchmark equilibrium data set in the SAM-framework to operationalize CGE. Then I specified the model's parameters – such as share and shift parameters in production, utility functions, constant elasticity of transformation (CET) function for the shift between export and domestic demand, and Armington functions for the substitution between imports and domestic goods (CES) – through the calibration procedure using SAM data to make the model operational. I also calculated tariff rates, tax rates, and savings from the SAM data. Elasticities are exogenous in the model. For the consumption function, I estimated household-specific income elasticities for each commodity based on the unitary household demand function using micro data from the HIES (Federal Bureau of Statistics 1993a). For the intrahousehold allocation of resources, I borrowed income elasticities from the unitary household demand function. This study sets income elasticities higher for women than for men by 2 percentage points, because as feminist economists emphasize, in the presence of discrimination female consumption is more vulnerable to changes in income and prices than male consumption (Elson 1995; Kabeer 2003). I took elasticities for the production function from Siddiqui and Kemal (2006). Elasticities that were not available from empirical studies are set at reasonable values consistent with those used in other CGE studies.

Calibration assumes that equilibrium exists in the economy under consideration in the presence of existing policies. Therefore, the procedure used in general equilibrium analysis is first to use the observed equilibrium to solve the model for parameter values such that the model reproduces the original equilibrium. I used the General Algebraic Modeling System (GAMS) software package to make these computations and solve and simulate the model to find new prices. These prices bring equilibrium in the market after the shock.

Poverty and welfare analysis

Macro policies affect poverty incidence that may differ by gender (Marzia Fontana and Yana van der Meulen Rodgers 2005). This study uses three indicators of poverty: capability,[19] income, and time to measure gender-specific impacts and welfare indicators EV1 and EV2 (Equivalent Variation). It measures impact at the household level using consumption of market goods only, and using consumption of market and nonmarket goods respectively.

Capability poverty

Infant mortality and literacy rates are the most appropriate capability indicators for a gender impact analysis because they measure composite effects of the satisfaction of basic needs (Kabeer 2003). The IMR captures satisfaction of several basic needs: nutrition intake, health services, shelter and safe drinking water, and sanitation facilities (Rizwana Siddiqui 2008a). The literacy rate (LR) measures the basic need for education, which enhances capabilities and choices. Both IMR and LR depend on per capita household expenditure (CH_{pc}) and per capita government expenditure on education and health (CG_{HEPC}). Using elasticities based on cross-district data (Siddiqui 2008a), I estimated the following indicators:

$$IMR = IMR_{\min} + \frac{(IMR_{base} - IMR_{\min})}{1 + A * CH^{\beta} * CG^{\gamma}} \tag{6}$$

$$LR = LR_{\max} - \frac{(LR_{\max} - LR_{base})}{1 + A * CH^{\beta} * CG^{\gamma}} \tag{7}$$

where β and γ are the elasticities with respect to per capita household expenditure (CH) and public expenditure on education and health (CG) respectively. IMR_{min} is the minimum value of IMR achieved worldwide.[20] LR_{max} is 100 – the maximum that can be achieved. I projected the base year values for IMR for each representative household using district-level estimates from Muhammad Arshad Mahmood (2003) and per capita household income. I calculated the literacy rate using HIES data (Federal Bureau of Statistics 1993a). With the logistic relationships between dependent and independent variables in equations (6) and (7), the gap between desired and actual levels of indicators decreases with increases in inputs.

Income poverty

Foster-Greer-Thorbecke (FGT) poverty indices (headcount ratio, poverty gap, and severity) have been calculated to measure the impact of trade liberalization on the poverty level prevailing in a country (James Foster, Joel Greer, and Erik Thorbecke 1984). The change in the gender composition of the poor population after the policy shock reveals the gender dimensions of income poverty.

I calculated the poverty level in the base year using a basic needs poverty line (V) based on an adult equivalent scale as follows:

$$V = \Sigma C_{i0} * P^{i}_{c0} \tag{8}$$

where C_{io} is quantity of good i necessary to satisfy basic needs, and P^{i}_{c0} is the consumer price index (CPI) for the ith good in the base period. I recalculated the poverty line after the shock with new consumer prices

$(C_{i0}{*}P_{c1}^{\,i})$. I used the following formula to calculate FGT indices (Foster, Greer, and Thorbecke 1984):

$$p_\alpha = \frac{1}{n}\sum_{j=1}^{j}\left[(V - Y_j)/Y\right]^\alpha \qquad (9)$$

where n is the total number of households, Y_j is household income for those below the poverty line, α is a parameter that takes values of 0, 1, and 2 to distinguish different measures of poverty, namely headcount ratio, poverty gap, and severity. Using the vector of simulated incomes and the new poverty line, I calculated FGT indices,[21] using the Distributive Analyses/Analyse Distributive (DAD) program before and after the shock (for more on the DAD program see Duclos, Araar, and Fortin [2001]). I obtained the relative income poverty among women and men by calculating the population by gender in poor households before and after the shock.

Time poverty

I measured time poverty in relative terms. The change in leisure time relative to base year value and the change in leisure of women compared to men determined the change in time poverty.

Finally, EV measured welfare using base year and post-simulation prices and consumption of goods. First, welfare was measured on the consumption of market goods only. Second, it included both the consumption of market and nonmarket goods.

SIMULATION RESULTS

Tariff reduction on imports and sales tax adjustment

In the 1990s, industry and agriculture in Pakistan were protected with average tariffs of 25.7 and 6.9 percent respectively. However, these averages reflected substantial variation within the sectors. In agriculture, fisheries and horticulture were heavily protected with 60 and 67 percent tariff respectively, compared to the crop sector with a low tariff of just 5 percent. Industrial commodities were protected with an average tariff of 25.7 percent, but the service sector was not protected at all. Therefore, trade liberalization would affect these sectors differently and have a gender-differentiated impact. The simulation is based on the actual average tariff cuts of 50 percent, which are compensated by an endogenous adjustment in average domestic taxes of 3 percent (ranging between 0 and 20 percent in the base period) so there is no loss in government revenue.

Macro effects[22]

The immediate effect of reduction in tariffs is a drop in import prices and a rise in imports of 2.9 percent (Table 3). The depreciation in the real exchange rate brings about an increase in exports of 3.9 percent, the so-called export-push effect of trade liberalization (John Cockburn, Bernard Decaluwé, and Veronique Robichaud 2008). These effects are mainly driven by changes in two industrial sectors: textiles and machinery. The former is an export-oriented sector with an export intensity of 42 percent, and the latter is an import competing sector with an import penetration ratio of 61 percent. In these two sectors, imports rose by 4.7 and 3.5 percent and exports by 4.6 and 6 percent respectively (Table 3).

Agriculture, which has a lower degree of import penetration (M/Q) at 3.5 percent and a small export share (E/XS) at 1.1 percent, is less affected (Table 3). The increase in domestic taxes on services raises their import price, thus negatively affecting imports of services (Table 3).

The decline in import prices exerts a downward pressure on domestic prices, most notably in industry. Hence, output falls noticeably in the import competing sector producing machinery. The depreciation of the real exchange rate makes export-oriented sectors more competitive, with an increase in the production of textile commodities of 2.6 percent (more than domestic sales), and an increase in textile exports of 4.6 percent.

Factor market effects

The price changes bring about a sectoral reallocation of resources, with employment changes following the same pattern as output described above. The increase in employment is greatest in the textile sector, over 5 percent. The increase in female employment in the textile sector outweighs the negative impact on demand for female labor in other industrial sectors. Hence, women's industrial employment rises by 2.2 percent, compared to a fall in men's industrial employment by 1.2 percent (Table 4).

Employment in the less import-intensive agriculture and service sectors declines more for women than men (Table 4). As a result, revenue-neutral trade liberalization reduces women's employment by 0.7 percent overall, and men's employment by 0.4 percent, corresponding to a decline in labor demand in the market economy of 0.5 percent at the national level.

The effects of trade liberalization on time allocation to nonmarket activities also vary, not only by gender but also by type of household, rich or poor. This confirms the findings of Jongsoog Kim and Lydia Zepeda (2004) that the intrahousehold time allocation on US farms is gender specific and the father's economic status has the largest impact on the time allocation of household members. Urban households with no education and all

Table 3 Revenue-neutral trade liberalization and variation in macro variables and domestic prices (percentages)

						Trade liberalization							
Sectors	*Tariff base value*	*Tax base value*	*Tariff cut*	*Imports/ domestic absorption of composite good*	*Exports/ domestic supply or output*	*Consumer price*	*Import price*	*Domestic absorption of composite good*	*Demand for domestically produced goods*	*Imports*	*Exports*	*Value added*	*Returns to capital*
Agriculture	6.9	0.4	0.5	3.5	1.1	-1.3	-2.5	-0.2	-0.3	1.5	3.5	-0.2	-3.1
Industry	25.7	5.8	0.5	26.8	15.2	-4.0	-8.5	0.03	-1.2	3.4	4.34	-0.2	-5.6
Textile	25.4	0.4	0.3	3.8	42.0	-2.2	-5.4	1.2	1.0	4.7	4.6	2.6	-0.4
Machinery	28.7	0.8	0.5	61.5	3.5	-8.0	-9.5	1.2	-2.4	3.5	6.0	-2.1	-8.2
Services	0.0	1.7	0.0	4.9	6.1	-1.8	0.7	-0.4	-0.08	-3.0	2.2	-0.2	-2.7
Total	22.4	3.0(1.3)[a]	0.5	14.0	9.1	-2.1	-0.01	-0.2	-0.50	2.9	3.9	-0.2	-3.4

Notes: [a]Uniform Adjustment in Tax Rate.

Table 4 Trade liberalization and employment by gender (percentage change over base values)

	Female labor					*Male labor*					
Market sectors	*No education*	*Low education*	*Medium education*	*High education*	*Total*	*No education*	*Low education*	*Medium education*	*High education*	*Total*	*Total labor demand*
Agriculture	0.2	-1.9	-2.5	0.0	-1.1	0.9	-2.4	-0.7	-4.6	-0.1	-0.4
Industry	6.2	4.6	1.7	-0.7	2.2	1.0	-1.9	-0.4	-5.6	-1.2	-0.4
Textile	7.0	4.7	4.2	1.8	4.3	7.9	4.5	6.4	2.4	6.1	5.3
Services	-4.0	-1.0	-1.7	-3.5	-2.7	3.9	0.9	1.5	-1.5	-0.3	-0.5
Total	0.8	-1.0	-1.6	-2.3	-0.7	-1.2	-4.2	-2.6	-6.2	-0.4	-0.5
Real wage rate	-2.1	1.5	2.9	6.6		-3.2	1.8	-0.2	5.8		0.7
Nominal wage rate	-4.9	-1.4	-0.1	3.5	-1.6	-6.0	-1.1	-3.1	2.7	-1.6	-1.6

Notes: No education = no formal education; low education = less than five years of education; medium education = five to nine years of education; high education = more than nine years of education.

households in rural areas, except female-headed households, have reduced labor input in both social reproduction and leisure (Table 5). Leisure decreases for urban households with no education and for all rural households, except female-headed households and employer households.

These households are relatively poor (see Table 8 for poverty incidence in the base year) and generally rely on their own unskilled labor (indicated by the category "no education").[23] The demand for unskilled women's labor increases in all market sectors by 0.8 percent (Table 4). Skilled labor (including those with low, medium, and high education), which is concentrated in relatively rich urban households, faces a decline in demand in the market sectors and an increase in non-traded nonmarket activities, social reproduction, and leisure. In addition, female-headed households (that receive a larger share of their income from remittances) also face an increased labor demand in nonmarket activities. Irrespective of type of household, female leisure changes less favorably – it declines more or increases less – than male leisure (Table 5). The overall results show that in urban areas social reproduction and leisure increase by 0.5 and 1.8 percent, respectively; in rural areas, they decline by 0.4 and 1.4 percent, respectively.

Capital cannot move from one sector to the other; therefore, change in demand for capital results in change in returns to capital (Table 3). Tariff reduction has less impact on agriculture and services sectors. Hence, returns to capital in agriculture and services decline less (-3.1 and -2.7 percent, respectively) than returns to industrial capital (-5.6 percent). The returns to industrial capital decline the most in the metallic industry (-16.3 percent), which is the most protected sector with a 43.8 percent tariff and very high import penetration ratio of 52.2 percent. On average, returns to capital decline more than wages (-3.4 versus -1.6 percent respectively), implying that trade liberalization hits the capital owners the hardest. However, on the labor side, trade liberalization hit unskilled labor harder, as the wage rates of unskilled labor declined more than skilled labor. The net change in households' income depends on their ownership and income shares from different sources (labor, capital, remittances, and transfers from government and firms) in the base period.

Household income effects

The exogenous shock of trade liberalization reduces the nominal income of all representative households over the base year values (Table 6). Table 6 shows that the poorest households (categorized as "no education" and "employee") are hardest hit, as their income declines by 3.4 percent in both areas. The nominal wage rate for unskilled labor falls by 4.9 percent for women and by 6 percent for men (Table 4), which is greater than the change in the wage rate for skilled labor as well as that in the return to

Table 5 Trade liberalization and labor in non-market activities (percentage change over base value)

	Female labor				*Male labor*					
Households	*No education*	*Low education*	*Medium education*	*High education*	*No education*	*Low education*	*Medium education*	*High education*	*Total*	*Ph*[a]
Social reproduction										
Urban households by education of the head of the household									0.5	
No education	-1.0	-2.2	-2.1	-3.5	-0.6	-2.3	-1.2	-3.3	-1.5	-2.5
Low education	5.2	3.8	4.0	2.3	5.5	3.7	5.0	2.6	4.0	-1.4
Medium education	1.5	0.2	0.2	-1.1	1.9	0.1	1.1	-0.9	0.3	-1.5
High education	5.2	3.8	4.0	2.4	5.6	3.7	5.0	2.6	3.0	-0.5
Rural households									-0.4	
Female-headed	3.6	2.2	2.3	0.9	4.0	2.1	3.3	1.1	2.8	-2.2
Male-headed households by employment status										
Employee	-0.9	-2.1	-2.4	-3.5	-0.6	-2.2	-1.5	-3.3	-1.6	-2.6
Self-employed	-0.6	-1.9	-1.8	-3.2	-0.3	-2.0	-0.9	-3.0	-1.1	-2.7
Others	-0.2	-1.6	-1.4	-2.8	0.1	-1.7	-0.5	-2.6	-1.2	-1.9
Employer	1.6	0.2	-0.2	-1.0	2.0	0.0	0.7	-0.8	-0.8	0.02
Total									-0.02	
Leisure										
Urban households by education of the head of the household									1.8	
No education	-0.6	-1.7	-2.0	-3.1	-0.3	-1.7	-1.0	-2.9	-0.8	-3.2
Low education	7.6	6.3	6.2	4.7	7.9	6.2	7.2	5.0	6.4	-1.8
Medium education	2.7	1.5	1.0	0.1	3.1	1.4	2.0	0.3	1.6	-2.2
High education	6.2	5.0	5.0	3.5	6.6	4.9	5.9	3.7	3.9	-0.5

(*continued*)

Table 5 (Continued)

Households	*Female labor*				*Male labor*					
	No education	*Low education*	*Medium education*	*High education*	*No education*	*Low education*	*Medium education*	*High education*	*Total*	*Ph*[a]
Rural households									-1.4	
Female-headed	5.4	4.0	4.0	2.6	5.8	3.9	5.0	2.9	4.8	-2.5
Male-headed households by employment status										
Employee	-1.2	-2.3	-2.9	-3.7	-0.9	-2.4	-2.0	-3.5	-1.8	-2.9
Self-employed	-0.9	-2.1	-2.4	-3.5	-0.6	-2.2	-1.5	-3.3	-1.4	-2.9
Others	-0.5	-1.6	-2.0	-3.0	-0.2	-1.7	-1.1	-2.8	-1.5	-2.2
Employer	3.0	1.8	1.1	0.5	3.3	1.7	2.0	0.7	1.2	-1.2
Total									0.16	

Notes: No education = no formal education; low education = less than five years of education; medium education = five to nine years of education; high education = more than nine years of education. [a]Ph is the price of social reproduction and leisure.

Table 6 Income effects of trade liberalization (percentage variation over base values)

	Urban households				*Rural households*				
	Education of head of the households					*Male-headed households by employment status*			
	No education	*Low education*	*Medium education*	*High education*	*Female-headed*	*Employee*	*Self-employed*	*Others*	*Employer*
Income	-3.4	-2.7	-2.8	-1.8	-1.9	-3.4	-3.3	-2.6	-3.2
Female wage income (real)	1.3	2.6	3.0	4.1	1.5	0.8	0.9	2.0	5.2
Male wage income (real)	-1.2	0.9	0.5	4.1	0.0	-0.3	-0.5	0.7	1.8

Notes: No education = no formal education; low education = less than five years of education; medium education = five to nine years of education; high education = more than nine years of education.

capital. Female-headed households receive 37 percent of their income from remittances. The value of remittance income rises in terms of domestic currency. So female-headed households are among the least affected with a drop in income of 1.9 percent.

Since prices decline more than nominal wages, real wages increase. Overall, the results suggest that trade liberalization favors women by increasing their real wage income for all skill levels in both urban and rural households (Table 6), which is likely to increase the bargaining power of women in their households. However, this conclusion needs to be further explored in a separate study.

Households with high education observe the largest wage income increase, which is equal for men and women in urban areas and greater for women than men in rural areas (Table 6).

Consumption by gender effects

On the consumption side, rural households consume more agricultural goods, whereas urban households consume relatively more services. Therefore, changes in the consumer price index differ by household type depending on the household's consumption pattern. The change in net income (total income minus savings) and relative consumer prices determines the change in consumption of men and women due to trade liberalization.

Total consumption of relatively better off households increases and consumption of poor households decreases (Table 7).[24] Women's consumption has higher income elasticity and so is more sensitive to changes in income. These consumption effects also depend on initial consumption shares and price and income elasticities. The size of the consumption effect varies by household type and commodity. In general, the consumption of women is more strongly affected by the policy shock, but this is not the case in rich households (Table 7).

In urban households categorized as having high education, expenditure on women's education and health after trade liberalization increases more than that on men: 5.4 and 4.9 percent respectively (Table 7). This confirms that prosperity reduces the gender gap in capability development. However, bias may exist in these households in other forms that are not included in this paper.[25]

Poverty and welfare effects

Table 8 shows that poverty increases in the households grouped as no education, employee, other, and self-employed, and poverty decreases in urban and rural area households with educated heads (low, medium, and high education) and those with an employer. Poverty also declines in female-headed households that receive a dominant share of their income

Table 7 Trade liberalization and demand for basic-needs goods by gender at constant prices (percentage variation over base values)

	Urban households				*Rural households*				
	Education of the head of household					*Male-headed households classified by employment status*			
Goods	*No education*	*Low education*	*Medium education*	*High education*	*Female-headed households*	*Employee*	*Self-employed*	*Others*	*Employer*
Crop									
Women	-1.7	3.0	0.6	2.6	1.2	-1.1	-1.6	-0.9	1.1
Men	-1.6	3.1	0.5	2.7	1.0	-1.2	-1.6	-0.9	0.9
Livestock									
Women	-2.0	2.3	0.2	3.4	1.7	-1.7	-1.7	-0.9	1.1
Men	-2.1	2.3	0.1	3.5	1.7	-1.8	-1.8	-1.0	0.9
Fish									
Women	-1.4	3.3	0.5	4.4	2.8	-2.2	-1.3	-0.7	1.1
Mmen	-1.4	3.3	0.5	4.1	2.8	-2.2	-1.1	-0.8	1.2
Food manufacturing									
Women	-1.3	1.5	0.3	3.0	1.1	-1.3	-1.7	-0.9	1.3
Mmen	-1.3	1.5	0.3	2.9	1.1	-1.3	-1.8	-0.9	1.4

(*continued*)

Table 7 (Continued)

	Urban households				*Rural households*				
	Education of the head of household					*Male-headed households classified by employment status*			
Goods	*No education*	*Low education*	*Medium education*	*High education*	*Female-headed households*	*Employee*	*Self-employed*	*Others*	*Employer*
Textile									
Women	-1.9	4.3	0.7	4.2	3.4	-2.2	-1.1	-0.4	1.9
Men	-2.2	4.4	0.7	4.2	3.3	-2.3	-1.2	-0.4	2.0
Social sector									
Women	-2.9	3.9	0.5	5.4	2.5	-3.0	-1.8	-0.9	0.9
Men	-2.7	3.6	0.4	4.9	2.6	-3.0	-2.0	-1.0	0.9
Household consumption									
Total	-1.7	3.5	0.8	4.1	1.6	-1.6	-1.5	-0.7	1.7
Consumer price index (CPI)	-1.6	-1.6	-1.7	-1.6	-1.7	-1.7	-1.7	-1.8	-1.7

Notes: No education = no formal education; low education = less than five years of education; medium education = five to nine years of education; high education = more than nine years of education.

Table 8 Trade liberalization, poverty, and welfare (percentage variation over base values)

		FGT indices			*Share in poor population (relative poverty)*		*Welfare*	
		Head count	*Poverty gap*	*Severity*	*Men*	*Women*	*(EV1)*[a]	*(EV2)*[b]
Urban households	*Head count base year*							
No education	39.8	3.7	5.6	6.9	-0.1	0.1	0	-0.03
Low education	35.0	-11.8	-11.1	-12.5	-1	1	0.03	-0.03
Medium education	35.0	-1.4	-1.2	-3.6	0.03	-0.03	0.01	-0.02
High education	13.3	-14	-13.8	-13.3	0	0	0.03	0
Urban total	32.2	-3.6	-2.6	-2.5	-0.08	0.08	0.01	-0.04
Rural households								
Female-headed households	26.5	-3.3	-5.6	-5.9	0.08	-0.08	0.02	-0.05
Male-headed households								
Employee	35.9	3	6.2	7.7	0	0	-0.01	-0.02
Self-employed	26.7	2.8	5.2	5.6	-0.03	0.03	-0.01	-0.04
Others	19.7	1.7	2.2	7.1	-0.07	0.07	-0.01	-0.03
Employer	15.3	-3.5	-5.4	-8.3	0	0	0	0
Rural total	29.3	2.3	4.6	5.7	0.02	-0.02	-0.004	-0.04
Pakistan	30.6	-0.3	1.3	2	-0.03	0.03	0.004	-0.037

Notes: No education = no formal education; low education = less than five years of education; medium education = five to nine years of education; high education = more than nine years of education.
Base year urban poverty line is Rs318 per capita per month, and rural poverty line is Rs264 per capita per month. EV = Equivalent Variation.
[a]Indicates that the figure is based on the consumption of market goods only.
[b]Indicates that the figure is based on the consumption of all goods: market goods, household goods, and leisure goods.

from remittances, which increases in rupee terms with the depreciation of the real exchange rate. Poverty decreases at the national level by -0.3 percent despite an increase in poverty in rural areas. The other two measures, poverty gap and severity indices, show an increase in poverty in Pakistan (Table 8).

Even though trade liberalization reduces income poverty, relative poverty (the share of women relative to men in the poor population) increases among women by 0.03 percent at the national level due to an increase in the share of women in the poor population in households representing the categories no education, low education, self-employed, and others (see Table 8). In all other households, women's shares decline (medium education and female-headed households) or remain constant (high education and employer). Women's share in the poorest rural households group also remains constant, where absolute poverty increases the most in rural households.

Leisure time for men increases more or decreases less than for women in all urban and rural households except in high education households, where the reverse pattern is found (Table 9). As a result, absolute as well as relative time poverty increases among women, meaning women's leisure time decreases by 0.09 percent and men's leisure time increases by 0.2 percent.

Trade liberalization does not reduce the welfare of urban households. In rural areas, only female-headed households are better off. Welfare based on consumption of market goods improves at the national level (EV1 in Table 8). However, when consumption of nonmarket goods is taken into account, the country is worse off, with welfare loss for all households except rich households (high education and employer households) (EV2 in Table 8).

Similar to income poverty effects, capability poverty increases in households classified as no education, employee, self-employed, and others, and decreases among better-off households (low, medium, and high education, and employer and female-headed households) – see Table 9. The effect on the IMR of boys and girls is the same quantitatively except in households with high education, where IMR declines more for females than males. However, the female literacy rate increases/decreases more than the male rate. This exercise again shows that the impact of trade liberalization (negative or positive) is largely absorbed by women in relatively poor households (Table 9). At the national level, the negative effect dominates; IMR and LR deteriorate for both men and women.

All indicators of poverty and welfare suggest that trade liberalization hurts the poorest households and remains gender neutral in the richest households. Thus, education, income growth, and poverty-targeted policies can be the most appropriate tools to counter the negative impact of trade liberalization.

Table 9 Trade liberalization, capability indicators, and time poverty (percentage variation in base values)

	Infant mortality rate			*Literacy rate*			*Time poverty*	
	Total	*Female*	*Male*	*Total*	*Female*	*Male*	*Men*	*Women*
Urban households								
No education	0.08	0.07	0.07	-0.8	-0.92	-0.6	-0.7	-1.3
Low education	-0.2	-0.2	-0.2	0.46	0.95	0.24	6.4	6.3
Medium education	-0.06	-0.06	-0.06	0.09	0.17	0.04	1.7	1.2
High education	-0.24	-0.24	-0.23	0.05	0.08	0.02	3.8	4.3
Urban total	-0.06	-0.05	-0.08	-0.29	-0.33	-0.20	1.87	1.74
Rural households								
Female-headed households	-0.1	-0.11	-0.11	0.75	1.57	0.49	4.8	4.8
Male-headed households								
Employee	0.08	0.07	0.07	-1.59	-3.33	-0.92	-1.7	-1.9
Self-employed	0.07	0.07	0.07	-0.57	-1.12	-0.3	-1.3	-1.5
Others	0.03	0.02	0.02	-0.11	-0.1	-0.04	-1.4	-1.5
Employer	-0.11	-0.1	-0.1	0.29	0.59	0.15	1.7	0.6
Rural total	0.06	0.05	0.04	-0.81	-1.69	-0.37	-1.49	-1.68
Pakistan	0.004	0.01	0.03	-0.58	-1.11	-0.29	0.20	-0.09

Notes: No education = no formal education; low education = less than five years of education; medium education = five to nine years of education; high education = more than nine years of education.

CONCLUDING REMARKS AND POLICY IMPLICATIONS

This study uses a CGE model specially constructed for investigating gender dimensions of the impact of trade liberalization in Pakistan. The model distinguishes not only women's from men's labor in four skill categories but also women's from men's consumption. Therefore, it examines the difference in the burden of trade liberalization for men and women from production and consumption aspects. It measures the impact by employing three indicators of poverty (capability poverty, income poverty, and time poverty), and it estimates welfare on the consumption of both market and nonmarket goods.

Revenue-neutral trade liberalization promises to increase the participation of unskilled female labor, but division of labor remains biased against them. The results indicate that the gender bias in the labor market participation of workers and in wage income decreases under revenue-neutral trade liberalization. With a greater increase in female wage income than male wage income for all categories, female income share in household income increases, which is likely to increase the bargaining power of women in their households – although this is not modeled explicitly in this study.

The results also show that the effects of trade liberalization on women and men differ in the richest and the poorest households. It adversely affects women in the poorest households by increasing their workload, reducing capabilities, and increasing relative income poverty. However, the effects remain gender neutral or favor women in the richest households, that is, households distinguished by high education and employer households.

The income poverty effects differ by area – rural or urban – and by type of household within the area. Trade liberalization reduces poverty in urban areas and increases it in rural areas. It benefits relatively rich households in urban areas (households grouped by low, medium, and high education). However, in rural areas poverty decreases in female-headed households (these receive a larger share of their income from remittances) and employer households (the richest households in rural areas); poverty increases in all other households. At the national level, trade liberalization reduces (absolute) income poverty. Despite decline in absolute poverty, relative income poverty among women increases. This indicates the need for disaggregated analysis to unveil the effects on the rich and the poor in rural and urban areas and by gender as well.

Trade liberalization improves welfare at the national level when measured with the consumption of market goods, but deteriorates when household work and leisure (nonmarket goods) are included in the analysis. The results confirm earlier policy recommendations for Pakistan and other developing countries that suggest the government should target poverty reduction, promote education, and make transfer payments or reduce taxes on basic needs to counter or even avoid the adverse impact of trade liberalization on poor households (see Siddiqui [2008a, 2008b, 2009]).

This work can be extended by incorporating the following: activities undertaken simultaneously by an individual; capital goods in home production; explicit modeling of the role of women not employed in market work; a linking of women's bargaining power with their earned income; and the feedback effect of capability development.

ACKNOWLEDGMENTS

This study was carried out with the aid of a grant awarded through the Gender Challenge Fund of the Poverty and Economic Policy (PEP) Research Network (www.pep-net.org), a joint venture of the Gender Network (Phase III) and the PEP Network, both financed by the International Development Research Centre (IDRC). I am thankful for the comments from discussants and participants in PEP Conferences in Colombo, Sri Lanka; Dakar, Senegal; and Addis Ababa, Ethiopia. Thanks are also due to Professors Bernard Decaluwé and John Cockburn from Université Laval, Canada for their comments. I would also like to acknowledge the valuable comments and suggestions by Dr. Marzia Fontana of the Institute of Development Studies at the University of Sussex. My special gratitude is due to Dr. Howard White, the executive director of International Initiative for Impact Evaluation (3ie), for his constant help commenting on different versions of this piece. Without his extensive help and encouragement, I would not have been able to prepare the study in this format. I am also grateful to anonymous referees at *Feminist Economics* for their very detailed comments on earlier versions of this piece. Last but not least, I am very grateful to the guest editors for their invaluable comments on many versions of this piece.

NOTES

[1] Rationalization of the tariff structure involves the simplification of the tariff structure, which includes reducing tariffs and reducing the number of duty rates (these were reduced to four in the 1990s). However, on some items such as petroleum, tariffs have increased.

[2] Women earned 43 percent less than men in 1993–4. A 55 percent wage differential between men and women is due to discrimination in the labor market (Rehana Siddiqui and Rizwana Siddiqui 1998).

[3] For details, see Erik Thorbecke (1992); Bernard Decaluwé, Jean-Yves Christophe Dusmond, Luc Savard (1999); and Siddiqui et al. (2008).

4 In 1989–90, the GOP introduced a general sales tax (GST) on both imports and domestic products to compensate for the loss in tariff revenue due to tariff reduction imports. Reduction in tariffs on imports along with tax rate adjustment on imported and domestic goods is called revenue-neutral trade liberalization.

5 The satisfaction of basic needs reflects (in aggregates) individual capabilities such as a long and healthy life, acquisition of knowledge, and having enough resources to buy food and other necessities. Empirical studies measure individuals' capabilities by various indicators such as IMR, life expectancy (LE), and literacy rate (LR) (Ravi Kanbur 1987; Siddiqui 2008b; Sudhir Anand and Martin Ravallion 1993). Infant mortality rate (IMR) is the best indicator to measure aggregates of capabilities and welfare, among other outcomes, because it measures the availability of several basic needs. It is an outcome variable of inputs such as health, nutrition, clean water, and sanitation facilities. The second capability development indicator is the literacy rate (LR). It indicates accumulation of knowledge. An increase/decrease in IMR implies an increase/decrease in capability poverty.

6 "Social Reproduction" describes household activities as classified by the system of national accounts such as cooking, cleaning, and looking after children and the elderly. However, my study includes fetching water as a household rather than market activity, and I use "household work" and "social reproduction" interchangeably.

7 The major difference between the Fontana and Fofana approaches is in the modeling of leisure time. Fontana and Wood (2000) assume men and women's leisure can be substituted for each other. In this approach, the model is calibrated assuming fourteen available hours for work and leisure and ten hours for personal care. Fofana, Cockburn, and Decaluwé (2003, 2005) use an explicit labor supply function, calculating maximum time available for work or leisure by using elasticities of labor supply with respect to income. The problem with this approach is that elasticities are not generally available. However, in the absence of time-use data, this approach would be preferred.

8 Trade liberalization such as tariff reduction on imports reduces domestic price of imports, and consumers increase the demand for imported goods and reduce demand for domestically produced goods. This reduces production in the domestic economy, and factors of production move toward relatively competitive sectors. The change in the structure of production changes the prices of domestic goods. As a result the prices of commodities produced in the domestic economy and the prices of factors of production change.

9 I calculated number of adults in a household using adult equivalent scale (see Deaton [1997] for details).

10 Other commodities such as housing, sanitation facilities, and utilities like water, electricity, and gas are public goods that men and women consume equally.

11 Table 8 reports poverty based on head count ratios (Po). In the urban area, households are categorized on the basis of the education of the head of the household – no education, low education (less than five years), medium education (five to nine years), and high education (more than nine years). In the rural area, households are first categorized by gender as female- and male-headed households, and male-headed households are further distinguished by the employment status of the head of the household – employee, employer, self-employed, and "others," which contains miscellaneous households.

These households are arranged on the basis of the incidence of poverty in ascending order as follows. Urban households: no education – poorest; low education – poor; medium education – poor; high education – richest. Rural households: employees – poorest; self-employed – poorer; female-headed – rich; others – richer; employer – richest. The ranking is based at the regional level.

[12] SAM consists of twenty market sectors in agriculture (crop, livestock, forestry, fisheries, and others); industry (mining, food and beverages, textile, wood and paper, chemical, non-metallic, metallic, machinery, and handicrafts); and services (utilities, wholesale, retail trade, education and health, other, sanitation and other, public administration, defense, and construction).

[13] For details of the social accounting matrix, see Appendix A.

[14] In practice, women frequently multi-task, in particular combining childcare with other tasks.

[15] Detailed results are available on request from the author.

[16] For a detailed discussion of neoclassical models and their assumptions, see Bernhard G. Gunter, Lance Taylor, and Eric Yeldan (2005) and Bernhard G. Gunter, Marc J. Cohen, and Hans Lofgren (2005).

[17] In the short run, we assume that capital cannot move from one sector to the other. If capital is also mobile (which is a long-run phenomenon), the country moves toward complete specialization.

[18] The real exchange rate is implicit in the model and is calculated in the following way: $er = e * (P^w/P_d)$, where er, e, P^W, and P_d, respectively, are the real exchange rate, the nominal exchange rate, world prices, and domestic prices.

[19] The satisfaction of basic needs reflects (in aggregates) individual capabilities such as the ability to have a long and healthy life, to acquire knowledge, and to have enough resources to buy food and other necessities. Empirical studies measure individual's capabilities by various indicators such as infant mortality rate (IMR), life expectancy (LE), and literacy rate (LR) (Kanbur 1987; Anand and Ravallion 1993; Siddiqui 2008b). Infant mortality rate (IMR) is the best indicator to measure aggregates of capabilities and welfare, because it measures the availability of several basic needs. It is an outcome variable of inputs, including health, nutrition, clean water, and sanitation facilities. Increase/decrease in IMR implies increase/decrease in capability poverty. The second capability development indicator is the literacy rate (LR). It indicates accumulation of knowledge.

[20] Japan achieved an IMR of 5 deaths per 1,000 live births in 1990 (World Bank 2005).

[21] For details of income poverty analysis in CGE, see Rizwana Siddiqui and Abdur-Razzaque Kemal (2006).

[22] Detailed results are available from the author.

[23] I have used skill and education interchangeably as follows: (1) no education = unskilled; (2) low education = low skill, medium education = medium skill, and high education = high skill.

[24] The same pattern is found in the consumption of basic needs items.

[25] Other forms may include mobility constraint, industrial and occupational choices, decision making, etc.

REFERENCES

Agricultural Census Organization. 1993. *Census of Agriculture 1990*. Islamabad: Statistics Division, Ministry of Finance and Economic Affairs, Government of Pakistan.

Anand, Sudhir and Martin Ravallion. 1993. "Human Development in Poor Countries: On the Role of Private Incomes and Public Services." *Journal of Economic Perspectives* 7(1): 133–50.

Arndt, Channing, Sherman Robinson, and Finn Tarp. 2006. "Trade Reform and Gender in Mozambique." *Nordic Journal of Political Economy* 32(1): 73–89.

Arndt, Channing and Finn Tarp. (2003). "Trade Policy Reform and the Missing Revenue: A Gendered Analysis for Mozambique." Paper presented at the 6th Annual Conference on Global Economic Analysis, Scheveningen, The Netherlands.

Browning, Martin, Pierri-Andre Chiappori, and Arthur Lewbel. 2003. ''Estimating Consumption of Economies of Scale, Adult Equivalence Scales and Household Bargaining Power.'' Centre for Applied Micro-econometrics, Institute of Economics, University of Copenhagen. http://www.econ.ku.dk/cam/Files/workingpapers/2003/2003-12_Martin_Browning.pdf(accessed November 2008).

Centre for Research on Poverty Reduction and Income Distribution (CRPRID). 2002. *Pakistan Human Condition Report – 2002.* UNDP: Islamabad, Pakistan.

Cockburn, John, Bernard Decaluwé, and Veronique Robichaud. 2008. ''Trade Liberalization and Poverty: Lessons from Asia and Africa,'' in John Cockburn, Bernard Ducaluwé, and Veronique Robichand, eds. *Trade Liberalisation and Poverty: A CGE Analysis of the 1990s Experience in Africa and Asia,* pp. 437–58. Ottawa: International Development Research Center.

Deaton, Angus. 1997. *The Analysis of Household Surveys: A Microeconomic Approach to Development Policy.* Baltimore, MD: Johns Hopkins University Press.

Decaluwé, Bernard, Jean Christophe Dumont, and Luc Savard. 1999. ''How to Measure Poverty and Inequality in a General Equilibrium Framework.'' CREFA Working Paper 9920, Laval University.

Duclos, Jean-Yves, Abdelkrim Araar, and Carl Fortin 2001. ''DAD-4: A Software for Distributional Analysis/Analyze Distributive, MIMAP Program.'' International Development Research Centre (IDRC), Government of Canada and CREFA, Université Laval.

Elson, Diane. 1995. ''Gender Awareness in Modeling Structural Adjustment.'' *World Development* 23(11): 1851–68.

Federal Bureau of Statistics. 1993a. *Household Integrated Economic Survey 1990–91.* Islamabad: Statistics Division, Ministry of Finance and Economic Affairs, Government of Pakistan.

Federal Bureau of Statistics. 1993b. *Labour Force Survey 1990–91.* Islamabad: Statistics Division, Ministry of Finance and Economic Affairs, Government of Pakistan.

Federal Bureau of Statistics. 1996. *Supply and Use Tables of Pakistan 1989–90.* Islamabad: Statistics Division, Ministry of Finance and Economic Affairs, Government of Pakistan.

Fofana, Ismail, John Cockburn, and Bernard Decaluwé. 2003. ''Modelling Male and Female Work in a Computable General Equilibrium Applied to Nepal.'' Paper distributed at a conference on Macro Adjustment Policies Gender-Network, Bangkok.

———. 2005. ''A Gender-aware Macroeconomic Model for Evaluating Impacts of Policies on Poverty Reduction in Africa: The Case of South Africa, Part II: Construction of the Model and Policy Simulation Results.'' African Centre for Gender and Development (ACGD), United Nations.

Fontana, Marzia. 2001. ''Modelling the Effects of Trade on Women: A Closer Look at Bangladesh.'' IDS Working Paper 139, Institute of Development Studies, University of Sussex.

———. 2002. ''Modelling the Effects of Trade on Women: The Case of Zambia.'' IDS Working Paper 155, Institute of Development Studies, University of Sussex.

Fontana, Marzia and Yana van der Meulen Rodgers. 2005. ''Gender Dimensions in the Analysis of Macro-Poverty Linkages.'' *Development Policy Review* 23(3): 333–49.

Fontana, Marzia and Adrian Wood. 2000. ''Modelling the Effects of Trade on Women, At Work and At Home.'' *World Development* 28(7): 1173–90.

Foster, James, Joel Greer, and Erik Thorbecke. 1984. ''A Class of Decomposable Poverty Measures.'' *Econometrica* 52(3): 761–6.

Gunter, Bernhard G., Marc J. Cohen, and Hans Lofgren. 2005. ''Analysing Macro-Poverty Linkages: An Overview.'' *Development Policy Review* 23(3): 243–65.

Gunter, Bernhard G., Lance Taylor, and Eric Yeldan. 2005. ''Analysing Macro-Poverty Linkages of External Liberalisation: Gaps, Achievements and Alternative.'' *Development Policy Review* 23(3): 285–98.

Haddad, Lawrence, John Hoddinott, and Harold Alderman. 1994. "Intrahousehold Resource Allocation: An Overview." Policy Research Working Paper 1255, The World Bank, Policy Research Department, Poverty and Human Resources Division, Washington, DC.

Haddad, Lawrence, and Ravi Kanbur. 1990. "How Serious is the Neglect of Intrahousehold Inequality?" *Economic Journal* 100(402): 866–81.

Hafeez, Amtul. 2000. "Determinants of Female Labour Force Participation Decision for Educated Married Women: A Case Study of the District Mani Bahauddin." MA Thesis, Quaid-i-Azam University.

Hertel, Thomas W. and L. Alan Winters. 2005. "Poverty Impact of a WTO Agreement: Synthesis and Overview," in Thomas W. Hertel and L. Alan Winters, eds. *Putting Development Back into the Doha Agenda: Poverty Impacts of a WTO Agreement,* pp. 1–44. Washington, DC: World Bank.

Jose, Sunny. 2003. "Gender Bias in Resource Allocation in India: Where Do Household Models and Empirical Evidence Intersect?" *Indian Journal of Gender Studies* 10(3): 405–29.

Kabeer, Naila. 2003. *Gender Mainstreaming in Poverty Eradication and the Millennium Development Goals: A Handbook for Policy-makers and Other Stakeholders.* Ottawa: International Development Research Centre (IDRC).

Kanbur, Ravi. 1987. "Structural Adjustment, Macroeconomic and Poverty: A Methodology for Analysis." *World Development* 15(2): 1515–26.

Kim, Jongsoog and Lydia Zepeda. 2004. "When the Work is Never Done: Time Allocation in US Family Farm Households." *Feminist Economics* 10(1): 115–39.

Lise, Jeremy and Shannon Seitz. 2004. "Consumption Inequality and Intrahousehold Allocations." Queen's IER Working Paper 1019, Queen's University. http://qed.econ.queensu.ca/pub/faculty/seitz/inequality05.pdf (accessed November 2008).

Mahmood, Muhammad Arshad. 2003. "Estimates of Mortality," in A.R. Kemal, Mohummad Irfan and Naushine Mehmood, eds. *Population of Pakistan: An Analysis of 1998 Population, and Housing Census,* pp. 121–44. Islamabad: Pakistan Institute of Development Economics and United Nations Population Fund (UNFPA).

Sathar, Zeba and Shahnaz Kazi. 1997. "Women's Autonomy, Livelihood and Fertility: A Study of Rural Punjab." Islamabad: Pakistan Institute of Development Economics.

Siddiqui, Rehana, Shehnaz Hameed, Rizwana Siddiqui, and Naeem Akhtar. 2003. "Gender and Adjustment Policies: Evidence from Pakistan,", in Swapna Mukhopadhyay and Ratna, M. Sudershan, eds. *Tracking Gender Equality Under Economic Reforms, Continuity and Change in South Asia,* pp. 153–95. Ottawa: International Development Research Centre (IDRC).

Siddiqui, Rehana, Shehnaz Hameed, Rizwana Siddiqui, Naeem Akhtar, and Ghulam Yasin Soomro. 2006. "Gender and Empowerment: Evidence from Pakistan." Islamabad: Pakistan Institute of Development Economics.

Siddiqui, Rehana and Rizwana Siddiqui. 1998. "A Decomposition of Male–Female Earnings Differentials." *The Pakistan Development Review* 37(4): 885–98.

Siddiqui, Rizwana. 2005. "Modelling Gender Dimensions of the Impact of Economic Reforms on Time Allocation among Market Work, Household Work, and Leisure." *The Pakistan Development Review* 44(4): 615–42.

———. 2007. "Modeling Gender Dimensions of the Impact of Economic Reforms in Pakistan." MPIA Working Paper 13, University of Laval, Canada.

———. 2008a. "Income, Public Social Services and Capabilities Development: A Cross District Analysis of Pakistan." Working Paper Series 43, Pakistan Institute of Development Economics.

———. 2008b. "Welfare and Poverty Implications of Global Rice and Agricultural Trade Liberalisation for Pakistan," in Mohammad A. Razzaque and Edwin Laurent, eds. *Global Rice and Agriculture Trade Liberalization: Poverty and Welfare Implications for South Asian Countries,* pp. 131–84. London: Commonwealth Secretariat and Academic Foundation.

———. 2009. "Do Dividends of Liberalization of Agriculture and Food (Manufactured) Trade Trickle Down to the Poor in Pakistan?," in Muhammed Mazhar Iqbal and Muhammed Idrees, eds. *Trade and Economic Growth Linkages: Conference Proceedings*, pp. 59–96. Department of Economics, Quaid-i-Azam University, Islamabad in collaboration with Social Sciences and Humanitarian Section, Higher Education Commission, Islamabad.

Siddiqui, Rizwana and Abdur-Razzaque Kemal. 2006. "Remittances, Trade Liberalization, and Poverty in Pakistan: The Role of Excluded Variables in Poverty Change Analysis." *The Pakistan Development Review* 45(3): 383–415.

Siddiqui, Rizwana. Abdur-Razzaque Kemal, Rehana Siddiqui, Muhammad, Ali Kemal. 2008. "Tariff Reduction, Fiscal Adjustment and Poverty in Pakistan: A CGE-Based Analysis," in John Cockburn, Bernard Decaluwé, and Véronique Robichaud, eds. *Trade Liberalization and Poverty: A CGE Analysis of the 1990s Experience in Africa and Asia*, pp. 303–43. Ottawa, Canada: International Development Research Centre.

Sinha, Anushree and N. Sangita. 2003. "Gender in a Macroeconomic Framework: A CGE Model Analysis," in Swapna Mukhopadhyay and Ratna M. Sudershan, eds. *Tracking Gender Equality under Economic Reforms, Continuity and Change in South Asia*, pp. 321–63. Ottawa: International Development Research Centre (IDRC).

Thorbecke, Erik. 1991. "Adjustment Growth and Income Distribution in Indonesia." *World Development* 19(11): 1595–614.

Weerahewa, Jeevika 2002. "The Influence of Garment Exports on Male–Female Wage Inequality in Sri Lanka." Unpublished paper, Department for International Development, UK.

White, Howard and Edoardo Masset. 2002. "Child Poverty in Vietnam: Using Adult Equivalence Scales to Estimate Income-Poverty for Different Age Groups." Young Lives, An International Study of Childhood Poverty, Working Paper 6, Institute of Development Studies, University of Sussex.

World Bank. 2001. "Engendering Development: Through Gender Equality in Rights, Resources, and Voice." Washington, DC: World Bank.

———. 2005. "World Development Indicators 2005." Washington, DC: World Bank.

APPENDIX

Salient features of gender-SAM

I prepared a detailed gender sensitive social accounting matrix for the year 1990 (SAM-1990). It has twenty market sectors with capital, eight types of labor identified by gender, and four education levels – no education, less than five years (low education), five to nine years (medium education), and ten years and above (high education). It has four institutions – households, government, firms, and rest of the world. In urban areas, I identified households by the education level (no education, low, medium, and high education) of the head of household. In rural areas, I grouped households as female-headed households and male-headed households. Then, I classified the male-headed households by employment status (employee, self-employed, employer, and others).

I compiled a matrix of time allocation among market, household (social reproduction), and leisure activities for the eight labor types in each of the nine representative households following the standard system of national accounts (SNA). The SNA defines productive activities (market activities) as those that produce goods and services for sale and for personal consumption (food, clothing, and other articles) and are included in GDP. The SNA defines social reproduction (household activities) as services that could be provided by others within households such as cooking, cleaning, collecting wood, fetching water, and looking after children and the elderly. These activities are defined as economic but not "productive." Leisure is non-economic and non-productive as it cannot be delegated to someone else.

After deducting ten hours (minimum time used for self-care) from twenty-four hours, fourteen hours are available for market, household, and leisure activities. I calculated hours used in market work using data from Supply and Use Tables 1989–90 (Federal Bureau of Statistics 1996); Census of Agriculture 1990 (Agricultural Census Organization 1993); Household Integrated Economic Survey 1990–91 or HIES (Federal Bureau of Statistics 1993a); and Labor Force Survey 1990–91 or LFS (Federal Bureau of Statistics 1993b). I took data for social reproduction services from the LFS for women, the gender planning network survey (Rehana Siddiqui et al. 2006), and a small rural household survey for men (Amtul Hafeez 2000). I assumed that the activities are separable. Therefore, I subtracted working hours (market and household) from fourteen hours to get hours used in leisure for each category of labor. I calculated the values of nonmarket activities assuming that the cost of production is purely labor costs – the weighted average wage of the labor used in these activities.

I adjusted labor use in market activities by including labor of own-account workers – self-employed and employers – earlier labor income of own-account worker is included in capital income. I calculated the labor share of own-account workers using hourly wage rates. I assumed that the wage rate of paid workers is the implicit wage rate of all workers. I further combined women's labor data based on old definition with data collected by the Federal Bureau of Statistics with new techniques to get improved participation by women. These adjustments increase the rate of female labor force participation (FLFP) from 11 percent to about 50 percent, because of considerable increase in female labor force participation in the textile and construction sectors. Male labor force participation increases in wholesale and retail trade. As a result, the gross domestic product increases by over 5 percent.

In the market sectors, both men and women laborers with no education and low education are largely employed in agriculture (50 percent of men laborers and three-quarters of women laborers with no education and one-third and two-thirds of low-educated men and women workers). Women with high education are concentrated in the textile and education and health sectors (they make up 27 percent and 26.7 percent of each respective sector). The import competing sectors employ more men laborers of all education levels compared to women laborers; while, the service sector is the major employer of highly educated men and women laborers (75 percent and 62 percent of the total respectively). With the exception of the social and public administration sectors, all other service sectors are capital intensive (Siddiqui 2007).

Labor and capital income from production activities are distributed among institutions. All labor income accrues to households. In rural areas, employee households earn about 80 percent of their income from men's and women's labor. Female-headed households receive 38 percent of their income from remittances. This indicates that, in the absence of senior male members in the household, women become heads of household. Own-account workers (self-employed and employers) receive, respectively, 60.9 percent and 93.8 percent of their income from capital (which includes land and livestock). The share of rural households in total consumption is 52 percent for about 70 percent of the total population. The share of urban households – 30 percent of total households – is 48 percent of total household demand. Among all household groups, those with no education or an employee head of household receive a relatively larger share of their income from illiterate labor and have the highest incidence of poverty: 39.8 percent and 35.9 percent respectively. Rich households are high-education households in urban areas and households where the head of household is an employer in rural areas; here poverty is very low (13.3 percent and 15.3 percent respectively). For further details, see Siddiqui (2007).

Gender, Monetary Policy, and Employment: The Case of Nine OECD Countries

Yelena Takhtamanova and Eva Sierminska

ABSTRACT

In many countries, low and stable inflation is the focus of monetary policy. Recent empirical evidence from developing countries indicates, however, that the costs of reducing inflation are disproportionately borne by women. This paper seeks to determine whether a similar pattern is evident in nine Organisation for Economic Co-operation and Economic Development (OECD) countries, using quarterly data for 1980–2004. The study examines economy-wide and sectoral employment effects by gender by utilizing two methodologies: single equation regression and vector autoregression analysis. Results indicate that the link between monetary policy instruments (short-term interest rates) and employment in the industrial countries under investigation is weak and does not vary by gender.

INTRODUCTION

In many countries, low and stable inflation is the focus of monetary policy, as price stability provides many benefits to the economy (John Taylor 2001; Frederic Mishkin 2007). Nevertheless, price stability can potentially come at the cost of exchange rate appreciation and declines in output and employment. There is a particular concern that the latter – employment losses – weigh more heavily on women and/or ethnic/racial minority groups, although the research on this issue is sparse, especially with regard to gender.[1]

There are several reasons why macroeconomic shocks and monetary policy may have a stronger negative effect on women's employment than men's. Job segregation, gender differences in labor market attachment and job tenure, and gender employment discrimination could all serve as mechanisms by which women and men experience different effects of monetary policy shocks. But these effects could work in either direction. On the one hand, in developed countries women tend to concentrate in sectors that are subject to milder cyclical fluctuations (such as administrative, public, and service sectors compared to agriculture and manufacturing for men). Within sectors, women tend to be in a range of occupations that are also less susceptible to shocks, for example, professional and technical jobs; hence, their employment could be less sensitive to macroeconomic shocks. On the other hand, women are more concentrated than men in temporary and part-time jobs, have shorter tenure (and consequently can be laid off faster than men), and are more likely subject to employer discrimination, all of which might make women's employment more sensitive to economic downturns and swings. Given the ambiguous effects of these labor market experiences, this paper explores whether women's employment in developed countries is more sensitive to macroeconomic shocks than men's. To our knowledge, this issue has not yet been investigated for a group of Organisation for Economic Co-operation and Development (OECD) countries.

Some recent research pays attention to gendered differentials in employment effects of monetary policy in developing countries. Elissa Braunstein and James Heintz (2008) find evidence that employment costs of inflation reduction are larger for women than men in developing countries. However, the results for developing countries may differ from those for developed countries. In developed countries, women tend to be concentrated in sectors that are less sensitive to macroeconomic fluctuations than men, and this leaves women less vulnerable to employment losses (Janet Rives and Kim Sosin 2002). Thus, it is possible that countries with differing patterns of job segregation exhibit different degrees of gender-specific employment responses to monetary policy. Additionally, gender differentials in employment response to monetary policy may be related to a more prolonged experience of high inflation in developing countries, as compared to modest inflation fluctuations in OECD countries.

This paper empirically assesses the impact of monetary policy shocks on women's and men's employment in nine OECD countries, providing useful information that allows us to determine whether there is need to address any such gender differences with more direct policies (that is, other than monetary policy). For example, if gender employment asymmetries are found due to women's concentration in jobs that have a higher probability of job loss, policy-makers may find it socially desirable to improve the social safety net to protect disadvantaged families.[2] Quarterly data for 1980–2004 are used to evaluate the impact of real short term interest rates, the preferred monetary tool in a sample of nine OECD countries – Canada, Finland, Italy, Japan, Norway, Spain, Switzerland, the US, and the UK. To control for varying interest-rate sensitivities of sectors, we use employment data disaggregated by three sectors: agriculture, industry, and services. As a robustness check, we look at two sub-periods, 1980–92 and 1993–2004, to account for the possibility of a structural break in the relationship between employment and interest rate that could have occurred as a result of the 1992 European Exchange Rate Mechanism (ERM) crisis.

We use two estimation methods: single equation and Vector Autoregression (VAR) analysis. With either approach, we find only weak evidence that the employment costs of tighter monetary policy are inequitably distributed across genders in the chosen group of OECD countries.

GENDER DIFFERENCES IN EMPLOYMENT AND MACROECONOMIC POLICY

In this paper, we question whether monetary policy changes have a gender-specific effect on employment. That is, when monetary policy tightens (or eases), does one gender's employment suffer (or gain) more? In this section, we discuss the link between monetary-policy tools and the labor market and then outline potential reasons for expecting differential employment responses between women and men resulting from monetary policy in the sample of OECD countries.[3]

For many central banks, including those in the countries used in this study, the short-term interest rate is the primary tool of monetary policy.[4] Changes in interest rates may affect employment through many channels. In the short run, changes in the short-term interest rate influence employment via the impact on aggregate demand. A lower short-term interest rate lowers borrowing costs and saving, which could have a positive effect on aggregate demand via consumption and investment expenditure. A boost to aggregate demand in turn will translate into job creation.

In the following sections, we discuss in more detail several possible reasons we had proposed previously why interests rates might have a gendered effect on employment in the short term in OECD countries: employment and occupation segregation, gender differences in labor market attachment, job tenure, and discrimination.

Employment segregation

Empirical evidence in OECD countries indicates that women tend to work in a different and narrower range of occupations than men, raising the possibility that changes in the interest rate will have unevenly distributed employment effects.[5] Traditionally, men are more likely to be employed in manufacturing and agricultural professions while women tend to concentrate in administrative, public, and service sector occupations in a more restricted range of professions. In OECD countries, recent shifts have occurred with both women and men increasing their employment in managerial and professional occupations. In terms of industries, in the US in the 1970s, for example, 28 percent of men were employed in manufacturing and 17 percent in services versus 21 percent and 42 percent respectively of women. In the 1990s, this number changed to 21 percent of men in manufacturing and 25 percent in services versus 11 percent and 47 respectively for women (Francine Blau, Marianne Ferber, and Anne Winkler 1998). In the 1990s, OECD countries saw the beginning of a greater demand for women in the labor market due to technological change that allowed substitution of men and women workers, the rise of the service sector and decline of the production sector, increased education levels of women, and effective anti-discrimination policy measures. As discussed in the next section, while women's labor market attachment increased, occupation and industry segregation, although declining, has remained an issue in these countries (Juan Dolado, Florentino Felgueroso, and Juan E. Jimeno 2002). Given the existence of occupational and industry segregation, a differential employment effect by gender due to changes in monetary policy may occur, if these sectors have differing degrees of interest rates sensitivity.

Cyclical properties of certain industries and occupations could also result in a gendered employment effect. For example, in European Union (EU) countries, women's relatively lower unemployment rates in the past have been attributed to female labor shifts from manufacturing to the service sector, as the latter is less affected by the business cycle. Hence, by concentrating in industries less sensitive to business cycle swings, women shelter themselves from both negative and positive business cycle effects (Hielke Buddelmeyer Gilles Mourre, and Melanie Ward 2004a). More recently, the influences of changes in occupational distribution, rather than distributions by industry, have been highlighted as having a greater effect on employment. Using UK data, Rives and Sosin (2002) show that although at times of recession unemployment rises for both genders, the occupational distribution favors women's employment. More specifically, within occupations, women's unemployment rates are consistently higher than men's. But the distribution of occupations favors women because low unemployment occupations have relatively higher proportions of women. This evidence suggests the possibility of gender-specific employment effects of interest rate changes, although the direction of that effect is ambiguous.

Labor market attachment

A differential sensitivity of men's and women's employment to interest rates can result from gender differences in the division of part-time and full-time work and labor market attachment (resulting from men's and women's different roles in the care economy) and its correlation with occupational segregation. In both Europe and the US, women have a considerably lower presence in full-time work compared to men (see for example, Rebecca Blank [1998]; Hielke Buddelmeyer, Gilles Mourre, and Melanie Ward

[2004b]; and Elena Bardasi and Janet Gornick [2008]) and concentrate in temporary and part-time jobs, which are more sensitive to economic downturns and upswings. Occupational segregation is also positively correlated with the share of part-time jobs, as these jobs tend to be in occupations traditionally held by women.

Job tenure

A third reason we could expect monetary policy to exert a differential employment response is the difference between genders in job tenure (Lalith Munasinghe, Tania Reif, and Alice Henriques 2008). Researchers have found that women have shorter tenure (one reason is that they leave work to start families) and consequently may be laid off faster than men (see Alison L. Booth, Marco Francesconi, and Carlos Garcia-Serrano [1999] for the case of the UK).[6] As a result, in times of economic downturns women may suffer more in terms of employment. However, workers with *substantial* tenure also may be disproportionately hurt in terms of employment during economic downturns. Christopher Ruhm (1987) finds that although the inverse relationship between job duration and turnover rates holds in the US, workers with substantial tenure in recently held jobs are more vulnerable during cyclical fluctuations. This effect is strengthened in sectors that are hit particularly hard by recessions. Overall, it is clear that there are differences in job tenure between men and women, and that tenure affects employment responses to economic conditions.

Gender discrimination

Employer gender discrimination can also result in employment segregation and cause a gendered employment effect resulting from changes in interest rates. Employers may perceive the productivity of men and women differently and prefer to hire one over the other, either in hiring/firing the more productive or hiring/firing the seemingly less productive and offering a lower wage. This type of behavior may not be evident when the economy is operating close to full employment but can certainly be in effect in times of economic downturns.

Although the argument of employer discrimination is difficult to maintain with the existence of widespread occupational segregation, there is empirical evidence for the US showing that in male-dominated occupations and industries, the unemployment rate for women has in the past increased more at the cycle troughs (see the literature review in Rives and Sosin [2002] and Ghazala Azmat, Maia Guell, and Alan Manning [2006]). More recently, Ajit Singh and Anne Zammit (2002) found that women in developing countries were fired at substantially higher rates than men after the Asian financial crisis. Another study also found that employers in developing countries may prefer to hire men as a means of reducing costs in recessionary times given that women are more likely to go on leave due to maternity or illness, despite the fact that they are perceived as reliable employees (Stephanie Seguino 2003).

THEORETICAL FRAMEWORK

To quantify the effect of monetary policy on employment, we use a theoretical framework that links the short-term interest rate, the preferred monetary policy instrument in the sample countries, to employment. We choose the IS curve, which represents the investment and saving equilibrium and therefore summarizes the relationship between aggregate output and interest rates, as the framework.[7]

In its most general form, the IS curve can be written as:

$$Y = f(Y, i - \pi^e, F), \qquad (1)$$

where Y is real output, i is the nominal interest rate, π^e is expected inflation, and F is the index of fiscal policy (see, for example, Olivier Blanchard and Stanley Fischer [1989] and David Romer [2006]). We assume that expected inflation is equal to last period's inflation, an approach that follows Glenn Rudebusch and Lars Svensson (1999) and Laurence Ball and N. Gregory Mankiw (2002).

$$\pi^e = \pi_{t-1}. \qquad (2)$$

Equation (2) represents expected inflation as determined through a process of the case of adaptive expectations.[8] Many students of inflation dynamics use models of rational expectations, which, while appealing on theoretical grounds, do not capture inflation inertia, putting them at odds with the data.[9] Although an assumption of adaptive expectations may not be fit in all circumstances, it is plausible for the time period considered in this paper during which inflation has followed a process close to a random walk (Robert B. Barsky 1987; Laurence Ball 2000; Ball and Mankiw 2002).[10] When inflation follows a random walk, forecasting future inflation using past inflation (the assumption of adaptive expectations models) is close to rational.

We work with a purely backward-looking IS curve in which past output affects current output. Although little work has been done on the relative importance of past and future output in determining current output, Glenn Rudebusch and Jeffrey Fuhrer (2004) estimate a forward-looking IS curve using alternative estimation techniques and find that expectations of future output have a relatively modest effect on current output, while the effect of lagged output is sizeable and empirically robust. As a result, we include only lagged output in our equation specification.

Since exchange rate fluctuations can also affect aggregate output via net exports, we control for real exchange rate effects on aggregate demand in order to extend the model to open economies (Laurence Ball 1999b; Lars Svensson 2000). We include four lags of dependent variables in our equation, the standard practice for quarterly data. The aggregate demand curve that serves as a basis to our empirical model is of the following form:

$$y_t = \sum_{i=1}^{4} \alpha_i y_{t-i} + \sum_{i=1}^{4} b_i (i_{t-i} - \pi^e_{t-i}) + \sum_{i=1}^{4} \delta_i e_{t-i} + \varepsilon_t, \tag{3}$$

where y is (log) real output, i is a short-term interest rate, π^e is expected inflation as defined above, and e is the (log) real exchange rate.

We are ultimately interested in the link between interest rates and employment. To formalize that link, we assume a simple production function:

$$Y = L^{\theta},$$

where L is employment, Y is output, and $\theta \; \varepsilon \; (0,1)$. Taking logs of the above, we obtain the link between employment and output:

$$y = \theta l, \tag{4}$$

where l is (log) employment. Next, we substitute equation (4) into equation (3) to capture the relationship between employment and short-term interest rates:

$$l_t = \sum_{i=1}^{4} \alpha_i l_{t-i} + \sum_{i=1}^{4} \frac{b_i}{\theta} (i_{t-i} - \pi^e_{t-i}) + \sum_{i=1}^{4} \frac{\delta_i}{\theta} e_{t-i} + \varepsilon_t.$$

Finally, let $\frac{b_i}{\theta} = \beta_i$ *and* $\frac{\delta_i}{\theta} = \gamma_i$:

$$l_t = \sum_{i=1}^{4} \alpha_i l_{t-i} + \sum_{i=1}^{4} \beta_i (i_{t-i} - \pi^e_{t-i}) + \sum_{i=1}^{4} \gamma_i e_{t-i} + \varepsilon_t. \tag{5}$$

The gender-specific equivalent of (5) is:

$$l^x_t = \sum_{i=1}^{4} \alpha^x_i l^x_{t-i} + \sum_{i=1}^{4} \beta^x_i (i_{t-i} - \pi^e_{t-i}) + \sum_{i=1}^{4} \gamma^x_i e_{t-i} + \varepsilon^x_t, \tag{5'}$$

where $x = m$ or f and $m =$ male and $f =$ female . We will use equation (5′) as the basis for the empirical investigation.

The coefficients on the real interest rate (β_i) capture the partial effect of changes in the real interest rate on unemployment shifts. The following relationship takes into account employment inertia, yielding the total effect:

$$\varphi^x = \frac{\sum_{i=1}^{4} \beta_i^x}{1 - \sum_{i=1}^{4} \alpha_i^x}. \tag{6}$$

Equation (6) is the total elasticity of employment with respect to the short-term interest rate, and this parameter is the focus of our empirical results discussion.

DATA

We use quarterly data from 1980–2004 for Canada, Finland, Italy, Japan, Norway, Spain, Switzerland, the US, and the UK, the OECD countries for which the longest time series of gender-specific employment and real effective exchange rate data are available.

Gender-specific employment data is available from the OECD's Quarterly Labor Force Statistics Database (OECD 2004).[11] The employment series are disaggregated by sector: agriculture, industry, and services. We employ the standard US Census Bureau multiplicative method to seasonally adjust the employment series (the Census X11.2 method).

We use the private consumption deflator (PCD) from the OECD Economic Outlook 80 database (OECD 2006a). The PCD is a chain price index, which represents changes in the consumer's cost of living more accurately than the Consumer Price Index (CPI), a fixed price index. The annualized inflation rate is computed as $\pi_t = 400 * (\ln P_t - \ln P_{t-1})$, where P is PCD. Real effective exchange rate data are from the OECD Main Economic Indicators (MEI) database (OECD 2006b). We use the CPI-based real effective exchange rate index, a chain-linked index.[12]

The data on interest rates comes from the International Monetary Fund's (IMF) International Financial Statistics (IFS; IMF 2007). We use the money-market rate, which is the interest rate that is directly influenced by monetary policy or closely tied to the interest rate influenced by the monetary authority.[13]

Figures 1 and 2 present selected summary statistics of the data for the whole sample and Table 1 for the two sub-samples, 1980:1–1992:4 and 1993:1–2004:4, considered in the paper. (The reasons for considering two sub-samples and the choice of the break date are discussed in the next section of the paper).

In Figure 1 we find the relative female and male employment rates by sectors. A ratio greater than 1 indicates the sector mostly employs women; a ratio less than 1 indicates the sector is male-dominated. Figure 1 indicates

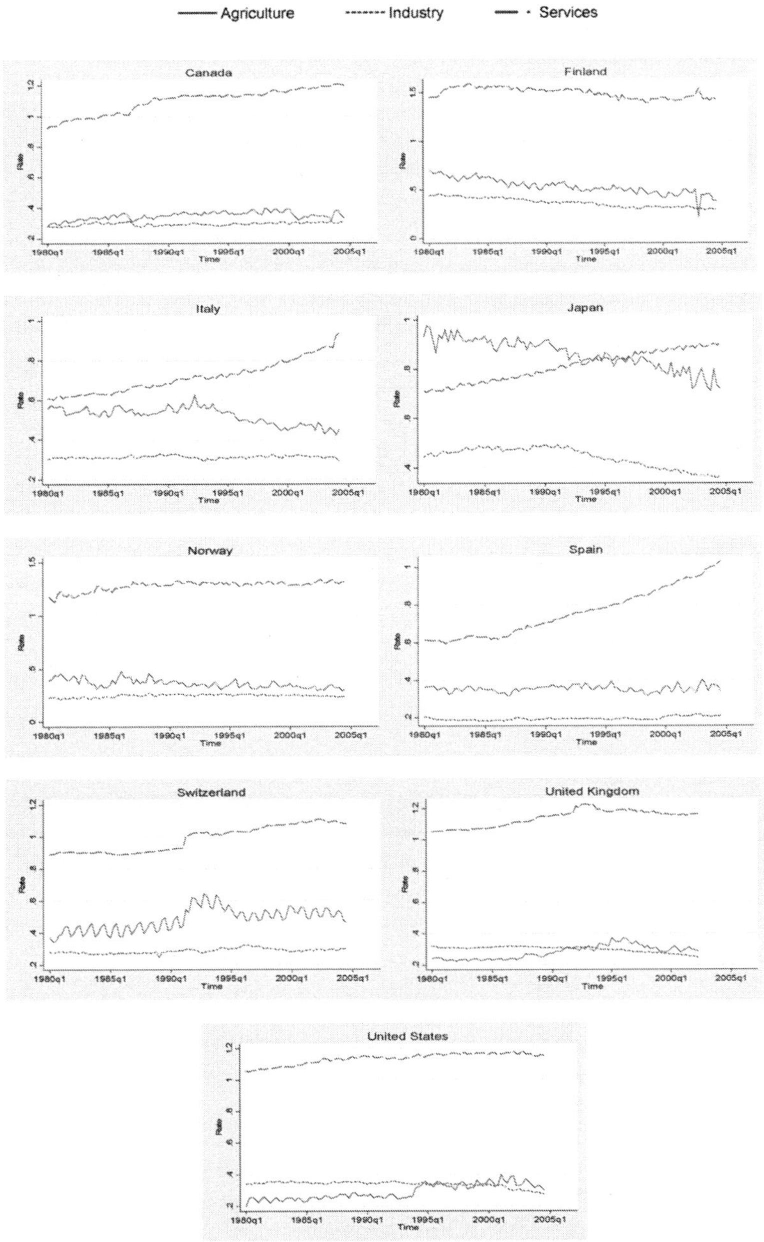

Figure 1 Relative female and male employment rates by sectors (1980–2004)

that in all countries employment in agriculture and industry is male-dominated and, for the most part, increasingly so over time, while women are mostly and increasingly concentrated in the service sector. The services

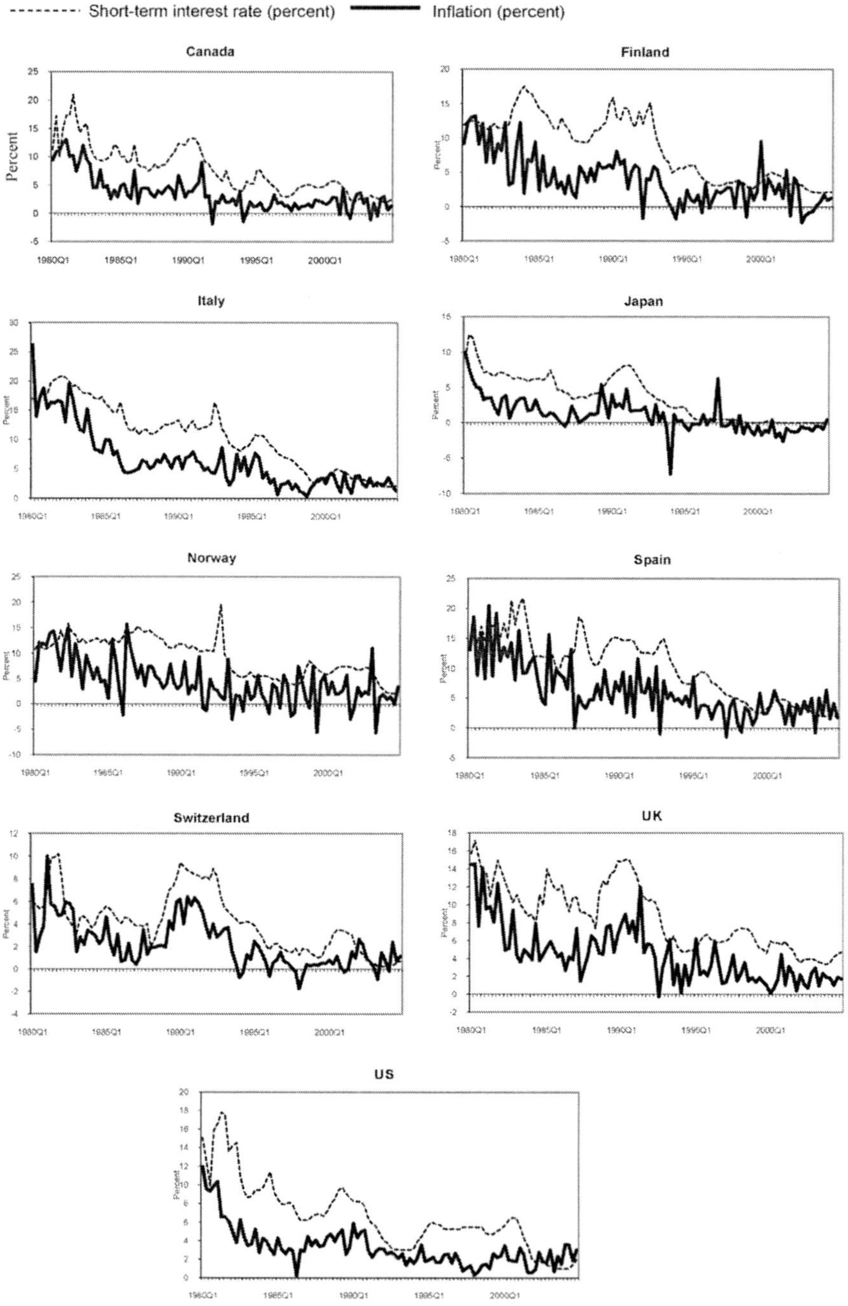

Figure 2 Inflation rate and money market interest rate (1980–2004)

Table 1 Summary statistics for the whole sample and two sub-samples (1980–92 and 1993–2006)

	Average explanatory variables and standard deviations											
	Overall	*sd*	*Sample 1*	*sd*	*Sample 2*	*sd*	*Overall*	*sd*	*Sample 1*	*sd*	*Sample 2*	*sd*
	Interest rates – money market rates						Inflation – PCD (annualized)					
Pooled	7.214	4.885	10.742	4.332	4.029	2.680	3.788	3.965	5.887	4.361	1.855	2.178
Canada	7.428	4.227	10.986	3.244	4.184	1.443	3.598	3.249	5.505	3.315	1.825	1.910
Finland	8.104	4.784	12.683	2.016	3.993	1.901	3.658	3.642	6.155	3.534	1.360	1.679
Italy	9.993	5.767	15.025	3.192	5.484	3.232	5.775	4.867	9.028	5.185	2.791	1.379
Japan	3.320	3.235	6.269	1.978	0.642	1.034	1.178	2.823	2.368	3.104	0.096	1.987
Norway	8.840	4.113	12.593	1.747	5.548	2.744	4.326	4.076	6.779	4.019	2.039	2.502
Spain	9.509	5.501	14.339	2.730	5.185	3.277	5.795	4.422	8.560	4.300	3.245	2.617
Switzerland	2.943	2.305	4.109	2.516	1.931	1.496	2.241	2.615	3.582	2.615	1.042	1.934
UK	8.390	3.681	11.677	2.344	5.320	1.106	3.904	4.357	6.198	4.982	1.783	2.062
US	6.428	3.684	8.997	3.501	4.024	1.720	3.618	2.736	4.810	3.182	2.517	1.592
	Growth rate of the real effective exchange rate index						Index					
Pooled	0.001	0.027	0.001	0.029	-0.001	0.026	0.071%	0.027	0.132%	0.029	-0.054%	0.026
Canada	0.000	0.021	0.000	0.018	0.000	0.024	0.043%	0.021	0.010%	0.018	0.003%	0.024
Finland	-0.001	0.022	-0.001	0.024	-0.003	0.024	-0.101%	0.022	-0.070%	0.024	-0.287%	0.024
Italy	0.001	0.021	0.003	0.020	-0.002	0.026	0.113%	0.021	0.251%	0.020	-0.204%	0.026
Japan	0.003	0.046	0.009	0.045	-0.001	0.047	0.328%	0.046	0.926%	0.045	-0.139%	0.047
Norway	0.001	0.019	0.001	0.015	0.000	0.022	0.073%	0.019	0.130%	0.015	-0.007%	0.022
Spain	0.000	0.020	0.000	0.023	-0.001	0.018	0.027%	0.020	0.036%	0.023	-0.098%	0.018
Switzerland	0.000	0.023	0.001	0.026	-0.001	0.019	0.015%	0.023	0.115%	0.026	-0.058%	0.019
UK	0.001	0.033	-0.001	0.043	0.001	0.026	0.101%	0.033	-0.109%	0.043	0.074%	0.026
US	0.000	0.025	-0.001	0.030	0.002	0.021	0.039%	0.025	-0.099%	0.030	0.230%	0.021

Note: PCD-personal consumption deflator. Sample 1 refers to the period 1980–92. Sample 2 refers to the period 1993–2006.

are female-dominated in Canada, Finland, Norway, Switzerland, the UK, and the US, and male dominated in Italy, Japan, and Spain. This latter group of countries, however, exhibits the largest increases in female concentration in the service sector among the sample OECD countries, suggesting convergence.

For all the countries in the sample, short-term interest rates and inflation are much lower in the 1993–2004 period than in the 1980s and early 1990s (see Figure 2 and Table 1). Notably, interest rates and inflation are less volatile in the later sub-sample (for a discussion, see, for example, Ben Bernanke [2004]).[14]

ESTIMATION METHODOLOGY

Single equation estimation

To examine the relationship between employment and interest rate, we first estimate a single equation model. Since the employment and real exchange rate series are non-stationary,[15] we estimate our model in first differences (except for the interest rate, which is in percentage point differences):[16]

$$\Delta l_t^x = \sum_{i=1}^{4} \alpha_i^x \Delta l_{t-i}^x + \sum_{i=1}^{4} \beta_i^x \Delta(i_{t-i} - \pi_{t-i}^e) + \sum_{i=1}^{4} \gamma_i^x \Delta e_{t-i} + \varepsilon_t^x. \tag{7}$$

Equation (7) is estimated by country, gender, and sector using the Newey-West covariance estimator, known to be consistent in the presence of both heteroskedasticity and autocorrelation of unknown form. The global effects of the 1992–3 ERM crisis provide a motivation to examine parameters in the pre- and post-ERM crisis sub-periods, 1980:1–1992:4 and 1993:1–2004:4, to test their stability (Edwin Truman 2002).[17] We compare and test the difference in the employment elasticity with respect to short-term interest rates, parameter φ in equation (6), for men and women.

The single equation approach differs from those utilized by others studying the link between gender-specific employment and interest rates, and does not call for taking a stand on a methodology to identify disinflationary episodes as in Braunstein and Heintz (2008), for example.

VAR estimation

While single equation estimation permits a straightforward interpretation of coefficients based on theory, it forces researchers to assume the exogeneity of some variables. A method for addressing the potential endogeneity of right-hand-side variables is VAR analysis, which treats every variable as endogenous. This is the predominant approach currently used to identify the effect of monetary policy shocks on other key variables, including gender and racial employment effects (Abell 1991; Willem Thorbecke 2001; Seth B. Carpenter and William Rodgers III 2004).[18]

In a reduced-form VAR, a vector of variables describing the general state of the economy, Z_t, is regressed on lags of this vector (Christopher Sims 1980). In a matrix form, the reduced VAR is:

$$Z_t = \zeta + \Gamma_1 Z_{t-1} + \cdots + \Gamma_k Z_{t-k} + u_t, \tag{8}$$

where ζ is the vector of constants, $\Gamma_1 \ldots \Gamma_k$ are matrices of coefficients, and u_t is a vector of uncorrelated white-noise disturbances. We obtained the estimates of ζ, $\Gamma_1 \ldots \Gamma_k$ by applying ordinary least squares (OLS) to each part of equation (8) separately; the sample covariance of OLS residuals gives the estimate of the variance-covariance matrix of the residuals Σ_u.

The identification of structural monetary policy shocks in both closed- and open-economy VAR analysis is controversial, however, as there are few highly credible identifying assumptions. Open economy VARs, appropriate for our analysis, are particularly problematic due to simultaneity issues. At a minimum, the open economy VAR must include short-term interest rates for each country and the exchange rate. Researchers have yet to find satisfactory identifying restrictions for sorting out the contemporaneous movements in these variables. Due to this difficulty associated with VAR analysis, we opted to utilize both single equation and VAR methodology.

This analysis, follows Martin Eichenbaum and Charles L. Evans's (1995) important work on open economy VAR estimation for the US, and uses orthogonalized components of the innovation to the short-term interest rate as a measure of monetary policy shocks. The estimated VAR includes the logs of domestic output, the domestic price level, and foreign real GDP, as well as the foreign short-term interest rate, the domestic labor market outcome (either the log of male and female employment or the log difference between the two), the domestic short-term interest rate, and the bilateral real exchange rate.[19] In the computations, we treat the US as a foreign country for all the countries other than the US itself. For the US, we follow Eichenbaum and Evans (1995) and experiment with Japan and the UK as foreign countries. As the results are very similar, we only present estimation results where the UK is considered the foreign country.

We estimate two VARs for each country and each sub-sector. In one set of regressions, the log of male and female employment is used in order to determine whether a gender differentiated employment response to a monetary policy shock exists. In the second, the difference of the logs of male and female employment tests the statistical significance of male and female employment responses to a monetary policy shock.

We compute bilateral exchange rates (S) as $S = \frac{E*P}{P^*}$, where E is the nominal exchange rate between the domestic and foreign currency, expressed as units of foreign currency per 1 unit of domestic currency, and P and P^* are the domestic and foreign price levels respectively (both measured with PCD). Note that here an increase in the real exchange rate indicates an appreciation of domestic currency.

The VAR ordering we adopt implies that actions of the central bank are informed by developments in the domestic and foreign economies (that is, domestic and foreign output, prices, foreign monetary policy, and domestic labor market outcomes), but policy affects these variables with a lag. Ordering exchange rate last implies that output, prices, labor market outcomes, and short-term interest rates affect exchange rates, but the effect of exchange rates on these variables is lagged, a standard assumption in the literature (Eichenbaum and Evans 1995; Jon Faust et al. 2003). Each VAR includes a constant and four lags.

ESTIMATION RESULTS

Single equation estimation results

The estimated elasticity of employment with respect to the short-term interest rate over the whole sample period – calculated from equation (7) and equation (6) – is shown in Tables 2a–d. The four tables report estimation results for different employment measures (total employment, employment in agriculture, industry, and services) and present the total employment elasticity of men (denoted with φ^{M}) and women (denoted with φ^{F}). The last row of each table shows the p-value for testing the hypothesis that there is no difference in the employment elasticity of men and women.

Estimation results in Tables 2a–d (last row) indicate that there are no statistically significant differences in male and female employment elasticity with respect to changes in short-term interest rates. In a few countries, the employment elasticity is found to be significantly different from zero. For total employment, interest rate changes are found to have a statistically significant effect on male employment in Finland (a 1 percent increase in the short-term real interest rate causes a 0.6 percent total decline in male employment). This result appears to be driven by the services sector: male services employment elasticity for Finland (Table 2d) is significantly different from zero (a 1 percent increase in the short-term real interest rate results in a cumulative male employment decline of 0.42 percent). We find statistically significant results in agriculture: in Italy, for male employment (Table 2b; a 1 percent increase in the short-term real interest rate causes a 0.31 percent cumulative loss in

Table 2a–d Elasticity of employment with respect to changes in short-term interest rate (sample period 1980:1–2004:4)

	Canada	*Finland*	*Italy*	*Japan*	*Norway*	*Spain*	*Switz.*	*UK*	*US*
(*a*) Using employment in all three sectors as a dependent variable									
φ^M	-0.11	-0.60*	-0.09	0.10	-0.09	-0.40	0.05	-0.41	-0.03
	(0.14)	(0.31)	(0.08)	(0.14)	(0.12)	(0.44)	(0.13)	(0.29)	(0.15)
φ^F	-0.10	-0.52	-0.03	-0.25	-0.02	-0.17	0.08	-0.06	0.15
	(0.13)	(0.61)	(0.08)	(0.17)	(0.10)	(0.29)	(0.14)	(0.32)	(0.11)
p-value	0.95	0.91	0.54	0.12	0.62	0.66	0.90	0.42	0.34
(*b*) Using employment in agriculture as a dependent variable									
φ^M	0.25	0.04	-0.31*	-0.09	0.16	-0.15	-0.13	-0.14	0.19
	(0.34)	(0.17)	(0.18)	(0.16)	(0.11)	(0.25)	(0.34)	(0.27)	(0.29)
φ^F	0.13	0.06	-0.42	-0.28	-0.13	0.02	-0.74*	-0.74*	2.19
	(0.49)	(0.23)	(0.30)	(0.22)	(0.48)	(0.34)	(0.43)	(0.40)	(1.71)
p-value	0.83	0.95	0.77	0.49	0.56	0.69	0.27	0.21	0.25
(*c*) Using employment in industry as a dependent variable									
φ^M	-0.27	-0.40	-0.07	-0.14	-0.21	-0.56	0.38	-0.06	-0.04
	(0.34)	(0.33)	(0.23)	(0.51)	(0.15)	(0.51)	(0.31)	(0.32)	(0.35)
φ^F	-0.08	0.06	0.11	-0.15	-0.01	0.07	0.15	0.10	0.22
	(0.27)	(0.25)	(0.19)	(0.50)	(0.19)	(0.47)	(0.27)	(0.46)	(0.31)
p-value	0.66	0.27	0.54	0.99	0.41	0.36	0.57	0.77	0.58
(*d*) Using employment in services as a dependent variable									
φ^M	0.02	-0.42*	0.15	0.12	-0.05	0.17	-0.19	0.13	0.00
	(0.05)	(0.25)	(0.15)	(0.11)	(0.12)	(0.14)	(0.19)	(0.48)	(0.10)
φ^F	-0.02	-0.26	0.13	-0.10	0.00	0.04	0.07	0.07	0.07
	(0.10)	(0.36)	(0.09)	(0.11)	(0.10)	(0.16)	(0.16)	(0.30)	(0.11)
p-value	0.68	0.72	0.90	0.17	0.76	0.54	0.30	0.90	0.63

Notes: Standard errors in parentheses. ***, **, * significantly different from 0 at a 1%, 5%, and 10% level respectively. φ^X is elasticity of employment with respect to interest rate for gender X. p-value is for H_0: $\varphi^M = \varphi^F$.

male employment), and in Switzerland and the UK for female employment (Table 2b; a 1 percent increase in the short-term real interest rate causes a 0.74 percent cumulative loss in female employment). These results are lost in the aggregate.

As a robustness check, we estimate the same model in equation (7) for two sub-samples: 1980:Q1–1992:Q4 and 1993:Q1–2004:Q4.[20] Tables 3a–d present the results for the four employment groups (total, agriculture, industry, and services). The first two columns report male employment elasticity for the two sub-samples (designated with φ_1^M and φ_2^M), and the next two columns show female employment elasticity (denoted with φ_1^F and φ_2^F). The next four columns report p-values for testing various null hypotheses. The first two columns of p-values correspond to the null hypotheses that male and female interest rate elasticity of employment is the same for a given period ($\varphi_1^M = \varphi_1^F$ and $\varphi_2^M = \varphi_2^F$). The last two columns

Table 3a–d Elasticity of employment with respect to short-term interest rate (sample period 1980:1–2004:4)

	Employment elasticity estimates				*p-values*			
	φ_1^M	φ_2^M	φ_1^F	φ_2^F	$\varphi_1^M = \varphi_1^F$	$\varphi_2^M = \varphi_2^F$	$\varphi_1^M = \varphi_2^M$	$\varphi_1^F = \varphi_2^F$
(*a*) Using employment in all three sectors as a dependent variable								
Canada	-0.33 (0.35)	0.01 (0.08)	-0.55 (0.34)	0.11 (0.12)	0.65	0.48	0.34	0.06
Finland	-0.21 (0.18)	-0.29 (0.48)	0.45 (0.81)	-1.11 (0.71)	0.43	0.32	0.88	0.16
Italy	-0.01 (0.09)	0.05 (0.17)	0.09 (0.13)	0.12 (0.13)	0.56	0.76	0.74	0.81
Japan	0.03 (0.06)	-0.17* (0.09)	-0.12 (0.10)	-0.22 (0.19)	0.21	0.79	0.08	0.61
Norway	-0.06 (0.09)	-0.61 (0.51)	0.20 (0.22)	-0.26 (0.27)	0.28	0.56	0.29	0.23
Spain	-0.47 (0.94)	0.12 (0.33)	-1.18 (1.23)	0.19 (0.66)	0.65	0.92	0.57	0.36
Switz.	0.04 (0.19)	0.09 (0.14)	0.11 (0.25)	0.02 (0.11)	0.84	0.67	0.83	0.73
UK	-0.54 (0.42)	-0.04 (0.07)	-1.35 (0.91)	-0.13* (0.08)	0.42	0.41	0.24	0.18
US	-0.91 (0.60)	0.28* (0.16)	-0.04 (0.31)	0.19 (0.29)	0.22	0.79	0.06	0.59
(*b*) Using employment in agriculture as a dependent variable								
Canada	-0.29 (0.32)	0.33 (0.52)	-0.22 (0.35)	-0.47 (1.22)	0.89	0.54	0.32	0.54
Finland	0.11 (0.40)	-0.20 (0.54)	0.68** (0.29)	0.59 (1.11)	0.27	0.52	0.65	0.94
Italy	-0.25 (0.24)	0.37** (0.17)	-0.55 (0.37)	0.09 (0.62)	0.50	0.67	0.03	0.38
Japan	-0.19 (0.46)	-0.06 (0.16)	-0.42 (0.43)	-0.04 (0.21)	0.72	0.93	0.80	0.43
Norway	-0.19 (0.29)	0.17 (0.13)	0.43 (0.71)	0.18 (0.41)	0.41	0.99	0.24	0.77
Spain	-0.27 (0.54)	0.51** (0.26)	-0.54 (0.38)	-0.22 (0.57)	0.68	0.23	0.20	0.64
Switz.	-0.09 (0.31)	-0.32 (0.92)	-0.71 (0.72)	-1.63 (1.23)	0.42	0.39	0.92	0.51
UK	-0.22 (0.41)	-0.51 (0.33)	-0.48 (0.32)	-2.74 (1.78)	0.63	0.21	0.57	0.21
US	0.16 (0.40)	0.33 (0.65)	-0.36 (0.30)	5.48* (3.26)	0.32	0.13	0.83	0.08

(*continued*)

Table 3a–d (Continued)

	Employment elasticity estimates				p-values			
	φ_1^M	φ_2^M	φ_1^F	φ_2^F	$\varphi_1^M = \varphi_1^F$	$\varphi_2^M = \varphi_2^F$	$\varphi_1^M = \varphi_2^M$	$\varphi_1^F = \varphi$
(*c*) Using employment in industry as a dependent variable								
Canada	-1.21 (1.41)	0.11 (0.17)	-0.33 (0.58)	0.38 (0.43)	0.56	0.57	0.35	0.33
Finland	-0.18 (0.30)	-0.02 (0.38)	0.60 (0.44)	-0.22 (0.60)	0.13	0.78	0.75	0.26
Italy	-0.31 (0.20)	0.10 (0.16)	0.55 (0.54)	0.24 (0.18)	0.14	0.55	0.10	0.59
Japan	-0.16 (0.46)	0.09 (0.21)	-0.15 (0.35)	0.55 (0.80)	0.98	0.58	0.62	0.43
Norway	0.01 (0.18)	-0.39 (0.32)	0.59 (0.39)	-0.11 (0.14)	0.18	0.42	0.27	0.10
Spain	-0.11 (0.45)	-0.42 (0.60)	0.40 (0.54)	0.81 (0.84)	0.47	0.25	0.67	0.68
Switz.	0.64 (0.85)	1.23* (0.66)	0.35 (0.35)	-0.21 (0.62)	0.74	0.11	0.61	0.43
UK	-0.16 (0.37)	0.50* (0.30)	-0.15 (0.41)	0.27 (0.50)	0.99	0.72	0.16	0.51
US	-1.90** (0.94)	0.56** (0.23)	-0.45 (0.72)	0.47 (0.88)	0.23	0.92	0.01	0.43
(*d*) Using employment in services as a dependent variable								
Canada	0.06 (0.08)	0.00 (0.07)	-0.23 (0.21)	0.06 (0.12)	0.19	0.66	0.58	0.21
Finland	0.11 (0.37)	-0.08 (0.34)	-0.03 (0.34)	-0.73 (0.54)	0.78	0.30	0.71	0.28
Italy	0.29 (0.23)	0.09 (0.23)	0.31 (0.20)	0.13 (0.14)	0.94	0.89	0.53	0.37
Japan	0.11 (0.12)	-0.17*** (0.05)	-0.06 (0.16)	-0.21* (0.12)	0.39	0.76	0.03	0.45
Norway	-0.03 (0.16)	-0.18 (0.23)	0.06 (0.19)	-0.19 (0.19)	0.71	0.97	0.60	0.39
Spain	0.10 (0.19)	0.12 (0.20)	-0.92 (0.87)	-0.24 (0.27)	0.25	0.29	0.94	0.46
Switz.	0.05 (0.21)	-0.28 (0.20)	0.05 (0.30)	0.07 (0.13)	0.99	0.15	0.26	0.94
UK	0.50 (1.44)	-0.26 (0.18)	-0.71 (1.00)	-0.18 (0.13)	0.51	0.75	0.61	0.61
US	-0.01 (0.10)	0.04 (0.29)	0.13 (0.25)	0.04 (0.30)	0.61	1.00	0.82	0.77

Notes: ***, **, * significantly different from 0 at a 1%, 5%, and 10% level respectively ϕ^X_T is elasticity of employment with respect to interest rate for gender X a sub-period T. T = 1 refers to sample period 1980–92. T = 2 refers to sample period 1993–2004.

report whether the elasticities for males or females have changed over time ($\varphi_1^M = \varphi_2^M$ and $\varphi_1^F = \varphi_2^F$).

We begin by discussing the results reported in the first two columns with p-values. Looking at total employment elasticity (Table 3a), we find no statistically significant differences between male and female employment elasticity for either sub-period. It is possible that aggregate employment numbers (that is, for all industries) mask gendered differences in employment sensitivity to short-term interest rates occurring in specific sectors; however, gendered differences in employment elasticity within each sector are not statistically significant (Tables 3b–3d). This is consistent with the estimation results for the whole sample.

We now turn to within-gender comparisons. Total employment sensitivity changes significantly for men in Japan from the first sample period to the next (Table 3a). Table 3d indicates this is driven by the services sector. The change in the employment elasticity suggests that total male employment sensitivity to short-term interest rates increased (in absolute terms) over time in Japan: it changed from insignificantly different from zero to negative and significantly different from zero at the 10 percent level. (In the earlier sub-period, short-term interest rates did not seem to exert pressure on male employment; in the second sub-period, a 1 percent increase in the short-term interest rate caused a 0.17 percent decline in male employment.) Total employment sensitivity also changed for women in Canada: a compounded effect of the industry and services sectors (from a negative response to a positive response). The change in male employment sensitivity to interest rates is also statistically significant in the US. This was driven by changes in the industry sector (Table 3c), where increases in the short-term interest rate caused a decline in male employment in industry in the first sub-period and an increase in the second sub-period. The effect in the aggregate in the US was diminished by the agriculture sector, where employment sensitivity remained positive for the two periods, although not significantly different from zero.

We also find significant changes in employment elasticity over time for men in Italy and women in the US in agriculture (Table 3b). Our results suggest that during the first sub-period, employment was not noticeably sensitive to the short-term interest rate in both countries, while during the second sub-period, short-term interest rate increases caused increases in employment for men in Italy and women in the US.

To summarize, our main conclusion from estimating a single equation is that we find no evidence of statistically significant differences in gender-specific employment responses to short-term interest rates in any of the three sectors, a result that holds for both sub-periods. We find some evidence of within-gender changes in employment elasticity across time, but the changes are not systematic and exist for only a few countries in the sample.

While investigating the source of differences in employment responses to interest-rate fluctuations between countries is beyond the scope of this paper, we believe that the finding of no gendered differences in interest rate elasticity of employment is an important one. The concern that the focus on low and stable inflation may lead to differential employment effects by gender is not supported by the estimation results presented here. In contrast, the evidence for the sample considered here implies that the link between employment and short-term interest rates is not strong and does not vary systematically by gender.

One concern with these results is that some of the independent variables may not be exogenous, especially exchange rates,[21] thus biasing coefficient estimates.[22] For that reason, gendered employment effects are also explored using VAR estimation techniques.

VAR estimation

In VARs, all variables in the system are treated as endogenous (that is, all variables in the system are allowed to influence each other). Recall that we call a shock to the domestic short-term interest rate a monetary policy shock (a positive innovation to the short-term interest rate is a contractionary monetary policy shock, meaning that it is expected to depress economic activity, including employment).

Figure 3a–d shows the differences in responses of male and female log employment to a contractionary monetary policy shock.[23] For clarity of discussion, we will refer to "log of employment" as "employment." We show responses for twenty periods (that is, five years, as each period refers to a quarter) after the monetary policy shock. The standard errors used in the computation of the confidence intervals are analytic (asymptotic). For each measure, the three sets of standard error bands indicate whether the response of employment to a one standard deviation positive innovation to the short-term interest rate is significantly different from zero at the 10, 5, or 1 percent levels. A negative response of the difference indicates that male employment falls more than female employment following an interest rate hike.

In the following paragraphs, we first discuss the results separately for male and female employment (results not shown and available from the authors upon request), which provide background information to the presented results in Figures 3a–d. Figure 3a provides estimation results for the difference in responses in total employment. We find male employment in Canada, Finland, Japan, Norway, Switzerland, and the US show statistically significant responses to short-term interest rate shocks (only the result for Finland is consistent with our single equation finding). We also observe statistically significantly responses of women's employment in Italy, Japan, the UK, and the US. In some cases, male and female employment responses to the interest rate shock are significantly different from each other, usually with a lag (see Figure 3a). For example, male

Confidence intervals: ------ 90% ——— 95% -·-·-·- 99%

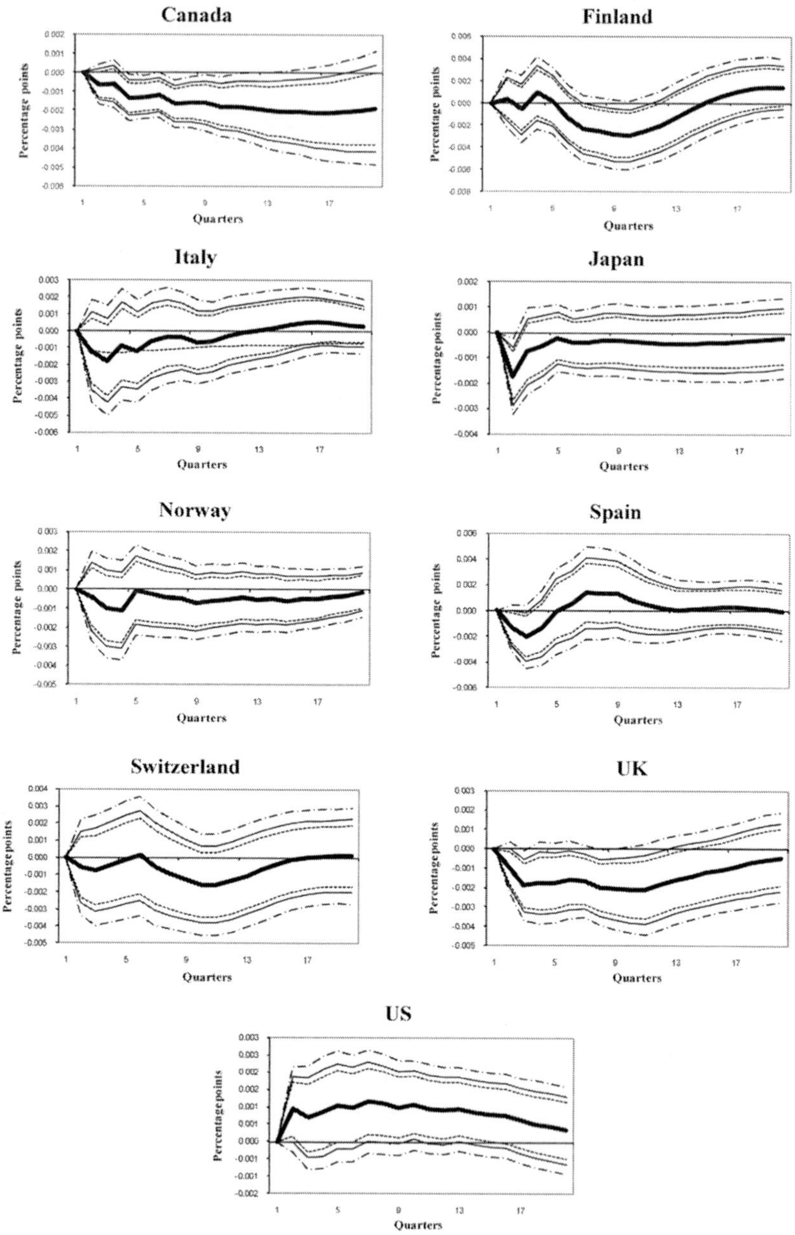

Figure 3a Difference in the impulse response of male and female total employment (in logs) to a 1 standard deviation innovation to the short-term interest rate

Confidence intervals: ------ 90% ——— 95% -·-·-·- 99%

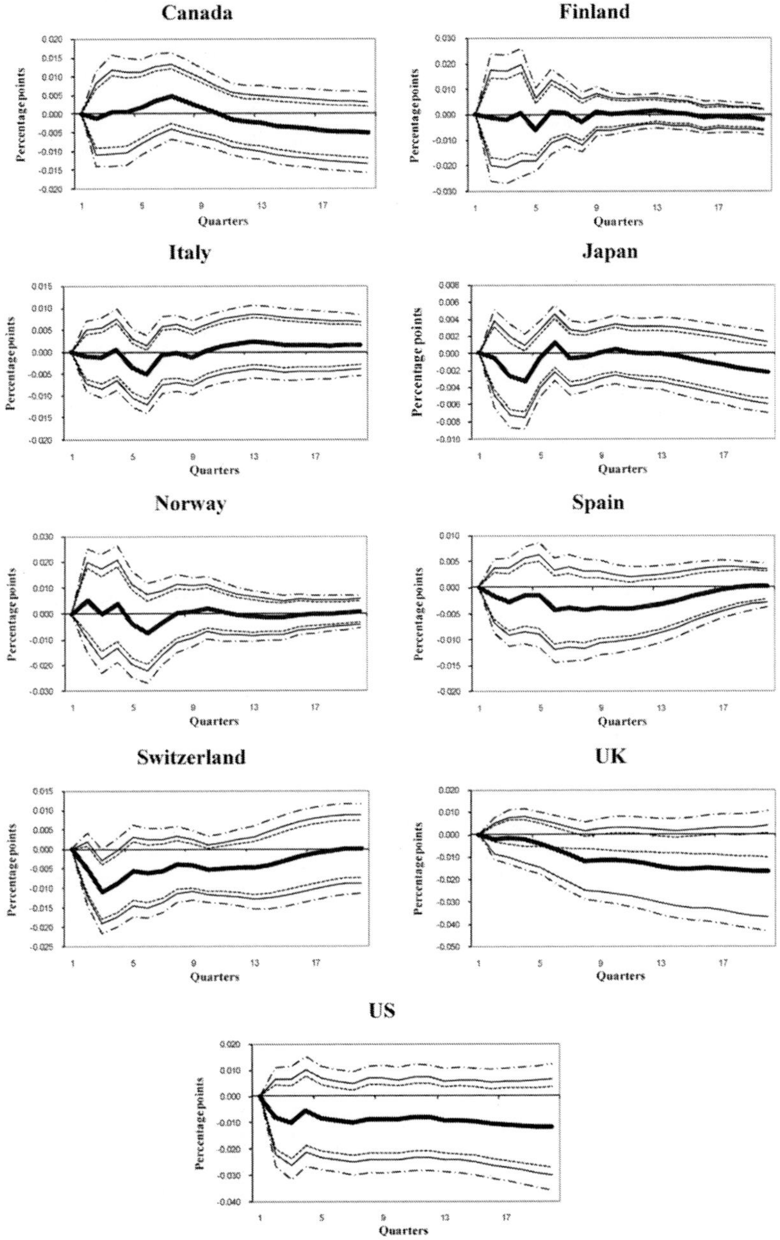

Figure 3b Difference in the impulse response of male and female employment (in logs) in agriculture to a 1 standard deviation innovation to the short-term interest rate

Confidence intervals: ------ 90% ——— 95% -·-·-·- 99%

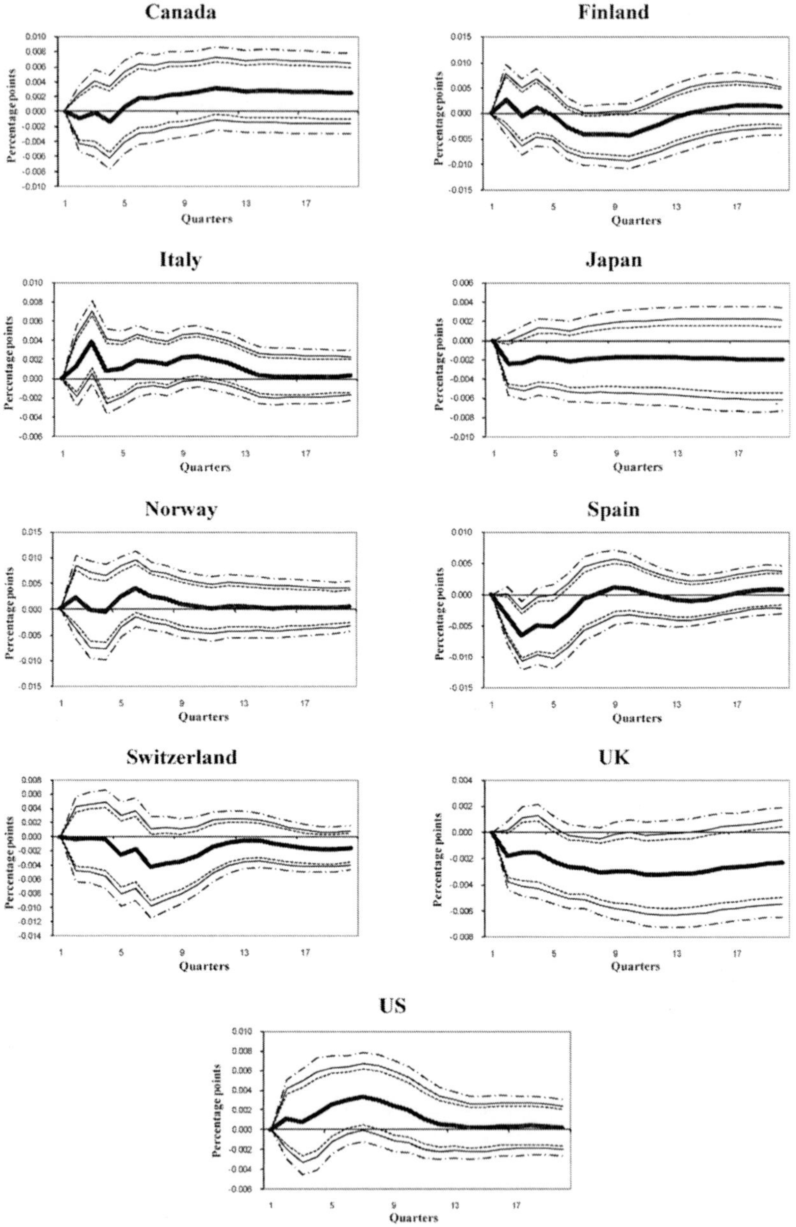

Figure 3c Difference in the impulse response of male and female employment (in logs) in industry to a 1 standard deviation innovation to the short-term interest rate

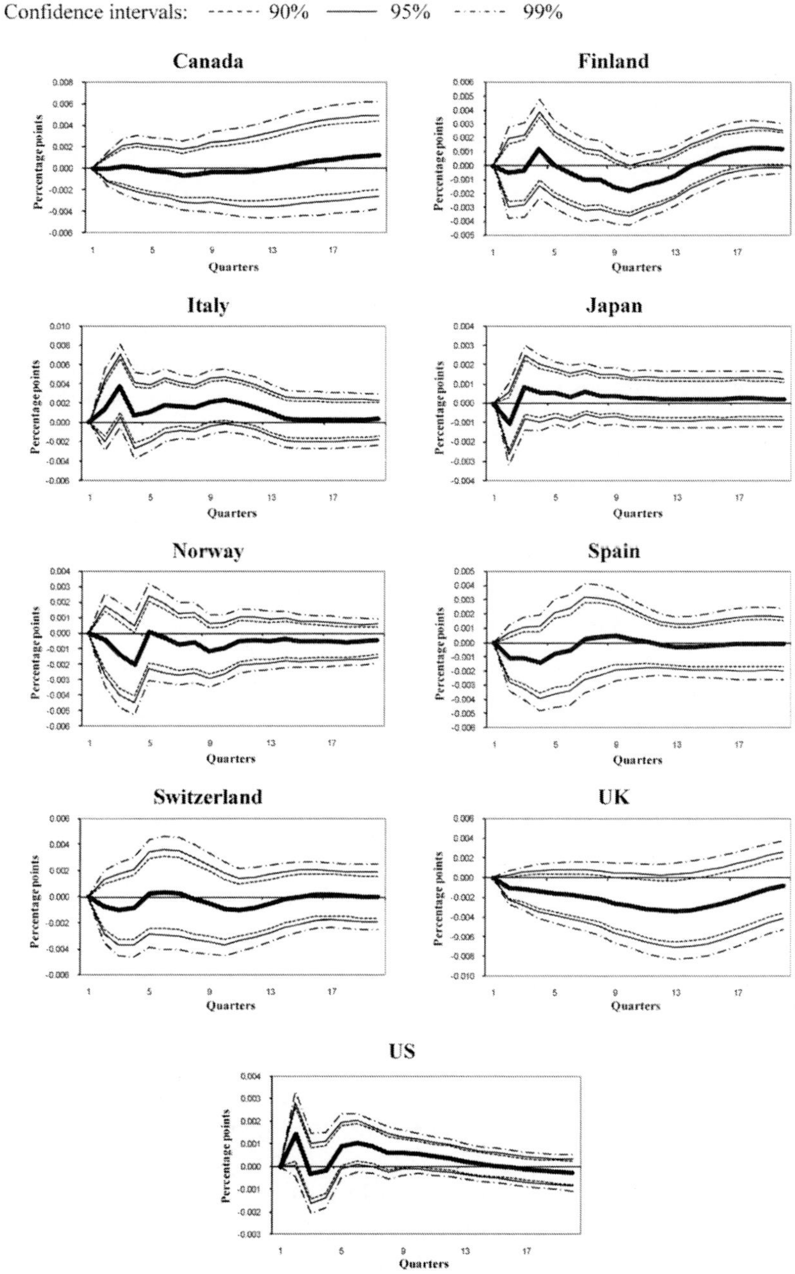

Figure 3d Difference in the impulse response of male and female employment (in logs) in services to a 1 standard deviation innovation to the short-term interest rate

employment is more sensitive to monetary policy shocks than female employment in Canada (with a one- to four-year lag), Finland (two- to three-year lag), Japan (only for the second quarter), Spain (for the second and third quarters), and the UK (up to three-year lag). In the US, female employment is more sensitive to monetary policy shocks than male employment. These are combined results from three sectors that, as will be shown below, hide statistically significant responses at a more dissagregated level.

Figure 3b shows differences in impulse responses for male and female employment in agriculture. We do not find many effects here; responses are significant only in Italy and the US for men (not shown). Results for Italy are consistent with the single equation estimation results presented in Table 2a. The difference in employment responses in Switzerland and the UK is significant but not persistent. In both cases, the statistically significant response is negative, indicating that male employment is more sensitive to monetary policy shocks than female employment.

Results indicate greater employment sensitivity in industry (Figure 3c) than in agriculture. Here, male employment responses to a monetary policy shock are statistically significant in almost all countries with the exception of Spain, Switzerland, and the UK (not shown). For women, statistically significant responses occur in all countries with the exception of Finland and Japan (not shown). In Figure 3c, male employment is seen as more sensitive than female employment in some countries with a lag: in Finland (with a two-year lag), Japan (first quarter), Spain (with a one-year lag), and the UK (with a one- to four-year lag). Female employment exhibited a higher sensitivity to monetary policy shocks than male employment in Italy (with a three-year lag) and in the US (with a two-year lag).

Lastly, responses of male and female employment in services are discussed. Male and female employment shows responses significantly different from zero in Finland, the UK, and the US, and for men in Canada and Norway, and for women in Italy (not shown). In Figure 3d, male employment is more sensitive to contractionary monetary policy than female employment in Italy (first quarter) and the UK (with a three-year lag). Female employment is more sensitive than male employment in the US (a statistically significant positive difference is found with a one- to three-year lag). In Finland, the difference is negative at shorter lags and then turns positive.

Consistent with the conventional wisdom on monetary policy lags, VAR estimation results suggest that monetary policy affects employment with a lag. Unlike single equation estimation results, VAR estimation results suggest that in many cases the differential of gender-specific employment responses to monetary policy shocks is statistically significant. In most cases, the difference is negative, implying that male employment is more sensitive to monetary policy shocks than female employment (except for the US).

These results might be attributed to employment segregation patterns as well as labor market institutions in the countries under investigation. Note, however, that in the cases where the employment response differences are statistically significant, they are very small, in most cases less than 0.01 percent, and therefore, in our judgment, not economically significant. Should the reader agree with this interpretation, the reader might also agree that the VAR results are actually consistent with our single-equation estimation results: that is, we do not find considerable differences in employment responses to monetary policy with either estimation technique.

SUMMARY AND CONCLUSIONS

This paper explores the data for gender-differentiated effects of interest rate changes on employment using single equation and VAR estimation techniques in OECD countries. Results indicate that the link between short-term interest rates and employment is weak for the majority of the sample countries. The estimation results do not support the hypothesis of gender differences in interest rate employment elasticity, nor do they support the claim that employment costs of inflation reduction are high. Our results are robust to stratifying by employment sectors (total, agriculture, industry, and services). Given this evidence and the transmission mechanism of monetary policy into employment, it may be that gender differentiated employment effects of monetary policy are negligible in other industrialized countries – although this is an empirical question that remains to be investigated.

Results presented here contrast with those obtained in previous research on developing countries that find differential employment effects by gender. This difference in results may be due to different patterns of job segregation in developed economies (and also different statistical methodologies).

We believe that our main finding is important, as the monetary authorities of all the countries investigated have signaled that low and stable inflation is on the top of their list of priorities (if not their only priority). The focus on price stability appears to have intensified in recent years, yet we have found little evidence to suggest there have been substantial changes of employment responsiveness to short-term interest rates from the 1980s through early 2000s.

Perhaps the recent volatility in financial markets that began in August 2007 and, as of this writing, threatens global economic growth will serve as an additional test to this finding in the future. As global economic growth slows, will labor markets in the UK and the Euro-zone suffer more than the US labor market because their central banks are more committed to low inflation than the US's Federal Reserve Bank, whose additional monetary policy goal is of maximum sustainable employment in addition to price stability? Will we see signs of a gender gap in employment sensitivity to recent monetary policy decisions?

We see several possible avenues for future research. One would be to stratify our result of gender asymmetries in the responsiveness of employment to interest changes by age and education with the use of micro data. Mary Daly, Osborne Jackson, and Robert Valletta (2007), for example, find that when it comes to unemployment and inflation tradeoffs modeled by the Philips curve, college-educated workers face a sharper trade-off than their less-educated counterparts. Another possible extension of this project would be to use a consistent methodology to estimate aggregate employment sensitivity to monetary policy changes in both developing and developed countries. Lastly, it would be useful to investigate the causes of between-country differences in interest rate employment elasticity using data on labor market institutions.

ACKNOWLEDGMENTS

The authors thank Renee Courtois, Mary Daly, Fred Furlong, Eric Swanson, Gary Zimmerman, the guest editors of the Special Issue of *Feminist Economics* on Inequality, Development, and Gender, the anonymous referees, and the participants in the Western Economic Association International (WEAI) 2007 annual conference for their useful comments. We also thank Charles Notzon for outstanding research assistance. All remaining errors are the responsibility of the authors. The views in this paper are solely the responsibility of the authors and should not be interpreted as reflecting the views of the Federal Reserve Bank of San Francisco or the Board of Governors of the Federal Reserve System.

NOTES

1 Gerald Epstein and Erinc Yeldan (2008) provide a summary of recent work that challenges the benefits of inflation targeting. Note that a focus on price stability does not necessarily imply inflation targeting.

2 At the same time, it is important to bear in mind that monetary policy is a national policy (or in the case of Euro-zone countries in our sample, Finland, Italy, and Spain,

the European Central Bank (ECB), set monetary policy in the interests of a group of countries), and cannot be used to address interests of one particular group. However, contractionary monetary and fiscal policies have adverse class and gender-differentiated effects, as explained by Diane Elson and Nilüfer Çagatay (2000) and documented recently for a group of Latin American and Asian countries (Günseli Berik, Yana van der Meulen Rodgers, and Ann Zammit 2008). That said, high inflation has considerable costs, as does deflation (as the recent Japanese experience reminds us). Thus, in our opinion, abandoning the current focus of central banks on low and stable inflation is not a solution, even if it is found that women more than men are negatively affected by contractionary monetary policy. A greater understanding of its economic implications for various social groups is warranted, in our view, as social policies can be designed to address these adverse consequences of national policies.

3 For a survey of evidence of gender differences in economic behavior and the implication for macroeconomic policy for developed and developing countries, see Janet Stotsky (2006).

4 For the purpose of this paper, our attention rests on the short-term effects of interest rates on employment. The theory of money neutrality posits that monetary policy cannot influence long-run employment, although this view has been challenged (see, for instance, Laurence Ball [1999a]).

5 Both demand- and supply-side explanations for employment segregation have been advanced. On the demand side, employer discrimination against women, including the perception that women are on average less qualified, could result in a greater willingness to hire men and a greater willingness to lay off women first during economic downturns. On the supply side, one explanation is that women self-select into occupations that require smaller human capital investment, due to lower penalties for career breaks. This could be attributed to "societal discrimination," whereby women are expected to bear the burden of raising children, thus requiring more flexible jobs.

6 Gender disparity in job tenure has been decreasing in the US, with men's tenure decreasing since the late 1990s and women's tenure remaining more or less stable since the early 1980s (Craig Copeland 2007: Figures 2 and 3). Booth, Francesconi, and Garcia-Serrano (1999) find that in the UK, although women are more likely to be laid off, the termination rates among men and women are similar.

7 One alternative to our approach would be to do an exercise similar to that of Braunstein and Heintz (2008) – that is, to identify deflationary episodes for a selected set of countries and then look at actual employment trends during each deflationary episode, comparing these actual employment trends to long-run employment trends. However, in that case it would be necessary to take a stand on our choice of deflationary episode identification methodology. Additionally, we would not be able to control for changes in other macroeconomic variables that can also affect employment (such as real exchange rate fluctuations).

8 We also experimented with a four-quarter inflation average ($\pi_t^e = \frac{1}{4}\sum_{i=1}^{4} \pi_{t-i}$) and obtained similar results.

9 For a detailed discussion of rational expectations models and the challenges they pose for empirical research, see Laurence Ball (2000).

10 The random walk model can be described as $y_t = y_{t-1} + \varepsilon_t$, where ε_t is white noise. When inflation behaves like a random walk, shocks to inflation have a long-lived effect on inflation. That is, when inflation goes up (down), it stays up (down).

11 The database was discontinued in 2004. For many countries, employment data is not available for the pre-1980 period.

12 We calculated percentage changes in the index by comparing the change in the index based on consumer prices for the country concerned (expressed in US dollars at

market exchange rates) to a weighted average of changes in its competitors' indices (also expressed in US dollars) using the weighting matrix of the current year. We then calculated the indices of real effective exchange rates from a starting period by cumulating percentage changes. This gives a set of real effective exchange rates based on moving weights.

13 The money market rate for Canada is the overnight money market rate; for Finland, it is the average cost of central bank debt; for Italy and Switzerland, the money market rate; for Japan, Norway, and Spain, the call money rate; for the UK, the overnight interbank rate; and for the US, the federal funds rate.

14 We also examine the sensitivity of employment sectors and interest rates by comparing statistically significant correlation coefficients (available from the authors upon request). These results indicate that agriculture is not correlated with changes in interest rates, but industry and services are. Employment in industry is most strongly correlated in Spain, Japan, Canada, and Finland in the whole sample and in the UK for the earlier period. Services exhibit a strong correlation in Spain, Norway, Finland, and the UK. Male employment in the industry sector is correlated with changes in interest rate in Canada, Finland, Japan (but with the opposite sign), and Spain. In Spain, the UK, and the US (with a positive sign) female employment also exhibits this correlation. For services, we find a correlation for both genders in Italy, Norway, and Spain, and also female employment in Finland and male employment in the UK.

15 We performed an augmented Dickey-Fuller unit root test on all the series and experimented with three different versions of the equation by including a constant, a constant and linear trend, or neither. We could not reject the null hypothesis of a present unit root in most cases for the employment and real exchange rate series.

16 Estimating an equation relating employment to other macroeconomic variables in log differences is standard in the literature. See, for example, Jose M. Campa and Linda S. Goldberg (2001) and William Nordhaus (2005).

17 This is discussed in greater detail in Yelena Takhtamanova and Eva Sierminska (2008).

18 Monetary policy shocks can arise due to a variety of random factors affecting monetary policy decisions. These include models employed by monetary policy-makers, measurement error in the data available at the time of decision making, and political factors.

19 There is a debate about whether the variables in a VAR need to be stationary. Some argue against differencing (even if the variables contain a unit root), as differencing "throws away" information concerning co-movements in the data (Sims 1980; Thomas Doan 1992). A similar argument applies to de-trending the variables. We calculated the VAR with both de-trended and differenced variables, and obtained qualitatively similar results to those obtained from neither de-trended nor differenced series. Thus, we only present one set of results.

20 The ERM crisis break data also coincides with large differences that have occurred in the labor market in the 1980s and 1990s, particularly for women.

21 Another may be that industry classifications are too broad to pick up some within-industry effects of monetary policy changes by gender. We are unable to address the latter concern due to lack of more detailed comparable quarterly cross-country employment data that is gender disaggregated.

22 While assuming exogeneity of exchange rates is hardly plausible from a theoretical standpoint, empirical studies show that macroeconomic variables have little explanatory power over exchange rates (Richard Meese and Kenneth Rogoff 1983; Kenneth Rogoff 1992; Walter Enders 1995).

23 Estimation results of the responses of male and female employment to a contractionary monetary policy, as well as the difference in the two responses in a

table format, and separate figures for the responses of male and female employment are available from the authors upon request.

REFERENCES

Abell, John D. 1991. "Distributional Effects of Monetary and Fiscal Policy: Impacts on Unemployment Rates Disaggregated by Race and Gender." *American Journal of Economics and Sociology* 50(3): 269–84.

Azmat, Ghazala, Maia Guell, and Alan Manning. 2006. "Gender Gaps in Unemployment Rates in OECD Countries." *Journal of Labor Economics* 24(1): 1–37.

Ball, Laurence. 1999a. "Aggregate Demand and Long-Run Unemployment." *Brookings Papers on Economic Activity* (2): 189–251.

———. 1999b. "Policy Rules for Open Economies," in John B. Taylor, ed. *Monetary Policy Rules*, pp. 127–44. Chicago: University of Chicago Press.

———. 2000. "Near-Rationality and Inflation in Two Monetary Regimes." Working Paper 7988, National Bureau of Economic Research.

Ball, Laurence and N. Gregory Mankiw. 2002. "The NAIRU in Theory and Practice." *Journal of Economic Perspectives* 16(4): 115–36.

Bardasi, Elena and Janet Gornick. 2008. "Working for Less? Women's Part-Time Wage Penalties across Countries." *Feminist Economics* 14(1): 37–72.

Barsky, Robert B. 1987. "The Fisher Effect and the Forecastability and Persistence of Inflation." *Journal of Monetary Economics* 19(1): 3–24.

Berik, Günseli, Yana van der Meulen Rodgers, and Ann Zammit. 2008. "Growth with Gender Inequity: Another Look at East Asian Development" in Günseli Berik, Yana Rodgers, and Ann Zammit, eds. *Social Justice and Gender Equality*, pp. 154–86. New York and London: Routledge.

Bernanke, Ben. 2004. "The Great Moderation." Remarks given at the annual meetings of the Eastern Economic Association, Washington, DC, February 20. http://www.federalreserve.gov/BOARDDOCS/SPEECHES/2004/20040220/default.htm (accessed February 2009).

Blanchard, Olivier and Stanley Fischer. 1989. *Lectures on Macroeconomics.* Cambridge, MA: MIT Press.

Blank, Rebecca. 1998. "Labor Market Dynamics and Part-Time Work," in Solomon W. Polachek, ed. *Research in Labor Economics*, vol 17, pp. 57–93. Greenwich, CT: JAI Press.

Blau, Francine, Marianne Ferber, and Anne Winkler. 1998. *The Economics of Women, Men and Work.* Upper Saddle Brook, NJ: Prentice Hall.

Booth, Alison L, Marco Francesconi, and Carlos Garcia-Serrano. 1999. "Job Tenure and Job Mobility in Britain." *Industrial and Labor Relations Review* 53(1): 43–70.

Braunstein, Elissa and James Heintz. 2008. "Gender Bias and Central Bank Policy: Employment and Inflation Reduction." *International Review of Applied Economics* 22(2): 173–86.

Buddelmeyer, Hielke, Gilles Mourre, and Melanie Ward. 2004a. "The Determinants of Part-Time Work in EU Countries: Empirical Investigations with Macro-Panel Data." Discussion Paper 1361, Institute for the Study of Labor.

———. 2004b. "Recent Developments in Part-Time Work in EU-15 Countries: Trends and Policy." Discussion Paper No. 1415, Institute for the Study of Labor.

Campa, Jose M. and Linda S. Goldberg. 2001. "Employment Versus Wage Adjustment and the US Dollar." *Review of Economics and Statistics* 83(3): 477–89.

Carpenter, Seth B. and William M. Rodgers III. 2004. "The Disparate Labor Market Impacts of Monetary Policy." *Journal of Policy Analysis and Management* 23(4): 813–30.

Copeland, Craig. 2007. "Employee Tenure, 2006." *EBRI Notes*, April.

Daly, Mary, Osborne Jackson, and Robert Valletta. 2007. "Educational Attainment, Unemployment and Wage Inflation." *FRBSF Economic Review* 49–61.

Doan, Thomas. 1992. *RATS User's Manual.* Evanston, IL: Estima.

Dolado, Juan, Florentino Felgueroso, and Juan E. Jimeno. 2002. "Recent Trends in Occupational Segregation by Gender: A Look across the Atlantic." Discussion Papers 524, Institute for the Study of Labor.

Eichenbaum, Martin and Charles L. Evans. 1995. "Some Empirical Evidence on the Effects of Shocks to Monetary Policy on Exchange Rates." *Quarterly Journal of Economics* 110(4): 975–1010.

Elson, Diane and Nilüfer Çagatay. 2000. "The Social Content of Macroeconomic Policies." *World Development* 28(7): 1347–64.

Enders, Walter. 1995. *Applied Econometric Time Series.* New York: John Wiley and Sons.

Epstein, Gerald and Erinc Yeldan. 2008. "Inflation Targeting, Employment Creation and Economic Development: Assessing the Impacts and Policy Alternatives." *International Review of Applied Economics* 22(2): 131–44.

Faust, Jon, John H. Rodgers, Eric Swanson, and Jonathan Wright. 2003. "Identifying the Effects of Monetary Policy Shocks on Exchange Rates Using High Frequency Data." *Journal of the European Economic Association* 1(5): 1031–57.

International Monetary Fund. 2007. *International Financial Statistics.* http://www.imfstatistics.org/imf/(accessed December 2007).

Meese, Richard and Kenneth Rogoff. 1983. "Empirical Exchange Rate Models of the Seventies: Do They Fit Out of Sample?" *Journal of International Economics* 14(1/2): 3–24.

Mishkin, Frederic. 2007. "Monetary Policy and the Dual Mandate." Speech given at Bridgewater College, Bridgewater, Virginia, on April 10. http://www.federalreserve.gov/boarddocs/speeches/2007/20070410/default.htm (accessed February 2009).

Munasinghe, Lalith, Tania Reif, and Alice Henriques. 2008. "The Gender Gap in Wage Returns to Job Tenure and Experience." *Labour Economics* 15(6): 1296–316.

Nordhaus, William. 2005. "The Sources of the Productivity Rebound and the Manufacturing Employment Puzzle." Working Paper 11354, National Bureau for Economic Research.

Organisation for Economic Co-operation and Development. (OECD). 2004. *Quarterly Economic Outlook,* release 4. Paris: OECD.

———. 2006a. *Economic Outlook* (2), Paris: OECD.

———. 2006b. *Main Economic Indicators* (12). Paris: OECD.

Rives, Janet and Kim Sosin. 2002. "Occupations and the Cyclical Behavior of Gender Unemployment Rates." *The Journal of Socio-Economics* 31(3): 287–99.

Rogoff, Kenneth. 1992. "Traded Goods Consumption Smoothing and the Random Walk Behavior of the Real Exchange Rate. Working Paper 4119, National Bureau of Economic Research.

Romer, David. 2006. *Advanced Macroeconomics,* 3rd ed. New York: McGraw-Hill.

Rudebusch, Glenn and Jeffrey Fuhrer. 2004. "Estimating the Euler Equation for Output." *Journal of Monetary Economics* 51(6): 1133–53.

Rudebusch, Glenn and Lars Svensson. 1999. "Policy Rules for Inflation Targeting," in John B. Taylor, ed. *Monetary Policy Rules,* pp. 203–53. Chicago: University of Chicago Press.

Ruhm, Christopher J. 1987. "Job Tenure and Cyclical Changes in the Labor Market." *Review of Economics and Statistics* 69(2): 372–8.

Seguino, Stephanie. 2003. "Why Are Women in the Caribbean So Much More Likely than Men to Be Unemployed?" *Social and Economic Studies* 52(4): 83–120.

Sims, Christopher. 1980. "Macroeconomics and Reality." *Econometrica* 48(1): 1–49.

Singh, Ajit and Ann Zammit. 2002. "Gender Effects of the Financial Crisis in South Korea." Paper presented at New Directions in Research on Gender-Aware Macroeconomics and International Economies: An International Symposium, Levy Economics Institute of Bard College.

Stotsky, Janet. 2006. "Gender and Its Relevance to Macroeconomic Policy: A Survey." Working Paper 233, International Monetary Fund.

Svensson, Lars. 2000. "Open Economy Inflation Targeting." *Journal of International Economics* 50(1): 155–83.

Takhtamanova, Yelena and Eva Sierminska. 2008. "Gender Differences in the Effect of Monetary Policy on Employment: The Case of Nine OECD Countries." IRISS Working Paper 2008–04, CEPS/INSTEAD, Luxembourg.

Taylor, John. 2001. "Low Inflation, Deflation, and Policies for Future Price Stability." *Monetary and Economic Studies* 19(S1): 35–51.

Thorbecke, Willem. 2001. "Estimating the Effects of Disinflationary Monetary Policy on Minorities." *Journal of Policy Modeling* 23(1): 51–66.

Truman, Edwin. 2002. "Economic Policy and Exchange Rate Regimes: What Have We Learned in the Ten Years since Black Wednesday?" Paper presented at the European Monetary Symposium, London School of Economics, London, September 16.

Index

absolute deprivation: *World Bank Development Report* (2006) 39
Africa: agrarian household gender and land 258–60; agrarian household labour 258–60; land reform debate and gender 260–1
Agarwal, B.: and Panda, P. 258
Amin, S.: and DaVonzo, J. 165
Annual Demographic Supplement (ADS) 141–2
assortative mating: China 169

Ball, L.: and Mankiw, N.G. 328
Bangladesh 287
Barro, R. 102; and Lee, J.-W. 96
Benería, L. 42
Blau, F.D. 139
Blecker, R.: and Seguino, S. 95
Bloom, D.E.: and Williamson, J.G. 94
Borensztein, E.: De Gregorio, J. and Lee, J.-W. 80
Boschini, A. 14–15
Bourguignon, F.: Ferreira, F. and Lustig, N. 47
Braunstein, E. 65; and Heintz, J. 324
Burtless, G.: and Karoly, L.A. 165
Busse, M.: and Nunnenkamp, P. 13, 16–17, 18, 22, 61–90; and Spielmann, C. 61, 80, 81, 97

Cagatay, N.: and Ertürk, K. 10, 17
Cambridge Journal of Economics 48
Canada: monetary policy and employment 323–48
Cancian, M.: and Reed, M. 170, 171–2, 180–1
capability poverty: Pakistan trade liberalization 297–8, 311–12
Carr, D.L.: Markusen, J.R. and Maskus, K.E. 68
Carr, M.: Chen, M.A. and Tate, J. 196
Cavalcanti, T.V. de: and Tavares, J. 94, 95
Chakrabarti, A. 67
Chang, H.-J. 42
Chen, M.A.: Carr, M. and Tate, J. 196; Sebstad, J. and O'Connell, L. 195
China 9–10, 163–90; assortative mating 169; childcare 168, 169; gender-differentiated retirement policy 168, 185; human-centred development program 185; personal connections and labor market 169, 185; public-sector downsizing 167–8, 184; state-owned enterprises (SOE) 166–7, 175; township village enterprises (TVE) 166; women's employment and family income inequality 163–90
Chinese Household Income Survey (CHIS) 165, 172–86
Cockburn, J.: Decaluwé, B. and Fofana, I. 289, 290
collective gardens: Africa 260–1, 271
compositional shifts: profitability and female employment 147–52
computable general equilibrium (CGE) framework: gender features 10, 295–9; model closure and calibration 296–7; poverty and welfare analysis 297–9; trade analysis 288–9
Conrad, C.: and Doss, C.R. 24
consumption expenditure: inequality 45–6
Convention on the Elimination of All Discrimination Against Women (CEDAW) 38
Country Gender Assessment 37

credit subsidies 19
Current Population Survey (CPS) 141–2
Custers, P. 194, 195
customary tenure: land rights 257, 260

Daly, M.: Jackson, O. and Valletta, R. 348
dams: Senegal River Valley 254–5, 262–4
Darity, W. 10, 17
DaVonzo, J.: and Amin, S. 165
De Gregorio, J.: Lee, J.-W. and Borensztein, E. 80
Deardoff, A.V. 67
Deaton, A. 290
Decaluwé, B.: Cockburn, J. and Fofana, I. 289, 290
decomposition analysis: *World Bank Development Report* (2006) 45–6
Deere, C.D.: and Doss, C.R. 257; and Leon, M. 258
Del Boca, D.: and Pasqua, S. 181
demographic gift 94, 107–8
Deng Xiaoping 167
developmental banking 19
Ding, S. 67; Dong, X.-y. and Li, S. 9–10, 12, 65–92
distributional shifts: profitability and female employment 339–44
Dong, X.-y.: Ding, S. and Li, S. 9–10, 12, 163–86
Doss, C.R.: and Conrad, C. 24; and Deere, C.D. 257
droughts: Senegal River Valley 254–5, 262–4
Duménil, G.: and Lévy, D. 134

East Asia: education gender gaps 115–17; employment gender gaps 115–17
East Asia and the Pacific (EAP): growth 98–9, 101, 106
Eaton, J.: and Tamura, A. 65, 73
economic growth: and education gender inequality 91–133; and employment gender inequality 91–133; and gender inequality theory and practice 93–7; and gender pay gaps 95, 96, 97
Economic Partnership Agreements (EPAs): EU 272
economic performance: education 98–102; employment 98–102; investment 106; labor force participation 98–102; panel regressions 102–3; population growth 106; regional growth rates 98, 100
education-related gender inequality 14–15, 17, 45, 47, 91–133; and economic growth 91–133; fertility levels 94; and foreign direct investment (FDI) 61–90; and GDP 96; human capital reduction 93, 110; international competitiveness 94–5
Eichenbaum, M.: and Evans, C.L. 335
Elson, D. 4–5, 35–60
employment gender inequality: corruption 95; demographic effects 94; and economic growth 91–133; family bargaining power 95; female labor and competitive advantages 94–5; fertility levels 94, 107–8; governance 95; international competitiveness 94; nepotism 95; pay gaps and economic growth 95, 96, 97; talent pool reduction 94
employment rates: Chinese men 173–4; Chinese women 173–4
employment segregation: monetary policy and employment 326–7
equal opportunity: *World Bank Development Report* (2006) 38–9
equitable development: and future policy 19–23
Ertürk, K.: and Cagatay, N. 10, 17
Esteve-Volart, B. 97
European Exchange Rate Mechanism (ERM) crisis 325
European Union (EU): Economic Partnership Agreements (EPAs) 272
Evans, C.L.: and Eichenbaum, M. 335

family income inequality: China 163–90; Chinese Household Survey (CHIS) 172–86; decomposition of change 182–3; education attainment 174–5; household income inequality measures 175–7; husbands' earnings 170–2; income quintiles 173, 174; industry sectors 175–7; modern reform period 169; occupation types 175–7; ownership types 175–7; radical reform period 169, 183, 184; wives' earnings 170–2; wives' employment impact 180–2
Feminist Economics 106
Ferreira, F: Bourguignon, F. and Lustig, N. 47
fertility levels: education 94

Filmer, D. 45
Finland: monetary policy and employment 323–48
Finoff, K.: and Jayadev, A. 134, 146
Floro, M.S. 52
Fofana, I.: Cockburn, J. and Decaluwé, B. 289, 290
Fontana, M.: and Wobst, P. 247; and Wood, A. 290
foreign direct investment (FDI) 6, 16–17, 22, 61–90; bilateral flows 69, 72; bilateral investment treaties 71, 73; colonial ties 70, 72; customs union 70, 73; and distance between host/source nation 72; education-related gender disparity 61–81; efficiency-seeking 63, 72; free trade agreement 70, 73; and GDP difference 69–70, 72, 77–8; gravity models 67–8; inflation 69, 73; knowledge-capital model 68; labor force participation rates 64–5; labor quality 63, 76, 78; market-seeking 63–4, 69; political constraints 70, 73; schooling and gender disparity 66, 71–2; and social factors 62–7; trade openness 69, 72; unilateral capital account liberalization 70–1, 72
Foster-Grear-Thorbecke (FGT) indices 290
Fuhrer, J.: and Rudebusch, G. 328

Galor, O: and Weil, D.N. 95
gender discrimination: monetary policy and employment 327–8
gender pay gaps 95, 96, 97; and profitability 134–55
globalization: gender and poverty 253–76
gravity models: and foreign direct investment (FDI) 67–8
Gross Domestic Product (GDP) 24; and education gender inequality 96
growth: *World Bank Development Report* (2006) 44–8
Gustafsson, B.: and Li, S. 166

Halpulaar agrarian system: Senegal River Valley 261–2
Hardy, M.A.: and Shuey, K. 142
Hartmann, H.I. 139
Hausman test 110
Heckman, J.J. 171
Heintz, J.: and Braunstein, E. 324
Henisz, W.J. 70
Hill, M.A.: and King, E.M. 96
HIV/AIDS 24
home-based work 8–9, 191–225; capital intensity 217, 219; caste 211–13; conceptual overview 191–5; definition 195–7; education level 211–13; fixed cost variables 206, 214; household head 214; housewife theory 194–5; India 8–9, 191–225; Indian trends 198–203; industry policy 218; International Labour Organization (ILO) 196, 197; literacy 211–12; macro determinants 216–18; macro model empirical results 218–20; macro variables 207, 214–18; Marxist perspective 194, 195; Marxist-Feminist theory 195; men 213, 215–16, 220, 221; micro determinants 203–7; micro model empirical results 207–11; Muslims 211–13; neoclassical model 194; participation probability models 207–11; piece rate system 194; production workers 199–203, 219–20; religion 213–14; rural areas 211–13; social status 211–12; theoretical framework 193–5; and trade policy 217–18; value added 217, 219; wage offer variables 205–6, 211–14; wage rate growth 217, 219; women with children 214, 221
household income distribution 164–5
Household Integrated Economic Surveys (HIES): Pakistan 291–2, 298

imports tariff reduction: Pakistan trade liberalization 243–4
income poverty: Pakistan trade liberalization 242–3
India: economic reforms 192, 216; home-based production workers 199–203; home-based work 8–9, 191–225; National Sample Survey Organisation (NSSO) 197, 207; sub-contracting 192–3; Survey of Unorganized Manufacture 197–8; trade categories and trade liberalization 198–9; trade and industrial policy liberalization 8
industry policy: home-based work 218
inequality: feminist perspectives 4–7; growth implications 13–19; macroeconomic policy impact 7–13; and macroeconomics 4–7; mainstream perspectives 4–7; *World Bank Development Report* (2006) 44–8

inequality traps 5, 43–4, 51
inflation rates: monetary policy and employment 332–3, 341
Institute for Women's Policy Research 140
interest rates: monetary policy and employment 332–3, 336–47; single equation estimation 334
International Classification of Status in Employment (ICSE) 196
International Labour Organization (ILO) 101, 102, 118; home-based work 196, 197
International Monetary Fund (IMF) 4, 7, 8, 20, 35, 330
intrahousehold resource allocation: Pakistan trade liberalization 291–3
investment: *World Bank Development Report* (2006) 44–8
investment performance requirements 19
Italy: monetary policy and employment 323–54

Jackson, O.: Daly, M. and Valletta, R. 348
Japan: monetary policy and employment 323–54
Jayadev, A.: and Finoff, K. 134, 146
job tenure: monetary policy and employment 327
Joireman, S.F. 258

Kabeer, N. 43–4
Kanbur, R. 45
Kandiyoti, D. 47
Karoly, L.A.: and Burtless, G. 165
Kenya 9, 227–52; agricultural production 229, 230, 234, 241, 243, 246; economic growth (1964–73) 229; economic structure and growth trends 229–31; employee compensation and exogenous injections 241–2; employment satellite account 236–7; employment structure and gender composition 231–4; external shocks (1974–89) 229; gender and economic growth 227–47; gendered employment creation and exogenous injections 243–6; health sector 230; household wage income distribution and exogenous injections 243; informal sector employment 230, 231–2, 233, 234, 243; land rights 230–1; liberalization (1990–2002) 229–30; manufacturing sector 233–4, 243, 245, 246; policy simulations and SAM approach 240–1; public sector employment 231; sectoral employment 233, 241–2; service sector 305; skilled labor 242, 245, 246; Social Accounting Matrix (SAM) approach 234–46; total employment statistics 231–2; urban employment rate 228; women's education and training 234
Kim, J.: and Zepeda, L. 300
King, E.M.: and Hill, M.A. 96
Klasen, S. 92, 93, 96, 102, 103, 105, 106, 107, 108, 110; and Lamanna, F. 13, 15, 17, 18, 22, 91–133
Koopman, J.E. 10–11, 12, 20, 21, 253–86
Kucera, D. 63, 65, 73
Kuznets hypothesis 47

labor force participation: and economic performance 98–102, 113–14
labor market attachment: monetary policy and employment 326–7
Lamanna, F.: and Klasen, S. 13, 15, 17, 18, 22, 91–133
land distribution 260
land rights 46–7, 48, 50; Africa 257–61; African land reform debate 260–1; gender inequalities 257–8; Kenya 230–1; Latin America 257; women's access 257–8
Latin America: gender inequality and growth 108, 110; land rights 257; schooling and gender disparity 66
Lee, J.-W.: and Barro, R. 96; De Gregorio, J.; and Borensztein, E. 80
Leon, M.: and Deere, C.D. 258
Lerman, R.L.: and Yitzhaki, S. 165
Lévy, D.: and Duménil, G. 134
Li, S.: Ding, S. and Dong, X.-y. 9–10, 12, 163–90; and Gustafsson, B. 166
Liu, J. 9
Long, C. 37
Lustig, N.: Bourguignon, F. and Ferreira, F. 47

macroeconomics: feminist perspectives 4–7; and inequality 4–7; inequality and policy impact 7–13; mainstream perspectives 4–7
Mahmood, M.A. 298
Mahoney, M.: and Zacharias, A. 11, 12, 134–62

Mankiw, N.G.: and Ball, L. 328
Mao, Zedong 165
market competition 41–2
market imperfections 41
market regulation: *World Bank Development Report* (2006) 51–2, 53
Markusen, J.R.: Carr, D.L. and Maskus, K.E. 68
Marx, K. 194
Maskus, K.E.: Carr, D.L. and Markusen, J.R. 68
Masset, E.: and White, H. 290
Mexico: PROGRESA 49
Middle East and North Africa (MENA): growth 15, 98–9, 100, 101, 102, 106, 109, 110, 114, 115, 117, 118
Mies, M. 194
migration: Senegal River Valley 262–4
Milanovic, B. 46
monetary policy and employment 12, 323–54; and employment segregation 325–6; estimation methodology 334–6; exchange rate fluctuations 329; gender discrimination 327–8; inflation rate and money market interest rate 332–3; job tenure 327; labor market attachment 326–7; sector employment and gender 330–1, 340; single equation estimation 334, 336–41; Vector Autoregression Analysis (VAR) 334–6, 341–7
Mozambique: schooling and gender disparity 66–7
multi-fiber agreement (MFA) 287

Niasse, M.: and Salem-Murdock, M. 271–2
Non-tariff barriers to trade (NTB) 217, 218, 219, 220
Norway: monetary policy and employment 323–54
Nunnenkamp, P.: and Busse, M. 13, 16–17, 18, 22, 61–90

O'Connell, L.: Chen, M.A. and Sebstad, J. 195
Oostendorp, R. 18
Organisation for Economic Co-operation and Economic Development (OECD) 12, 323–54
Organisation Pour la Mise en Valeur du Fleuve Sénégal (OMVS) 268–9
Organization of Petroleum Exporting Countries (OPEC) 161

Pakistan trade liberalization 10, 287–321; basic-needs goods demand and gender 308–9; capability indicators 311–12; capability poverty 297–8; CGE model and gender features 295–313; consumption and gender effects 307; employment and gender 300, 302; factor market effects 300–3; gender effects 287–321; gender inequality literature review 289–90; gender and time allocation 293–5, 300, 303; general sales tax (GST) 291; household income effects 303, 306, 307; imports tariff reduction 299; income poverty 298–9; intrahousehold resource allocation 291–3; macro effects 300; non-market activities labor 304–5; poverty and welfare 310–11; poverty and welfare analysis 297–9; poverty and welfare effects 307, 311–12; sales tax adjustment 299; structural adjustment program 286, 288; time poverty 299, 312
Panda, P.: and Agarwal, B. 258
Pasqua, S.: and Del Boca, D. 181
pension rights: women 48
Phillips, A. 38
Polanyi, K. 41–2
Pong, S.-l. 165
Portes, R.: and Rey, H. 67
Poverty Reduction Strategy Paper (PRSP) 37
privatization 50–1
profitability and female employment 11, 133–62; bargaining power 144; collective bargaining 144; compositional shifts 147–52; decomposition technique 152–5; distributional shifts 147–52; functional distribution 139–47; gender segregation 140; national income and product accounts (NIPA) 141–2; post-1997 trend 154–5; private sector gross profit rate 136–7; profitability trends 135–8; real hourly compensation 144, 151; sectoral analysis 149–54; women's aggregate hours work 143–5; women's pay increase 139–40
PROGRESA: Mexico 49

Rani, U.: and Unni, J. 8–9, 11, 24, 191–225
Ravazi, S. 36
Rawlings, L. 49

Reed, M.: and Cancian, M. 170, 171–2, 180–1
Rey, H.: and Portes, R. 67
Rodrik, D. 20
Round, J.I. 237
Rudebusch, G.: and Fuhrer, J. 328; and Svensson, L. 328
Ruhm, C. 327

Salem-Murdock, M.: and Niasse, M. 271–2
sales tax adjustment: Pakistan trade liberalization 299
schooling: gender disparity 66, 71–2, 74–8
Sebstad, J.: Chen, M.A. and O'Connell, L. 195
Seguino, S. 15, 61, 94, 97, 143–4; and Blecker, R. 95
Senegal River Valley 10–11, 253–86; 1970s 262–4; 1980s 265–7; 1990s 267–70; 2000s 268–70; dams 262–4, 268–9; droughts 262–4; electricity 269; food security 275; household agricultural labor distribution 265–7; irrigation schemes 254–6, 262–4, 265; land rights and gender inequalities 257–61; migration 262–4, 269; modernization plan 254–6, 262–4; rice production 263–4, 265, 267–8, 270–2; small farm prosperity and gender bias reduction 273–4; structural adjustment programmes (SAPs) 254, 255, 265, 269; traditional livelihood system 261–2; women and vegetable production 270–3; women's land rights 263–4, 270–2
sharecropping 261–2
Shatz, H.J. 62–3, 65, 68, 73, 74
Shorrocks, A.F. 165
Shuey, K.: and Hardy, M.A. 142
Siddiqui, R. 10, 13, 287–322
Sierminska, E.: and Takhtamanova, Y. 12, 20–1, 323–54
Singh, A.: and Zammit, A. 327
Social Accounting Matrix (SAM) approach 9, 13, 227–54; employment satellite account 236–7; endogenous/exogenous accounts 238; Kenya 234–46; model 237; multiplier analysis 239–40, 246; multiplier derivation 237–9; policy simulations 240–1
social protection: *World Bank Development Report* (2006) 50
South Asia: education gender gaps 115–17; employment gender gaps 115–17; gender inequality and growth 108, 109, 110, 117, 118
Sow, F. 273–4
Spain: monetary policy and employment 323–54
Spielmann, C.: and Busse, M. 61, 80, 81, 97
Structural Adjustment Programmes (SAPs) 254, 255, 265, 269
Sub-Saharan Africa: gender inequality and growth 106, 108, 109, 110, 113
Svensson, L.: and Rudebusch, G. 328
Sweden: inflation targeting 21
Switzerland: monetary policy and employment 323–54

Takhtamanova, Y.: and Sierminska, E. 12, 20–1, 323–54
Tamura, A.: and Eaton, J. 65, 73
Tate, J.: Carr, M. and Chen, M.A. 196
Tavares, J.: and Cavalcanti, T.V. de 94, 95
taxation: *World Bank Development Report* (2006) 49
time poverty: Pakistan trade liberalization 299, 312
trade liberalization: Pakistan 287–321
trade policy: and home-based work 217–18
Tzannatos, Z. 37

United Kingdom (UK): monetary policy and employment 323–53
United States Agency for International Development (USAID) 35, 176
United States of America (USA) 11, 134–62; Annual Demographic Supplement (ADS) 141–2; Current Population Survey (CPS) 141–2; female employment and functional distribution 139–47; gross profit rate 136–7; monetary policy and employment 323–53; national income and product accounts (NIPA) 141–2; profitability and employment gender disparities 325–53; profitability trends 135–8
Unni, J.: and Rani, U. 8–9, 11, 24, 191–226

Valletta, R.: Daly, M. and Jackson, O. 348

Vector Autoregression Analysis (VAR): monetary policy and employment 12, 334–6, 341–7
Von Werlhof, C. 194

Wanjala, B.M.: and Were, M. 9, 13, 227–52
Washington Consensus 35, 53
Weil, D.N.: and Galor, O 95
Welfare Monitoring Survey (1997) 236
Were, M.: and Wanjala, B.M. 9, 13, 227–52
White, H.: and Masset, E. 290
Williamson, J.G.: and Bloom, D.E. 94
Wobst, P.: and Fontana, M. 247
Wolff, E.N. 134
women's employment: China 163–90
Wood, A.: and Fontana, M. 290
World Bank 4, 7, 20, 35, 36, 37, 255, 265
World Bank Development Report (2006) 4–5, 35–60; absolute deprivation 39; capital-labor relations 40–1; conceptual framework 38–44; decomposition analysis 45–6; equal opportunity 38–9; equality 38, 39; equity 38, 39, 40, 41; equity/prosperity complementarity 41–3; fairness 39–40; gender 40; gender equality 35–60; growth 44–8; human capacities 49–50; inequality 44–8; inequality traps 43–4, 51; inequitable political institutions 41; investment 44–8; level playing field notion 41, 42, 51; macroeconomic policy 52; market competition 41–2; market imperfections 41; market regulation 51–2, 53; policy recommendations 49–53; social class 40; social protection 50; taxation 49
World Trade Organization (WTO) 7, 20

Yitzhaki, S.: and Lerman, R.L. 165

Zacharias, A.: and Mahoney, M. 11, 12, 134–62
Zammit, A.: and Singh, A. 327
Zepeda, L.: and Kim, J. 300
Zhu Rongji 167